The BIG Book of
KITCHEN
GARDENS

WITHDRAWN

TIME®
LIFE
BOOKS

Alexandria, Virginia

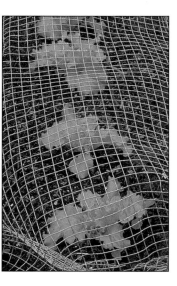

CHAPTER ONE

Kitchen Garden Styles

Many gardeners find no reason to banish veg-etables or culinary herbs to a remote corner of their property. If your garden of edible plants is well designed, and especially if it includes ornamentals borrowed from the flower border, it can be an attractive feature.

An appealing garden style for traditional houses is the formal jardin potager, or kitchen garden. The four-square layout features sym-metrical beds separated by paths. The Pennsyl-vania garden at left, featuring container-grown topiaries and frilly leaf-lettuce borders, is a classic example of this style. Informal kitchen gardens can be beautiful as well, as evidenced by the charming "edible landscape" shown on pages 12-13. This modern free-form planting of vegetables, culinary herbs, and ornamentals yields both visual pleasure and a bountiful harvest.

For a detailed list of plants and a planting guide for these two gardens as well as other gardens shown in this chapter, see pages 14-17.

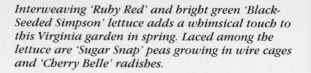

Interweaving 'Ruby Red' and bright green 'Black-Seeded Simpson' lettuce adds a whimsical touch to this Virginia garden in spring. Laced among the lettuce are 'Sugar Snap' peas growing in wire cages and 'Cherry Belle' radishes.

A rustic arch draped with 'Scarlet Runner' beans and a wall of tomatoes trained on high stakes add vertical interest to the formal layout of this Long Island kitchen garden. The birdbath at its center echoes the wells that were often the focus of kitchen gardens of the past.

A Victorian-style fence surrounds this long rectangular plot in Pennsylvania, which is divided into four beds by neatly manicured grass pathways. A tall, lush cone of vining 'Blue Lake' green beans thrives in the bed in the foreground, along with a large patch of 'Clarimore' zucchini, three varieties of green peppers, and blue-leaved 'Premium Crop' broccoli. Across the path is a small cutting garden where white 'Mt. Fuji' phlox, thinleaf sunflower, 'Autumn Sun' rudbeckia, and the bright orange-and-gold blossoms of 'Whirlybird Hybrids' nasturtium provide a vivid focal point. Culinary herbs occupy the bed in the far corner, and vegetables fill the fourth bed. The wrought-iron bench and the standard roses on either side of it reinforce the period look.

9

Intensively planted in fall for harvest over the mild California winter, cool-weather vegetables and annuals—some with edible flowers—make a dense, colorful patchwork. Rot-resistant redwood boards contain the double-dug raised beds, which are replenished before every planting with compost.

Ornamental kale and billowy sweet alyssum decorate a rock retaining wall in a terraced five-level vegetable garden in Santa Barbara, California. Beyond the wall are 'Green Ice' lettuce, young filet bean plants, and 'Silver Queen' corn.

This imaginative island garden overflowing with vegetables, herbs, and flowering ornamentals is the focal point of a front yard in California. Dominated by imposing, bold-leaved 'Purple Sprouting' broccoli, the vegetables in the bed's center contribute a variety of shapes, heights, textures, and foliage colors. They also act as a foil for the alluring burst of bright purple pansies, red and yellow Persian buttercups, and dainty white paludosum daisies in the foreground. The narrow brick path beckons strollers and also provides easy access for tending the plants.

A Guide to the Gardens

pages 4-5

A. 'Green Ripple' English ivy
B. Hen-and-chickens
(Sempervivum sp.)
C. 'Red Salad Bowl' lettuce
D. 'Albus' white creeping thyme
E. Joseph's-coat
(Alternanthera ficoidea)

F. 'Elegans' Siebold plantain lily
G. 'Green Joe' lettuce
H. Rosemary
I. 'Crimson Pygmy' barberry
J. Japanese painted fern
K. 'Telecurl' English ivy
L. Sweet bay tree *(Laurus nobilis)*

M. 'Argenteus' common thyme
N. 'Pagoda' parsley
O. Boxwood
P. English ivy

page 6

A. 'Ruby Red' lettuce
B. 'Black-Seeded Simpson' lettuce
C. 'Cherry Belle' radish
D. 'Sugar Snap' peas

pages 6-7

A. 'Lavender Lace'
Chinese wisteria
B. 'Joseph's Coat' climber rose
C. Nasturtium
D. 'Hidcote' English lavender
E. Italian flatleaf parsley
F. Sweet basil

G. Purple basil
(Ocimum basilicum cv.)
H. Common sage
I. 'Silver Carpet' lamb's ears
J. Common thyme
K. 'Truly Yours' geranium
L. Purple sage

M. 'Early Girl', 'Big Boy', and
cherry tomatoes
N. Wild marjoram
O. Grccn bell pepper
P. Cucumber
Q. Rhubarb
R. 'Scarlet Runner' beans

pages 8-9

A. Wisteria
B. Thin-leaf sunflower
(Helianthus decapetalus)
C. 'Autumn Sun' rudbeckia
D. 'Mt. Fuji' phlox
E. 'Blue Lake' green beans
F. 'Roc d'Or' ycllow beans
G. 'Clarimore' zucchini
H. 'Ariane', 'Nory Charm',
and 'Purple Bell' peppers

I. 'Premium Crop' broccoli
J. 'Whirlybird Hybrids' nasturtium
K. 'Tres Fin Maraichiere' endive
L. Rose
M. 'Cayenne', 'Texas Joe Parker',
'Jalapeño', and 'Sweet Banana'
peppers
N. 'Rosa Bianco' and 'Agora'
eggplants
O. 'Haricots Verts' filet beans

P. Sorrel
Q. Lovage
R. Lemon balm
S. 'Oakleaf' lettuce
T. 'Ruby' Swiss chard
U. 'Paros' Swiss chard
V. Arugula
W. 'Pink Mist'
pincushion flower

Note: The key accompanying each garden diagram identifies the plants by letter.

page 10

A. Snapdragon
B. Johnny-jump-up
C. 'Rocambole' garlic, French shallots, 'Italian Red Bottle' and 'Walla Walla' onions
D. Pinks
E. Marigold
F. 'Buttercrunch' lettuce

G. 'Jewel Hybrids' nasturtium
H. Petunia
I. 'Rouge d'Hiver' lettuce
J. Arugula
K. Ornamental kale
L. 'Four Seasons' lettuce
M. 'Romanesco' and 'Premium Crop' broccoli

N. 'Yukon Gold' potato
O. 'Scarlet Nantes' carrot
P. 'All-America' parsnips
Q. 'Ruby' Swiss chard
R. 'Finocchio' bulbing fennel
S. 'Bounty Shelling' and 'Old Spice' peas
T. 'Scarlet Ball' turnip

pages 10-11

A. 'Early Sunglow' corn
B. 'Green Comet' broccoli
C. 'Sensation Hybrids' cosmos
D. Filet beans
E. 'Carpet of Snow' sweet alyssum

F. 'Nagoya' ornamental kale
G. 'Crystal Palace' lobelia
H. 'Green Ice' lettuce
I. 'Silver Queen' corn
J. 'Richgreen' zucchini
K. Lavender

L. 'Red Ace' beet
M. Arugula
N. Dittany-of-Crete *(Origanum dictamnus)*

A. 'Tecolote Giants Red' Persian buttercup
B. 'Tecolote Giants Yellow' Persian buttercup
C. Sweet alyssum *(Lobularia maritima)*
D. Paludosum daisy *(Chrysanthemum paludosum)*
E. 'Blue Princess' horned violet
F. 'Universal Antique Mix' pansy
G. Marguerite *(Chrysanthemum frutescens)*
H. 'Touchon' carrot
I. 'Green Sprouting' broccoli
J. 'Sugar Snap' peas
K. 'Slo Bolt' cilantro
L. 'Joy Choi' pak-choi
M. 'Black-Seeded Simpson' lettuce
N. Wallflower *(Erysimum 'Bowles' Mauve')*
O. 'Chioggia' beets
P. 'Burpee's Golden' beets
Q. 'Purple Sprouting' broccoli
R. Euryops daisy *(Euryops pectinatus 'Viridis')*
S. 'Beverly Sills' bearded iris
T. Curly parsley

Note: The key accompanying each garden diagram identifies the plants by letter.

CHAPTER TWO

Kitchen Gardening the Organic Way

Nothing tastes better than something you've grown in your own garden. And if your vegetables and herbs are raised organically, they are as healthful as they can be, free of contamination from synthetic pesticides and other possibly harmful substances.

Far from being an arcane or difficult science, organic gardening is a common-sense blend of traditional techniques and modern advances for building a fertile soil and creating a healthy garden environment. Like the owner of the New Jersey garden at left, who prepared the soil carefully, then planted crops in neat raised beds, you'll want to tackle organic kitchen gardening methodically. Assess your site, your climate, and your needs, and then concentrate on feeding the soil that will feed your plants. By following the techniques presented in this chapter and relying exclusively on organic amendments, fertilizers, pesticides, and fungicides, you'll not only protect your health and that of the environment, you'll also enjoy a robust, productive garden.

Siting a Successful Vegetable Garden

A south-facing slope provides the Wisconsin garden below with the double benefit of long hours of sunshine and shelter from chilling northerly winds. In a sunny spot at the garden's center, a latticework trellis awaits the climbing tendrils of late-summer pole beans. Lettuce, which enjoys some protection from the sun, has been planted in the shade cast by trees at the east end of the garden.

An orderly plot of dark, crumbly soil brimming with vigorous, carefully tended vegetables and fruits is a handsome expression of the gardener's art, as beautiful in its own way as an artfully composed perennial border. Before you begin the appetizing task of deciding which varieties to grow, however, you need to do some thoughtful planning so that the venture will be a productive one.

The first order of business is to choose the best site your property has to offer for this purpose. Although such matters as the size, convenience, and appearance of a vegetable garden are important factors to keep in mind, growing conditions should be at the top of your list of concerns as you compare the possibilities your yard offers.

Soil and Microclimates

The foundation of a successful organic garden is, literally, a fertile, well-drained soil teeming with microorganisms. If yours doesn't fill the bill in its present condition, this chapter details some reliable methods organic gardeners can use to turn inferior soil into a good growing medium *(pages 23-33)*. Climate, the other variable critical to garden success, is far less amenable to manipulation and control. In this instance, your goal is to find the microclimate on your property with the sunlight, temperature range, and air circulation your vegetables need to flourish.

The Primacy of Sunlight

Of the climatic variables, sunlight is the most important. Except for a handful of shade-tolerant crops—lettuce, for one—vegetables require at least 6 hours of direct sun per day for optimal growth; if you have a spot that is in full sun for 7 or 8 hours, so much the better.

If a survey of your property turns up several

places with ample sunlight, look for differences in their microclimates that can tip the balance in favor of one over the others. For gardeners in cold climates, an especially desirable location is a gentle, open slope that faces south and receives a full day of sun. Because the sunlight strikes the surface of the slope at an angle, the soil will warm up earlier in the spring and remain warm longer in the fall, making it more productive than it would be if the ground were level. A northern exposure has a very different set of conditions—fewer hours of direct sunlight, cooler soil temperatures, and, in many parts of North America, prevailing northwesterly winds that remove heat from the soil and shorten the growing season.

High Winds and Frost Pockets

From whatever direction they come, strong winds are harmful to the garden: They rob the soil of moisture, and they can also uproot plants and topple the supports that hold vining vegetables. As a rule, an exposed site at the top of a slope or hill is especially vulnerable to the cooling and drying effects of the wind, effects that are exacerbated in freezing weather or during a period of drought. If you have no alternative to such adverse conditions, you could plant a windbreak of two or three staggered rows of closely spaced evergreen trees or shrubs, then site your garden on the lee side and far enough away to avoid any root competition or shade from the windbreak.

Frost pockets can be equally destructive to tender plants. The result of cold, heavy air settling in low areas or on the uphill side of a building or a hedge running across a slope, frost pockets are colder in winter and prone to frost later in spring and earlier in fall, greatly shortening the growing season. If you have a dense, solid hedge that blocks air flow, you can alleviate the problem by removing a section of it to allow cold air to continue its downward movement.

Size, Looks, and Convenience

Next, you'll need to decide how much space you wish to devote to your garden plot or, if space is limited, how much you can spare for this purpose. If you are new to raising vegetables, it's prudent to keep the plot small the first year to avoid taking on more work than you bargained for. An area measuring no more than 10 feet square, for instance, can yield upwards of 60 pounds of vegetables a year and will give you a good idea of how much

time and effort tending your garden will require. After a season's trial run, you can always expand the size the following year. The chart on page 41 provides information on how much you can expect to harvest in a season from a 10-foot row of 30 different kinds of vegetables.

When it comes to how visible a vegetable patch should be, people differ in their opinions. Some may enjoy having a burgeoning plot in full view of the terrace, while others prefer to tuck theirs out of sight behind the garage or along one side of the house. But if you're a gardener for whom convenience outweighs aesthetics, a plot close to the kitchen has many advantages. For one, you'll be more likely to visit the garden every day, checking its progress, pulling weed seedlings, and harvesting vegetables at their peak. And you won't have to carry your prized produce more than a few short steps.

The vegetable garden should also have easy access to water. From planting time to harvest, watering is one chore that can't get short shrift. You'll also find it very handy to have the compost

In late summer, an edging of frilly green parsley and colorful marigolds decorates a raised bed that contains a mature clump of blooming basil, onions, and rows of romaine seedlings for fall salads (below). The clipped yews in the background protect the vegetables and herbs from the cold northeast winds that buffet this New Jersey garden.

Indigo-colored Lobelia erinus and mixed zinnias mingle with edible species—including pink-flowering garlic, a stand of yellow peppers, Phaseolus coccineus (scarlet runner bean) in full crimson bloom, and broad-leaved eggplant—rendering this California garden both practical and beautiful.

pile—an integral part of organic gardening—close to the vegetable plot and the kitchen, since both generate waste for composting.

A Tailor-Made Design

The classic layout for a vegetable garden is a rectangular plot, often fenced to keep animals out. The plot may be divided into a series of rows, but many gardeners prefer to divide it into two or more individual beds separated by paths of hardened earth, mulch, flagstone, or turf grass.

Dividing a plot into separate beds makes it easy to group vegetables that have similar soil, moisture, and nutritional requirements. Although the surface of a bed can be level with the surrounding soil, there are great advantages to mounding the soil so that the surface is elevated by 4 inches or more. Mounding not only ensures good drainage, it also allows the soil to warm up more quickly in the spring because more of it is exposed to the air; this lets you begin planting earlier than usual.

A raised bed is also the ideal space for applying intensive gardening techniques. Because the soil in the bed is tailored to meet the nutrient requirements of the vegetables you plant there, they can be placed very close to one another without suffering the adverse effects of competition. You will reap more produce from your initial planting and can also feel confident that a subsequent crop won't be shortchanged.

A plot with multiple beds is the most efficient way to grow vegetables. If space doesn't permit this layout, however, you can disperse beds around your property, fitting them in wherever there is room and the conditions are appropriate. Planting vegetables—especially dwarf varieties—in containers is another way to expand your growing area *(pages 76-77)*. And if you're still hungry for edible plants, consider making room among the perennials and annuals of an ornamental border for such attractive vegetable varieties as a ruffly bright chartreuse lettuce or purple broccoli *(pages 50-51)*. Like your vegetables, the flowering plants will thrive on an organic regimen.

Soil: Your Garden's Foundation

A vegetable garden imposes high demands on soil: It must nourish a succession of closely spaced plants with a variety of nutritional needs; produce a harvest within a few months; and, if the gardener wants to coax the highest yield possible from the plot, provide good growing conditions from very early spring until well after fall frosts arrive.

The raw material you have to work with may not seem promising. The typical city or suburban gardener in North America has inherited a soil that has been changed, seldom for the better, by activities such as farming, lumbering, and construction. The topsoil's natural fertility may have been depleted. Worse, the topsoil itself may have been bulldozed away, exposing the underlying, largely infertile, subsoil layer *(right)*. With the right organic techniques, however, even the most discouraging plot can be made productive.

Sand, Silt, and Clay

Many gardeners think of soil as a purely mineral substance, but in fact the mineral component of loam—the ideal soil for growing vegetables—accounts for somewhat less than 50 percent of its volume. Air and water each account for around 25 percent, and organic matter for 5 percent.

About half of the mineral component of loam is sand; the other half is clay or silt, or a mixture of the two. What distinguishes these three kinds of particles from one another is size: Sand particles, visible to the naked eye, are the largest; silt particles are the next largest, and clay the smallest.

How a soil feels to the touch and how loose or dense it is will help you determine what kind of soil you have. The best time to examine it is 2 or 3 days after a heavy rain or a thorough watering; the soil should be moist but not soggy. Dig a hole several inches deep with a trowel and scoop out a handful of soil. Rub some between your thumb and fingers, then let it all fall between your fingers to the ground. If the soil feels rough and gritty and slips quickly through your fingers, it is predominantly sand. If it feels smooth and floury and adheres slightly to your fingers, it is predominantly silt. Soil that feels rather slick and tends to make a sticky lump is mostly clay. If the soil is loam, it will be loose, crumbly, and slightly moist.

Next, test how well or how poorly the soil drains: Dig a hole 10 to 12 inches deep and wide,

Soil from Top to Bottom

A section of earth several feet deep reveals four distinct layers *(below)*. The surface of the soil is covered with a leafy litter, which decomposes to become part of the topsoil **(A)**. Usually measuring 4 to 8 inches in depth, topsoil owes its rich color and fertility to the organic matter it contains. Vegetable roots are largely confined to this layer. The next layer, mineral subsoil **(B)**, is as deep as 30 inches, has very little organic matter, and is inhospitable to vegetables unless it is deeply tilled and amended. The lowest soil layer **(C)** contains rock fragments broken off from the bedrock below **(D)**. Over time these fragments migrate upward and break down into particles that become part of the subsoil and, ultimately, the topsoil.

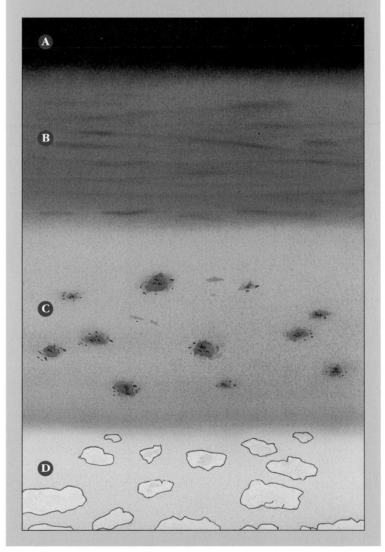

pour in a gallon of water, and note how long it takes for all of the water to drain out of the hole. The water will disappear in about 5 minutes in a sandy soil and in 5 to 15 minutes in loam. If it takes longer than 15 minutes to disappear, you have a silty or clayey soil. Sandy, silty, and clayey soils all need improvement if vegetables are to thrive.

The Importance of Drainage

A prime virtue of a loamy soil's blend of large and small particles is that water drains neither too quickly nor too slowly, so plants aren't routinely subjected either to overly dry conditions or to waterlogging. Moisture imbalances hamper plant growth in several ways. In a very fast-draining, sandy soil, plant tissues are not only parched but also undernourished; plants can absorb nutrients only when they are dissolved in water, so applying fertilizer to a soil that is habitually dry won't be at all effective. By the same token, as water drains through a sandy soil, dissolved nutrients are quickly carried out of the reach of plant roots.

In a heavy, waterlogged, clay soil, air is the element in short supply. Air and water alternately occupy the network of spaces running through the solid part of soil. When water is removed—for example, when it drains away, is taken up by plant roots, or evaporates—air flows in to fill the empty spaces, delivering essential carbon, hydrogen, and oxygen to roots. If the soil's spaces remain filled with water, plants will suffocate.

Soil Nutrients and pH

The nutrient elements used by plants in the greatest quantities—nitrogen, phosphorus, and potassium—are supplied by the mineral and organic parts of the soil. Nitrogen is responsible for healthy leaf and stem development, phosphorus for strong root systems, and potassium for flowers and fruits. A secondary trio of elements—calcium, magnesium, and sulfur—are needed in smaller amounts. Plants require only tiny quantities of boron, zinc, and the other trace elements, so gardeners rarely, if ever, need to be concerned about them.

Whether the nutrients present in a particular soil are available to plants depends on the soil's pH, which is a measure of how acid or how alkaline the soil is. On a scale of 1 to 14, with 7 being the neutral point, the soil becomes progressively more acid below 7; above 7 it becomes increasingly more alkaline. Much as a refrigerator operates at an ideal temperature so that food neither spoils nor freezes, an optimal pH range enables soil to release just enough nutrients to keep plants well fed. Too high or too low a pH either blocks needed nutrients from being released or delivers the nutrients at toxic levels. A pH between 6 and 7 is ideal for the majority of vegetables.

The Role of Organic Matter

Organic matter has an influence that is far out of proportion to the small amount of it found in garden soil, even in loam. In the form of partially decomposed compost, leaves, straw, and other readily available materials, organic matter can dramatically improve the structure of a deficient soil and help achieve a good balance of air, water, and nutrients. Added to a sandy soil, it helps bind the large sand particles together, shrinks the volume of empty space in the soil, and makes the soil more water retentive. Added to clay in conjunction with sand, organic matter enlarges the soil's network of spaces, allowing water to drain more freely and air to circulate.

Still another benefit of organic matter is the nutrients it releases into the soil as it decomposes. Decaying organic matter is a food source for the array of creatures that reside in a healthy soil, including earthworms, insects, beneficial nematodes, bacteria, and fungi. This population plays a critical role in making a soil fertile and keeping it that way. One of the important contributions of these organisms is converting plant and animal tissue into a dark, crumbly material called humus, which gives good soil its rich, deep color. Humus can absorb up to 90 percent of its weight in water, so boosting the amount of humus in a poor, dry soil will help keep plants steadily supplied with moisture.

Testing Your Soil

To find out how your soil measures up in terms of pH, organic matter, and nutrients, you'll need to test it. To measure pH, you can use a hand-held electronic pH meter or litmus paper. For more detailed information on both pH and nutrient levels, analyze your soil with a ready-to-use testing kit. All of these devices are available at any large garden or home center.

To obtain a comprehensive professional analysis, submit a soil sample to your state Cooperative Extension Service or a commercial laboratory. The report you receive should state the type of soil you have and its pH level, organic matter content, and nutrient availability. It will also include recommendations for amendments and fertilizers you can use to improve the soil, so be sure to specify that you prefer organic products.

Organic Soil Enrichment

An amendment is a material that, when added to a soil, improves its structure by changing the way mineral particles adhere to one another. Sometimes it is necessary to add two or more amendments at the same time to get the desired effect.

For example, you can work shredded leaves and a substance called greensand into a clay soil to help improve drainage. The greensand, a dark green, grainy mineral, loosens the clay particles, and the newly created open spaces allow air and water to move more freely through the soil. The shredded leaves nourish soil life and prevent the combination of clay and greensand from producing a soil so hard that roots and water can scarcely penetrate it.

Organic fertilizers supplement the soil's level of available nutrients, notably nitrogen, phosphorus, and potassium, and they also contribute to the

Building a Compost Pile

A well-made compost pile is an ideal habitat for microorganisms, providing the food, water, air, and warmth they need to grow and reproduce at top speed. A thriving population quickly converts ordinary kitchen and garden waste into an invaluable fertilizer and soil conditioner.

The microorganisms need a balanced diet of carbon and nitrogen. Fibrous materials such as dry leaves, straw, and sawdust provide plenty of carbon, while nitrogen is furnished by green materials such as grass clippings, wastes from the vegetable garden or flower bed, and kitchen scraps (vegetables and fruits only).

To start a compost pile, spread a layer of brown fibrous material several inches deep and at least 3 feet wide and 3 feet across on bare soil. Add a layer of green material and sprinkle

it with soil or a commercial compost activator to introduce microorganisms. Water until the materials are damp like a sponge. Continue in this fashion until the layered pile is at least 3 feet high—the size necessary to generate sufficient heat. Turn the pile once or twice a week with a garden fork to aerate it and rid the center of excess moisture. Water as needed to keep the pile slightly moist. The compost is ready to use when it is dark and crumbly.

The three-bin composter shown below can produce a large, steady supply of compost. The decomposing pile in the center bin is flanked by a newly assembled pile *(right)* and a bin containing finished compost *(left)*. Wire mesh on three sides and the gaps between the slats on the bin's front help keep the pile aerated. The slats are removable, making it easy to turn the pile. Several smaller compost bins are shown on the next page.

25

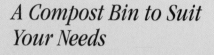

Decomposing waste occupies one of the two cinder-block bins at left; the other stores finished compost. The spaces between the blocks allow air to circulate. You can mortar the blocks at the back and the sides of the bins, but leave the front blocks free so you can remove the compost.

A Compost Bin to Suit Your Needs

Even the simplest compost bin keeps decomposing wastes tidy and compact. And as long as you have the right mix of ingredients and enough of them, it will generate the heat needed to ensure speedy decomposition. For free-standing compost piles or those in open bins, you should start with a pile measuring 3 feet wide, deep, and high. For the ready-made bins available at home and garden centers, simply fill them according to the manufacturer's instructions.

Each of the composters shown here can be easily constructed or purchased for less than a hundred dollars. Some require that the debris pile be turned manually, while others need little or no attention from the gardener.

To create the bin at right, wrap a length of hardware cloth 4 feet wide and 12 feet long around two stakes hammered into the ground. Secure the ends of the hardware cloth with wires. To aerate the compost pile, unfasten the cylinder, reposition the stakes adjacent to the loose pile, reassemble the cylinder, and turn the pile with a fork.

The plastic barrel composter at left is designed to produce finished compost in a month or less. The barrel rests on rollers; turning a handle rotates the barrel and aerates the contents thoroughly. Finished compost is removed through a hinged door on the barrel; a finished batch must be removed before starting a new one.

A compact plastic compost bin like the one at left is an excellent choice where space is limited. Fresh waste material can be added continually to the top of the bin while older material is decaying. Compost is retrieved from the pull-out drawer at the bottom of the bin. Enough air enters the bin through the large slots to make turning the pile unnecessary.

soil's volume of organic matter. All of the fertilizers organic gardeners use are made of animal and plant materials such as blood, fish, and seaweed.

An organic fertilizer's nutrients are released into the soil slowly; most of them become available for use only after soil microorganisms, mainly bacteria, have broken the material down. Synthetic fertilizers, on the other hand, typically supply fast-acting shots of nutrients that stimulate rapid spurts of growth. With repeated use, synthetics eventually kill much of a soil's population of valuable organisms and can also acidify the soil. Commercial organic fertilizers are labeled to show the percentages by weight of nitrogen, phosphorus, and potassium, in that order. A labeling of 5-3-4, for example, means that the product contains 5 percent nitrogen, 3 percent phosphorus, and 4 percent potassium. See the chart on page 33 for information on organic fertilizers and amendments.

All-Purpose Compost

Of the many soil amendments and fertilizers you can use, the best one for an organic garden is com-post. Consisting mainly of partially decayed plant wastes, it is an excellent source of organic matter and a reservoir for many nutrients.

As an amendment, compost can convert a sandy or clayey soil into loam. And, because it has a nearly neutral pH value, it helps keep soil in the range vegetables prefer. As a fertilizer, finished compost provides a good balance of 2 parts nitrogen to 1 part each of phosphorus and potassium. If it is made from a large variety of materials, compost will contain a healthy balance of trace elements as well as the major nutrients.

To make compost properly, gardeners combine two kinds of plant materials—fibrous materials such as leaves, straw, and sawdust (often referred to collectively as "browns"), and succulent "greens" such as grass clippings and kitchen scraps. The browns are the source of the carbon required for decomposition, while the greens furnish nitrogen. The greens and browns are assembled in a pile of alternating layers *(page 25)*.

When the pile is kept about as moist as a well-squeezed sponge and its layers are turned and mixed regularly to incorporate air, the decay microorganisms are very active. The energy released

The sandy soil of this Long Island vegetable garden is enriched with regular additions of compost and mulched with seaweed from nearby beaches. Before the seaweed is spread, it is washed to remove the salt; as it decomposes, it will add organic matter to the soil.

27

Starting a Vegetable Garden

A sunny patch of lawn is often the best place to site a new vegetable garden, and the best time to begin the work of creating it is the season prior to planting. Clearing and tilling the plot at that point, as described in the first two steps on this page, gives the soil time to fully incorporate any amendments and fertilizers you have added; the result is a more fertile medium for seeds and seedlings when planting season arrives. Several weeks in advance of planting, till the soil lightly with a garden fork or broadfork *(box, page 32)*. Then build the beds and mulch the paths, as described in Steps 3, 4, and 5. Shaping the prepared soil into raised beds is well worth the effort required; better drainage and more room for root growth mean more vigorous plants and a more bountiful harvest.

1. Mark the perimeter of your vegetable plot with stakes and string. *Using a sharp square-bladed spade and working just inside the string, slice down through the sod to the depth of the spade (above); do this all the way around the plot. Next, use the spade to cut the sod into sections small enough to lift easily. Pry each one loose with the spade or a garden fork and knock the topsoil off the roots. Remove the stakes and string.*

2. Till the plot with a rotary rear-tined tiller *(above) to the depth of one tiller blade—approximately 8 to 12 inches. Work your way up and down the length of the plot, then repeat the process across the plot. After you have tilled the soil, remove any large stones, roots, weeds, or bits of sod. Incorporate amendments or fertilizers as needed to correct soil deficiencies, working them into the top 6 to 8 inches of soil with a spading fork.*

3. Using stakes and string, measure and mark off the tilled plot *into individual beds and pathways (above). Make each bed 3 to 5 feet wide so the plants in the center will be within easy reach. For convenience in moving around the beds, make them no more than 15 to 20 feet long. Pathways 2 feet or more in width allow room to maneuver tools and equipment, such as a garden cart, between the beds.*

4. To mound up the soil for a raised bed, *first place a 1-by-4 board in the center of the bed: If you need to step into the bed, the board will distribute your weight, minimizing soil compaction. Standing on one side of the space you've staked out, use a raised-bed builder (below) or a flat rake to reach across the bed and rake tilled soil from the path area into the bed. Repeat from each side of the bed, sloping the sides a bit to minimize erosion. Then, with the back of the tool, smooth and level the surface of the bed (right). The bed should be 4 to 5 inches higher than the surrounding paths.*

5. Mulch the paths with straw, *as shown here, or another organic material to suppress weeds and conserve soil moisture. Spread straw, pine needles, and other loose, airy mulches 3 to 4 inches deep; for a denser mulch such as woodchips or ground bark, 1 to 2 inches is enough. By the end of the growing season, the mulch will have decomposed enough to be dug into the soil.*

Double Digging for Deeper Soil

Double digging a vegetable garden is doubly heavy work, since the soil is tilled in two steps to a total depth of 2 feet instead of the usual 8 to 12 inches. But the work is worth it, especially in heavy clay soils prone to compaction. Water, air, and nutrients move much more freely, and roots spread more widely, through the deep layer of loosened soil. If you combine double digging with intensive planting techniques, you'll be rewarded with very large harvests.

Choose a time when the soil is moist but not wet; if you're ready to plant and the soil is dry, water it deeply. Beginning at one end of the bed, use a heavy-duty spade to dig a trench about 1 foot wide and deep; move the topsoil to a tarp or wheelbarrow. Next, push the tines of a spading fork as far into the exposed subsoil as you can and move the fork back and forth to loosen the soil. For an extra-rich soil, spread a layer of manure or compost over the subsoil. Then dig a second trench parallel to the first, moving its topsoil to the first trench and letting it slide off the spade right side up so that the topsoil structure remains undisturbed.

Loosen the subsoil of the second trench *(above, left)* and slide over topsoil dug from a third trench *(above, right),* being careful to keep the soil right side up. Repeat the sequence until you reach the end of the bed. Use the topsoil set aside from the first trench to fill in the last.

during decomposition raises the mound's internal temperature to as much as 160°F, which in turn stimulates chemical processes to break the material down even further. With this method, called "hot composting," the finished product will be ready in as little as a month; at the end of that time, the mass of material will have shrunk to approximately one-third of its original size.

Some gardeners prefer the "cold composting" method, which is less work: Once the pile is assembled, it is left undisturbed. However, the materials will decay slowly, and it may be 2 years before you have finished compost. Unless you have room for several piles in different stages of decomposition, this method probably won't provide enough compost for your vegetable garden.

Timing Soil Improvements

Enriching the soil is an ongoing chore for the vegetable gardener. When establishing a new plot *(pages 28-29),* dig in a 2- to 3-inch layer of compost to improve soil structure; at the same time, correct any deficiencies uncovered by soil testing.

In most parts of the country, applications of 1 to 2 inches of organic matter twice a year, in spring and fall, are sufficient to maintain good soil structure and to ensure a healthy population of soil organisms. In the Deep South, however, where summers are hot and humid and winters are short and mild, organic matter decomposes at a much faster rate, so gardeners need to replenish it at least three times a year.

Tilling the Garden

Tilling or cultivating the soil at least twice a year, in spring and in fall, is a task that can't be avoided. It is the time to work in fertilizers and amendments, and the simple act of turning the soil is itself beneficial in several ways: It restores lightness to compacted soil so plant roots get the water and air they

Closely spaced rows of lettuce grow to near perfection in the rich, well-drained soil of this Idaho garden. The raised bed has been double dug (box, above) and planted with such varieties as 'Red Sails' (second from left) and the ruddy-leaved 'Red Salad Bowl' (far right). Purple-flowered Allium schoenoprasum (chives) edges the straw-covered path in the background.

A Tool for Easy Tilling

A bed that has been prepared and then left to rest for weeks or months will inevitably undergo some compaction because of rain, snow, and gravity. For loosening the soil at planting time, many organic gardeners prefer to use a broadfork *(below)*, a tool that alleviates the work of lifting and turning the soil required by the more commonly used garden fork. The broadfork, also called a U-bar, has long handles and five or six tines attached to a horizontal crossbar. The tines vary in length from 10 to 18 inches; the long-tined models are designed for the deeply cultivated soil of double-dug beds, the short-tined ones for single-dug beds.

To use the broadfork, hold it upright and step up and onto the crossbar, using your weight to push the tines down into the soil. Step off and pull the broadfork's handles toward you until the tips of the tines lift out of the soil. Repeat this process at 6-inch intervals across the area to be planted, moving backward to avoid stepping on soil you have already cultivated.

need. The increased oxygen content also stimulates the activity of soil life. And in spring, the loosened soil warms up more quickly, giving the gardener a jump on the new growing season.

There are a variety of tools for tilling, including rotary tillers and hand tools such as spades, spading forks, and broadforks. A rotary tiller makes sense for large plots, and it makes the work of preparing a new garden or turning under a cover crop *(pages 130-131)* much easier. However, using this tool on the garden more than twice a year tends to compact the soil. For that reason, choose hand tools for tilling work during the growing season.

When you are ready to till, spread any amendment or fertilizer over the entire area to be cultivated *(see chart at right for application rates)*. If you are using a spade or a spading fork, push the blade or the tines all the way into the soil, then lift the soil and turn it over. Use a broadfork as described in the box at left. If you can't avoid stepping in the area you are tilling, stand on a board to distribute your weight more evenly.

Beds versus Rows

A tilled plot is almost ready for planting. The last step is to subdivide the plot into either narrow rows or rectangular raised beds like those on page 28. Although row planting has its adherents, it has at least two major drawbacks. For one thing, an alternating pattern of rows and paths is an inefficient use of space because much less of the total area is actually devoted to crops. When you arrange your plants in beds, on the other hand, you greatly reduce the area occupied by paths. In addition, shrinking the area taken up by paths keeps the potential for soil compaction to a minimum.

Another advantage of raised beds is that their greater depth of topsoil provides better drainage and more space for the roots of vegetables to grow downward. The additional soil needed to raise the beds 4 or 5 inches is furnished by digging out the paths between the beds *(page 29)*.

The center of each bed should be within easy reach so that there's no need to step into the bed when you are tending plants or harvesting vegetables. Beds with access from two sides should be no wider than 4 or 5 feet. If there is access from one side only, limit the width to 3 feet. The length of a bed is more flexible, but don't make it so long that you'll be tempted to take a shortcut across it instead of sticking to the paths surrounding it. Be sure to make the paths that run between the beds at least 2 feet wide so there will be enough room for a garden cart.

ORGANIC AMENDMENTS AND FERTILIZERS

Below is a selection of widely available organic amendments and fertilizers. In most cases, they can be worked into the soil during tilling in either fall or spring; fresh manures are best applied in the fall so they can partially decompose over the winter. Fertilizers can be applied once or twice during the growing season for crops needing a nutrient boost or for new plantings. Unless otherwise noted, amendments that change pH should be used as often as soil tests indicate.

Name	Function	Application Rate	Comments
Blood meal	Fertilizer. Provides nitrogen.	2 lbs./100 sq. ft.	Also called dried blood. When using as a side dressing, keep 2 to 3 inches away from plant stems.
Bone meal	Fertilizer. Provides phosphorus, calcium.	2 lbs./100 sq. ft.	Work into topsoil immediately after applying; otherwise, the pungent odor may attract rodents.
Chicken manure, rotted	Amendment/fertilizer. Adds organic matter. Provides nitrogen, phosphorus, potassium.	1-inch layer	Work into topsoil in fall or compost before using.
Compost	Amendment/fertilizer. Loosens clay soils, binds sandy soils, increases water-holding capacity. Adds organic matter. Provides nitrogen, phosphorus, potassium.	2- to 3-inch layer	Best all-purpose amendment.
Cottonseed meal	Fertilizer. Provides nitrogen, phosphorus, potassium.	2.5 lbs./100 sq. ft.	May be contaminated by pesticides.
Cow manure, rotted	Amendment/fertilizer. Adds organic matter. Provides nitrogen, phosphorus, potassium.	1- to 2-inch layer	Work into topsoil in fall or compost before using.
Fish emulsion	Fertilizer. Provides nitrogen.	¼ oz./100 sq. ft.	Sold as concentrated liquid that is diluted for use. Can also be applied as a foliar spray.
Fish meal	Fertilizer. Provides nitrogen, phosphorus.	2 lbs./100 sq. ft.	Also called fish scrap, fish tankage. Apply just before planting or as a side dressing during the growing season.
Greensand	Amendment/fertilizer. Retards soil compaction, loosens clay soils, increases water-holding capacity. Provides potassium, trace elements.	5 lbs./100 sq. ft.	Use in conjunction with organic matter to amend clay soil.
Gypsum	Amendment. Loosens clay soils, balances pH. Provides calcium, sulfur.	2 lbs./100 sq. ft.	Also called land plaster, sulfate of lime. Pellets easier to use than powder.
Horse manure, rotted	Amendment/fertilizer. Adds organic matter. Provides nitrogen, phosphorus, potassium, trace elements.	1- to 2-inch layer	Work into topsoil in fall or compost before using.
Leaf mold	Amendment/fertilizer. Builds up soil humus content quickly. Adds organic matter. Provides nitrogen, phosphorus, potassium.	2-inch layer	Also called woods-soil when sold commercially. Can also be used as a mulch; apply a 2- to 3-inch layer.
Limestone	Amendment. Raises pH. Provides calcium, magnesium.	6 lbs./100 sq. ft. for clay 4 lbs./100 sq. ft. for loam 2 lbs./100 sq. ft. for sandy	Also called ground limestone, dolomitic limestone. Avoid hydrated lime or quicklime—they dissolve too quickly in the soil and burn plant roots and kill soil life.
Peat moss	Amendment. Loosens clay soils, lowers pH, increases water-holding capacity. Adds organic matter.	1- to 2-inch layer	Also called sphagnum peat moss. Work into topsoil.
Rock phosphate	Amendment/fertilizer. Raises pH. Provides phosphorus, trace elements.	2.5 lbs./100 sq. ft.	Most effective if applied to acid soils.
Sawdust	Amendment. Adds organic matter. Provides nitrogen, potassium.	1-inch layer	Apply only well-rotted sawdust to soil. Best if added to the compost pile.
Seaweed meal	Fertilizer. Provides nitrogen, potassium, trace elements.	1 to 2 lbs./100 sq. ft.	Also called kelp meal. Apply in early spring and work into topsoil.
Straw	Amendment. Adds organic matter. Provides nitrogen, phosphorus, potassium.	2- to 3-inch layer	Buy straw labeled "weed free." Can also be applied as a mulch, then turned under when it decays.
Sulfur	Amendment. Loosens clay soils, improves water-holding capacity, lowers pH.	Up to 1 lb./100 sq. ft. applied every 8 weeks	Also called soil sulfur. After working into topsoil, water thoroughly.
Wood ashes (leached)	Amendment/fertilizer. Raises pH. Provides potassium, calcium.	2 lbs./100 sq. ft.	Keep stored wood ashes dry to prevent nutrients from leaching out. When using as a side dressing, keep 2 to 3 inches away from plant stems.

Siting a Successful Herb Garden

Both culinary herbs and ornamentals thrive in this formal Mobile, Alabama, garden. The growing conditions offered by the site support a variety of plants, including yellow-flowering dill and fennel in the four outer beds and low-growing hollies surrounding the sundial. White flowering tobacco blooms at the edge of the lawn.

As with vegetables, the first step in growing herbs successfully is to assess the growing conditions in your garden. Variations in soil, microclimate, and light exposure will produce several different habitats that are congenial to different kinds of herbs. Although some herbs are very choosy about their soil requirements, most will grow vigorously in an open, loamy, well-drained soil. If drainage is too slow—usually because the soil is clayey—the oxygen that is vital for normal growth will be replaced by water. Plants may suffocate or, in less extreme conditions, produce weak shoots that tend to wilt or die back at the tips.

Only a few herbs tolerate waterlogged soil. If you have a drainage problem in a spot where you want to plant a wide variety of herbs, you'll need to loosen the soil. Begin by laying out your bed in the fall and digging the soil to a depth of 12 to 18 inches. In early spring, work in a 1- to 2-inch layer of builder's sand or poultry grit and about 1 inch of organic matter such as compost or leaf mold. Let the bed settle for several weeks before planting. If amending the existing soil is too big a job, you may prefer to build a raised bed *(pages 68-69)*.

Some Like It Sandy

If your garden has a coarse, sandy soil, it will provide the fast drainage some herbs demand, no-

tably those that are native to the Mediterranean region. These include such favorites as rosemary, thyme, and oregano. To accommodate herbs that prefer moist, fertile soil, incorporate about 2 inches of organic matter; this will enhance the soil's ability to hold water and will prevent nutrients from draining away too quickly. Be diligent about watering, and replenish the supply of organic matter periodically.

Picky Eaters

Fast-growing annual herbs that are harvested repeatedly for their leaves and stems require high levels of nutrients to continue producing new growth. They should be fed with liquid fertilizer every 2 weeks. You can make your own fertilizer from the potassium-rich foliage of comfrey (*Symphytum officinale*), a perennial herb. Pour 4 cups of boiling water over a handful of fresh comfrey leaves. Steep them for at least 10 minutes, then strain the liquid through cheesecloth and let it cool before using. Along with potassium, this infusion will provide phosphorus, nitrogen, trace elements, and minerals. The leaves of a number of other herbs, such as tansy, goosefoot, nettle, yarrow, dill, and coltsfoot, can also be made into liquid fertilizer.

Restraint is called for when you fertilize perennial and woody herbs, which will respond to small doses of organic fertilizer with increased vigor and health. Bone meal, blood meal, fish emulsion, and kelp are all excellent choices. Working compost into the soil at the beginning of the growing season will also boost the level of nutrients.

Testing the Soil's pH

As with vegetables, before planting herbs it's prudent to determine the soil's pH, which is a measure of its acidity or alkalinity *(page 24)*. You can do it yourself with a kit bought at a garden center, or you can send a soil sample to your Cooperative Extension Service for testing. Most soils in the eastern half of the country are acidic because of high rainfall levels that leach alkaline elements from the soil. Conversely, alkaline soils are common in the drier West.

The majority of herbs grow well in soils ranging from 6, which is slightly acid, to 7.5, which is mildly alkaline. If the pH falls outside this range, nutrients in the soil may not be available to plants. To raise the pH level, dust the soil with dolomitic limestone at least 1 month before planting, fol-

lowing the directions on the package. An application of sulfur will lower the pH level if your soil is too alkaline. For gardeners in the eastern part of the country who want to grow any of the Mediterranean herbs, soil testing is essential. Although these plants will grow in slightly acid soil, their preference is for a pH range of 7 to 8.2.

Light and Climate

Most herbs are sun worshipers, requiring at least 6 hours of direct light each day. Ideally, then, an herb bed should have a southern exposure. When

This rustic dooryard garden in Texas provides the perfect spot for sun-loving herbs. Fennel and bay laurel grace the front of the bed, while silver artemisia and a border of lavender-flowered onion chives lead the eye toward the house. Mexican oregano, growing behind the fennel, is a native herb used in Southwest cuisine.

assessing how much light a site receives, be sure to factor in shade cast from structures such as sheds, trellises, and walls, as well as hedges, shrubs, and trees. Luckily for gardeners who lack full-sun sites, several culinary herbs—among them parsley, chives, chervil, and hot peppers—can be planted in partial shade (4 to 6 hours of sun a day).

The intensity of light is as important as the number of hours of sunshine. Herbs that prefer fewer than 6 hours of sun grow best with direct morning light and dappled light or shade during the afternoon. Bright afternoon sun may be filtered by planting herbs on the northeast side of a trellis covered with a quick-growing vine.

Climate is another factor to consider when growing herbs. Winter cold presents special challenges to gardeners who want to grow an herb that isn't reliably hardy in their zone. To greatly increase the prospects for winter survival:

• Locate your herb bed near a wall or an evergreen hedge for protection from winter winds.

• Avoid fertilizing or pruning borderline-hardy herbs late in the season; the new growth this stimulates will be more susceptible to winter injury than growth that has had time to mature.

• Mulch the bed with evergreen boughs after the ground has frozen.

• Pot up tender plants in the fall for overwintering indoors. Shrubby herbs like rosemary are good candidates for this treatment *(page 83)*.

Gardeners in the South have the advantage of a long growing season. There are, however, a few cultural practices that are critical for healthy herbs in the typically hot, steamy southern summers.

Improving air circulation is important for all herbs cultivated in high humidity, which favors fungal diseases such as powdery mildew. Allow plenty of growing space between plants, and thin them to keep the interior airy.

Herbs with gray or silver leaves are difficult to grow in muggy climates; the little hairs that give the leaves their grayish cast also slow evaporation. This trait is a boon in hot, dry climates but a drawback where the moisture level is high. Give these plants a sunny site and mulch them with a 2-inch layer of light-colored sand or gravel, which will reflect light and heat onto the plants.

Herbs that cannot tolerate the intense heat of midsummer can be planted in early spring and harvested as long as temperatures re-

Herbs for Hot, Humid Climates

Allium ampeloprasum **var. *ampeloprasum*** (elephant garlic)
Artemisia dracunculus **var. *sativa*** (French tarragon)
Cymbopogon citratus (lemon grass)
Foeniculum vulgare (fennel)
Ocimum **spp.** (basil)
Rosmarinus officinalis (rosemary)
Salvia elegans (pineapple sage)

Salvia officinalis **'Berggarten'** (sage)
Tagetes lucida (sweet marigold)
Thymus **spp.** (thyme)

Note: The abbreviation "spp." stands for the plural of "species"; where used in lists it means that many, but not all, of the species in a genus meet the criterion of the list.

***Ocimum basilicum* 'Dark Opal' (basil)**

In the Texas herb garden below, a tall brick wall shelters plants from buffeting winds and creates a hospitable microclimate of reflected warmth for sun-loving herbs, including garlic chives and wormwood (lower left), rosemary and pink 'Fairy' roses (center), and Spanish lavender (lower right).

main moderate. After a midsummer break, a second planting can be made in early fall. Remember, too, that an herb that thrives in full sun in the North may perform well in the South only if it is sheltered from the blazing afternoon sun.

Finding a Home for Herbs

Herbs have traditionally occupied a separate and distinct place in the garden. In the monastery gardens of medieval Europe, for example, kitchen herbs were segregated from other plants and organized by type—say, leafy culinary herbs in one bed, and onions, garlic, and shallots in another. Similarly, herbs in dooryard gardens of Colonial America were grouped according to how they were used in the household.

Today, many gardeners continue this tradition by keeping valued culinary herbs close at hand. Foremost are flavorings and garnishes for the kitchen, including herbs for salads and soups, colorful and strong-flavored herbs to enliven bland

dishes, and herbs that ease digestion, such as fennel, dill, and caraway. In addition, herbs for the teapot—chamomile, mint, hyssop, lovage, and lemon balm, to name just a few—are often only a few steps from the kitchen.

Culinary herbs needn't be relegated to a separate plot, however. In fact, many kitchen gardens contain both vegetables and herbs—and perhaps fruits as well. And like vegetables, many culinary herbs mix well with ornamental plants in beds and borders *(pages 50-51)*. If gardening space is limited, kitchen herbs are especially well suited to growing in containers, too *(pages 78-88)*.

In this New Jersey garden, kitchen herbs create a feast for the eyes as well as the palate. Curving blades of lemon grass arch over spiky rosemary, while broad-leaved borage elbows for space with neat mounds of lemon basil and orange mint. White-flowering cilantro brightens the scene.

CHAPTER THREE

Designing Your Garden

One of the most common misconceptions about growing vegetables and culinary herbs is that you don't have to spend much time planning or designing the garden before you plant: All you need to do is put the seeds or transplants in the ground, and you'll soon be rewarded with a bountiful crop.

On the contrary, kitchen gardens can require as much forethought as ornamental beds and borders—sometimes more. At its simplest, planning an edible garden means deciding what you'd like to grow, how many plants you'll need, and where and when to put them in the ground. A well-conceived garden plan can mean the difference between an abundant harvest and very little to show for a season of hard work. For example, the tidy network of beds in the Vermont garden at left was carefully designed to ensure a healthy yield at harvest time.

This chapter describes the various stages involved in the planning process, including plant selection and drawing a garden plan, as well as design techniques for using space efficiently and for keeping crops healthy.

Planning a Vegetable Garden

Planning is particularly important for the organic gardener. Providing the best environment for healthy and productive plants without using synthetic fertilizers requires preparation and forethought. Laying out your garden on paper, for example, allows you to use all of your available space to best advantage. Other techniques help you increase yield and improve the quality of your produce. Succession planting and interplanting, for instance, allow you to harvest two or more crops from the same space in one growing season, and crop rotation minimizes pests and diseases and slows the depletion of soil nutrients.

In this section, you'll learn specific techniques for planning and designing gardens consisting primarily of vegetables. For information on selecting culinary herbs and designing herb gardens, see pages 47-49.

Choosing Which Vegetables to Plant

To decide what crops to grow in your garden, begin with a list of the vegetables that you and your family most like to eat. You may also want the list to include vegetables that are picked by commercial growers before they reach maturity, such as tomatoes, or those that don't travel well and have lost some flavor by the time you purchase them in the grocery store. Or you may want to treat yourself to unusual vegetable varieties such as golden tomatoes, watermelon with bright yellow flesh, blue potatoes, and other exotic produce that is not widely available. Another addition to the list might be heirloom vegetables that were grown by our forebears and have been rescued from extinction by groups working to save and distribute the seed.

Go over your list and make sure your selections are ones that will grow well in your area. If some are questionable, check with other gardeners or your local Cooperative Extension Service. Keep in mind that by making minor adjustments in planting times, you can often expand the number of crops that will thrive in your garden. If you live in a very hot climate, for example, you can still grow crops such as lettuce and cabbage, which prefer cooler temperatures and a mix of sun and shade. You'll just need to plant them in spring and autumn, not in the middle of summer.

If you live in the part of the North where the

The pairing of 'Salad Bowl' and 'Red Sails' lettuce with onions in this garden not only makes a striking visual combination, it makes good sense as well. The dense growth of the lettuce plants keeps weeds at bay, and their shallow roots don't compete with the young onions for space. By the time the onions need more room, the lettuce will be finished.

growing season is no more than 90 days long, choose varieties that mature quickly so that you can harvest a ripe crop before cold weather arrives. In regions where a specific pest or disease is a problem, look for named varieties that are resistant to that particular affliction *(box, page 97)*. For example, the cucumber 'Fanfare' is resistant to powdery and downy mildews, angular leaf spot, anthracnose, scab, and cucumber mosaic virus, making it an ideal vegetable for places with humid summers where fungal diseases are prevalent.

Deciding How Much of Each Crop to Plant

Given the delightfully varied selection of vegetables, it's easy to overbuy seeds and plants. Before you make any purchases, it pays to find out what you can expect to harvest from one mature plant. Although the yield will depend in part on your growing conditions, certain vegetables and specific varieties are known to be strong producers. For example, one plant of the spaghetti squash 'Tivoli' is expected to produce three to five squashes during the growing season, each weighing between 3 and 5 pounds. By contrast, one plant of the yellow scalloped squash 'Sunburst' can produce 35 squashes *each month* during the peak of the growing season. In either case, a family of four—depending on their taste for squash—could be

Low-growing, rambling pumpkin plants make excellent intercropping partners with tall-growing corn, which has been planted at 2-week intervals to extend the harvest season. Both vegetables are heavy feeders, however, so the soil should be amended with generous amounts of organic material.

HOW MUCH TO EXPECT FROM YOUR GARDEN			
Vegetable	**Length of Harvest**	**Average Yield per 10' Row**	**Average Harvest per Week**
Asparagus	4-6 weeks	3 lbs.	0.6 lbs.
Bean, green (bush)	2 weeks	3 lbs.	1.5 lbs.
Bean, lima (bush)	3 weeks	2 lbs. with pod	0.7 lbs.
Bean, lima (pole)	4 weeks	4 lbs. with pod	1 lb.
Bean, pole	6 weeks	10 lbs.	1.7 lbs.
Beet	4 weeks	2.4 dozen	7 beets
Broccoli	4 weeks	4 lbs.	1 lb.
Cabbage	3-4 weeks	4 heads	1 head
Cantaloupe	3 weeks	9 melons	3 melons
Carrot	4 weeks	4 dozen	1 dozen
Chard	8 weeks	5 lbs.	0.6 lbs.
Corn, sweet	10 days	10 ears	1 ear/day
Cucumber	4 weeks	8 lbs.	2 lbs.
Kale	4-20 weeks	5 lbs.	0.5 lbs.
Lettuce, head	4 weeks	10 heads	2.5 heads
Lettuce, leaf	6 weeks	9 lbs.	1.5 lbs.
Okra	6 weeks	9 lbs.	1.5 lbs.
Onion	4-24 weeks	10 lbs.	0.8 lbs.
Parsnip	4 months	8 lbs.	2 lbs.
Pea, green	2 weeks	7 lbs. with pod	3.5 lbs.
Pepper, sweet	8 weeks	40 peppers	5 peppers
Potato	4 months	12 lbs.	0.8 lbs.
Potato, sweet	6 weeks	10 lbs.	1.7 lbs.
Pumpkin	1 month	10 lbs.	2.5 lbs.
Radish	2 weeks	7 dozen	3.5 dozen
Rhubarb	4-6 weeks	6 lbs.	1.2 lbs.
Spinach	4 weeks	5 lbs.	1.25 lbs.
Squash, summer	4 weeks	20 lbs.	5 lbs.
Tomato	8 weeks	30 lbs.	3.75 lbs.
Watermelon	3 weeks	4 melons	1.3 melons

A Three-Season Garden Plan

A vegetable garden that produces continuously from early spring to late fall by using succession planting would be most successful in Zones 5 to 7 and in the Pacific Coastal area. Each bed in the plan at right measures 2 feet by 4 feet, and the plants are drawn to scale.

To follow this three-season plan, plant bed No. 1 in the spring with a soil builder, such as rye. Till the rye under to make way for the summer pole beans. When the beans are spent, plant the bed with clover, the last crop of the growing season. Plant each of the other beds with the succession of crops shown in the three diagrams. To rotate the crops the next year, plant the soil builders in bed No. 2, and move each crop over by one bed. The plan schedules cabbage-family crops, which are vulnerable to the same soil-borne diseases, so that one member of the family does not follow another member either from season to season or from year to year.

Adaptations of this scheme are required in Zones 3 and 4, where the growing season is only 90 to 120 days long. There, two crops rather than three could be grown in the same space. Since northern summers tend to be shorter and cooler, spring vegetables will continue to bear through midsummer. After they are finished, replace them with a new crop of cool-season vegetables for fall, although it's wise to select frost-hardy ones such as kale, kohlrabi, and mustard greens. Start warm-season crops indoors so they can be harvested before the end of August, when early frosts may threaten. Leave space for them in the spring garden so you have somewhere to put them when it is safe to plant them outside.

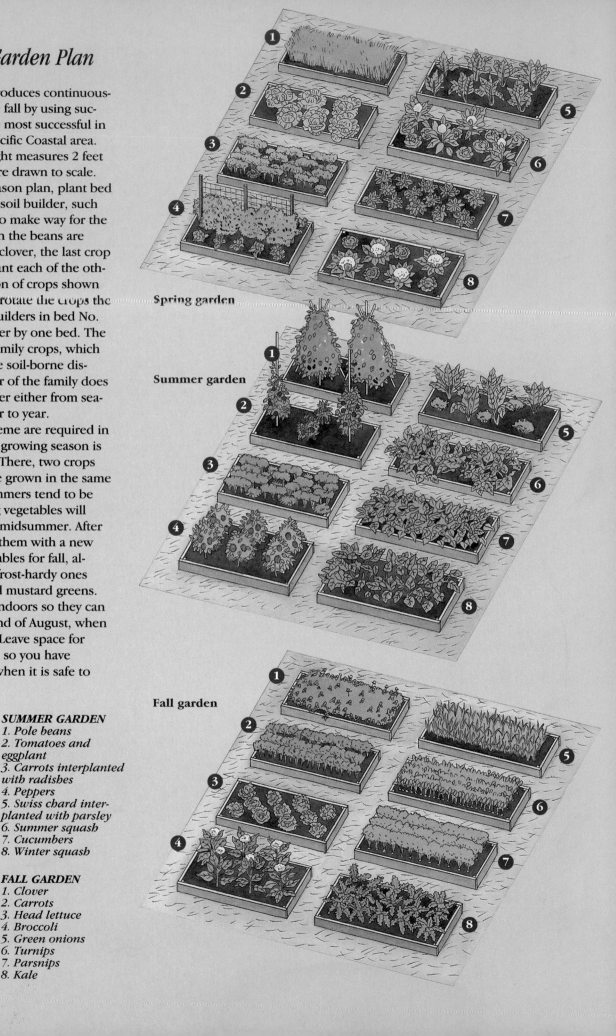

Spring garden

Summer garden

Fall garden

SPRING GARDEN
1. Annual rye
2. Cabbage
3. Carrots interplanted with spring radishes
4. Peas interplanted with salad greens
5. Swiss chard
6. Broccoli interplanted with lettuce
7. Spinach
8. Cauliflower interplanted with lettuce

SUMMER GARDEN
1. Pole beans
2. Tomatoes and eggplant
3. Carrots interplanted with radishes
4. Peppers
5. Swiss chard interplanted with parsley
6. Summer squash
7. Cucumbers
8. Winter squash

FALL GARDEN
1. Clover
2. Carrots
3. Head lettuce
4. Broccoli
5. Green onions
6. Turnips
7. Parsnips
8. Kale

satisfactorily fed by just one plant. To find out more about expected crop yields for particular plants, refer to the chart on the previous page.

If you plan to freeze, can, dry, or pickle some of your vegetables so that your family can enjoy the garden's bounty all year, you'll need to plant extra. Some varieties are better suited to preserving than others. The green bean 'Derby' is known to freeze well, as is the sweet corn 'Honey 'n' Pearl'. Cucumbers are divided into slicing and pickling types; choose varieties from both groups if you plan to preserve some of your crop.

If you have only a small plot for your vegetables, you may have to pare your list down to a number of plants that will fit comfortably. There are a few techniques that will help you get the most out of a small plot *(box, page 46)*, but overcrowding a bed is not one of them. Cramped plants will yield less produce than those given ample room to grow, and are more susceptible to disease and infestation by insects.

Laying Out the Garden in Advance

Drawing a plan of your garden will give you the opportunity to think through important factors such as space requirements and nutrient needs before you put seeds or plants into the soil. Advance planning will also boost the results of using special techniques such as crop rotation, succession planting, and interplanting. You probably will need to work and rework the plan until you get it right, but it is much easier to erase a pencil line than to move a row of growing plants.

Artistic skills are not required for this task. Simply draw the outline of the plot to scale (using graph paper makes this easier), mark which direction is north, and then indicate plants and planting rows with circles and lines.

To begin, arrange tall plants to the north of the bed so they don't shade shorter plants, or use them to provide screening for crops that need the shade. Vining vegetables that like to sprawl across the ground, such as pumpkins, do well along the edges of a bed, where they can creep without encroaching on other plants. Group early-maturing plants together; once harvested, they will create space for another crop. Arrange perennial vegetables—those that come back year after year, such as asparagus and rhubarb—so that they aren't disturbed when the time comes for you to till the soil for the annual plantings. Cluster plants that demand especially large amounts of water so that you can water them all at once. And try to

A recent planting of cucumbers (center) has replaced a bed of harvested spring vegetables in this New Jersey garden. After the cucumbers are finished, a fall crop of turnips will follow in the same bed. Young fennel plants and red-ribbed Swiss chard flourish in the foreground.

keep vegetable families (cabbage and its relatives, legumes, squashes and melons, onions, and tomatoes and their relatives) together to simplify crop rotation.

Rotating Crops for Garden Health

Crop rotation has two enormous advantages for the organic gardener: It puts nutrients back into the soil, and it helps prevent attacks by pests and diseases. At its simplest, crop rotation means planting each crop in a different place in the garden each time you plant. (This technique applies only to annual vegetables; perennials should not be disturbed.)

Rotation is fairly easy to implement for crops that occupy the same bed for an entire growing season; simply move each crop over by one bed every time you plant it. Rotating vegetables that finish midseason and are succeeded by a different crop requires a little forethought. When laying out your garden, bear in mind whether plants are

WHAT VEGETABLES NEED TO GROW

	Vegetable	Soil Temp. to Germinate	Feeding Requirements	Primary Nutrient Needs
COOL SEASON	Beet	45 - 85	Heavy	Phosphorus (P), Potassium (K)
	Broccoli	45 - 85	Heavy	Nitrogen (N)
	Brussels sprouts	45 - 85	Heavy	Nitrogen (N)
	Cabbage	45 - 95	Heavy	Nitrogen (N)
	Carrot	45 - 95	Light	Potassium (K)
	Cauliflower	45 - 85	Heavy	Nitrogen (N)
	Celery	45 - 75	Heavy	Nitrogen (N), Potassium (K)
	Endive	45 - 75	Heavy	Nitrogen (N)
	Kale	40 - 90	Heavy	Potassium (K)
	Leek	50 - 95	Light	Potassium (K)
	Lettuce	40 - 75	Heavy	Nitrogen (N)
	Onion	50 - 95	Light	Potassium (K)
	Parsnip	45 - 85	Light	Potassium (K)
	Pea (soil builder)	45 - 85	Light	Potassium (K)
	Radish	45 - 95	Heavy	Potassium (K)
	Spinach	45 - 75	Heavy	Nitrogen (N)
	Swiss chard	45 - 95	Light	Nitrogen (N)
	Turnip	45 - 95	Light	Potassium (K)
WARM SEASON	Bean (soil builder)	60 - 90	Light	Potassium (K)
	Corn	55 - 105	Heavy	Nitrogen (N)
	Cucumber	60 - 105	Heavy	Nitrogen (N), Phosphorus (P)
	Eggplant	75 - 90	Heavy	Phosphorus (P)
	Melon	65 - 105	Heavy	Nitrogen (N), Potassium (K)
	Pepper	65 - 95	Light	Phosphorus (P)
	Pumpkin	65 - 105	Heavy	Phosphorus (P)
	Squash	65 -105	Heavy	Phosphorus (P)
	Tomato	60 - 85	Heavy	Phosphorus (P)

heavy or light feeders or are soil builders *(chart, left)*, then arrange the crops according to their nutrient demands. For example, in one bed, first plant spring peas, which are light feeders that release nitrogen into the soil; after harvesting the peas, follow with summer squash, a heavy feeder that uses lots of nitrogen. Conversely, follow a heavy feeder such as summer squash or corn with a legume that releases nitrogen or with a cover crop that will be turned back into the soil to nourish it. Alfalfa, clover, and soybeans are examples of soil-building cover crops.

Varying where you plant your crops each season also minimizes problems caused by diseases that attack particular plants *(box, page 98)*. These diseases settle into the bed where the plant is growing and overwinter in the soil, surviving to do their damage later on. Rotation of crops also discourages insect pests, even though they are more mobile than most diseases.

The Technique of Succession Planting

Succession planting, or planting one crop after another during the same season, maximizes your garden space and extends your harvest of certain crops. Instead of planting all your lettuce seeds at once, for example, and ending up with salad for a crowd, you can plant some of the seed, then wait 2 or 3 weeks and plant again. The different sections of the bed can then be harvested over a longer period of time. This technique works best with vegetables that do not produce continuously throughout the season, such as corn, carrots, radishes, bush green beans, cabbage, beets, spinach, and onions.

To use limited garden space most efficiently, you may want to try mixed crop succession. With this technique, you follow one season's harvest with a different crop in the same space. For example, in regions that have a long growing season, you can follow a cool-season crop such as lettuce with heat-loving summer squash. When you have harvested the squash in autumn, plant another cool-season vegetable, such as turnips. The Three-Season Garden Plan on page 42 offers additional examples of mixed crop succession practiced throughout the growing season.

'Winterbore' Kale

Interplanting: Making the Best Use of Space

Interplanting, or combining two plants in the same space, allows you to fit more vegetables into your allotted space. The practice, also called intercropping, can be mutually beneficial to the plants involved. A classic example of intercropping is the Native American custom of planting corn, squash, and pole beans together. This combination, called the Three Sisters of the Cornfield by the Indians, is ideal for nutrient exchange. As they grow, the beans release nitrogen into the soil for the squash and corn. In addition, the three crops use a minimum of space: Vining bean plants are supported by the tall cornstalks, while the squash spreads out along the ground.

Another way to exploit a small space is to combine fast-maturing, early crops with larger, slow-growing vegetables. For example, plant Brussels sprouts among spinach plants; by the time the slow-growing Brussels sprouts need more room, the spinach will have been harvested. To mark a row of seeds that are slow to germinate, such as parsnips, interplant radishes, the fast-sprouting wonder of the vegetable world. As an added bonus, when you pull the radishes, you are cultivating the soil for the nearby plants.

The practice of interplanting can also extend the growing season of spring vegetables if you combine them with taller warm-season plants. Sow spinach or lettuce on the east side of a row of trellised beans, a stand of sunflowers, or a bed of corn; the shade from the tall plants will protect the lettuce from going to seed or wilting in the hot afternoon sun. You can also extend your harvest by interplanting fast- and slow-maturing varieties of the same vegetable at the same time. The growing season will last longer, and you will have the opportunity to taste the different flavors of each vegetable type.

Sources for Seeds

Once your planning is done and you are ready to purchase seed, you should follow one basic rule: Do not make your choices based on price. Often,

As summer gives way to autumn, perennial crops such as the feathery asparagus at upper left have long since peaked. Newly planted crops such as Swiss chard and mizuna (center) take over the space vacated by harvested summer vegetables. Widely cultivated in China and Japan, mizuna's leafy tops make an excellent addition to soups or may be combined with other mild greens in salads.

In this intensively planted raised bed, cabbage, beans, lettuce, and carrots grow shoulder to shoulder; yarrow and daylilies nestle in the gaps; and vining tomatoes climb a simple trellis in back, using every available inch of ground.

retailers mark down seed because it is old and less likely to germinate. It makes no sense to put in hours of labor preparing your soil, planning your garden, and planting it, only to end up with weak plants—or no plants at all—because of faulty seed. Check the freshness date on seed packets and only buy seed that has been packaged to be sold in the year you are buying it.

Hardware stores, home and garden centers, and mail-order catalogs are the primary sources of vegetable seed for home gardeners. Local shops are often cheaper and more convenient, but catalogs offer a greater selection of plant varieties. Moreover, local or regional seed-catalog companies feature seed that is particularly suited to your area.

As you read descriptions of the various vegetables, look for the qualities that are most important to you. You may want early-maturing plants for a short growing season, compact plants for containers, or plants that are resistant to disease, heat tolerant, exceptionally flavorful, unusual looking, or a combination of these qualities. No doubt you will have to compromise on some features, but with the wealth of selections available, you should be able to find what you want. For good all-around performance, look for vegetable varieties listed as AAS, or All-America Selections, which have proved superior in gardens throughout the United States.

TIPS FROM THE PROS

Getting the Most from a Small Garden

Even the smallest of spaces can produce a lot of vegetables when you use intensive gardening methods. Your first consideration in a scaled-down garden must be to prepare and enrich the soil, since a large number of plants in a small area will compete for nutrients. See pages 23-33 for information on how to build healthy soil.

When planning your garden, emphasize vertical crops. Peas, pole beans, cucumbers, some melons, and some tomatoes are vining crops that

actually perform better when they are kept off the ground. These can be grown on an attractive trellis, tied to stakes, or trained to follow twine that is anchored to the ground and an overhead frame.

Also, to reap as much harvest as possible from each plant, choose compact varieties or prolific producers. 'Tom Thumb', a "midget" head lettuce, requires comparatively little room, for example, and 'Jade Cross' Brussels sprouts yield an early, boun-

tiful crop. As a rule, the smaller the fruit, the more the plants tend to produce, so make most of your selections from small varieties such as cherry tomatoes.

Avoid the temptation, though, to plant too many hugely prolific vegetables, such as zucchini. If you have extra plants, give or throw them away and save your space for other crops. When laying out the garden, make use of succession planting and intercropping to maximize your growing space.

Planning an Herb Garden

While many gardeners plant culinary herbs among vegetables and fruits, you may decide you'd like to devote a separate bed or two just to herbs. Most successful herb gardens use a combination of annuals, biennials, perennials, and woody subshrubs. Because perennials and subshrubs give an herb garden its structure, it's especially important to satisfy their cultural needs so that you can count on their long-term presence.

The short life span and rapid growth of annuals and biennials make them ideal subjects for sampling unfamiliar culinary herbs. Some annuals and biennials can be more or less permanent residents if they are allowed to sow themselves. But they don't necessarily stay put: Between the wind and birds scattering the seeds, sometimes the plants pop up in surprising places from year to year.

Making the Right Choices

It's best to start small when deciding how many culinary herbs to grow for the first time. One or two plants of any one kind are usually enough, though you'll want to make room for more if you develop a taste for a specialty such as pesto, which calls for large quantities of fresh basil.

Don't overbuy: Plants pinched for space are likely to grow tall and spindly, and the lack of air circulation may result in disease. Remember to factor in a particular variety's mature height and spread, growth rate, and any tendency toward invasiveness. For example, lovage, a perennial herb that takes its time reaching maturity, may surprise—or dismay—the unwary gardener when it eventually shoots up to a dizzying 6 or even 8 feet.

Herbs purchased at a local nursery or from a mail-order nursery in your region will often be better suited to your climate than plants raised farther afield. This is especially true for cultivars, which may not be quite as vigorous, hardy, or disease resistant as their parents. When purchasing container-grown herbs, look for plants that have brightly colored foliage, undamaged leaves, and bushy, full growth with no signs of insect infestation or disease. Check that no more than a few roots are growing out of the bottom of the pot; a root-bound plant is often weaker because it has depleted the nutrients in its container.

A few popular herbs for kitchen gardens are listed at right. For a more complete list, including plant size and cultural requirements, see the Encyclopedia of Herbs on pages 250-279 at the back of this book.

Choosing a Style

If your taste leans toward the formal, consider planting a knot garden, composed of intertwined bands laid out like a bas-relief carpet in a mirroring symmetry. Achieved with careful planning (page 48), it is beautiful even in winter, embossed with a blanket of snow. Herbs for each band of the knot garden should be of markedly different foliage colors to create a strong contrast between the intertwining areas of the design.

Choose plants that are roughly the same height at maturity—less than 24 inches tall and wide—and dense enough to create a seamless and solid design when pruned. Some naturally compact herbs are dwarf basil, curly chives, and burnet (Poterium sanguisorba), as well as the more traditional knot-garden members like hyssop, lemon thyme, and dwarf sage. Fill in the ground between the bands with low-growing flowers or herbal ground covers such as creeping thyme, pennyroyal, or curly parsley, which makes an interesting ground cover when mass-planted. Or spread woodchip mulch, slate, crushed brick, tile, seashells, or colored sand.

If you prefer an informal herb garden, remember that it will still need careful planning. Although such gardens don't contain any strict geometric lines, they take on a satisfying sense of balance with sinuous lines of beds and paths that lead you to a focal point. Without this focal point, the garden will appear jumbled and formless. Consider adding a garden bench or an ornament to draw the eye and create atmosphere. Traditionally, a sundial, a

Herbs for Kitchen Gardens

Agastache foeniculum (anise hyssop)	**Mentha spicata** (spearmint)
Allium schoenoprasum (chives)	**Ocimum basilicum** (sweet basil)
Allium tuberosum (Chinese or garlic chives)	**Origanum majorana** (sweet marjoram)
Aloysia triphylla (lemon verbena)	**Origanum onites** (Greek oregano)
Artemisia dracunculus var. sativa (French tarragon)	**Petroselinum crispum** (parsley)
Cymbopogon citratus (lemon grass)	**Rosmarinus officinalis** (rosemary)
Foeniculum vulgare (fennel)	**Rumex acetosa** (sorrel)
Foeniculum vulgare 'Purpurascens' (copper fennel)	**Salvia officinalis** (sage)
Levisticum officinale (lovage)	**Satureja hortensis** (summer savory)
Melissa officinalis (lemon balm)	**Thymus x citriodorus** (lemon thyme)
Mentha x piperita (peppermint)	**Thymus vulgaris** (thyme)
	Tropaeolum majus (nasturtium)

How to Construct and Plant a Knot Garden

The 10-by-10-foot closed knot garden described below consists of three bands of contrasting plants that make interlocking rectangles with a circle weaving through them. Site your knot garden in full sun on level ground; shade may cause the plants to grow unevenly.

To obtain true 90° square corners, lay out your bed using a process known as triangulation, as shown below. Materials you will need include wooden stakes and pegs; string; and sand, bone meal, or powdered lime to mark lines on the soil.

After marking the bed's perimeter, prepare the soil (*pages 34-35*), and install a brick or wooden edging to keep the garden looking neat and trim.

Space the plants closely, and buy several extra plants in case you need replacements during the season. You will also need to mulch the ground between the bands with woodchips or gravel, or, alternatively, plant a low-growing ground-cover herb such as caraway thyme. Install a dwarf boxwood near each corner to finish the design.

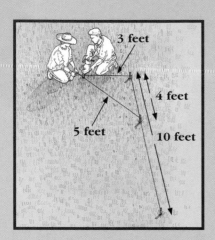

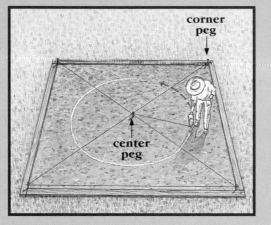

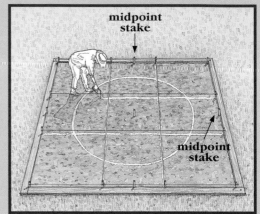

1. To create square corners, mark off one 10-foot side of the bed with stakes and string. Then, with a helper, set a peg 4 feet from the first stake and tie a string to it; mark the string at a point 5 feet from the peg. Tie a string to the first stake and mark it 3 feet from the stake. Cross the strings at the marks and set a new peg at that point. To stake off the next side, run a string from the first stake out to a length of 10 feet; repeat the squaring process. Repeat for remaining corners. Install edging along the string line and prepare the soil for planting.

2. Run string to link opposite corners; set a peg where the strings intersect at the center of the square. Next, to mark a circle at the garden's center, tie a string to a nail in the top of the center peg. Mark your string at a point that is half the distance from the center peg to a corner stake. Tie a sand- or lime-filled bottle to the string at the mark and, keeping the string pulled taut, walk around the peg with the bottle inverted so the sand pours out and marks a circle.

3. To outline the two interlocking rectangles, set stakes at the midpoint of each side of the bed. Then set two pegs on either side of each midpoint stake, 1½ feet away, so that the pegs are 3 feet apart. Run string between each of the opposite pegs to make two sets of parallel lines. Then mark the lines on the ground by dribbling sand or lime along the string lines. Remove the string, but keep the stakes and pegs in place.

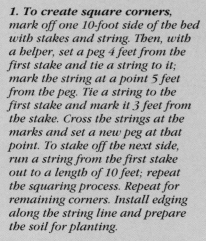

4. Working outward from the center, space the plants 3 to 6 inches apart along the sand lines, adding a dose of slow-release fertilizer for each plant, following package directions. Plant a same-sized dwarf box at each corner, as shown in the diagram. In the spaces between the bands of plants, spread gravel or woodchips, or plant a ground cover. As the garden matures, trim the herbs every few weeks so that the bands appear to go under or over each other, like a lattice piecrust (inset).

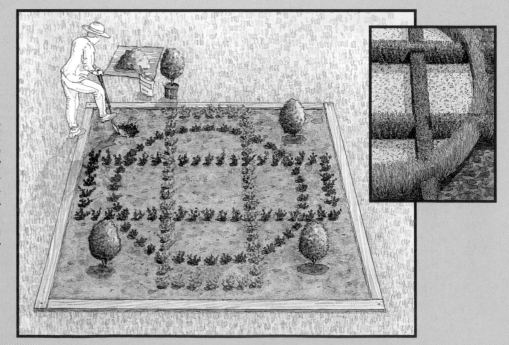

A small statue draws the eye and adds a decorative touch to the kitchen herb garden at left, which features a neat row of compact globe basil alongside green-and-purple sweet basil. Marjoram, tarragon, parsley, chives, and sage visually anchor the end of the bed.

A pot of sweet basil flanked by two sages—furry-leaved 'Berggarten' sage on the right and purple sage on the left—occupy a place of honor on the deck outside a Maryland gardener's kitchen door (below). Under the purple sage, lemon thyme cascades over its container, jockeying for space with silvery lavender and bright green sweet marjoram. A pot on the deck holds oregano, Italian parsley, and more purple sage.

stone or iron urn, or a small statue serves as a focal point, but a birdhouse or birdbath would also be effective, especially in an informal setting.

Once you have decided on the ideal place for your herb garden, you're ready to lay it out. Either plot your design on paper, or plan your garden at the site itself. Mark the outer corners of the garden with stakes, and tie string from one stake to the other to approximate the garden's perimeter. This will allow you to "see" the finished garden from all angles and to determine the best location for your plants. At the same time, mark features such as benches, ornaments, and pathways, keeping in mind that for two people to walk side by side—or to accommodate a wheelbarrow—your paths will need to be at least 4 feet wide.

Plan for a sheltering enclosure to keep out the wind and hold in the herbs' scents. Even one wall or hedge can make a difference. A trimmed boxwood hedge nicely complements formal architecture, while lattice or low walls of wattle—vines woven between stout branches driven into the earth—are especially well suited to informal or naturalistic settings.

Once you have planned the layout and the hard structures of your garden, go over your list of herbs, noting their heights so that you can assign their positions in the garden. Also take into account their bloom times; with a little planning, you can have flowers all season long. Finally, consider including evergreen herbs such as *Thymus vulgaris* (common thyme) and *Gaultheria procumbens* (wintergreen), which will maintain a presence all through the winter when the rest of the garden is bare.

Keep in mind that even a containerized garden like the one shown at right requires planning and forethought. For tips on designing container gardens with herbs, see pages 78-83.

Mixing Edibles and Ornamentals

Note: The abbreviation "spp." stands for the plural of "species"; where used in lists it means that many, but not all, of the species in a genus meet the criterion of the list.

This southern California garden produces a delightful array of cool-weather annuals that are ready to serve as either decoration or dinner. Displaying their varied forms and foliage as they cluster in harmony are marigolds, carrots, lettuce, rose-toned ornamental kale, organically grown pansies, and purplish stands of red mustard. Regular harvesting of leaves and flower heads ensures a long season of productivity.

More and more, gardeners are discovering that many garden vegetables and culinary herbs can be beautiful as well as delectable. Likewise, some plants that are usually grown as ornamentals, such as marigolds and pansies, are now appearing in the salad bowl. A bed that combines attractive vegetable plants, herbs with interesting or colorful foliage, and edible flowers can both dress up your property and enhance your meals.

Many edible plants rely on unusual coloration and texture for their visual appeal. Among these are ornamental cabbage and kale—varieties of *Brassica oleracea* that are indispensable in cool-season borders—and rhubarb chard, a variety of *Beta vulgaris* whose ruby red stems and glossy green foliage are spectacular in indoor arrangements as well as in the garden. Butterhead lettuce makes a charming early-spring edging at the front of a flower border, while taller edibles, such as burgundy-colored 'Rubine' Brussels sprouts, add interest in the midborder. For a range of color, plant ornamental peppers *(Capsicum annuum),* whose fruits ripen in shades of red, orange, purple, yellow, and green. At the back of the bed,

use annual sunflowers to vary the scale of your flowers; they can also screen an unwanted view and supply next winter's bird feeders to boot.

The sculptured foliage of *Cynara cardunculus* (cardoon) and its relative, the purple artichoke *(C. scolymus),* provide dramatically different accents. If you prefer fine detail, plant a minigarden of *Ocimum* (basil), including varieties with bright green tiny-leaved mounds of foliage and bushlike plants with leaves of rich purple.

When choosing any part of a plant for the dinner table, always be certain that it's safe to consume. Check seed packets, catalogs, and other literature, keeping in mind that some species in a genus are edible while others are not. Even some peppers are too fiery to eat—or even to handle.

Useful as well as beautiful, the backdoor garden at right combines ornamentals and culinary herbs in a tightly woven tapestry of contrasting colors and textures. Sage and rosemary mingle happily with irises, lamb's ears, pinks, and other perennials in neat raised beds. Handsome brick paths between the beds provide easy access for maintenance and harvesting.

CHAPTER FOUR

Getting Started

There is no rule book or single set of instructions for putting in and caring for an organic kitchen garden. At first, the task can seem a bit daunting: You must decide whether you will purchase seedlings from a nursery, start plants indoors, or direct-sow seeds outdoors. Once you've started your garden, you'll need to make decisions about staking and supporting the plants, as well as mulching, watering, fertilizing, and other maintenance tasks. And if you're growing herbs, you may want to consider increasing your stock of healthy plants by using various propagation methods.

In the end, your garden will be unlike any other, reflecting your choices, your experiences, your land. The garden at left, for example, represents one gardener's approach to growing pole beans: Twine stretched vertically between wooden poles provides support for the clinging tendrils as the plants mature.

Keep a journal of your observations, challenges, and solutions. Besides the sheer delight of watching tiny seeds grow into food, learning to work with nature will give you some of the greatest rewards under the sun.

Planting Your Vegetables

Vegetables Best Started Indoors

Broccoli, 6-8

Brussels sprouts, 4-8

Cabbage, 6-8

Cauliflower, 6-8

Celeriac, 6-8

Celery, 6-8

Eggplant, 8-10

Leeks, 8-12

Lettuce, 4-6

Onions, 10-12

Peppers, 8-10

Tomatoes, 6-8

(Note: The numbers after each vegetable indicate how many weeks before the date of the last frost the seeds should be started.)

After all the soil tilling, catalog perusing, and garden planning, at last the time has come to plant your seeds. Depending on the climate in your area and the type of vegetables you want to grow, you may decide to start plants indoors, buy seedlings from a nursery, or sow seeds directly into the ground.

Starting Seeds Indoors

In northern zones where the growing season is 90 days or less, starting seeds indoors is imperative, especially for warm-season crops such as tomatoes, melons, and peppers. Gardeners farther south can start seedlings to get a jump on the season. It is possible, however, to start seeds too early, and that can foil well-laid plans. For example, if you start tomato seeds indoors 10 weeks before the last frost date instead of the recommended 6 to 8 weeks, the plants will be ready to go outside too soon, and will become leggy and unhealthy while waiting for warmer weather.

You can start seeds indoors either by planting each seed in its own container, which will save you from having to repot them separately later on, or by planting many seeds together in a flat. If you're planting each seed separately, any sort of recycled container will do—waxed-cardboard milk cartons, yogurt cups, egg cartons, or cell packs saved from last year's purchases—as long as you poke drainage holes in the bottom. You can also buy peat pots and peat pellets. These containers are designed to be planted directly in the ground and work especially well for plants that do not like having their roots disturbed, such as cucumbers. One type of peat pellet is held together with netting. Although the netting disintegrates with time, many gardeners prefer to take it off to free the roots before putting the plant in the ground. Other pellets are held together with a built-in binder that disintegrates quickly once the container is planted.

Another excellent medium for starting seeds is a homemade soil block, created by compressing a peat-compost mixture into a cube using a blocking tool, available from mail-order catalogs. Larger vegetables, such as melons, cauliflower, broccoli, cabbage, eggplant, squash, peppers, and tomatoes, benefit from being started in peat pots, pellets, or soil blocks because the seedlings have plenty of room to develop their root systems and can be transplanted directly into the ground.

If you prefer to plant your seeds in a flat or are planting many seeds of smaller vegetables, splurge on plastic seed-starting trays. These handy trays have three components: a planting tray with holes for drainage, a liner to catch water that drains off, and a domed, clear plastic lid to maintain moisture while the seeds germinate.

Seed-Starting Soil

The ideal medium for starting seeds is fine grained and loosely packed so that a seedling can push through it without difficulty. It should also be as free as possible of weeds, harmful

Seedlings and seeds that have yet to sprout share a warm, sunny, south-facing window with pots of marigolds. Once the seeds have sprouted, turn the plants daily to give them even exposure to the light.

Making a Seed-Starting Mix

Many gardeners swear by a favorite seed-starting medium, each a little different, though the basic ingredients remain the same. Experiment to find the mix that works best for you.

RECIPE 1

1 part sterilized compost

1 part sand, vermiculite, or perlite

1 part peat moss

RECIPE 2

4 quarts shredded sphagnum peat moss

4 quarts vermiculite

1 tablespoon superphosphate

2 tablespoons ground limestone

RECIPE 3

1 quart sphagnum peat moss

1 quart vermiculite

1 quart perlite

insects, and disease-causing contaminants such as fungi and other pathogens.

Seed-starting mixes usually consist of vermiculite and perlite for aeration and drainage, sphagnum moss or peat moss for bulk and moisture retention, and compost. You can make your own growing medium using any of the recipes given above or purchase it ready-mixed in bags from garden centers. If you do not wish to use peat moss, you can put together a satisfactory mix from 50 percent vermiculite or perlite and 50 percent screened compost. If you buy your mix, be sure to get the type formulated for seeds, rather than regular potting mix.

After Growth Begins: Seedling Care

Once your seeds are planted and covered with plastic *(right)*, they'll need a warm spot in which to germinate. Most seeds sprout faster in warm conditions, and warm-season vegetables won't germinate at all until the soil reaches a temperature of 60° to 65° F. If the interior of your home in early spring tends to be cooler than this at

Starting and Transplanting Seeds

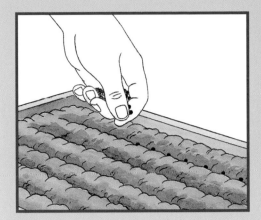

1. Fill each container to within ½ inch of the rim with moist seed-starting mix. *Gently press the soil to level it, but do not compact it. Make furrows in the soil to the appropriate depth for the seeds you are planting. Drop the seeds into the furrow, spacing them as recommended on the seed packet. Cover the seeds and gently tamp the soil along the furrow to make good contact between seed and soil.*

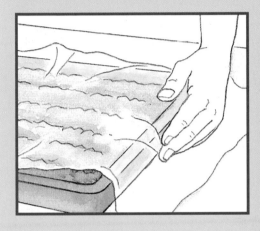

2. Mist the top layer of soil. *Cover the container to hold in moisture, using a plastic dome from a seed-starting kit, a grocery-store produce bag, or plastic wrap. Do not water again once the container is covered. Keep the seeds in a warm spot until they sprout. When the first sprouts appear, remove the cover and place the seedlings in a spot where they will get 12 hours of light a day.*

3. Repot crowded seedlings by scooping them out with a spoon. *Immediately replant the tiny seedlings into a large container filled with lightweight potting soil. Water carefully to make good contact between the roots and the soil, but avoid swamping the plants. Place the seedlings in a spot where they will get 12 hours of light a day.*

4. To remove a young plant from a cell pack or plastic container, *grasp the stem between your index and middle fingers and tip the container. Ease the plant out; do not pull on the stem. If the plant does not slide out easily, try tapping the bottom of the container gently on the ground or squeezing the sides of the container.*

Sheltering Plants from the Cold

Plant protectors such as cold frames, portable greenhouses, and cloches provide a sheltered setting for starting plants early, hardening off seedlings, and extending the growing season of autumn vegetables. They work by transmitting light and retaining heat.

A cold frame can be as simple as a bottomless box covered with clear glass or plastic, or as sophisticated as an elaborate high-tech creation with temperature sensors that automatically open and close the lid as needed. A cloche can be small enough to protect just one plant or large enough to cover an entire row of vegetables, and can be devised from overturned bushel baskets or 1-gallon plastic milk containers with the bottoms cut out.

The large portable greenhouse at right *is made from clear plastic sheeting stretched over arched wire fencing. Versatile and inexpensive, the greenhouse protects young vegetables, like these lettuce plants, from cold weather.*

night, you must provide additional heat. A waterproof heating mat designed to go under pots and containers works well for this purpose. A less costly option is to place pots on top of a refrigerator or a clothes dryer.

When the seeds have sprouted, remove the plastic covering to allow air to circulate; otherwise, you may lose the seedlings to damping-off, a disease caused by several soil fungi. At this point, seedlings also need a lot of light—at least 12 hours a day. Lack of light creates thin, leggy plants and will affect a plant's vigor and productivity for the rest of the season.

For best results, place the plants in front of a south-facing window that gets direct sun most of the day. Be sure to rotate the containers every day so that the plants receive even exposure. If you must use artificial light instead, opt for fluorescent or "grow" lights rather than incandescent ones, which do not generate the ultraviolet light required by plants. Position fluorescent lights about 2 to 4 inches from the top of the plants. Hang the lights from chains for easy height adjustment as the plants grow.

To keep the soil moist without damaging fragile seedlings, mist plants daily or set the containers on top of several layers of wet newspaper; the water in the newspaper will be drawn up and absorbed through the drainage holes in the bottoms of the pots. Feed the seedlings with a weak mixture of liquid fertilizer every 2 weeks. Experienced gardeners regulate seedlings' rate of growth by the amount of food they provide. If the seedlings are coming along quickly and cold weather is lingering longer than expected, the plants' growth can be slowed by cutting back slightly on fertilizing. Conversely, if warm weather comes early, you can accelerate growth by feeding with a richer mixture of fertilizer.

Seedlings that have sprouted too closely together will need to be thinned. If you have more seedlings than you need, simply snip off the weaker specimens to give more growing space to the vigorous ones. If you want to use all of the seedlings, carefully lift the excess from the container and transplant them to pots filled with a seed-starting mixture. Before removing a seedling, poke a hole in the mixture with the eraser end of

Cloches of water-filled plastic tubes surround plants in this New Jersey garden. The water in the plastic cloches absorbs heat and radiates it to the plants, protecting them from killing frosts in fall and early spring, thus extending the growing season. For best results, use water cloches for single upright plants such as tomatoes, peppers, and eggplant.

a pencil. Either lift the seedling out with a spoon, as shown on page 55, or use the technique called pricking out. To do this, hold the top leaves of a seedling between your thumb and forefinger as you use the pencil or other narrow object to gently lift the seedling from the container. Ease it carefully into the planting hole and press the mixture around the plant.

Buying Healthy Plants from the Nursery

For those who don't have the time or the space to start their own seeds, buying seedlings from a nursery can be a satisfactory substitute. However, not all nursery transplants are healthy, so it's imperative to examine them carefully.

First, check the seedlings for insects or insect eggs. Favorite insect hiding places include under leaves, where the leaves meet the stem, and at the growing tip of the plant, where the young leaves are most tender. Also, don't forget to look underneath the container for night-feeding pests

that like to congregate or hide in the crevices.

Choose young and vigorous plants. Avoid those that are oversized and too well established. If plants are already in flower or bearing fruit, don't be misled into thinking they will give you an earlier or more bountiful harvest. In fact, quite the opposite is true: The stress of transplanting is likely to reduce the main crop. Likewise, tall and leggy plants often fail to fill out and produce well. Instead, look for well-proportioned seedlings; plants that are ready to be transplanted will be about as wide as they are tall.

Reject plants that have roots growing several inches out of the bottom of their container; these plants have been in their pots too long and have become root-bound. In the case of cole crops such as kale, gently scrape away a little soil to check for swollen, distorted roots, which are an indication of a condition called clubroot. And any roots that are yellow, soft, or too woody also indicate an unhealthy plant.

Tricks for Easier Seed Sowing

- When sowing seeds outdoors, run a strip of white toilet tissue down the length of each furrow and lay the seeds on top. The whiteness of the paper will make it easier to see the seeds and to gauge their spacing and depth. The fine tissue will degrade quickly into the soil.

- To make it easier to distribute tiny seeds, such as those of carrots, mix them with sand and sprinkle the mixture over the ground using a clean salt shaker. For easier handling, carrot seeds are also sold on seed tape and in pellet form about the size of buckshot.

- Plant bean seeds with the scar side facing down; bean roots grow into the ground out of the scar point. Planting them all this way means they will surface at about the same time.

- To presprout seeds, space them on a double layer of damp paper towel, roll it up, and keep it moist in an open plastic bag. In 2 or 3 days the seeds will sprout. Then plant them in pots or put them into the ground, taking care not to break the fragile roots.

Hardening Off

Before transplanting any seedlings outside, you must prepare the young plants for the transition from a protected environment to the harsher conditions of the outdoors. This process is known as hardening off. A week or two before you plan to transplant the seedlings into your garden, take them outside and place them in a protected spot for about an hour. Repeat this process daily during the transition period, increasing the time by 1 hour each session.

Putting Transplants Into the Ground

If you can, plant young seedlings on a cool, misty day; cooler temperatures are less likely to cause stress to new plants. If that isn't possible, transplant in the evening when the temperature begins to drop. The plants will have all night to settle in before they are exposed to the hot sun.

Three Ways of Supporting Plants

To construct a tripod plant support (below), push three poles measuring 6 to 8 feet long firmly into the ground to form a circle; tie them together at the top. Plant vining vegetables such as peas, pole beans, squash, and pumpkins at the base of each pole. Within the circle, grow lettuce and other crops that welcome shade.

For a support of crisscrossed poles, push 6- to 8-foot poles into the ground in two parallel rows about 12 inches apart as shown, and tie pairs together about 4 inches from the top. For stability, give the end units an extra leg to create a tripod, and tie a pole along the length of the support on top.

To create a simple trellis for vining vegetables such as peas, squash, pumpkins, pole beans, and cucumbers, choose sturdy poles that are 6 to 8 feet long and at least 1 inch square. Space them an equal distance apart and sink them about 12 inches into the ground. Staple wire fencing or nylon netting to the poles.

Once you have removed each plant from its pot or cell pack, examine the roots carefully. If they are crushed tightly against the edge of their container or curled in a circle around the bottom of the pot, gently massage the rootball in your hand to loosen the clump.

If your beds are bare or mulched with straw or any other loose, organic material, simply dig through the mulch and soil to create a planting hole. If the beds are covered with plastic mulch, use a penknife to cut through the sheeting. For each plant, cut an X in the plastic big enough to fit the rootball, then dig the hole and place the plant in it. To create the best possible contact between the soil and the roots, press the soil down firmly around each plant.

Space the plants far enough apart to allow ample growing room, but choose an arrangement that makes efficient use of the land. For example, you might place the plants in wide beds with staggered rows. A bed that is 30 inches wide could have three lettuce plants in the first row and two lettuce plants in the second row positioned between the plants in the first row. In the third row, there would be three lettuce plants parallel to the ones in the first row, and so on. Such a pattern will accommodate a few more plants without crowding. Once the seedlings are in the ground, be sure to water promptly and well, especially when using plastic mulch, which acts as a barrier to rainwater. (For more on using plastic mulch, see page 63.)

While the transplants are adjusting to their new environment, they may need shelter from strong sun. If the sun is particularly intense the first few days after planting, make a temporary shade structure with a beach umbrella, cloth anchored to cinder blocks or mounted on stakes, or even an overturned basket or box that allows some light to penetrate. During hot weather, be prepared to water your transplants daily until the roots are established and you see signs of growth.

Direct-Sowing Outdoors

Not all seed-grown vegetables are suited for early sowing indoors. The heading types of Chinese cabbage will go to seed from transplant stress, for instance, and carrots will die. Root disturbance to corn, peas, beans, and okra plants hinders their growth. These crops and others *(list, page 56)* are simply easier to start outdoors.

When sowing seed outdoors, keep in mind that the soil temperature must be within the range required by the plant type for germination to occur. Fortunately, surface soil temperature does not

fluctuate as radically as air temperature because of the thermal insulation provided by the earth. Once the soil is warm enough in spring to nurture the seeds, it's likely to stay that way until autumn. A soil and compost thermometer with an extended spike can help you determine when the soil is warm enough to begin planting. To use the thermometer, insert the spike into the soil to the planting depth of the crop to be sown there. Check each bed with the thermometer, as temperatures may vary significantly within a garden.

Before you plant, rake the soil's surface in one direction to make it smooth. Break up large clods and remove any stones, weeds, and grass roots Then rake in the other direction to smooth and level the bed. To avoid compacting the soil, walk on the beds as little as possible. Mark each planting row with string stretched across the beds and

The clinging tendrils of pole beans spiral around these vertical support wires as the plants reach upward. A heavy cord stretched between two poles runs across the top of the structure and holds up the wires, which are also anchored to the ground with stakes. When the growing season is over, the gardener will take down the wire and string and store them for reuse.

Helpful Hints for Planting Tomatoes

To train a vining tomato plant, pound a sturdy 8-foot-tall stake at least 1 foot into the ground, then plant the tomato at its base. Tie the plant to the stake with string or twine. To avoid damaging the stem, first loop the string around the stake and tie it tightly, then loop it around the vine and make a loose knot (inset). Continue to tie the tomato to the stake as the plant grows.

To keep cutworms from feasting on a tomato stem, cut a collar measuring 3 inches square from 3 layers of newspaper. Wrap the collar around the stem next to the rootball and position the tomato in the planting hole so that half of the collar is above ground (above, left). To plant a leggy tomato transplant, remove the lower leaves and lay the plant on its side in a trench. Gently bend the top of the stem upward and cover the roots and the horizontal section of stem with soil.

tied at either end to stakes. Using the string as a guide, dig a shallow furrow in the earth with a trowel or hoe.

Sowing the Seeds

Sow seeds in rows according to the recommended spacing on the package; do not overcrowd them. Then cover the seed with soil. As a rule of thumb, you should bury seeds three times deeper than their width. Under certain conditions, though, you may have to adjust the planting depth slightly. Seeds require a little less covering when soil is very wet and heavy, and more when the soil is sandy or the weather is dry.

Hill planting is preferred for crops that need more warmth to germinate, such as corn, cucumbers, melons, pumpkins, and squash. To create a rich reservoir for them, dig a hole 12 inches deep and wide. Fill the hole with 8 inches of well-rotted compost or manure and top with 8 inches of soil. After watering, the hill should be about 3 inches high. Plant seeds at the appropriate distance and depth along the top and sides of the hill.

The technique called broadcasting, or scattering seed over a bed, works best for cover crops such as clover and annual rye, and for large beds planted with the same crop. Prepare the bed as you would for row planting, but without furrows. On a windless day, broadcast the seed by shaking it out of your hand in a loose spray. Then rake the bed lightly with a fine rake or a spike-toothed rolling cultivator to settle the seed into the soil and cover it slightly.

Label each row, hill, or bed with the vegetable's complete name and the planting date. Do not use the paper seed packet as a label; rain will make it illegible, and besides, it will be far more useful in your garden-record notebook *(page 67)*. Instead, purchase wooden tags at a garden center or nursery and write the information on them with a waterproof pen.

Once planted, seeds need to be kept continually moist in order to germinate. If you have planted rows of seeds in moist soil, it isn't necessary to water at planting time, but keep a watchful eye on the beds and sprinkle them daily, if necessary, to keep them moistened. For seed that has been broadcasted, water immediately after planting to ensure good contact between the seed and the soil, and sprinkle daily until the seeds have sprouted. Use only a gentle spray of water; a strong spray may dislodge the seeds and wash

Wire cages can support bush or vining tomatoes, but the cages for vining types need to be larger, about 24 inches across and 60 inches tall. Place a cage over the tomato when you plant it, and tie the cage to a tall stake so it will not topple under the weight of ripening fruit.

To encourage tomato vines to produce earlier and larger—but fewer—fruits, prune the side shoots. Once three leaves appear on the shoot, pinch off the top leaf (below), stopping the shoot's growth. Leave some foliage on the plant to protect ripening fruit from harsh sun.

them away completely or cause them to congregate in tight clumps.

Staking and Support Systems

Using stakes or other support systems to grow plants vertically does more than save space. When lifted off the ground, vining and trailing plants tend to be healthier and more productive. Supported in an upright position, they receive more sunlight and increased air circulation, which prevents fungus and rot. In addition, the produce stays cleaner and is easier to monitor and harvest. Cucumbers, melons, summer and winter squash, peas, pole beans, and tomatoes are all good candidates for training upward.

If you plan to stake plants, place the stake in the ground before you sow, or when you put transplanted seedlings into the ground. Do not wait until the plant grows larger, or you run the risk of damaging the roots when you insert the stake. Choose sturdy supports and bury them deep enough to bear the weight of the growing plant and its produce.

Vegetables that have twining tendrils, such as beans, will grip onto the support, but other vining plants, such as tomatoes and squash, need to be secured. Be careful not to tie the plant too tightly to the support, however, or you may damage the stem. Instead, first tie a tight loop around the support and then a looser one around the stem of the plant, as shown in the illustration opposite. Use string, cloth strips, or other biodegradable materials to tie the plants; when the season is over, both plants and ties can be thrown onto the compost pile.

Support systems for vegetables range from small and simple to large and fairly elaborate, depending on the gardener's preference and the space available. One common method for supporting vining vegetables such as pole beans, squash, and peas is the tripod plant support, consisting of three poles pushed into the ground to form a circle, with the ends tied together at the top. Another way to support vining vegetables is with a trellis, made of nylon netting or wire fencing stretched between poles sunk into the ground. For details on constructing these supports, see page 58.

Heavy with ripening red tomatoes, the 1984 All-America Selections tomato, 'Celebrity', is supported by a wire cage. This bush variety grows to maturity in 70 days, producing a generous crop of firm, flavorful fruits, each weighing 7 to 8 ounces. Known for its outstanding disease resistance, the cultivar adapts to most parts of the country.

Caring for Your Vegetables throughout the Season

A vegetable garden does not run on a set schedule. Although some tasks do need to be performed at certain times of the year, many maintenance chores will be in response to clues that your plants provide. Try to walk through your garden every day, preferably early in the morning or in the evening. Allow yourself time to enjoy the progress your crops are making and to watch for any problems. Carry a trowel and clippers so that you can perform the odd weeding or transplanting job on the spot. Your observations during these daily rounds will do much to keep your garden healthy.

Heading Off Problems with On-the-Spot Fixes

Early in the season, tend to crops that need thinning, since plants that are spaced an optimum distance apart will reward you with an abundant harvest. Conversely, if you come across a little extra room in a bed, tuck in a plant for some quick intercropping. Be on the lookout for weeds poking through the soil or mulch, and dig or pull them promptly. Likewise, nip insect problems in the bud before they become serious. (For more information on pests and diseases, see Chapter 6 or, for help with a specific problem, consult the Troubleshooting Guide on pages 228-235.)

If the weather has been dry, check the soil to make sure you've given your plants enough water. Probe the soil with your fingers to discover how deep the dry surface layer is; if it is dry down to the root mass of a crop, it's time to water. Remember that once plants show signs of water stress, the problem has gone too far.

Before long, your diligence in the garden will begin paying off in the form of plump, healthy produce. Take a basket or other container with you on your walks so you can collect vegetables at their peak. Keep a close eye on crops like zucchini, which can be harvested when they are only as big as your finger. These vegetables grow so fast that if you leave them an extra day or two, they'll be noticeably bigger and their taste and texture may have changed. (See Chapter 7 for information on how to tell when vegetables are ripe for harvesting or, for a specific variety, check the encyclopedia that begins on page 280.)

Routine Tasks

In addition to the chores you perform on your daily inspections of the garden, your vegetable plot will require such regular maintenance as mulching, watering, fertilizing, and weeding.

Your best ally in keeping your garden healthy and productive is a layer of mulch. It insulates the ground, keeping the soil warm in cool weather and cool when temperatures turn hot. It cuts down on the need for watering because it holds moisture, and it also discourages the growth of weeds. And organic mulches such as bark, grass clippings, and newspapers (black-and-white newsprint only) break down into the soil, adding nutrients and improving soil structure.

Applying Organic Mulch

For best results, apply a layer of mulch in the spring after the soil has warmed. A good rule of thumb is to wait until seedlings are up and growing, since putting down mulch too early may pre-

Cucumber plants with woodchip mulch (belo

Good Organic Mulches for Vegetables

Compost

Cottonseed hulls

Grass clippings

Ground corncobs

Hay and straw

Newspapers
(no colored inks)

Peanut hulls

Pine needles

Rotted manure

Shredded leaves

Black plastic mulch warming a melon patch

Winter squash 'Orangetti' on grass-clipping mulch

vent the ground from warming sufficiently for heat-loving plants. For effective weed control, apply organic mulch about 4 to 6 inches thick. Half that amount will suffice in shady areas where weeds struggle to grow. Take care not to pile the mulch against the stems of the plants, since this can promote rot. As the mulch thins and decays during the growing season, replenish it.

When you put the garden to bed for the winter, till the organic mulch into the ground; it will continue to break down during the cold months, improving the soil's nutrient value and structure. If your soil is nitrogen-poor, however, tilled-in mulch—especially one with a high carbon content like shredded bark—can further deplete the nitrogen level as it decomposes. To combat this problem, dig in nitrogen-rich cottonseed meal or blood meal in autumn, or plant a winter cover crop such as clover or annual rye.

Inorganic Mulch

Even the most devoted organic gardeners sometimes rely on an inorganic mulch like heavy black plastic sheeting because of its superior weed control and insulating properties. Weeds cannot penetrate it, and as a bonus, vegetables grown on or near the surface of the ground stay cleaner and are less prone to rot. In northern climates, cover beds with black plastic before you plant to hasten the warming of the soil. The dark color absorbs heat during the day and conducts it into the soil. After you have planted the beds, the dark plastic radiates warmth back to the plants at night. Obviously, this extra heat is a disadvantage in hot climates; there, the plastic should be covered with an organic mulch to keep the soil cool.

To use black plastic, lay the sheeting over a bed that has been watered, and weight the edges down with boards or large stones. The plastic will hold in the moisture, but little additional rainwater will get through. To water the beds, you'll need to install a drip-irrigation system or set up soaker hoses under the sheeting. When you're ready to plant, cut slits in the plastic and insert the seedlings. At the end of each season, if the plastic is still in good shape, remove it from the bed, wash it off, fold it when it has dried, and reuse it the following year.

Watering the Garden

You cannot always count on Mother Nature to water your vegetables. As a rule, a garden should receive 1 inch of water per week, including rainfall,

although more may be needed if you have fast-draining, sandy soil or if your area is experiencing extreme heat. To keep track of the amount of rain that falls, invest in an inexpensive rain gauge. Empty it after each rain and keep a tally of the measurements. Then supplement when necessary by hand watering, or with drip- or soaker-hose irrigation or sprinklers. Whenever possible, water early in the morning or in the evening to reduce the loss of moisture through evaporation.

Hand watering is time-consuming, but for a small garden it may be the most practical method. Aim the water at the plants' roots rather than at the foliage, and keep the flow of water light enough so that the water soaks in deeply and doesn't run off. A hand-held wand that attaches to a hose makes the job of directing the water easier; such wands come with a variety of spray nozzles, including one with a very fine mist for newly planted seeds.

Overhead sprinkling works well for germinating seeds because it keeps the surface of the ground continuously moist until the seeds sprout. Once the plants are well on their way, however, it is best to choose another method of irrigation.

Drip Irrigation/Soaker Hoses

Large vegetable gardens profit greatly from drip irrigation or soaker hoses. A drip system works best for plants that are spaced fairly far apart, like tomatoes. Soaker hoses are better for closely spaced crops like salad greens. Both systems operate with low water pressure, delivering water directly to the plants' roots at rates as slow as half a gallon per hour. The slow delivery of water to the areas that need it allows moisture to soak in deeply. As a result, plants tend to grow faster and more uniformly. And because the foliage doesn't get wet, there are fewer problems with fungal diseases, which are often spread by water.

Drip-irrigation and soaker systems can be installed by the home gardener and are easily modified throughout the season as the garden changes. Basic kits are available that include all the valves, feeder lines, and other attachments necessary to set up either type of system. In addition, new feeder lines may be added, old lines removed, and holes opened or plugged as the need arises. You may also purchase a timer that turns

The feeder lines of a drip-irrigation system snake through a recently planted bed in the garden above, but in a short time they will be completely covered by the growing vegetable plants (opposite). Such a setup can be designed to fulfill immediate watering needs and can also be adapted to meet new requirements simply by adding new feeder lines or removing old ones.

the water on and off automatically according to a programmed schedule.

If you use drip-irrigation lines in conjunction with black plastic mulch, lay the lines down under the plastic. Mark each drip emitter with a shovelful of compost to make a visible mound under the plastic sheeting, and plant accordingly.

Weed Control: Every Gardener's Problem

One of the great ironies of gardening is that while it takes a great deal of effort to produce a beautiful and productive garden, weeds flourish with virtually no attention at all. Although their persistence might tempt the gardener to give up the battle against them, they must be destroyed because they compete with crops for growing space, soil nutrients, and water, and often harbor damaging insect pests.

Weeds can be controlled effectively through mulching, which denies them the sunlight they need to grow. A few determined weeds will make their way through mulch, but the numbers will be drastically reduced. You can add to the effectiveness of any organic mulch by putting a thick layer of newspaper (with no colored ink) underneath it. Few weeds can penetrate that barrier, and eventually the newspaper will decompose, improving the soil's structure and nutrient value in the process.

Unfortunately, some mulches can actually increase your weed problem. For example, hay, compost made from seedy plants, or manure from animals grazing in seedy pastures can contain viable seed that has the potential to sprout among your vegetables. Opt for seed-free straw rather than hay, and be sure any compost or manure you use does not contain seedy materials.

Removing and Preventing Weeds

Early eradication is another weapon an organic gardener can use in the war against weeds. When weeds are young and their root systems are just developing, they are easier to pull or hoe, and if they are removed before they set seed, many more weeds will be prevented.

Digging with a hoe or other cultivating tool—the traditional way to weed a large vegetable garden—serves the dual purpose of uprooting weeds and aerating the soil. Be careful, though, not to disturb the roots of nearby vegetables. When hoeing around corn, squash, tomatoes, and potatoes, pile up a little extra soil around the base of the plants to protect their shallow roots.

If you do not use mulch, begin tilling the bed about 3 days after you sow your seeds. This preemptive strike will damage germinating weed seeds before they take root and become established. Continue tilling or hand pulling weeds as necessary throughout the season.

Pulling weeds by hand can be a backbreaking job, but it is a necessary one if weeds grow too large to be uprooted by the hoe. Take solace in knowing that each time you pull a weed you're aerating the soil, and remember that weeding does at least get your hands in the dirt. Throw pulled weeds into the compost pile if it reaches at least 140° F, or dispose of them in accordance with local ordinances for plant debris.

Another way to control weeds is by planting cover crops such as clover, annual rye, vetch, barley, and alfalfa. These crops, sometimes called green manure, thickly carpet the ground, choking out weeds as they grow. To minimize the possibility of wind-borne weed seeds taking hold in your soil, try planting hedges along the border of your vegetable plot.

Fertilizing the Garden Midseason

Weed-free, nutrient-rich soil can sustain many crops throughout the growing season without the addition of fertilizer. But some plants that produce fruits (as opposed to edible leaves, stems, or roots), such as tomatoes, eggplant, and peppers, benefit greatly from a boost in midseason, when the fruits are developing and maturing. And vegetables grown in containers require a steady diet of diluted nutrient supplements throughout the growing season *(page 76)*.

If the soil is not rich enough to begin with, nutrients—especially nitrogen—can leach out with watering or can be depleted by plants that are heavy feeders. Nitrogen deficiency shows up in plants as yellowing leaves and stunted growth. Watch your plants closely; if you catch the problem early and apply a midseason fertilizer, you may be able to save your crop. Unfortunately, the warning signs sometimes become obvious only after it is too late to save the plants. When that happens, your only option is to prepare for the next growing season by amending your vegetable beds with plenty of nutrient-rich organic material such as compost and rotted manure.

When you go looking for fertilizers, you'll find two types—synthetic and organic. Synthetic fertilizers, which are produced by industrial processes, eventually decrease the organic matter in soil and change the biological activity. In addition, they contain mineral salts that acidify the soil and repel earthworms. By contrast, organic products, which are derived from animal or plant remains, or from mined rock minerals, actually build the soil as they feed the plants. Examples of these are dried blood, meat and fish meal, bone meal, com-

post, cottonseed meal, and well-rotted manure *(chart, page 33).*

Potassium-hungry crops, such as turnips, parsnips, beets, carrots, and cabbage, all benefit from an application of wood ashes during the growing season. Nitrogen feeders, including corn and tomatoes, are stimulated by a dose of rotted manure, fish emulsion, or manure tea. You can prepare your own fertilizer from compost or a combination of other ingredients, or you can purchase organic fertilizers that will provide the nutrient concentration you need.

Applying Supplemental Fertilizer

Fertilizers appropriate for established plants are sold in either solid or liquid form. Solid materials are best applied by top- or side-dressing, that is, by spreading the fertilizer around the base or beside the plants. Avoid getting solid fertilizer directly on plants, since it can burn tender shoots and stalks. Lightly rake or hoe the dressings into the soil, and water immediately to help them penetrate the soil.

Spray diluted liquid fertilizers, such as manure tea *(recipe, below)* or fish emulsion, directly onto the plant's leaves, which will absorb the nutrients quickly. Or pour the fertilizer onto the soil so that it soaks down to the plant's roots. Drip-irrigation systems have attachments that release measured amounts of liquid fertilizer while the system is running. The irrigation systems come with safety backflow preventers that stop water in the irrigation pipes from flowing back into the house drinking water.

Manure and Compost Teas

Fill a bucket two-thirds full of water. Add manure or compost to fill the container to the top, and steep for a day or two. Leaving the solid material at the bottom, pour off the liquid into another container and dilute it with more water to the color of weak tea. (To use the tea in small amounts, dip off what you need and dilute it.) Pour about 1 pint of tea around each vegetable plant that will benefit from extra nitrogen. Do not use on root vegetables, which require potassium for healthy growth.

Keeping Records of Your Garden

Keeping a complete record of your garden allows you to build on accumulated knowledge and experience so that you can repeat triumphs and avoid errors. Use a loose-leaf notebook for your garden journal; you can add pages when necessary and move them around if you choose. You'll need graph paper for garden plans, ruled paper for your notes, and heavy paper or photo-album refills for mounting photographs, invoices, and catalog descriptions. To get the most out of your record book, treat it as a combination journal and scrapbook. Collect and keep the following kinds of information:

- **Your garden plan.** This will help you keep track of crop rotations from year to year.
- Lists of the vegetables you planted. Save your invoices, receipts, and seed packets so you can go back to the seed vendor to reorder or seek help with problems. If you ordered from catalogs, paste in their cultivar descriptions. Over the course of the season, note the performance of each plant and how you liked it. Pictures of the vegetables, such as the eggplants above, will jog your memory.
- The number of plants you grew of each vegetable and the yield. This information will assist you in making future decisions about how many plants you want or need of any vegetable or variety.
- Temperature. A daily log of high and low temperatures will give you a good sense of the weather in your area. Also note soil temperatures during the planting season.
- Rainfall. Check your rain gauge weekly and record the results. This information, along with the temperature records, will give you a clear picture of weather trends.
- Dates, especially planting, harvest, and the last spring and first fall frost dates. Note if you seeded too early or too late.
- Pests and diseases. Record the date the problem began, what you did to treat it, and how successful you were.

Planting and Caring for Your Herbs

Herbs—adaptable, undemanding, and forgiving of mistakes—are perfectly suited to beginning and busy gardeners. Just be sure there's a good match between the herbs you choose and your garden's growing conditions, and that you get them off to a good start with proper planting. After that, you'll find them remarkably easy to care for.

Planting Primer

If your schedule and the weather give you a choice, a cool, cloudy day is ideal for planting herbs. And it's best to wait a few weeks after the last frost date to minimize the chance that an unusually late cold snap could damage the young plants. Before removing the herbs from their pots, arrange them in the bed according to your garden plan to see whether you want to make any last-minute adjustments. Once the herbs are placed to your satisfaction, you are ready to begin planting.

Dig each planting hole several inches wider and deeper than the container. Fill the hole with water, allow it to drain, then add a few inches of soil, tamping lightly to prevent excessive settling.

Gently ease your herbs from their containers. Using a garden knife or your fingers, loosen compacted soil around the roots of large container-grown herbs. Seedlings in large flats should be divided into fist-sized clumps with a trowel; leave as much soil around the roots as possible. If the seedlings were grown in peat pots, they can be planted, pot and all, directly in the garden. Just be sure to tear off the top half-inch or so of the peat pot, since any portion of the rim that is exposed above the surface of the soil will soak up water and nutrients, to the seedling's disadvantage.

Place each plant in the prepared hole and add

Building a Raised Bed of Stone

The raised bed described here can be planted from the side as well as the top, since a soil mixture fills the spaces between the stones. The stone walls rest on footings and are further stabilized by being stepped. Use large, flat stones 12 inches or more across for the footings; smaller or more rounded stones are fine for the rest of the structure. This bed stands 18 inches above ground level. For a higher bed, seek the advice of a mason.

2. Lay the second row of stones on top of the first, stepping their outer edges in slightly from the outer edge of the footing stones. Pack the gaps with soil. Continue laying stones in this manner until they are a maximum of 18 inches above ground level. Fill the gaps in the aboveground portion of the walls with a planting mix of equal parts of soil, leaf mold, and sand or poultry grit.

1. Mark off the outline of the bed with lime. Dig a trench about 15 inches deep and as wide as the footing stones. Next, put 10 inches of crushed stone into the trench. Lay the footing stones on this base so that they slope at a slight angle toward the bed's center; the ends of the stones should touch one another. Pack soil tightly into any spaces between and around the stones.

3. To plant in the wall pockets, remove each seedling or cutting from its container just before planting and wrap its tiny soil ball in damp sphagnum moss to protect the roots. Make a planting hole in the pocket with a widger—the spatula-shaped tool shown at left—or a tongue depressor. Lay the plant on the tool, ease it into place, and gently tamp soil mix around its roots.

enough soil to fill it. Firm the soil around the plant, and water thoroughly with a fine spray.

A number of popular herbs, including basil and chives, are very easy to grow from seed sown directly in the garden. And direct-sowing is the preferred method for herbs with fleshy, sparse roots or long taproots that make them difficult to transplant, such as coriander, chervil, dill, parsley, nasturtium, and summer savory.

Sow seeds according to the packet instructions for spacing and depth. If no instructions exist, a good rule of thumb is to plant in shallow trenches at a depth of twice the seed's diameter. Cover the seeds lightly with soil, and water well with a fine spray. To keep birds, insects, and other pests from feasting on your herbs-to-be, consider covering your seedbed with a floating row cover, which will let in rain, light, and air while protecting the seeds.

The soil must remain moist for the seeds to germinate, so check the seedbed frequently. When the seedlings emerge, thin them according to the directions on the seed packet. Don't allow the soil to dry out, and apply a water-soluble fertilizer every other week for approximately 6 weeks.

Thriving between a Rock and a Hard Place

Many herbs will flourish where other plants might not survive. For example, try tucking small thyme plants in gaps between stones (*photo, below*). Creeping thyme (*Thymus praecox* ssp. *arcticus*) and caraway-scented *T. herba-barona* are good low-growing varieties for crevice planting.

For most gardeners, steep inclines are troublesome areas to cultivate. You can turn hot, dry banks into an asset by planting them with drought-resistant herbs such as lavender, creeping savory (*Satureja spicigera*), or winter savory. Easy-care herbs with fibrous, spreading roots such as calamint (*Calamintha grandiflora*) and wild marjoram (*Origanum vulgare*) will clothe a bank with foliage and flowers as they slow erosion.

Herbs for Crevice Planting

Crocus sativus
(saffron)
Gaultheria procumbens
(wintergreen)
Origanum vulgare 'Aureum'
(golden oregano)
Rosmarinus offici-

nalis 'Prostratus'
(prostrate rosemary)
Thymus herba-barona
(caraway thyme)
Thymus praecox ssp. *arcticus*
(creeping thyme)
Thymus pulegioides
(broad-leaved thyme)

Below, a raised bed overflowing with catmint is home to creeping thyme rooted between stones (right, center). The yellow-tinted shrub is a dwarf false cypress.

4. To prepare the interior of the bed for herbs that prefer light, fast-draining soil, add garden soil to a depth of 6 to 8 inches. Then fill the bed to within 3 inches of the top with a mixture of 1 part each of gravel, loam, and sand or grit. After planting, mulch the herbs with a 2-inch layer of sand or pea-sized gravel to help keep their crowns dry, retain soil moisture, and thwart weeds.

Weeding and Mulching

When preparing your beds for planting, it's important to pull or dig out the roots of perennial weeds, since even small fragments will resprout if left behind. Bindweed, couch grass, and goutweed are particularly difficult to remove when they invade a planting of creeping herbs like chamomile or thyme. Be vigilant and pluck out weed seedlings as soon as you spot them.

To suppress weeds around tall herbs, spread a 2- to 4-inch layer of organic mulch around your plants. This will also help retain soil moisture and enrich the soil as it decays. Remember to keep the mulch an inch or two away from the crowns of the plants, however, to prevent rot. For plants that prefer a drier, leaner soil, use a mulch of sand, pea-sized gravel, or poultry grit.

In cold climates, an airy winter mulch of evergreen branches, straw, or salt hay will help plants survive low temperatures and drying winds. Remove the mulch in the spring to allow the soil to warm up and the sun to reach new sprouts. If you are growing alkaline-loving herbs, it is especially important to remove evergreen branches before they shed their needles because they will acidify the soil as they decay.

The Fine Art of Watering

Knowing when to water your plants is a skill acquired by carefully attending to the requirements of the particular herbs in your garden. Species adapted to dry conditions are likely to perform poorly in soil that is constantly moist, while others require even moisture and must be checked frequently during dry weather *(list, below)*. Wilting is

usually considered a sign that a plant is short of water, but looks can be deceiving. On hot days, some thin-leaved herbs such as basil and hot peppers (*Capsicum* spp.) will wilt dramatically by early afternoon, even if the soil around their roots is moist. In the cool of the evening, the plants will perk up again. Always check the soil before watering herbs that wilt easily.

Although watering is largely a summertime chore, it may also be necessary in the winter. If there is no precipitation in your area for 3 or 4 weeks, give your beds a deep soaking to keep dormant herbs healthy. The following tips on when and how to water will help keep established herbs in good condition:

• For most herbs, allow the top inch or so of soil to become somewhat dry between waterings. To check whether it's time to water, dig down 3 to 4 inches with a trowel to see if the soil is still moist. If not, watering is in order.

• Drought-resistant herbs need no more than a half-inch of water per week. Other herbs should receive approximately 1 inch per week. Use a rain gauge to determine how much supplemental watering is needed.

• Give plants slow, deep soakings. Frequent light sprinklings encourage plants to produce shallow root systems, making them more vulnerable to drought.

Pointers on Pruning

Pruning, pinching, or deadheading your herbs at the right time will repay you with more attractive and productive plants. For example, periodically pruning away deadwood from shrubby herbs like sage and lavender encourages stronger, bushier growth. Remember, however, to stop pruning woody herbs approximately 4 weeks before the first expected frost in your area. Otherwise, the plants may waste their energy putting out new growth that could be damaged or killed by the cold.

Pinching back some herbs not only helps maintain a rounded, compact shape, it can also preserve flavor. Many culinary herbs valued for their foliage, such as basil, chervil, lemon balm, and oregano, will diminish in flavor if allowed to produce flowers. But if you promptly pinch off any new flower buds, the herbs will maintain their full flavor and aroma and continue to produce new foliage.

Unless you want to harvest seeds for cooking, you should remove spent flowers promptly. Deadheading prevents seeds from forming, so that the plants have more energy to spend on producing new flowers and foliage.

Herbs for Moist Soil

Angelica archangelica
(angelica)
Anthriscus cerefolium
(chervil)
Gaultheria procumbens
(wintergreen)
Laurus nobilis
(sweet bay)
Levisticum officinale
(lovage)

Lindera benzoin
(spicebush)
Melissa officinalis
(lemon balm)
Mentha x piperita
(peppermint)
Monarda didyma
(bee balm)
Myrrhis odorata
(sweet cicely)
Nepeta spp.
(catmint)
Ocimum basilicum
(sweet basil)

Panax quinquefolius
(American ginseng)
Polygonum odoratum
(Vietnamese coriander)
Viola odorata
(sweet violet)

Note: The abbreviation "spp." stands for the plural of "species"; where used in lists it means that many, but not all, of the species in a genus meet the criterion of the list.

Propagating Your Herbs

The fastest way to get an herb garden going is with nursery-grown plants, but don't overlook using your own mature plants to increase your stock. Dividing overcrowded clumps is simple, and growing new plants from cuttings is only a little more involved. If you need large numbers of plants for kitchen use or for a large knot garden, seeding is a low-cost alternative. Most annual herbs are easy to grow from seed, and starting the cold-sensitive types indoors will give you a head start on the growing season.

Good light is vital for growing healthy seedlings indoors. A very sunny window sill may suffice for winter sowings, but if the intensity of the sunlight is too low, the seedlings will be weak and leggy. If you plan to raise seedlings every year, it's smart to establish a propagation area in your basement or in a spare room. The setup can be as simple as a light fixture with two standard 4-foot-long fluorescent tubes suspended over a table or a sheet of plywood on sawhorse supports. Position the tubes so they will be about 4 inches above the seedlings. A timer set to 16 hours of light followed by 8 hours of darkness is a convenient way to ensure that the plants will get the light they need every day.

Planting the Seed

A soilless growing medium, which you can buy or mix yourself *(page 72, bottom),* is the best choice for starting seeds. For containers, you can purchase inexpensive seed-starting trays with domed plastic lids that let in light and retain warmth and moisture. Individual plastic pots or cell packs with a covering of clear plastic wrap work just as well and are a good choice when you will be sowing only a few seeds of a variety. To minimize the chances of transmitting a disease to your seedlings, sterilize previously used containers with a solution of a half-cup of bleach to a gallon of water.

When you are ready to plant, moisten the growing medium and fill the containers no more than 2½ inches deep. Plant the seeds according to the instructions on the packets. Herbs that have a low rate of germination, such as lavender and parsley, should be sown so thickly that the seeds touch one another. Make a label for each container with the name of the variety and the date of planting. Water thoroughly with a fine spray, then cover the container to keep the seedbed moist and warm.

When using plastic wrap, choose the thinnest you can find and drape it loosely over a support of sticks, pencils, or arched hoops so that it is several inches above the seedbed.

Care of Seedlings

Place the containers in a warm (70° to 80° F), bright room out of direct sunlight. After a week, begin checking for signs of germination. As soon as a few seeds have sprouted, place the containers in a sunny window or under fluorescent lights and remove the covering. Seedlings left under cover in moist, warm conditions may be stricken with damping-off, a fungal disease that can quickly destroy an entire flat of young seedlings. To help prevent damping-off, try misting seedlings with an infusion of German chamomile: Add a handful of fresh chamomile or 2 tablespoons of the dried herb to 4 cups of boiling water. Steep the mixture for 10 minutes, strain it through cheesecloth, and let it cool before using.

Be careful not to overwater the seedlings; soggy roots make them susceptible to root rot and foliage diseases. Water once each day in the morn-

Double Potting for Easy Watering

For an effective way to keep your herb cuttings constantly moist, first fill a 6-inch clay pot halfway with moistened soilless growing medium. Plug the drainage holes of a 3-inch clay pot and set it on top of the medium. Fill the space between the pots with more of the growing medium and tamp it lightly. Plant the cuttings in the larger pot, then fill the small pot with water; it will seep through the pot and water your herbs.

PROPAGATION METHODS FOR 23 POPULAR HERBS

Herb	Propagation Method
Allium schoenoprasum (chives)	seed, division
Aloysia triphylla (lemon verbena)	seed, cuttings
Anethum graveolens (dill)	seed
Angelica archangelica (angelica)	seed
Anthriscus cerefolium (chervil)	seed
Artemisia dracunculus var. *sativa* (French tarragon)	cuttings, division
Calendula officinalis (calendula)	seed
Chamaemelum nobile (Roman chamomile)	seed, cuttings, division, layering
Foeniculum vulgare (fennel)	seed
Laurus nobilis (bay laurel)	cuttings
Lavandula spp. (lavender)	seed, cuttings, layering
Melissa officinalis (lemon balm)	seed, cuttings, division
Mentha spp. (mint)	cuttings, division
Monarda didyma (bee balm)	cuttings, division
Myrrhis odorata (sweet cicely)	seed
Ocimum basilicum (sweet basil)	seed, cuttings
Pelargonium spp. (scented geranium)	seed, cuttings
Petroselinum crispum (parsley)	seed
Rosmarinus officinalis (rosemary)	cuttings, layering
Salvia spp. (sage)	seed, cuttings, layering
Satureja montana (winter savory)	seed, cuttings, layering
Thymus spp. (thyme)	seed, cuttings, division, layering
Tropaeolum majus (nasturtium)	seed

Note: The abbreviation "spp." stands for the plural of "species"; where used in lists it means that many, but not all, of the species in a genus meet the criterion of the list.

Making a Soilless Growing Medium for Herbs

A soilless growing medium gets seedlings and cuttings off to a healthy start. Air and water penetrate it easily to reach growing roots and, unlike garden loam or commercial potting soil, it is free of disease organisms and weed seeds. To make a good mix yourself, combine 3 parts each of vermiculite, composted pine bark, and sphagnum moss with 1 part leaf mold. To each gallon of the mix add a heaping tablespoon of ground limestone and a half-cup of a slow-release fertilizer such as 17-6-10. Store in dry, clean containers or plastic bags. Just before using, dampen the mix with warm water.

ing, then allow the growing medium to dry out until the following morning. Once a week, feed the seedlings with a water-soluble organic fertilizer, diluted as directed on the package.

Seedlings are ready for transplanting when they have two sets of leaves. Lift them carefully by their leaves, not by their fragile stems, and place them in 2- to 2½-inch plastic pots filled with dampened growing mix. After 3 to 6 weeks, the seedlings will be ready to be hardened off. Set them outdoors in a sheltered, sunny spot for the day and bring them back inside at night. In a week they will be ready for planting out in the garden.

New Plants from Cuttings and Division

If you have plants with long taproots that are hard to divide, you'll need to propagate them from stem cuttings. This method is also best for cultivars that don't come true from seed; the cuttings will yield offspring identical to the parent.

Spring is generally the best time to take cuttings, since fresh green growth roots quickly. First, prepare flats, trays, or shallow pots with dampened soilless growing medium. Using scissors or a sharp knife, make a clean cut just below a node or leaf 3 to 5 inches from the tip of the stem. If you will be taking cuttings for more than a few minutes, wrap each one as you go in dampened newspaper and place in a plastic bag to keep it moist and cool.

When you have enough cuttings, move to a shaded area to prepare them for potting. Strip all leaves from the lower half of the stem and pinch off all flowers or flower buds. To stimulate root formation, dip the base of the cuttings in rooting hormone, then plant the cuttings about an inch deep. Space them several inches apart to allow for air circulation. Water deeply and cover the container loosely with plastic wrap or a plastic bag held several inches above the cuttings by sticks or other supports. Keep the cuttings in a cool spot that gets plenty of bright, indirect light. Frequent misting—several times daily, if possible—will help maintain the high humidity needed to prevent wilting. Cuttings root most quickly when the air temperature is in the 60s and the root-zone temperature is around 75° F. For a steady source of bottom heat, set the container on an electric mat purchased at a garden center or through a garden supply catalog.

The appearance of new growth on a cutting signals that it has taken root and is ready to be transplanted to its own container and placed in a sunny window or under fluorescent lights. The new plant can be set out in the garden when a network of roots has developed on the surface of the rootball; this will take several weeks. To check its growth, gently slip the plant from its pot.

If you wish to propagate such herbs as basil, lemon verbena, mint, pineapple sage, and Vietnamese coriander, you can also root them in water. Fill a clear glass jar with enough water to submerge only the stripped portion of the cutting's stem. Place it in bright, indirect light and change the water daily to keep it free of the bacteria that cause rot. When a cutting has roots ¼ to ½ inch long, which generally takes about 2 weeks, pot it in a soilless growing medium and place it under fluorescent lights or in direct sunlight. In a few weeks, the cuttings can be planted in the garden.

Division is the easiest and quickest way to increase your stock of healthy established herbs many times over. In cold climates, spring is the best season to divide plants; in milder climates you can choose between spring or fall. Work on a cloudy day, if possible, and dig up the plant with a sharp spade. Using your hands, a trowel, or a knife, divide the plant, roots and all, into several clumps. As a rule, a large clump will be less stressed than a small one and will establish itself more quickly after planting. If a division has an ample root system and the weather is cool, it can be planted directly in the garden. Otherwise, plant the division in a container so that it can develop a larger root system before it is transplanted to a permanent place. Water well with a soluble organic fertilizer to reduce the stress of transplanting.

The Simplicity of Layering

Creeping herbs often put down roots on their own wherever stems or branches touch moist soil. This process, known as layering, can be helped along by a gardener who wants new plants. Choose a young, flexible stem and strip the growth from a 5- to 6-inch section growing close to the ground. With a sharp knife, nick the bare section, then bury it 2 to 3 inches deep; leave several inches of the stem's tip exposed above the soil. You may need to anchor the buried stem with a small stone or a U-shaped wire to keep it in place. Mulch the layered area and water deeply. In about a month, check for roots by gently tugging on the buried stem. If you meet with resistance, roots have probably formed. Sever the stem from the parent plant, lift it gently, and transplant it to a pot or directly to the garden.

A special version of layering is used to propagate herbs that have upright, woody stems. This process, which is called mound layering, is explained in the box at right.

Mound Layering Shrubby Herbs

The stems of a number of shrubby upright herbs with woody bases will take root when mounded with soil, yielding new plants for the garden. Lavender and other plants that are slow to root need to be cut back, as shown below in Step 1, then mounded with soil. You can skip this step with thyme, sage, rosemary, and other herbs that root easily, and proceed to Steps 2 and 3.

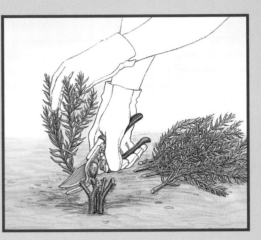

1. In early spring, cut the stems of the plant to be mound layered back to within 2 to 3 inches of the ground. Within several weeks after pruning, new shoots should appear.

2. When the new shoots are about 5 inches long, mound a mixture of equal amounts of sand, peat moss, and soil over the plant's center, until only the tips of the new growth are showing. Keep the mound slightly moist. As the shoots continue to grow, add soil to the mound until it is 6 to 8 inches high. Be sure not to cover the tips of the shoots.

3. On an overcast day in late summer, gently wash away the mounded soil. Using hand pruners, cut each rooted stem at its base to separate it from the parent plant. Plant the rooted stems immediately in a well-prepared bed. The following year, you can mound layer the parent plant again or leave it to grow back into a healthy rejuvenated shrub.

CHAPTER FIVE

The Portable Kitchen Garden

Container-grown vegetables, fruits, and herbs can transform even the smallest space into a garden. You can locate the garden wherever the plants will thrive and look their best, and rearrange or move it as you wish. Potted herbs are especially versatile: Depending on the season, you can set them inside on a window sill or outside on a porch or patio.

With a bit of pampering, most herbs and many small vegetables and fruits adapt well to containers. And—in addition to providing food for the table—some offer delicious fragrances, while others display handsome foliage or colorful fruit or flowers. In the California patio garden shown at left, pots of pineapple mint, sage, and cilantro, backed by bright pink roses, are a feast for the eyes as well as the palate.

On the following pages, you will learn the basics of designing and caring for portable kitchen gardens, from choosing plants and containers to feeding, watering, and pruning the plants once they are established.

Vegetable Gardening in Containers

A colorful array of containers filled with red and green varieties of lettuce (foreground), silvery leaved sage, a large tomato plant with ripening fruit, and rich red peppers spills down the steps of a Los Altos, California, terrace. Many favorite vegetables are now available in dwarf varieties that grow well in containers.

If your only space or sunny spot is on a patio or deck, containers can serve as a garden for your vegetables. Many vegetables—especially dwarf varieties—will grow in boxes, tubs, or other planters, although they will require more attention than plants in the ground. Because the soil in containers dries out quickly, you'll need to water these plants regularly. The best watering setup is a drip-irrigation system with spaghetti lines to each pot and a timer to regulate the water flow. This system works especially well if you have lots of containers, if you plan to be away for several days at a stretch, or if you are growing vegetables that are extremely sensitive to moisture variation, such as cauliflower.

Every time you water container-grown plants, soil nutrients leach out, so plan to fertilize frequently. Start the plants off in a good-quality potting mix and supplement it on a weekly basis with fish emulsion, liquid seaweed, or other organic fertilizers.

The volume or depth of soil needed for the roots of a plant determines the size of the container required. For example, deep-rooted vegetables like leeks or beets need a container the size of a whiskey barrel to provide enough depth for healthy growth. By contrast, plants with shallow roots, such as peppers, green onions, and bok choy, do well in 8- to 12-inch pots. Window boxes make suitable containers for leafy vegetables, in-

cluding spinach, leaf lettuce, mustard greens, and arugula. You can plant a single plant type or a mixture of vegetables in one container, if you like; check the spacing and cultural requirements of different plants in the Encyclopedia of Vegetables at the back of this book *(pages 280-323)* and plant your pots accordingly.

If you have a sunny spot on a porch, place a vining vegetable in a pot there. Tie one end of a string to the pot and the other to the roof or the eaves, and train the plant up the string. Pole beans, vining tomatoes, vining cucumbers, and cantaloupes are good choices for this treatment. 'Super Sweet 100' tomato plants, which bear bright red cherrylike fruit, and the 'Yellow Pear' variety, with its golden pear-shaped crop, are particularly decorative.

Minimum Container Sizes for Compact Gardening

Artichoke: whiskey barrel

Arugula: window box

Beets: whiskey barrel

Bok choy: 8" pot

Broccoli: 12"-18" pot

Brussels sprouts: whiskey barrel

Cabbage: 12"-18" pot green-leaved: 'Early Jersey Wakefield', 'Stonehead' red-leaved: 'Ruby Ball'

Carrots: 12"-18" pot 'Baby Spike', 'Babette', 'Little Finger', 'Minicor', 'Marmet', 'Planet', 'Thumbelina'

Cauliflower: 12"-18" pot

Chard: 12"-18" pot 'Charlotte', 'Perpetual Spinach'

Cucumber, bush: 12"-18" pot

vining: whiskey barrel, trained up string

Eggplant: 12"-18" pot

Endive/Escarole: 12"-18" pot

Garlic: 12"-18" pot

Kale: 12"-18" pot

Kohlrabi: 12"-18" pot

Leeks: whiskey barrel 'King Richard'

Lettuce, leaf: window box or 12"-18" pot

Melons: whiskey barrel *muskmelon:* 'Sweet Bush' *watermelon:* 'Bush Baby II' *cantaloupes:* trained up string

Mustard greens: window box

Onions, green: 8" pot

Peppers: 8"-12" pot

Radishes: 12" pot

Rhubarb: whiskey barrel

Shallots: 8"-12" pot

Spinach: window box

Squash, summer: whiskey barrel

Squash, winter: whiskey barrel *acorn:* 'Bush Table' *butternut:* 'Butterbush'

Strawberries, alpine: 8" pot

Tomatillo: 12" pot

Tomato, determinate varieties: 18" pot *indeterminate (vining)* varieties to train up string: 'Super Sweet 100', 'Yellow Pear', 'Gardener's Delight' 8"-12" pot: 'Florida Basket', 'Tiny Tim', 'Toy Boy'

Turnips: 12"-18" pot 'Tokyo Cross'

Container-grown tomatoes, peppers, parsley, and basil flourish among pots of flowering alyssum, lobelia, marigolds, and periwinkle on a backyard patio. Though overflowing, the small pots provide enough soil for these shallow-rooted plants to thrive.

77

Container Gardening with Herbs

Planting herbs in pots allows you to grow a garden wherever and whenever you choose. If your in-ground growing space is small, containers can expand it by incorporating surrounding areas—such as a walkway or a set of stairs—into your overall scheme. And if you have a roomy garden, you can still use container-grown herbs as accents and fillers or for indoor enjoyment.

Whether you allow them to develop their natural form or train them as espaliers or topiaries (*pages 89-91*), herbs in containers are excellent accents in a garden. A pair of large containers filled with tall herbs can add a dramatic touch at the entrance to a garden path, for example. And matching topiaries can be set up to march in a rhythmic geometric pattern across a bare wall or along a stockade fence.

A Portable Visual Feast

The simplest way to create a lovely display of container-grown herbs is to cluster together small pots holding different plants. A grouping of culinary herbs, for instance, can be situated right outside your kitchen door. A more ambitious design technique is to plant a large container with a variety of complementary herbs to form what is essentially a movable garden. You can take the container to any part of the property or, if it suits you, take it into your home or greenhouse. Using a dolly to transport your pots makes even heavy concrete containers portable.

Inside, the kitchen is a logical setting for a grouping of culinary herbs. In cold climates you can grow long-lived tender herbs such as sweet bay laurel and lemon grass outdoors in pots dur-

A winter garden provides a palette of fresh tastes for the Virginia cook who tends these herbs (right). At far left are slim-leaved garlic chives and thyme. Two kinds of oregano crown the strawberry pot at center, and a small variegated sage is tucked in its side pocket. A pot of catnip and a basket with curly parsley and dwarf basil complete the garden.

At the edge of a brick patio (below), culinary plantings of thyme, oregano, fennel, sage, tarragon, and mint share space with ornamental daisies, pinks, heliotrope, and alyssum in a trio of containers.

Long-Lived Container Herbs

Aloysia triphylla
(lemon verbena)
Citrus aurantium
(bitter orange)
Citrus limon
(lemon)
Cymbopogon citratus
(lemon grass)
Laurus nobilis
(bay laurel)
Myrtus communis
(myrtle)
***Pelargonium* spp.**
(scented geranium)
Punica granatum* var. *nana
(pomegranate)
Rosmarinus officinalis
(rosemary)
Tulbaghia violacea
(society garlic)

Note: The abbreviation "spp." stands for the plural of "species"; where used in lists it means that many, but not all, of the species in a genus meet the criterion of the list.

Culinary herbs are kept close at hand on a New Jersey deck (above) and outside a Washington State kitchen door (below). The rustic planter filled with thyme and the clay pots containing mint, oregano, and other herbs also create different design effects.

ing the summer months and move them indoors when temperatures drop and nights grow cold.

Containers also allow you to bring herbs that are at the peak of their season and are looking their best into prominent spots in the garden for viewing. For example, if you want to dress up a shady spot for a party, you can move containers planted with sun-loving herbs, display them there for the few hours they are needed, and then whisk them back to their original location.

Selecting Plants for Containers

Choosing different herbs to mix in a container can be as much of a creative challenge as designing a garden bed or border. Keep in mind the growth habits of the plants as well as which ones look good together. As a starting point, perennials are logical companions for other perennials, annuals for other annuals. For best results, combine plants with similar needs. Mediterranean herbs such as sage, lavender, and rosemary require well-drained soil and can tolerate a degree of drought. Don't mix them with plants like parsley, peppers, or ginger, which prefer rich, moist conditions.

Also consider the mature shape and size of each herb so the finished effect will show off all of the plants to best advantage. Be careful not to set a slow-growing or naturally small plant next to one that will quickly envelop its smaller companion in foliage. For example, marjoram, nasturtium, French tarragon, and parsley tend to get choked out by vigorous plants such as lemon verbena and lovage, which reach heights of 6 feet or more if allowed to grow unchecked.

Most herbs need a minimum of 6 hours of sunlight to flourish. When you plan your container garden, make sure sun-loving plants aren't shaded by taller neighbors. One likely trio for a sunny site would feature sweet basil, lemon basil, and sweet marjoram. Herbs that tolerate some shade include angelica, nasturtium, lovage, mint, and tarragon. Chervil, coriander, and parsley all enjoy a cool, moist environment.

Designing Plant Combinations

As you work out plant combinations based on similar growing requirements, use your imagination to create displays of herbs that are beautiful as well as functional.

Plant herbs with trailing habits on the edges of pots, where they can drape over the sides. Among your choices might be silver or golden lemon thyme, marjoram, and prostrate rosemary. To cover bare soil in a container planted with a tall plant or a standard, use low-growing herbs such as creeping thyme or Roman chamomile (*Chamaemelum nobile*).

Pairings for Color and Texture

Consider planting a container with a color theme, combining, for example, the variegated pink, green, and cream foliage of tricolor sage with pink-flowering chives. Tricolor sage would also look stunning against the deep purple foliage of purple basil. For a golden motif, you might choose gold-leaved forms of sage (*Salvia officinalis* 'Icterina'), marjoram (*Origanum vulgare* 'Aureum'), and thyme (*Thymus* x *citriodorus* 'Aureus'). Herbs with gray or silver foliage include silver thyme and lamb's ears. For a large container, consider silver horehound (*Marrubium incanum*), which can grow 2 feet or more in height.

To create a look that is subtle but no less striking, combine herbs that have contrasting leaf textures. For example, allow the large leaves of purple sage (*Salvia officinalis* 'Purpurea') to intermingle with delicate thyme foliage.

Perfuming the Air with Geraniums

If you're looking for kitchen herbs that are not only attractive but also highly aromatic, scented geraniums are the perfect choice.

Scented geraniums, tender perennials native to Africa's Cape of Good Hope, were introduced in England around 1795. Growers soon found that the plants would thrive indoors in winter if given ample light. The geraniums were an instant success because of their diverse, fascinating leaf forms—the herb mutates readily, and bee-crossed hybrids are common—and distinctive scents.

Today, although nursery catalogs may advertise scents as diverse as clove, apricot, and coconut, most experts agree that the possibilities are limited to variations of lemon, mixed citrus (combining lemon, lime, and orange), mint, rose, rose-lemon, apple, pepper, and a pungent odor—more or less pleasant, depending on the cultivar—that can only be described as spicy.

Fragrant geraniums boast leaf forms to satisfy just about any gardener. Size varies from the crinkly ½-inch-wide leaves of lemon-scented *Pelargonium crispum* 'Minor' to the pungent *P. hispidum*, with leaves that measure 4 to 5 inches across. Leaf shapes range from the ruffled, round foliage of apple geranium (*P. odoratissimum*) to the deeply indented leaves of rose geranium (*P. graveolens*). Leaves come in many shades of green, some with a light brush of velvet, as well as variegated mixtures of green with cream, white, brown, and even maroon.

The most useful varieties of scented geranium for cooking are those with citrus-, rose-, or mint-scented foliage; use the fresh leaves in teas or as a flavoring for jam, baked goods, syrup, or vinegar. The resinous leaves of other varieties may be used to flavor pâté and sausage.

Pelargonium quercifolium 'Fair Ellen' (oak-leaved geranium)

Comely clay pots on a Virginia kitchen window sill keep dill (left), parsley, lemon balm, purple basil, sage, thyme, and rosemary (far right) convenient for flavoring a winter dinner. A sunny south-facing window is ideal for growing them; just remember to rotate the pots weekly so the herbs will grow evenly.

Herbs with Good Taste

If you'd like to make flavor your theme, create a lemon-scented garden in a large container. Plant lemon-scented gum *(Eucalyptus citriodora)* at the center, then surround it with a selection of edible herbs such as lemon grass *(Cymbopogon citratus),* golden lemon thyme *(Thymus* x *citriodorus* 'Aureus'), lemon basil *(Ocimum basilicum* 'Citriodorum'), and lemon-scented geraniums *(Pelargonium crispum* 'Prince Rupert' and *P. c.* 'Mabel Grey').

Many herbs are delicious brewed as tea, and some are said to have health-giving properties as well. To add to your pleasure, grow a tea garden in containers planted with bee balm, chamomile, mint (peppermint, apple mint, and orange mint have distinctive flavors), lemon balm, and lemon verbena.

Herbs to Start from Seed Indoors

Allium schoenoprasum
(chives)
Allium tuberosum
(Chinese or garlic chives)
Anthriscus cerefolium
(chervil)
Capsicum
(pepper)
Lavandula
(lavender)

Melissa officinalis
(lemon balm)
Nepeta cataria
(catnip)
Ocimum basilicum
cultivars
(basil)
Origanum majorana
(sweet marjoram)

Melissa officinalis (lemon balm)

Enjoying Rosemary Year Round

Pine-scented rosemary lives for years if it is planted in gardens as temperate as those of its native Mediterranean. In summer, it will flourish in any sunny garden in well-drained soil if given a modicum of water. Though most rosemaries succumb to prolonged freezes, some varieties such as *Rosmarinus officinalis* 'Arp', 'Hill Hardy', 'Salem', 'Dutch Mill', and 'White Flowered' can survive winter temperatures as low as -10° F.

Indoors, potted rosemary does best in a cool, sunny spot. Dry indoor heat in winter will cause the plant to dry out and die. Rosemary plants are under the greatest stress in late January, when the stronger sun begins to draw moisture out of plants more quickly. But too much moisture in the air can promote powdery mildew.

To give your rosemary a fighting chance under such trying conditions, begin by potting the plant in a light growing medium of peat moss mixed with perlite and vermiculite. Then water your plant only when the mix is dried out—the pot will feel light, and the mix will have turned a pale brown; make sure to let all the excess water drain out. Brown leaves at the plant's base are a sign that your rosemary has been overwatered, whereas wilted terminal shoots indicate a thirsty plant.

As the plant grows, pinch off long shoots and branches to use in cooking and to promote bushiness. Flowers in lavender-blue, pink, or white will appear from winter through spring. Among the earliest bloomers are 'Beneden Blue' and 'Tuscan Blue', flowering in late winter; prostrate rosemary can bloom almost continually if it is given enough light.

Root-bound plants should be transplanted in spring to a slightly larger pot; too large a pot prevents the plant from using up the moisture in the soil and encourages rot. Fertilize your plant once every 2 weeks during the growing season with a balanced fertilizer. Stop fertilizing in autumn, a few weeks before you bring the plant indoors.

Annual Herbs in Winter

Many annuals that are valued for seasoning food germinate quickly from seed and are thus well suited for growing indoors *(list, opposite)*. Although the plants won't last as long as they would outdoors—about 6 weeks is the maximum life span, even under the best conditions—you will be able to harvest a steady supply of fresh herbs throughout the winter by making three or four successive sowings, spaced about 3 weeks apart. That way, new plants will be mature enough to use at about the time you're ready to throw the old ones away.

A top-quality, homemade soilless potting mix *(recipe, page 72)* should contain enough nutrients to satisfy the plants. If you want to supplement the mix, use an organic houseplant fertilizer, applying it at only half the recommended rate. A fertilizer with a low nutrient analysis of 3-6-4 or 5-5-5 will suffice; giving the plants more fertilizer than that may cause them to produce excess foliage and lose flavor.

Once the plants sprout, they will need the same light conditions as would any herb grown indoors. (For instructions on growing herbs from seed, see pages 71-72.)

Potting and Caring for Herbs

Once you have decided on which herbs to grow, your next step is to choose the containers in which to grow them. Almost any container will do as long as it is clean and has one or more holes in the bottom for ample drainage. However, there are some differences worth considering between the two main container types, plastic and clay.

Plastic pots hold moisture well, but plants in them must be monitored carefully—especially if they are in the shade—to make sure the soil doesn't stay too wet. By contrast, clay containers are porous, providing plants with good air circulation and drainage. For just these reasons, however, plants in clay pots need to be watered frequently, especially in hot weather, so that the soil doesn't dry out.

Cleaning and Reusing Clay Pots

Before using an old clay pot for a new plant, first check the pot for chips or cracks that might allow moisture to seep away. Then give the pot a good cleaning. To remove algae and fungi as well as any disease that may be lurking, scour the pot under cold running water with a nylon scrubbing pad, then soak it for several hours in a solution of 1 part bleach to 5 parts water. Rinse the pot thoroughly. If you won't be using the container right away, let it dry completely before storing it.

Even such a thorough cleaning may not remove the white salts—residue from alkaline water—that sometimes streak clay pots. Soak these pots in undiluted vinegar (buy it in gallon jugs to save money) for a day or two. Rinse them under cold water and scrub with a nylon pad. If salt streaks persist, repeat the process, using fresh vinegar. Gardeners with time to spare can set the salt-streaked containers outside; rain will leave them fresh and clean within a few months.

The square tiles used to line the inside of a chimney are imaginatively employed as containers—planted with parsley, purple basil, peppers, marigolds, and scented geraniums—in this Georgia garden. Other possibilities for unusual containers include decorative watering cans, discarded wheelbarrows, large shells such as those of giant clams or conchs, and weather-beaten, hollowed-out logs.

Ideal Potting Soil Mixtures

Soil collected directly from the garden should not be used in containers. In most cases it is too heavy, and it often harbors harmful insects and diseases. Soilless, commercially packed container mixes, on the other hand, tend to be so light that fast-growing roots soon make herbs potbound. These mixes also dry out very quickly.

To give a packaged potting mix more substance, blend it with sterilized compost (2 parts potting mix to 1 part compost).

Or, if you have access to top-quality loam soil from a mulch or landscape company, you can prepare a container mix by blending 1 part loam soil and 1 part soilless potting medium, such as a peat/perlite mix. Moisten with fish emulsion diluted at the rate of ¼ cup per gallon of water.

TIPS FROM THE PROS

Tricks to Retain Moisture in Containers

During the hot months of summer, container-grown plants dry out quickly and may need watering once—even twice—a day. Here are some ways to escape the tyranny of tending pots:

• Choose a container that retains moisture. The materials with the lowest evaporation rate are plastic, fiberglass, metal, and glazed ceramic, often called terra cotta. The most porous materials are clay (unglazed ceramic), wood, and concrete. Generally, plants in porous pots need watering three times more often than those in plastic or metal containers.

• Pick white containers, which tend to reflect heat, thus somewhat reducing the rate of evaporation. Dark-colored pots, on the other hand, absorb heat, causing the soil to dry out faster.

• Find a pot that is slightly larger than the plant requires. The extra soil will hold more moisture.

• Blend soil polymers—available at most garden centers—into your container mix to aid moisture retention.

• Place decorative bark or pebbles on top of the soil to slow surface evaporation. Or cover the soil with an organic mulch of compost or grass clippings and top with the bark or pebbles.

• Group containers together to shade and humidify each other. Place the small pots, which are likely to dry out first, in the center of the cluster.

• Shelter pots from the wind, which can dry out plants.

• Install an automatic irrigation system with a line running to each container. The initial effort may seem great, but so will the rewards.

The Well-Watered Strawberry Pot

To obtain even moisture throughout a large strawberry pot with six or more pockets, turn PVC (polyvinyl chloride) pipe into a watering tube. Choose pipe 2 to 4 inches in diameter and 4 inches less in length than the pot's height. Place the pipe upright in the pot and mark the location of each pocket on the pipe. This ensures that water will reach the roots of every plant directly. Drill ½-inch holes at those marks. Cover the bottom of the pipe with a square of plastic mesh and secure it by wrapping wire around the pipe. Fill the pipe with pebbles, tamping them as you go, then cap the top of the pipe with mesh. Next, put a mesh square over the pot's drainage hole, and center the pipe on the hole. Align the drilled holes with the pockets. Add soil to the pot to the level of the first pockets.

With a chopstick or screwdriver, gently push the first plant's rootball into the lowest pocket, roots pointed down. Keep the crown of the plant level with the lip of the pocket to allow for settling; add more soil to the level of the next pocket. Repeat until all the pockets are full and soil reaches to within 1 inch of the rim. Then center a plant over the pipe and fill in the rest of the pot with soil.

Set the container in a pan of water to soak up moisture. Then water the top and pockets with a fine spray.

Planting the Containers

Before you plant a new clay pot, soak it in water overnight. Then, for any type of container, cover the drainage hole with a piece of mesh screen, a large pebble, or a pottery shard. Fill the bottom of the container with potting medium and position the plant in the pot so that the soil level will be below the pot's rim. Then fill the pot with soil and tamp firmly to remove air pockets. Finally, water thoroughly.

If you are replanting a container of mixed herbs in the spring, first remove any perennials so you can work the soil without interference. Replenish the potting mix by adding a 1-inch layer of well-rotted chicken manure; mix it in thoroughly, aerating the soil at the same time. Replant the perennials and add new annual herbs.

Feeding Hungry Container-Grown Herbs

Herbs planted in the ground typically have a more intense flavor and a more pungent aroma if they are fertilized with a light hand. By contrast, those planted in containers require extra nourishment. Frequent watering leaches nutrients from the soil, and the problem is compounded when several plants are grown in one pot and they are all competing for food.

During the growing season, feed herbs in containers every 2 weeks with an organic fertilizer that is high in nitrogen; seaweed and fish emulsion are two good choices. Follow the directions on the package to measure out and dilute the fertilizer. At the end of summer, cut back on the feeding, and stop altogether in late fall.

Grooming Potted Herbs

Plants will grow bushier and be more attractive if stem tips are pinched off regularly to encourage more branching. In the case of container-grown herbs, this care is especially important to

Herbs for Strawberry Pots

ON TOP

Lavandula dentata (French lavender)
Lavandula stoechas (Spanish lavender)
Pelargonium graveolens (rose geranium)
Petroselinum crispum (parsley)
Salvia officinalis 'Nana' (dwarf sage)
Tropaeolum minus (dwarf nasturtium)

IN POCKETS

Allium schoenoprasum (chives)
Mentha requienii (Corsican mint)

Ocimum basilicum 'Minimum' (bush basil)
Origanum majorana (sweet marjoram)
Pelargonium odoratissimum (apple geranium)
Petroselinum crispum (parsley)
Thymus caespititius (tufted thyme)
Thymus x *citriodorus* (lemon thyme)
Thymus x *citriodorus* 'Silver Queen' (silver lemon thyme)
Thymus herba-barona (caraway thyme)
Thymus praecox ssp. *arcticus* (creeping thyme)
Viola tricolor (Johnny-jump-up)

control plants like sage and lemon verbena that tend to grow large and sprawl. Even less vigorous herbs benefit from being trimmed when they share a container.

Make it a habit to carry clippers with you when you check on your container-grown herbs, and take a few moments to snip and shape the plants. Use the harvested pieces for the evening meal, for potpourri, or in flower arrangements.

Repotting Root-Bound Perennials

Over time, perennial herbs outgrow their containers. If roots protrude from the bottom of the pot, or if you notice that water doesn't soak through the soil properly, the plant has become root-bound and needs to be repotted. If possible, do the job in spring, when the plant is ready to begin a growth spurt. The least desirable time to repot is late autumn or winter, when the plant is dormant and will be slow to generate new roots.

Increase the container size gradually rather than in big jumps. Choose a pot 2 inches larger in diameter than the old one, and prepare it for planting by covering the drainage hole and spreading a layer of container mix in the bottom.

Remove your plant from its old pot and gently loosen the roots. Position it so it will sit at the same level in the pot as before. Fill in the gaps with soil, and water well.

Some herbs—tender perennials, trees, and shrubs such as myrtle or bay laurel—can live in a container for years. However, you'll need to refresh and replenish the soil annually. This can be as simple as carefully removing the top layer and replacing it with fresh potting mix enriched with a slow-release fertilizer. However, some experts recommend lifting the plant out of its pot and carefully scraping soil from the sides and bottom of the rootball as well, then replenishing with fresh soil mix as you replant the herb.

For a severely root-bound plant, lift the herb from the pot, slice off the outer layer of roots, and loosen the rootball before replacing the plant in its original container. Add fresh potting mix to fill the extra space, then trim back the foliage to compensate for the loss of roots.

Winter Care for Outdoor Containers

In the northern climate zones, even hardy herbs will need winter protection if they are grown

These long wooden planters take little space yet drape this Maryland deck with a lush curtain of herbs. The planters brim with (from left) lovage, redmint (Mentha x gracilis), madonna lily, nasturtium, lavender, lemon balm, Jerusalem sage, rose-lemon-scented geranium, lemon-scented geranium, and comfrey. Swags of wild yam (Dioscorea bulbifera) festoon the railing.

above ground. If you prefer to overwinter your hardy perennials outdoors, one option is to replant them in the ground in autumn or to bury the containers so that the roots are better insulated. Alternatively, you can cluster the pots together in a sheltered spot away from the wind and pile mulch around them. Otherwise, not only your plants but also your containers will be at the mercy of the vagaries of winter: Unglazed clay pots, for example, have a tendency to crack and flake when they freeze and thaw.

If you want to bring your container-grown herbs indoors, start getting them ready in early autumn. Cut back the plants by about half their new growth, trim back the roots if the plant is rootbound, and repot with fresh soil. Then move the plants to a sheltered area such as a patio or terrace to help them make the transition to their new environment. When the weather begins to turn cold, move the pots indoors.

You can also pot up tender perennials growing in the garden—rosemary, lemon verbena, lemon grass, and the like. If a plant is too large for the pot you want to use or the indoor space you have, trim the foliage back to a manageable size before you dig it up. Then, a few weeks before you put the plants into pots, trim the roots: Use a shovel to slice through the earth all around the rootball, cutting off the outer edge of the roots. This pruning will encourage the growth of new feeder roots that will help the plant cope with the transition indoors.

Overwintering Pots Indoors

Once indoors, your herbs will still need their 6 hours minimum of direct sunlight; a sunny, south-facing window is best. If you don't have a location with adequate natural light, purchase special "grow" lights or use ordinary fluorescents. (Incandescent lights give off too much heat.) Hang two to four light tubes 5 to 6 inches above the plants. If you mount the lights on chains, you can easily adjust the height as the plants grow. Ideally, the lights should be color-balanced to replicate natural light, but you can simulate the sun by pairing cool-white and warm-white tubes. Turn the lights on for 14 to 16 hours a day, which is the equivalent of 6 hours of sun.

The air inside your home during the winter is likely to be very dry and can take a toll on plants. Set each pot on top of pebbles in a water-filled tray or dish, making sure that the pot itself isn't sitting in the water; as the water evaporates, it will humidify the air. If the humidity level indoors drops below 40 percent, give the herbs a misting.

Because the plants are dormant during winter, you won't need to water as frequently as you would during the growing season. However, take care not to allow the soil to dry out completely.

Herbs for Hanging Baskets

Nepeta mussinii
(catmint)
Ocimum basilicum
'Minimum'
(bush basil)
Ocimum basilicum
'Minimum
Purpurascens'
(purple bush basil)

Origanum majorana
(sweet marjoram)
Origanum onites
(Greek oregano)
Petroselinum crispum
var. crispum
(curly parsley)
Rosmarinus officinalis
'Prostratus'

(prostrate rosemary)
Satureja spicigera
(creeping savory)
***Thymus praecox* ssp.**
***arcticus* cultivars**
(creeping thyme)
Tropaeolum majus
(nasturtium)

Tropaeolum majus 'Double Gleam' (nasturtium)

Topiaries and Espaliers

Like trees and shrubs, dozens of sturdy herbs can be grown in marvelous shapes and forms using the techniques developed for producing topiaries and espaliers. The training process is creative and fun, and with fast-growing herbs you can enjoy the results of your efforts within months rather than several years.

There are many advantages to growing trained herbs in containers rather than in the ground. Since they are portable, you can move them to create special effects in different garden spots at different times, and any tender herbs can be taken indoors for the winter. In addition, most herbs have shorter lives than trees or shrubs. As older trained plants begin to decline, replacement plants can be trained behind the scenes and positioned in the garden when they are at their peak.

Tied Topiaries

Topiaries are simple to make; the process just involves bending supple new plant growth and tying it onto a wire frame. Shapes suitable for training plants include spirals, globes, hearts, teardrops, wreaths, and animals or birds with simple outlines. You can buy these wire forms or make your own using No. 8 or No. 9 gauge wire.

Tied topiaries make ideal tabletop decorations, but remember that most herbs require a lot of light (full sun for a minimum of 6 hours a day) a benefit from good air circulation. After use, carry them back outside as soon as possible.

Ornamental Standards

An easy topiary to create is the so-called standard, which doesn't require a wire frame. Resembling a stylized miniature tree, the simplest standard has one globe-like crown of foliage atop a single stem. The "poodle" variation has two or three balls of foliage growing on branches out of the straight, central stem at regular intervals.

Either type is easy to train *(pages 90-91)* and makes a striking garden accent. Put a pair of standards at the entrance to your home or garden for dramatic effect. If they are placed against a building, turn the pots regularly to ensure that all sides are exposed to the light. Or

consider featuring a standard topiary instead of a birdbath, statue, or sundial as the focal point in the center of a low-growing flower bed.

Standard topiaries tend to be top-heavy. You can provide a counterbalance by adding an attractive top dressing of pebbles to the soil in the container. (A top dressing will also help keep the soil moist.) Or try placing the pot inside a larger container and filling in the gap with pebbles. Just make sure the size of the outer container is in pleasing proportion to the plant.

Training a Tied Topiary

Using your topiary frame as a reference, plant one young herb for every leg of the frame. Place the frame in the pot with its legs next to the plants; remove any leaves that rub against the frame. Then gently bend the plants' stems to follow the wire. Taking care not to crush the leaves, tie the stems at about 1-inch intervals with ½-inch strips of nylon hose, cut horizontally. Continue to tie new growth until the frame is covered, and replace ties as they get too tight. When the plant becomes woody, it will keep its shape on its own and you can remove the ties. Prune regularly to accentuate the desired form, and pinch off the tip, or leader, of the central stem when it reaches the length you need.

Herbs Suitable for Training

AS STANDARDS

Aloysia triphylla
(lemon verbena)
Laurus nobilis
(bay laurel)
Lavandula dentata
(French lavender)
Lavandula x intermedia
(lavandin)
Lavandula stoechas
(Spanish lavender)
Myrtus communis
(myrtle)
Pelargonium crispum
(lemon geranium)
Pelargonium graveolens
(rose geranium)

Rosmarinus officinalis 'Arp', 'Tuscan Blue'
(rosemary)
Salvia officinalis
(sage)
Thymus vulgaris
(upright form)
(thyme)

AS TIED TOPIARIES AND ESPALIERS

Myrtus communis
(myrtle)
Rosmarinus officinalis
(rosemary)

Rosmarinus officinalis (rosemary)

Decorative Espaliers

Because they are grown flat against a support, espaliered herbs make appealing decorations for a wall, fence, or trellis. Like a tied topiary, the plant is trained on a frame; the pattern can be casual and free-form or symmetrical and formal. Among the classic designs are the fan pattern known as palmette oblique, and the cordon, in which the plant is trained into several tiers of parallel horizontal rows. Other popular patterns include the candelabra, diamond, V-shape, U-shape, and triangle.

Pruning Trained Herbs

Some gardeners prune their trained herbal topiaries and standards every day—using nail scissors—to ensure absolutely perfect specimens with no leaf or branch out of place. Such commitment is hardly essential, although these plants do require frequent grooming. Anytime you notice branches growing long enough to distort the desired shape of the topiary, get out your scissors or clippers and do some trimming.

Don't shear plants, or you'll end up with ugly, blunt edges and maimed leaves. Instead, trim back each branchlet to a leaf node, cutting at a 45° angle just above a bud or node. Every time you cut back a branch to a bud, two new shoots will develop, eventually creating a beautiful, bushy plant.

In addition to maintaining a standard's shape, you must periodically clean out the inside of the foliage globe. Remove dead twigs and thin the crown so that light and air can penetrate.

New Pots for Topiary

To keep your topiary's root system from outgrowing its container, repot it annually—preferably in autumn or spring, when weather conditions are optimum for new root growth. Remove the plant from the container and gently loosen the rootball, shaking away the loose soil. Trim back any extra-long roots. If the rootball has grown very tight, cut off the outer edge of the roots, on the sides and the bottom, with scissors or a knife, reducing the rootball by about one-third. Use fresh soil to replant the herb in the same pot.

Water repotted herbs immediately. You can water from the top as usual, but you should also set the pot in a pan of water so it can draw up moisture from the bottom. That way, any loose soil around the roots will settle, preventing air pockets.

How to Train a Standard Topiary

Herbs amenable to training as standards have central stems that grow straight up until the plant reaches its full height. However, pinching off the tip, or leader, at any time encourages lateral buds along the stem to sprout branches and form a crown.

To create a standard, find a young plant with a stem that has never been pinched. Start in early spring so that the plant has a long season of favorable weather to grow tall and strong.

Before pinching the stem tip, consider how you want the topiary to look. The final height should be in proportion to the size of the pot as well as the crown.

1. Insert an 8- to 10-inch-long stake next to the plant in the pot. Remove side shoots along the plant's stem, but leave the primary leaves in place; remove any leaves that rub against the stake. Tie the stem to the stake at 1- to 1½-inch intervals, taking care not to damage the stem. As the plant grows, continue to tie the stem to the stake; when the plant outgrows the stake, replace it with a taller one. Also replace ties that have tightened as the stem has grown.

2. As the plant approaches the desired height, pinch off the tip of the central stem. Allow the side branches near the top of the plant to continue growing; when they are about 4 inches long, pinch each of these just above a node (right) to encourage vigorous growth. Continue pinching as needed to keep the head of the plant bushy and well branched.

Two rosemary stand-ards flank a tiered ivy topiary in this formal planting. Perfect as fo-cal points or standing sentry at the entrance to a home or garden, standards add a regal air to a setting. The up-right form of rosemary is particularly suited to growing as a standard, and its narrow, needle-like leaves give off a strong fragrance remi-niscent of pine.

3. Once the top growth has filled in and you are happy with the way the topi-ary looks, remove the primary leaves grow-ing along its central stem. Repot the plant, if necessary, in a con-tainer appropriate for its size. Pinch as need-ed to maintain the plant's shape. If you like, you can under-plant the topiary with small herbs.

Controlling Pests and Diseases

Gaining the upper hand on pests and diseases begins before they ever appear in the garden. Building and maintaining a fertile, well-drained soil as described in Chapter 2 is your first line of defense, along with the tips found in Chapters 3 and 4 on planning your garden and caring for your plants. Well-cultivated crops grown in a healthy environment will be robust and less vulnerable to devastating infestations or infections. Other tips and techniques for preventing problems are discussed on the following pages. These include choosing plant varieties bred for disease resistance; protecting plants with various types of barriers; and making the garden hospitable to beneficial insects that prey on pests like the larval-stage and adult Colorado potato beetles at left.

When preventive action doesn't work, first try simple, safe methods for dealing with the problem, such as trapping the pests or using homemade sprays (pages 102-105). The commercial chemicals described on pages 106-107 should be reserved for serious problems.

Spotting Potential Problems

Managing pests and diseases organically depends on your ability to identify a threat to your garden so that you can take steps to prevent or eradicate it. You may already have successfully diagnosed attacks on your vegetables or herbs by pests or diseases. However, it's a good idea to contact your local Cooperative Extension Service for a list of the culprits common in your area; that way, you'll be forewarned of problems you haven't encountered personally. Such a list, along with the information on the following pages and in the Troubleshooting Guide on pages 228-235, will help you choose appropriate preventive measures.

A keen eye is crucial for heading off problems or solving them quickly. Make it a habit to examine your plants methodically every week, turning over their leaves and checking their stems—a 10-power hand lens will help you with this task. If you discover chewed or yellowing leaves or other signs of trouble, describe the damage and record the date in your garden diary *(page 67)*. Along with the other items in your diary, such as the date a vegetable was planted, rotation schedules, or unusual weather, this information will help you identify the cause of a problem. Good records will also help you anticipate seasonal outbreaks.

Pests and diseases can be hard to identify, even for a seasoned gardener, so consult your local Cooperative Extension Service agent if you are stumped. A plant specimen and your diary will help the agent make the correct diagnosis.

Clinging to a wire support for peas, a raccoon on a nighttime raid surveys a garden's bounty. In the background is a stand of corn, a favorite food of this pest.

Chewing and Sucking Insects

Most of the insects that harm plants fall into two basic categories—chewing insects and sucking insects. Among the most voracious chewing pests are beetle larvae and caterpillars, which are the larvae of moths and butterflies. If chewing pests have invaded your garden, you'll see nibbled edges of leaves or holes chewed between leaf veins. Little piles of excrement, or drass, deposited on the leaves are another telltale sign.

In large enough numbers, chewing insects can defoliate a plant or completely devour a seedling, and they also open a plant's tissues to infection. There may be several generations of a particular pest in one season, so you have to be continuously on the alert for signs of chewing. If you find holes in foliage, look for eggs on the undersides of the leaves; remove any you find and drop them into a bucket of soapy water to keep them from hatching.

Sucking insects, such as aphids and leafhoppers, feed on juices in leaves, stems, or roots. Besides weakening a plant, a sucking insect can inject deadly pathogens as it feeds. Typical kinds of damage include wilting; stunted growth; yellowed, brown, or blotchy leaves; and misshapen leaves, shoots, or fruit. Aphids leave sticky trails of sugars and sap, known as honeydew, on the leaves.

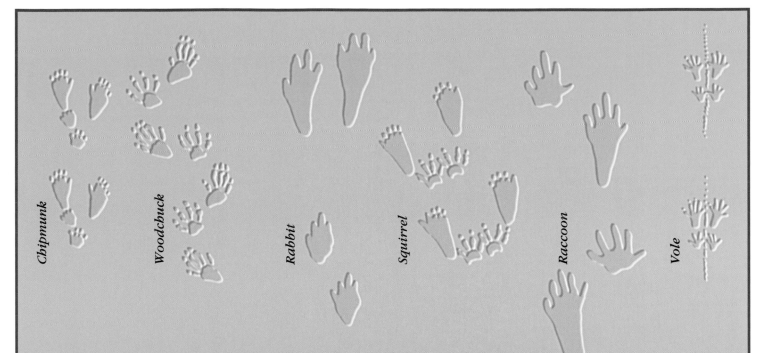

Identifying Animals by Their Footprints

Most wild animals are very shy and some are nocturnal, so you may not catch sight of a pest that has been raiding your garden. However, footprints will reveal the forager's identity and allow you to take steps to prevent repeat visits *(pages 99 and 101)*. To get a clear footprint, smooth the earth near the plants that are being eaten and, in the evening, lay wide bands of flour around them. The next morning, check the flour bands for footprints. Compare any you find with the drawings shown here of the prints of six common animal pests.

Diseases

Like other living creatures, plants occasionally fall victim to infectious diseases. Pathogens such as fungal spores, viruses, bacteria, and parasitic nematodes can be transported into your garden on the feet of insects or in their saliva, on infected plants bought at a nursery, or by way of wind or birds. Once in your garden, a disease organism may not manifest itself for years, remaining dormant until conditions become more favorable.

Your hands, shoes, and tools can also spread pathogens from place to place within the garden, and the simple act of accidentally nicking a stem when you are cultivating around a plant can provide an entryway for a disease organism. As a precaution, don't work in the garden when it is wet, since pathogens, especially fungal spores, are easily spread from plant to plant in drops of water.

Not all garden diseases are caused by pathogens. They also arise from environmental disorders such as mineral deficiencies or air pollution. The symptoms of noninfectious and infectious diseases can be confusingly similar, and close scrutiny is required to tell the difference. One way to distinguish the two is to examine how the symptoms are distributed. If most or all of the plants growing in the same area have the same symptoms, an environmental cause is likely. An infectious disease, by contrast, tends to attack one plant first and then spread in a random pattern to a few plants nearby. See the Troubleshooting Guide on pages 228-235 for help in diagnosis.

Animal Pests

The plants in a kitchen garden are just as appealing to a number of animals as they are to humans. Such common animals as raccoons, rabbits, and woodchucks, for example, are capable of devastating a crop in short order. As with insects or diseases, different species call for different control measures. If you suspect that an animal pest is slipping in and out of your garden unseen, the information in the box above may help you identify the elusive culprit.

One easy way to stop problems before they start is to fill your garden with plants that have been bred to resist one or more diseases without compromising flavor. Resistance is often indicated on plant labels or in catalogs by coded abbreviations of diseases. For instance, DMPM means that the plant is resistant to downy mildew and powdery mildew. In addition to the many disease-resistant cultivars, there are a smaller number that are resistant to attack by certain insects.

Not quite as trouble free but still very desirable are plants that are rated tolerant of a particular disease or pest. Although a tolerant variety may suffer infection or an infestation, the damage won't be bad enough to cut its production significantly.

Crops on the Move

Pests and pathogens that live in the soil will continue to multiply as long as their preferred food supply is present, so putting the same plants in the same bed year after year is asking for trouble. But if you shift crops from place to place every time you plant, an insect, bacterium, virus, or fungus that has established itself in your garden will be deprived of its food source and will die out.

A crop rotation scheme must be based on families of plants, since closely related species are likely to be attacked by the same pests and diseases. The chart on page 98 groups widely grown vegetables and herbs by family and will help you plot out a rotation scheme. Since the pathogens responsible for bean anthracnose, verticillium wilt, fusarium wilt, and other diseases can survive in the soil for up to 3 years, waiting at least that long before replanting a bed with the same family of crops will give you maximum protection.

It is also a good practice to work soil-building crops like clover and rye into your rotation plan to ensure a regular replenishment of nutrients and organic matter. The chart on page 131 provides information on six soil-building crops, including when to sow, seeding rate, and how each crop improves the soil.

Keeping the Garden Clean

Another way to interrupt the life cycle of pests and disease organisms is to develop good gardening habits. As soon as a plant reaches the end of its productive life, pull it up and add it to the compost pile; debris left in the garden can harbor insects or pathogens from one season to the next. After clearing away crop debris, till the soil to bring eggs and larvae to the surface, where birds, snakes, or other predators can find them. Turning the soil of an empty bed several times in late winter will expose insects such as corn ear worms and cutworms to freezing cold. Keeping weeds under control in and

This 'Whopper Improved' green bell pepper plant is heavy with unblemished fruit and foliage. It is resistant to the tobacco mosaic virus, a common disease that can cause yellowing of leaves, stunting, and reduced yield.

around the garden is also important. Besides competing with your plants for water, nutrients, and light, some weeds are hosts to harmful garden pests and disease organisms.

Encouraging Beneficials

All pests have natural predators. Known collectively as beneficials, these include toads, snakes, lizards, moles, songbirds, and a number of insects, such as parasitic wasps. You can buy certain insect predators, but it's also wise to make your garden attractive to native beneficials. For instance, including plants with pollen- and nectar-rich flowers, such as dill and yarrow, will draw the beneficial insects that depend on them for food. A constant water supply is also essential. A birdbath can do double duty if you make a little island of pebbles or float a piece of wood in the water for insects to alight on. See the chart on page 100 for other ways to encourage beneficials.

Barriers to Stymie Pests

A number of simple but effective barriers do a good job of keeping flying and crawling insects, slugs, raccoons, and other hungry pests away from vegetables and fruits. A sheet of black plastic or a thick layer of organic mulch will not only moderate soil temperatures and suppress weeds, it will also disrupt the life cycles of thrips, leaf miners, and other soil-borne pests. For example, 6 inches of straw mulch will deter Colorado potato beetles that have overwintered in the soil from emerging in time to feed on potato seedlings.

Plants covered by a lightweight, translucent fabric are shielded from a wide variety of flying and crawling insect pests, such as aphids, leafhoppers, and caterpillars. While these row covers offer no protection against soil-borne eggs, larvae, or adult pests that are already in the soil, they do prevent flying and crawling adults from laying a new generation of eggs in the soil. Another benefit of row covers is the protection they provide plants against bacteria and viruses transmitted by insects.

The most versatile materials for row covers are spunbonded polyester, polypropylene, and polyvinyl fabric. Because these fabrics are very lightweight, they can be draped directly over the plants—hence the name "floating row cover." They transmit to the plants about 85 percent of available sunlight, along with ample water and air. Floating row covers also slow the evaporation of soil moisture and shield plants from drying winds.

In this benign environment, plants grow as well—or better—than they would if they were fully exposed to the elements.

Some spunbonded row covers are designed to trap enough heat to protect plants from light frosts in spring and fall. There are also summer-weight row covers so airy that they can be left in place throughout the growing season without the risk of overheating your plants. These row covers are an especially good choice for protecting cool-

Pest- and Disease-Resistant Varieties of Vegetables

In addition to vegetables that resist particular diseases and pests, the list below includes several tolerant varieties, which can grow fairly well in spite of an infestation or infection.

CABBAGE
'Danish Ballhead', *'Early Jersey Wakefield'*—tolerate cabbage looper and imported cabbageworm; *'Golden Acre'*—tolerates fusarium yellows; *'Red Acre'*—tolerates cabbage looper and imported cabbageworm; *'Wisconsin All Seasons'*—fusarium yellows

CARROT
'Napoli'—tolerates alternaria blight

CHINESE CABBAGE
'Blues'—alternaria, black speck, downy mildew, soft rot

CORN
'Lancelot'—corn rust, Stewart's bacterial wilt; *'Miracle'*—corn rust; *'Silver Queen'*—northern corn leaf blight, southern corn leaf blight, Stewart's bacterial wilt; *'Tuxedo'*—corn rust, corn smut, Stewart's bacterial wilt

CUCUMBER
'Little Leaf'—angular leaf spot, anthracnose, cucumber mosaic, downy mildew, target leaf spot; *'Marketmore 76'*—scab; tolerates cucumber mosaic, downy mildew, powdery mildew; *'Salad Bush'*—cucumber mosaic, scab; *'Space Master'*—cucumber mosaic, scab; *'Sweet Slice'*—tolerates cucumber mosaic, powdery mildew, watermelon mosaic, zucchini yellows mosaic; *'Sweet Success'*—cucumber mosaic, scab, target leaf spot

GREEN BEANS AND POLE BEANS
'Kentucky Wonder'—rusts; *'Provider'*—bacterial blight, common bean mosaic, downy mildew, powdery mildew, white mold; *'Tendercrop'*—bacterial blight, downy mildew, powdery mildew, white mold

LETTUCE
'Ithaca'—brown rib, lettuce mosaic, tipburn; *'Paris Island Cos'*—lettuce mosaic, tipburn

ONIONS
'Early Yellow Globe'—onion smudge; *'Northern Oak'*—fusarium yellows, pink root; *'Texas Grano'*—pink root

PEPPERS
'Bell Boy'—tobacco mosaic; *'California Wonder'*—cercospora leaf spot; *'Gypsy'*—tobacco mosaic; *'Whopper Improved'*—tobacco mosaic; *'Yolo Wonder'*—tobacco mosaic

SQUASH
'Cocozelle'—aphids

TOMATOES
'Ace 55'—fusarium wilt, verticillium wilt; *'Beefmaster'*—alternaria, fusarium wilt, gray leaf spot, nematodes, verticillium wilt; *'Better Boy'*—alternaria, fusarium wilt, root knot nematodes, verticillium wilt; *'Celebrity'*—alternaria stem canker, fusarium 1-2, gray leaf spot, nematodes, tobacco mosaic, verticillium wilt; *'Early Cascade'*—alternaria stem canker, fusarium, gray leaf spot, verticillium wilt; *'Roma VF'*—alternaria, fusarium wilt, verticillium wilt; *'Sweet Million'*—fusarium wilt, nematodes, septoria leaf spot, tobacco mosaic

YELLOW BEANS
'Cherokee'—common bean mosaic, rust; *'Roc d'Or'*—anthracnose, common bean mosaic

weather greens like lettuce and spinach that tend to bolt when the temperature is too high.

Heavier row covers of polyethylene and polystyrene plastic are more efficient heat traps than any of the spunbonded fabrics. They are excellent for getting the garden started earlier in the year and keeping crops growing longer in the fall, but can easily overheat crops in milder weather. Also, these plastics need wire hoops or some other support to keep them from crushing the plants.

Before you drape a floating row cover over a planting, weed the area thoroughly and use the techniques described on pages 102-105 to get rid of as many insects as you can. Place the fabric over the row immediately after planting; if the day is breezy, the job will be easier to do if you have a helper. Leave plenty of slack in the cover so the plants will have growing room. Weight the edges down securely with soil, rocks, or boards, and check to be sure there are no gaps that insects could slip through.

For cucumbers, beans, tomatoes, and other fruiting vegetables that must be pollinated to develop, remove the row covers when the crops begin to bloom. Vegetables that don't need pollination can remain covered until harvest. When you need to remove a cover for weeding and thinning, replace it as soon as you have finished the chore.

Some young vegetable plants require special protection. For example, to defend members of the cabbage family against cabbage maggots that feed on their roots, you can make a barrier that prevents adults from laying eggs in the soil at the base of the plant. Use a piece of heavy cardboard, plastic, or tarpaper measuring 6 inches square. Make a slit from one edge to the center of the square and cut out a small circle at the inner end of the slit to make room for the stem. Slip the square around the stem of the seedling at planting time. For a barrier that discourages cutworms, which chew on the stems of young vegetables at soil level, place a collar around the seedling's stem at planting time. Use a small paper cup with the bottom removed, a toilet paper roll, or a square of newspaper rolled into a tube, as shown on page 60. Bury the collar 1 to 1½ inches below ground level.

Slugs and snails are very destructive, chewing large, ragged holes in leaves and feeding on onion bulbs, strawberries, and tomatoes. Deter them by laying down a strip of abrasive material 2 inches wide and a quarter inch deep around a plant; when the animal crawls on the scratchy surface, its skin is damaged and it dies of dehydration. Particularly effective is diatomaceous earth, a commercial product derived from fossilized plankton. Wood ashes, talc, lime, and crushed eggshells also work well.

For a permanent barrier, surround a garden bed with a strip of copper sheet metal 4 inches wide. Bury the strip 1 to 2 inches below ground level and bend the top half-inch of the strip away from the bed. When a slug or snail touches the copper strip, a chemical reaction occurs that creates an electric current and gives the pest a shock.

A Family Plan for Crop Rotation

A reliable way to minimize or even eliminate soil-borne pest and disease problems is to plant a particular patch of ground with the same vegetable or its close relatives only once every 3 to 5 years. In the lean years, without their favored hosts to feed on, organisms that typically plague a certain vegetable family will decline in numbers. Use the family groups below to help you plot out a long-term rotation scheme for your garden.

BEET FAMILY

beets, chard, orach, spinach

CARROT FAMILY

carrots, celeriac, celery, fennel, parsley, parsnips

COMPOSITE FAMILY

cardoon, celtuce, chicory, endive, escarole, Jerusalem artichoke, lettuce, radicchio, salsify, sunflower

LEGUME FAMILY

beans, peas, peanuts, soybeans

MUSTARD FAMILY

arugula, broccoli, Brussels sprouts, cabbage, cauliflower, Chinese cabbage, collards, cress, kale, kohlrabi, mustard greens, radishes, rutabaga, turnips

ONION FAMILY

chives, garlic, leeks, onions, shallots

SQUASH FAMILY

chayote, cucumbers, melons, pumpkins, squash

TOMATO FAMILY

eggplant, peppers, potatoes, tomatillo, tomatoes

Mammals: Friends and Foes

A few mammals are actually more helpful than harmful in the garden, despite their reputation. For instance, skunks will eat berries and ears of corn that grow close to the ground, but they also catch insects, voles, mice, and rats. Moles ignore plants altogether; they dine on slugs, Japanese beetles, white grubs, and other pests in the soil. But some mammals, including rabbits and voles, are truly pests. Most organic gardeners prefer nonlethal methods, such as fences and repellent chemicals, to control them. Live traps are another option, but be careful you don't release an animal where it will become a headache for another gardener or where it cannot survive. Before using a trap, make sure your state does not have laws against transporting and releasing wild animals. The following is a list of a few mammals that can do damage in your garden, as well as some of the controls you can use to deter them:

Rabbits—A 3-foot-high fence of ¾-inch wire mesh will keep rabbits out of the garden. Dried blood meal, cow manure, or wood ashes sprinkled near plants will repel them; replenish after a rain.

Raccoons—To deter these animals, you can cover individual ears of corn or melon fruits with nylon stockings or net bags, but an electric fence—the only kind that works with raccoons—is easier. Two strands of electrified wire or cord around the garden are usually enough. Position the upper strand about a foot from the ground and the lower strand within 6 inches of the ground.

Woodchucks—Also called groundhogs, they eat almost anything succulent and rip up entire plants. The electric fence described above will discourage them, as will a wire-mesh fence that is at least 3 feet tall and extends 2 feet underground.

Squirrels—These animals relish tomatoes, sweet corn, and sunflower seeds. Try covering corn ears and sunflowers with nylon stockings or net bags, or spray the ears with a red pepper spray (the husks will shield the kernels from the spray).

Looming above its unwitting victim, a praying mantis prepares to strike a grasshopper, a pest that takes an especially heavy toll on seedlings. Though often helpful, praying mantises are indiscriminate predators, feeding on beneficial insects as well as destructive ones.

In search of a meal, a hungry green snake glides among bee balm blossoms ornamenting a vegetable garden. Nonpoisonous snakes like this one are a boon, hunting down insects and slugs as well as larger pests such as mice and voles.

99

BENEFICIALS THAT PREY ON VEGETABLE AND FRUIT PESTS

Beneficial	Pests Controlled	Comments
Aphid midges	More than 60 species of aphids	Attract with pollen- and nectar-producing plants. Buy six to 10 cocoons per plant and release half in early spring and the remainder 2 weeks later.
Assassin bugs	Flies, mosquitoes, beetles, caterpillars	Provide permanent beds in or near the garden for shelter. Purchase commercial attractant.
Braconid wasps	Aphids, moth and beetle larvae, flies, codling moth, cabbageworm, hornworm, corn borer, armyworm, other caterpillars	These wasps feed on the nectar of dill, parsley, mustard, white clover, yarrow, and other small-flowered plants. Also available by mail order.
Flower flies, syrphid flies	Aphids, mealybugs, mites, thrips	These predators are attracted by daisylike flowers that produce nectar and pollen.
Lacewings	Aphids, mealybugs, mites, moth eggs, scales, small caterpillars, soft-bodied insects, thrips	Attract with nectar- and pollen-producing plants such as goldenrod. Purchase eggs and distribute in the garden. Purchase commercial attractant.
Ladybugs, ladybeetles	Aphids, mealybugs, soft scales, spider mites, whiteflies	Plant pollen- and nectar-producing plants. Buy adults collected in spring only. Ladybugs collected at other times of year will migrate from your garden. Buy commercial attractant.
Nematodes, beneficial, type HH	Soil-borne insects, including armyworm, black vine weevil, cabbage root maggot, chafers, Colorado potato beetle, corn rootworm, cucumber beetle, cutworms, fungus gnat larvae, Japanese beetle grubs, mole cricket, root weevils, white grubs, and wireworms	Keep soil moist. Available by mail order.
Nematodes, beneficial, type NC	Soil-borne insects, including armyworm, cabbage root maggot, chafers, Colorado potato beetle, cutworm, earwig, Japanese beetle grubs, onion maggot, root weevils, seed corn maggot, sowbug, white grubs, and wireworms	Keep soil moist. Available by mail order.
Pirate bugs	Aphids, insect eggs, leafhoppers, rust mites, spider mites, small caterpillars, thrips	Attract with pollen-rich plants such as goldenrod, and provide a water source such as a birdbath.
Praying mantises	Aphids, beetles, bugs, caterpillars, flies, leafhoppers, and other insects	Available by mail order, but try other controls first because praying mantises eat beneficials.
Predatory mites	European red mites, rust mites, thrips, two-spotted spider mites	These mites prefer high humidity and rich soil and do not thrive in hot, dry areas.
Rove beetles	Aphids, fly eggs, maggots, mites, parasitic nematodes, slugs, snails, springtails	Provide organic mulch for shelter.
Soldier beetles	Aphids, beetle larvae, butterfly larvae, caterpillars, grasshopper eggs, moth larvae	Attract by growing goldenrod and other nectar- and pollen-producing plants.
Spiders	Most insects	Encourage by leaving webs intact.
Tachinid flies	Many kinds of caterpillars, including cutworms, codling moths, cabbage loopers, squash bugs, and grasshoppers	Attract by growing nectar-producing plants such as dill, parsley, sweet clover, and yarrow.
Trichogramma wasps	Eggs of many moths, including corn ear worm, cutworm, cabbage looper, corn borer, codling moth, tomato hornworm	Several species that prey on different pests are available by mail order; be sure you buy the appropriate one. Use pheromone traps to determine when the pest is at its peak, or release wasps every week for a month around the peak season.
Bats	Nocturnal flying insects	Install a bat house and provide water.
Birds	Many kinds of insects	Install birdhouses, provide water, and plant fruit-bearing shrubs and trees.
Snakes	Insects and small rodents	Provide shallow containers of water and shelter.
Toads, lizards, turtles	Slugs and most insects	Provide shallow containers of water and shelter.

Firmly weighted down by soil and logs, floating row covers shield young vegetables from pesky insects early in the growing season in the Maine garden above. The row covers also trap enough heat overnight to protect the plants against late, light frosts. Once all danger of insect infestation has passed, the covers can be removed.

Voles—Sprinkle household ammonia on the ground around plants to repel these rodents. Also try a small-mesh wire fence, bent horizontally so that it stands at least 18 inches high with 12 inches or more lying flat on the ground, to discourage voles from burrowing into the garden.

Deer—A fence is one option, though even a 7-foot fence may not keep the best jumpers out. (The top of the fence should slant outward at a 45° angle.) First, however, experiment with net bags filled with mothballs or hair (animal or human) hung every 20 feet throughout the garden; blood meal sprinkled around the perimeter; or sweaty clothes hung on stakes. You can also try laying chicken-wire fencing on the ground around the garden; the deer may become discouraged if their feet get tangled in the wire.

Birds—Songbirds are generally beneficials, eating hundreds of insects in a single day. Most other kinds of birds, however, eat vegetable seedlings, lettuce, berries, and other crops. Scare tactics such as inflatable owls and balloons on which you've

Rain, sunlight, and air pass easily through the translucent floating row cover protecting the cabbage plants at upper right. A sturdy wire cage that can be lifted for weeding and harvesting keeps the lettuce plants at right out of the reach of birds, rabbits, and other greens-loving animals.

drawn large eyes work fairly well; place them every 30 to 40 feet around the garden and change them often to keep the birds from getting used to them. A surer method is to cover vulnerable plants. Several weeks before the fruits ripen, drape berry plants with broad-mesh plastic netting with a ½- to ¾-inch grid. For seedlings and crops like lettuce that continue to attract birds as they mature, use spunbonded floating row covers.

Minimizing Damage in Your Garden

A trap set amid cucumber plants is peppered with pests that were drawn to its color and became entangled in its coating. Yellow sticky traps snare numerous small insect pests, including aphids, whiteflies, and leafhoppers.

Sometimes even your best efforts to curb pests and diseases aren't enough. An outbreak occurs, and you may find your vegetables rotting, wilting, or chewed to shreds. Fortunately, there are ways to prevent a problem from getting out of hand without resorting to chemicals.

The first step is to physically remove as much of the problem as possible. If a plant is diseased, get rid of it, roots and all. Put it in a plastic bag and throw it out with your household trash. Do not compost diseased debris; pathogens may survive the decay process and reinfest the garden when you use the finished compost.

In the case of a plant with a soil-borne disease, dig it up with a garden fork, taking care not to knock the soil from the rootball. Put the plant and the soil clinging to its roots in a plastic bag for disposal. Replant with a resistant variety or a different vegetable that is immune to the disease.

After handling a diseased plant, clean your tools and gloves with a 10 percent bleach solution to avoid spreading the disease to other plants.

Handpicking Pests

An infestation of pests usually doesn't call for total removal of the plant. If the intruders are confined to a stem or two, cut back to clean, uninfested tissue, put the plant parts in a plastic bag, and discard with the household trash. Large pests like caterpillars and snails can be picked off plants and dropped into a bucket of soapy water.

Some beetle pests, such as Japanese beetles or Colorado potato beetles, can be shaken out. Spread a sheet of plastic or a cloth on the ground under the plant to catch the pests as they fall. Gather up the cloth and shake them off into a bucket of soapy water. This method works best in the early morning, when the beetles are sluggish.

Handpicking and shaking don't work for insects like aphids and spider mites that cling tightly to plants, but you can injure or kill many of them with a stream of water from a hose. Adjust the strength of the stream so it won't damage your plants, then spray all of the plant's leaves, top and bottom, repeating as often as necessary. Don't spray a plant that shows symptoms of a fungus, however, since the water could spread pathogens further. Also, it's better to spray in the morning or the evening if the weather is hot and sunny—water droplets can act like magnifying glasses and burn the leaves.

Trapping Insects

Another fairly easy way to get rid of insect pests is to lure them away with traps. The best traps imitate certain sights or smells that insects associate with food or potential mates. Many flying insects—particularly aphids, thrips, whiteflies, cabbage root flies, carrot rust flies, cucumber beetles, and imported cabbageworms—are attracted to the color yellow. A simple, effective trap for these insects is a bright yellow strip or rectangle coated with a sticky glue. You can purchase such traps at garden centers or make them yourself. Paint pieces of sturdy cardboard, wood, or plastic with two coats of a paint containing a pigment known as Federal Safety Yellow No. 659. After the paint dries, use a putty knife to spread the surface with a commercial sticky glue, which should remain tacky for about 2 weeks; leave one corner uncoated so that you can handle the trap without your fingers sticking to it. Affix the trap to a stake and place it beside the infested plant; the trap should be about level with the top of the plant. Set out one trap for every five or six plants and add more if the damage continues.

One disadvantage of using color as a lure is that it may draw not only pests but also beneficials. To be sure that your traps attract only those species infesting your plants, you may want to consider using pheromone lures.

Pheromones are chemicals emitted by females of the species to attract mates, and flying insects can sense these chemicals from great distances. Pheromones that lure about 40 moth species, including cabbage loopers, corn ear worms, and leaf rollers, have been identified and commercially reproduced. The lures are placed in traps lined with a sticky substance to catch the insects. Scented traps must be used with care, since they can attract pests to your garden from miles away. To avoid making your pest problem worse, place the traps outside and upwind of the garden.

Controlling pests is not the only function of traps. Pheromone traps, for instance, are excellent for monitoring changes in the size of a particular pest population. They can warn the gardener of a problem before it becomes serious. For example, if your tomatoes have been troubled by hornworm caterpillars in past seasons, you can set out a pheromone trap to draw adult male hornworm moths; their arrival will signal the start of the season for mating and egg laying. Then you can take action, such as releasing trichogramma wasps, which parasitize the eggs.

You can keep tabs on flea beetles and tarnished plant bugs with white sticky traps; blue sticky traps will attract thrips. A good rule of thumb is to check a monitoring trap twice a week. It's also a good idea to continue checking it after you've started using a control measure so you can gauge its effectiveness.

Fighting Pests and Diseases with Heat

Solarization is a simple technique that uses the strong summer sun and a sheet of 3- to 4-mil clear plastic to kill soil-borne pests and diseases. This process raises the temperature of garden soil to 120° F or higher—high enough to kill pests and pathogens to a depth of 3 to 5 inches. When air temperatures average 90° F, solarization takes about 4 weeks; it can take up to 8 weeks when temperatures are in the 70s. Raised beds will heat faster than level ground.

To begin, clear the bed of vegetation and debris, and add any amendments the soil needs. Rake the bed smooth, dig a trench a few inches deep around it, then soak the soil to a depth of at least 12 inches. To trap heat and moisture, cover the bed snugly with the plastic, tuck the edges into the trench, and bury them with soil.

Measure the soil temperature periodically, pulling back the plastic just far enough to insert a soil thermometer. Record the temperature at several different spots. A few days after the temperature has stabilized at 120° F or higher, remove the plastic.

To replace beneficial microorganisms killed by solarization, add microbe-rich material such as aged manure or compost to the bed. Do not cultivate it below 4 inches, or you risk reinfecting the solarized soil with surviving pathogens.

Coping with Slugs and Snails

If slugs and snails have eluded the preventive barriers you have placed around vulnerable crops, you can set traps for them. Garden centers and mail-order companies sell baited traps, but you can make your own by filling a shallow container with beer or with yeast dissolved in water. Sink the trap to its rim in the soil and empty it every few days in an inconspicuous place in the garden. Then refill the container with fresh bait.

Slugs and snails are night feeders and seek refuge in moist, cool, dark places during the day. To take advantage of this behavior, provide them with boards or upside-down flower pots, melon rinds, or grapefruit rinds as shelter. Collect the pests that congregate under the trap and crush them or place them in the trash.

Microbial Pesticides

Like other creatures, pests are susceptible to fatal infections, and a bacterium called *Bacillus thuringiensis,* or Bt for short, is an invaluable pesticide for the organic gardener. There are some 30 different strains of this microbe, each one a magic bullet that attacks a single species of caterpillar or beetle larva; all other organisms are immune to that particular strain. Among the common pests susceptible to infection are cabbage loopers, tomato hornworms, European corn borers, and beetle larvae that feed on leaves.

Homemade Pesticides and Fungicides

If you have used the full arsenal of cultural, physical, and biological controls against a pest or disease without success, your remaining weapon is an organic pesticide or fungicide. The mildest and safest of these—and for that reason the ones to try first—are homemade preparations based on common, readily available ingredients. A spray made from baking soda, for instance, is effective against fungal diseases, especially powdery mildew, leaf blight, and leaf spot.

Recipes for baking soda fungicide and three other sprays are given below. The garlic and hot pepper sprays control insects. The soap-and-oil spray prevents fungal spores from germinating and is also an insecticide.

Before applying any of the preparations to an entire plant, spray it on a few leaves to test for sensitivity. After 2 days, examine the leaves to see whether there are any spots of discolored or dying tissue. If the leaves are damaged, dilute the spray with a little more water and test the plant again to see if it is safe to use.

When you spray a plant, be sure to cover the top and bottom of all of its leaves (box, left). Repeat every 5 to 7 days until the pests are gone or the disease symptoms have disappeared. To prevent a repeat outbreak of a disease the following year, begin spraying in the spring and continue until the fall.

Baking soda spray—Dissolve 1 tablespoon of baking soda in 1 gallon of water and add ⅛ to ¼ teaspoon of insecticidal soap to help the solution spread and adhere to the foliage.

Soap-and-oil spray—Mix 1 teaspoon of liquid dishwashing soap with ⅓ cup of corn, soybean, sunflower, safflower, or peanut oil. To apply, combine 1 to 2 teaspoons of this mixture with 1 cup of water in a hand sprayer.

Garlic spray—Combine 15 garlic cloves with 1 pint of water in a blender and purée. Alternatively, mince the garlic cloves and steep them in the water for 24 hours. Strain the liquid through cheesecloth and add a few drops of insecticidal soap.

Hot pepper spray—Purée ½ cup of hot peppers and 2 cups of water in a blender. Strain the liquid through cheesecloth. Wear gloves when handling the peppers and be careful not to get the liquid on your skin or in your eyes—it will sting and burn.

Commercial Chemicals

If a homemade preparation doesn't take care of a stubborn problem, you may decide that stronger measures are called for. Although the natural chemicals that organic gardeners use are derived from plants or minerals, they can have adverse effects and should be considered only as a last resort. Some are toxic not only to certain pests or diseases, but also to humans, mammals, birds, reptiles, fish, harmless insects, or soil microorgan-

Spraying for Complete Coverage

To make sure that a plant is thoroughly covered by a chemical, spray methodically from the plant's base to its top, aiming the sprayer at the underside of the leaves as shown below. Spray until the liquid just begins to drip off the foliage. When you reach the top of the plant, reverse direction: Aim the sprayer downward to coat the upper surface of the leaves, and work your way back down to the base of the plant.

isms. Nevertheless, they are preferable to synthetic, or manufactured, chemicals because the natural substances break down quickly. In addition, they have no long-lasting detrimental effects on the environment. Synthetic chemicals, by contrast, may remain active for months or years and can be extremely harmful. The chart on pages 106-107 provides information on organic pesticides and fungicides that are safe to use on food crops. Whatever the pest or disease you are battling, always try the least toxic chemical first, apply it sparingly, and follow directions carefully.

Handling Chemicals Safely

Before you use a pesticide or fungicide, read the label thoroughly and follow all of the instructions to the letter. Whenever you handle one of these chemicals, wear long pants, a long-sleeved shirt, and rubber gloves to protect your skin. For added security, wear goggles and a dust mask or a respirator to protect your eyes and lungs from irritation.

Before tackling a job, have the right equipment on hand. For chemicals that come in the form of dust, a good choice is a duster with a rotating blower and a long, adjustable nozzle that makes it easy to thoroughly cover both sides of a plant's leaves. For spraying liquids, a hand-held pump sprayer is all most home gardeners need. However, if your garden is 400 to 500 square feet or more, a pressurized backpack sprayer with a hand pump will save you time and effort.

To lessen the risk of exposing yourself to the chemical, wait for a windless day before applying a pesticide or fungicide. Mix only what you need for a single application so you won't have to dispose of any leftovers; you can always mix a second batch if necessary. Be careful not to spill any of the chemical on your skin or clothes or on the ground when you are filling the duster or sprayer.

Keep children and pets away until the dust settles or the spray dries. Follow the directions on the label for rinsing and disposing of containers.

A planting of African marigolds (above) can clear infested soil of root knot nematodes in one season. When the nematodes feed on the roots of these plants, they take in a chemical that keeps them from reproducing. At season's end, the marigolds can be turned under to improve the soil's texture.

A Guide to Commercial Organic Pesticides and Fungicides

The 13 organic products included in this chart are your last line of defense against pests and diseases in the garden. When using any of them, always read the label on the container, heed all warnings, and follow all directions. Before treating an entire plant, test the product on a small portion to see if it does any damage. Apply controls in the early morning or evening, and only when the air is still. Cover a plant thoroughly, including the undersides of leaves. If your local merchants don't stock a control you wish to buy, all those listed here can be ordered from mail-order nurseries or garden supply companies.

	Name	Type	Target Pests or Diseases	Form	Shelf Life
PESTICIDES	*Bacillus thuringiensis* (Bt)	Biological insect control; infectious bacteria	Cabbage loopers, cabbageworms, tomato hornworms, and other leaf-eating caterpillars; Colorado potato beetle larvae	Dust; wettable powder; liquid concentrate	Dry form: 2-4 years; liquid concentrate: 2-3 years
	Beneficial nematodes	Biological insect control; roundworms found naturally in soil	Soil-dwelling pests such as borers, cutworms, cucumber beetle larvae, root maggots, wireworms, white grubs	Sold in semidormant state on sponges, mixed with gel, or in granules. Products are mixed with water before applying.	Up to 2 months in refrigerator; dehydrated forms up to 6 months at room temperature, longer if refrigerated.
	Diatomaceous earth (DE)	Abrasive, desiccating pesticide; finely ground fossilized marine algae	Most soft-bodied insects and pests such as aphids, caterpillars, cabbage root flies, corn borers, leafhoppers, mites, pill bugs, slugs, snails, sowbugs, thrips	Dust; can be mixed with water to make a spray.	Lasts indefinitely if kept dry.
	Horticultural oil	Contact insecticide and miticide; ultrafine petroleum	Most pest eggs, larvae, and soft-bodied adults such as aphids, leafhoppers, leaf miners, mealybugs, mites, scales, thrips, whiteflies	Liquid concentrate	Indefinite
	Insecticidal soap	Contact insecticide	Most effective against soft-bodied and sucking insects such as aphids, mites, leafhoppers, mealybugs, scales, spider mites, thrips, whiteflies	Liquid concentrate; ready-to-use spray	Up to 5 years. Keep tightly sealed.
	Neem (azadirachtin)	Botanical broad-spectrum insecticide and repellent derived from neem tree	Aphids, beetles (cucumber, flea, Japanese, Mexican bean, potato), corn ear worms, leaf miners, loopers, mealybugs, spider mites, tomato hornworms, thrips, whiteflies. Kills juveniles; repels adults.	Liquid concentrate	Minimum of 18 months
	Pyrethrum (pyrethrins)	Botanical contact insecticide containing pyrethrin compounds derived from the pyrethrum daisy	Aphids, beetles (asparagus, Colorado potato, cucumber, flea, Japanese, Mexican bean), caterpillars (cabbage loopers, corn ear worms, European corn borers, fall armyworms), leafhoppers, mites, stink bugs, tarnished plant bugs, thrips, whiteflies	Dust; liquid concentrate; ready-to-use spray	Dust: up to 1 year. Liquid concentrate and spray: 1-3 years
	Repellents, garlic and hot pepper	Botanical insect and animal repellents	Aphids, cabbage loopers, leafhoppers, squash bugs, whiteflies; birds, cats, deer, dogs, rabbits	Both available as liquid concentrate	2 years
	Rotenone	Botanical broad-spectrum contact and stomach-poison insecticide; derived from South American cube plant	Aphids, beetles (asparagus, Colorado potato, cucumber, flea, Japanese, Mexican bean), cabbage loopers, corn ear worms, European corn borers, leafhoppers, mites, spider mites, stink bugs, thrips, whiteflies	Dust; wettable powder; liquid concentrate, usually with pyrethrin	Dust: 2-3 years; liquid: 3 years or more
	Sabadilla	Botanical broad-spectrum contact insecticide; derived from a South American lily	Aphids, armyworms, beetles (Colorado potato, cucumber, flea, Mexican bean), cabbage loopers, caterpillars, diamondback moth larvae, European corn borers, grasshoppers, leafhoppers, squash bugs, stink bugs, thrips	Dust; wettable powder	5 years or more
FUNGICIDES	Copper	Mineral fungicide and surface protectant	Anthracnose, bacterial leaf spot, black rot, blights, downy mildews, leaf spot, powdery mildews, rusts, scabs	Dust; wettable powder; liquid concentrate	Up to 5 years
	Lime sulfur	Mineral fungicide, insecticide	Anthracnose, brown rot, leaf spot, powdery mildews, rusts, scabs	Liquid concentrate	3-5 years. Keep from freezing.
	Sulfur, elemental sulfur	Mineral fungicide, surface protectant, miticide	Black spot, botrytis molds, brown rot, leaf spot, powdery mildews, rusts, scabs	Dust; wettable powder; liquid concentrate; ready-to-use spray	Dust and powder: indefinite; concentrate and spray: 3 years

Toxicity	When & How Often to Apply	How Soon Effective	Effective Period/ Biodegradability	Time Required Between Last Use & Harvest	Comments & Precautions
Low. Harmless to mammals, fish, and nontarget insects.	Spring and summer, when pest is actively feeding. Reapply every 10-14 days if necessary and after rain.	Feeding stops within 1 hour of ingesting; pest dies in 1-3 days.	Short. Ineffective if ingested more than 48 hours after application.	No restrictions	Different strains of Bt are effective against different pests, so read label carefully. Avoid inhaling when applying, because of possible allergic reaction.
Nontoxic	When soil is very moist and soil temperature is over 60° F. Single application may be effective up to 1 year.	Nematodes begin feeding on pests within 24-48 hours.	Feeding continues until food source is exhausted.	No restrictions	Follow storage and mixing directions very carefully. Spray or pour directly onto moist soil in the root zone of affected plants. Nematodes need constantly moist soil to survive.
Nontoxic to humans, mammals, birds, and earthworms; harmful to beneficial insects and bees.	When plants are still wet from dew, rain, or watering; reapply after every watering, rainfall, or heavy dew.	Within 48 hours	Works as long as it remains dry.	No restrictions	Eye and lung irritant; avoid breathing dust, and wear mask and goggles. Use only natural DE, not pool-filter grade, which is much more toxic.
Very low for mammals; beneficials in larval stage may be harmed.	Use weekly in spring and summer when pests or eggs are present and temperature is between 40° and 85° F.	Kills newly hatched insects within a day; smothers eggs to prevent hatching.	Continues working until it dries.	1 month	Use only the lighter-grade horticultural oils for vegetable crops and brambles. The heavier-grade dormant oils are for use on dormant plants only and will burn vegetable crops.
Virtually nontoxic to humans, mammals, and birds; larvae of beneficials may be affected, but not adults.	Every 7-10 days when pest is present. Spray three times at 2-day intervals for severe aphid or mealybug infestation.	Immediately on contact	Breaks down quickly; effective only while still moist.	No restrictions	Works only when wet spray contacts insect. Do not apply in direct sun or when the temperature is above 85° F. To avoid damage to plants, do not use at concentrations higher than recommended. Not effective if mixed with hard water.
Active ingredient very low, but stabilizers make it harmful if swallowed. May affect beneficials in juvenile stages.	Every 7-10 days when pest larvae are present, or as needed to repel adults.	Death occurs in 3-14 days.	Lasts up to 7 days; breaks down rapidly in sunlight.	No restrictions	Lung, skin, and eye irritant
Highly toxic to fish, aquatic insects, and some beneficials. Moderately toxic to mammals, birds, and bees.	When pest is present. Can be repeated at 3- to 4-day intervals.	Within 2 hours of direct contact	Broken down within 1 day by sunlight, air, moisture, and heat.	No restrictions	A pest is killed only when hit directly. If it receives an inadequate dose, it may appear dead at first, then revive. Do not confuse natural pyrethrins with the synthetic compounds called pyrethroids.
Garlic oil has low toxicity; hot pepper is an extreme eye and skin irritant.	Before pests begin feeding. Apply garlic twice each season. Reapply pepper spray after rain or overhead watering.	Immediate	Both break down rapidly.	Garlic: 1 day. Hot pepper: No interval needed, since spray should never be applied to edible portion of crops.	These sprays may kill some pests, but their main effect is to repel them and deter them from feeding. Protect eyes while mixing and using hot pepper spray.
Very toxic to fish, aquatic insects, birds, beneficial insects; moderately toxic to humans, mammals.	When pest populations cause unacceptable damage. Reapply in 7 days if necessary.	Pests quickly stop feeding and die within several hours to a few days.	Breaks down in 2-7 days.	5-7 days unless label recommends otherwise	Avoid using near ponds, streams, or wherever runoff may contaminate bodies of water. Avoid inhaling.
Moderately toxic to humans, mammals, bees.	When pest populations are excessive or as soon as eggs hatch, at 5- to 7-day intervals and after rain or overhead watering.	Pest may be killed immediately or be paralyzed for several days before dying.	Breaks down in 2 days when exposed to sunlight and air.	1 day	Sneezing is sign of overexposure to skin or lungs. Wear mask, goggles, and protective clothing. Sale and use not permitted in some states.
Moderately toxic to humans and mammals; little risk to insects.	Before disease appears; apply every 7-10 days.	Regular treatments needed to prevent disease or slow spread of existing disease.	Does not degrade; can build up in soil, causing toxicity to plants.	1 day	Liquid concentrate may settle; shake well. Spray early on dry, sunny day. Copper hydroxide will burn leaves in damp weather and may leave visible residue. Wash produce well before eating.
Very high to fish. Caustic and corrosive.	Once a year in early spring while plants are dormant is usually sufficient. If needed, reapply in fall as a preventive.	Immediate; lasts several weeks.	2 or more weeks	Not applicable; used before or after growing season.	Use only in cold weather on dormant raspberries, blackberries, and other bramble fruits. May burn some varieties. Wait 2-3 weeks after using oil spray to apply lime sulfur.
Low toxicity for humans, mammals. May be harmful to bees.	Early in spring and as needed for protection; when rain is forecast, to protect against waterborne disease spores.	Use as preventive or to slow spread of existing disease.	Does not break down; naturally present in soil and required by plants for normal growth.	1 day	Do not use on squash family. Repeated applications may acidify soil. Do not apply when temperature is over 85° F. Lung, eye, and skin irritant. Corrosive; wash metal sprayer after each use. Never use within a month of applying horticultural oil.

CHAPTER SEVEN

Reaping the Harvest

Harvesting a bountiful crop is your reward for many months of hard work in the garden. After carefully preparing the soil and tending your plants, you can finally reap the benefits in the form of delicious, fresh-picked vegetables and fruits, and flavorful herbs still warm from the sun.

On the following pages, you will learn how to judge when various vegetables are ready to be picked and how to store them so that you can continue to enjoy homegrown produce— like the 'Red Leaf' garlic at left curing in the shade of a walnut tree—long after the growing season is over. This chapter also provides tips on picking, processing, and storing herbs to ensure optimal flavor. In addition, you'll find information on extending the growing season into late fall and even into winter, by planting the cold-tolerant varieties recommended here or by using protective devices for late-maturing plants as described on pages 125-128. The chapter closes with advice on mulching, leaf composting, and planting cover crops, which will help rebuild the soil and prepare the garden for the coming year.

Gathering and Storing Vegetables

Knowing when and how to pick vegetables helps safeguard their flavor, texture, and nutritional value. To be sure you pick at the optimal time, keep track of the expected dates of maturity for your crops and begin checking them for ripeness approximately 1 week earlier. Remember that ripening may be hastened or delayed by the weather, the condition of the soil, and the effects of pests and diseases.

Determining Ripeness

Fruiting vegetables tend to deepen in color and develop a gloss or sheen as they ripen; then, as the vegetables age, their skin becomes dull. Exceptions to this rule include most eggplant cultivars, which do not change color, and the rinds of water-melons, which look dull when ripe. Root crops such as carrots often protrude slightly from the soil when mature, and the foliage becomes somewhat dry and flattened. Leafy crops like lettuce can be harvested and eaten at any time, but will become bitter if they begin to bolt (produce flowers or seeds). In fact, many vegetables can be eaten before they are fully mature, with a marked difference in taste and texture. To decide what you like best, sample vegetables at different stages of growth.

Within these guidelines, a hands-on approach is the best way to determine ripeness. Gently press tomatoes to see if they are softening; feel along the shoulders of root vegetables to check their size; or pull a carrot to taste. In time, you will be able to tell when your crops are ripe and, perhaps more important, you will be able to harvest at the stage of maturity and flavor you prefer for each vegetable.

Carrots from a late planting in this garden have been pulled for fall eating. A mulch laid down later in the season will protect the remaining roots so that they can be harvested throughout the winter. Planted behind the carrots are Egyptian onions that overwinter in the ground and mature the following year.

TIPS FROM THE PROS

Crop-by-Crop Harvesting Techniques

Asparagus—Begin harvesting after one season of growth. Choose firm, tightly closed spears 4 to 8 inches high. Snap spears off or cut with a dandelion digger slightly below ground level.

Beans—Harvest every 2 to 3 days to keep plants productive. Pick shell beans when the pod is plump and full, green beans when small and tender, and dry beans when they rattle in the pod.

Carrots—If root tops are above ground, harvest before a hard freeze. Loosen soil alongside the row with a garden fork and gently pull on the leaves just above the root. For easier pulling, water beforehand to soften soil.

Corn—Pick when the ears are plump and full and the corn silk is brown. To test for ripeness, make a small slit in the husk and press a kernel with your fingernail; the kernel will spurt milky fluid if ripe. To pick, hold the main stalk in one hand and pull down and twist the ear with the other hand.

Lettuce—Cut individual leaves of loose-leaved varieties as needed 1 inch above the ground. Cut butterhead and romaine lettuce when the heads are firm and full.

Onions—Harvest scallions when green leaves are 12 inches tall. Dig bulb onions when leaves turn brown and begin to fall over. To increase storage life, stop watering bulb onions a week before digging.

Peppers—Begin picking sweet peppers as soon as they are large enough to be usable. Cut stems 1 inch from the fruit with a sharp knife or pruning shears. Most sweet peppers become sweeter as they mature.

Potatoes—Dig new potatoes when vines begin to flower. For mature potatoes, dig when stems and leaves turn brown. Carefully loosen soil with a spading fork 2 feet from the plant's center. Work the fork toward the plant and slide it under the tubers so you can lift them without piercing them.

Squash—Harvest before the first frost. Most kinds of summer squash are ready to pick when fruits are 4 to 6 inches long and skins are still soft. Winter squash is ready when a fingernail cannot dent the rind and the stem is dry and woody. With a sharp knife or pruning shears, cut off winter squash at the juncture of the stem and vine. Leave the stem attached and handle carefully.

Tomatoes—Pick when evenly colored and firm. To ripen at room temperature, pick when the color is just beginning to develop. Twist fruit off gently; pulling may damage or uproot the plant.

Timely Harvest

Most crops respond to frequent picking by producing more vegetables. As a result, you get more vegetables onto the table, or into storage, while they are at their prime. As a rule of thumb, you cannot overpick a fruiting crop once it begins to bear mature vegetables. Root crops are usually once-only harvest plants, but you can enjoy a more sustained yield if you plant and thin a plot in stages. Leafy vegetables can be harvested as soon as the leaves form, but picking more than a third of a plant's leaves at one time can retard productivity.

Diligent and timely harvesting can be critical for many crops. For example, cucumbers, peas, beans, and summer squash plants will quit producing altogether if the vegetables are not picked

A Double Harvest from Cabbage and Broccoli

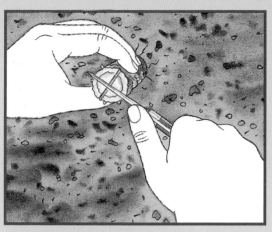

To encourage another crop from a cabbage plant that has a mature head ready for harvesting, cut off the head with a sharp knife at a point about an inch above the soil. To avoid disturbing the roots, hold the stem firmly as you cut, but do not tug on it. Then carve an X in the cut surface of the stub (left). Within a few weeks, the stub will sprout several small cabbage heads (left, below).

For a second harvest of broccoli, remove the first central head the plant produces by using a sharp knife to cut through the stem about 4 inches below the head (left); take care not to pull on the plant, or you might disturb the roots. Several small side shoots will subsequently develop around the stub at the plant's center (left, below). Continue cutting the side shoots as they mature to encourage production.

can avoid inadvertently spreading disease-causing fungi and bacteria, which travel in water particles, to other plants. When bad weather is predicted, harvest tender crops that might be damaged by hard rain, wind, or hail.

Tools and Containers

A gentle hand at harvest time will contribute greatly to the quality of your produce. Tearing vegetable stems and yanking fruits from vines can damage and uproot plants, decreasing or eliminating further yield from those plants. To handpick properly, support the plant with one hand and carefully take off the vegetables with the other.

As an alternative to handpicking, certain tools can make the process of separating vegetables from plants simpler, quicker, and less traumatic for both the plant and the produce. Utility knives help prevent damage to roots when you are gathering vegetables that form heads, such as cabbage and broccoli. Knives or pruning shears cut cleanly through the heavy stems of tomatoes, eggplants, bell peppers, pumpkins, squash, cucumbers, and okra. Scissors are useful for harvesting leafy crops like lettuce, whereas digging tools are essential for extricating root vegetables that are embedded in the ground or growing in soil that is hard and dry.

It's also a good idea to have on hand a variety of clean, dry containers for sorting and carrying vegetables. Place soft, fleshy vegetables that bruise easily in shallow containers with flat bottoms. Plastic buckets, crates, bushel baskets, and laundry baskets work well for firmer vegetables.

Washing the Vegetables

Cleaning the crop is important for prolonging storage life and for retaining flavor, texture, and nutritional value. And although you are unlikely to have exposed your organic garden to dangerous chemicals, even low-toxicity organic pesticides must be thoroughly washed away before you consume the food. Cleaning not only removes dirt and other unwanted substances, in some cases it also actually helps to preserve freshness. Greens, for instance, will quickly dry out unless they are rinsed in cool water, dried, and placed in an unsealed plastic bag before refrigeration. Be sure they are thoroughly dried before storage, since water droplets may harbor fungus spores that cause rot.

Vegetables grown on trellises or covered with floating row covers do not typically require much cleaning. Similarly, vegetables whose edible parts

These winter squash and pumpkins will sit in a sunny window for a week or so to toughen their skins and reduce their moisture content. After this period of sunning, they will keep all winter if stored in a dry, airy place at 50°F.

as soon as they ripen. Some vegetables, such as winter squash, pumpkins, and root crops, must be allowed to mature fully; otherwise, they will not keep well in storage.

Also, crops vary in their ability to retain flavor after ripening. Steady picking and prompt eating, drying, canning, or freezing are essential for tasty tomatoes, peas, beans, peppers, corn, cucumbers, and summer squash. Other vegetables, such as potatoes, carrots, onions, and winter squash, can be harvested in a more leisurely manner.

In general, harvesting is best done in the early morning because vegetables gathered before the sun warms them are less susceptible to spoilage and wilt. You should also try to harvest on clear, cool days when the foliage is dry. That way, you are protected by thick skins, husks, or pods do not usually need to be washed if the exterior covering will be discarded. Vegetables to be stored, such as root crops, should simply be wiped off with a clean, dry cloth. Dip winter squash and pumpkins (including stems) in a solution of 1 part bleach to 10 parts water to kill surface bacteria and fungi.

Planning for Storage

Preparation for storage begins in the garden. Many of the cold-hardy plants, such as root vegetables, cabbage, onions, and winter squash, will last until spring if properly stored. When choosing varieties for your fall garden, look for traditional "good keepers" such as 'Long Season' beets, 'Yellow Globe' onions, and 'Kennebec' potatoes. To increase their storage life, do not fertilize vegetables for about a month before harvesting, since vegetables growing in nitrogen-rich soil late in the season tend to keep poorly. Likewise, withhold water for a month before harvesting; otherwise, the vegetables' tissues will be watery and more likely to spoil quickly.

All the produce you store should be free of blemishes. Even small breaks in a vegetable's skin can open the way to bacteria and fungi that cause rot.

Curing enhances the storage life of these vegetables. By drying and hardening the skin, shell, or rind, you protect the inner flesh from bacteria and fungi. Pumpkins and winter squash should be cured in a sunny room for 7 to 10 days. Most root vegetables need only a few days in a warm, sunny, well-ventilated room before storing. Potatoes, however, should be dried for 2 weeks in an area protected from the sun; in direct light, a toxin that turns the skins greenish often develops.

Storing Root Vegetables

Even though few homes today have root cellars, it is easy to adapt an area of your home for short-term storage. (For vegetables that prefer drier air and warmer temperatures, such as winter squash and pumpkins, an attic or spare room makes a good storage area.) Root vegetables such as beets, carrots, leeks, and turnips keep best at temperatures of 32° to 40°F and can be stored in sheds, garages, porches, or barns for up to a month after harvest. For longer storage, however, these vegetables need an area that mimics their underground growing environment—cool temperatures and high humidity. You can experiment with converting a corner of an unheated basement into

Storing Onions and Garlic

For onions and garlic that will keep all winter, select late-maturing types with thin necks and, if you plan to braid and hang them, long, strong stems. Gently dig the vegetables and brush off any soil. If the weather is dry, place the bulbs outdoors in a lightly shaded area; otherwise, choose an airy, dry shelter such as a carport. Spread the bulbs on wire mesh set on a support so that air can circulate on all sides. When the outer skins are dry and brittle and the stems have withered, the bulbs are ready to store. Either braid the stems together for hanging, or cut them off an inch above the bulbs and put the onions and garlic in mesh bags or other airy containers. For best results, store in a dry area at 36°F.

TECHNIQUES FOR A LONG STORAGE LIFE

Crop	Temperature/ Humidity	Storage Life	Comments
Beets	32° F; 95%	2-5 months	Clip tops to 1 inch and layer in boxes with sawdust, sand, or peat moss in a basement or other cool, humid area. Can also be left in the ground and dug up as needed.
Cabbage	32° F; 90%	2-4 months	Store in separate area due to strong odor. Cut off damaged or rotten leaves. Wrap heads in paper or layer in straw and store in a basement or other cool, humid area.
Carrots	32° F; 95%	4-5 months	Cut off tops and layer in boxes with moist sand or sawdust and store in a basement or other cool, humid area. In mild climates carrots can be overwintered in the garden.
Potatoes	40° F; 90%	3-8 months	Harvest before the first hard freeze. Potatoes that have been frozen will rot in storage. After curing, pack loosely in well-ventilated boxes or mesh bags and store in a dark, cool, humid area such as a basement.
Winter squash	50° F; 60%	3-8 months	Choose unblemished high-quality fruits and store in a warm, dry area such as an attic or unheated spare room. Check often for signs of mold or spoilage and promptly remove damaged fruits.

a root cellar. Mount a humidity meter and thermometer in the area (see the chart above for the ideal temperatures and humidity levels). Place vegetables in well-ventilated containers such as mesh bags, baskets, or slatted wooden boxes, or hang them in braids and bunches. Open outside vents or windows periodically to let in cool air on fall nights. If your basement is dry, sprinkle water on the floor as needed. If you have trouble maintaining humidity levels, pack root vegetables in damp sand or sawdust to help them stay crisp.

Root vegetables can also be stored outdoors in a cold frame. To protect the frame from wind, place it adjacent to the foundation of your house or garage. Layer the produce in loose, clean straw or sawdust surrounded with rodent-proof wire mesh. For extra protection against cold, stack hay bales around the frame and cover the top with several layers of heavy canvas and a final layer of straw.

Even if you have stored only high-quality produce, you'll still need to check regularly for signs of spoilage. Promptly remove any vegetable that has gone bad, along with the straw or sawdust immediately around it. As a precaution, wipe off adjacent vegetables with a dry cloth and, if necessary, add clean sawdust or straw.

Saving Seed

Gathering seed was a standard gardening task before the proliferation of seed companies in the 19th century. Although the seeds of premium hybrids may not reproduce or may revert to one of the parent types, collecting seed is a fairly simple process and is especially worthwhile if you are growing unusual varieties that may be difficult to obtain elsewhere.

Harvesting your own seeds also lets you develop varieties that are suited to your particular garden and tastes. When choosing plants for seed, look for specimens that are healthy and possess the variety's best features. Over time, you can have a hand in improving the quality of your vegetables by collecting seed from plants in your garden with exceptional yield, flavor, keeping quality, or resistance to pests and diseases.

Determining when to harvest vegetables for seed will depend on what type of crops you are using for seed collection. In general, you will be gathering two types of seeds—wet and dry. Tomatoes, cucumbers, squash, and melons bear fleshy fruit and wet seeds. To collect seed from these plants, wait till the fruit is slightly overripe, then pick it and remove the seeds. Dry seeds are harvested from crops such as beans, peas, and corn. These should be left to mature several weeks past their prime before picking for seed collection.

The next step in seed collection is cleaning. To clean fleshy fruits, scoop the seeds into a strainer, rinse with cool water, and dry on paper towels for a week or two. Seeds in pods can be shelled and spread to dry on a wire-mesh screen in a well-ventilated room.

Once they are thoroughly dry, the seeds of most vegetables can be stored in glass jars or in cans with tight-fitting plastic lids in a cool, dry area of your home. Do not use plastic bags and containers, because they may be permeable to air and could expose the seeds to moisture, thus reducing their viability. Beans and peas, however, need different handling because they are susceptible to fungus if stored in airtight containers. Keep them instead in small cloth bags or paper envelopes. As a preventive measure, you can give seeds a light sprinkling of silica gel. This desiccant, which is available at craft stores, hardware stores, and camera supply shops, will absorb moisture and help keep the seeds dry.

Harvesting Herbs

When harvested and handled with care, home-grown fresh and dried herbs are far superior to any you can buy. Knowing when to harvest them ensures intense flavor, scent, and color. And storing herbs to retain their just-picked savoriness doesn't have to be a long, involved process; it can be as simple as drying or freezing them.

Keep in mind that you don't necessarily need a large herb garden for a bountiful harvest. Even a few pots or a small bed near your back door can yield a plentiful supply of herbs for the kitchen. For example, just a few plants of parsley, chives, and mint can provide a wealth of flavor for soups, salads, and teas—and they will taste much better than their store-bought counterparts.

Most herbs—including basil, borage, parsley, angelica, chives, and sage—may be picked at any time. Harvesting a few leaves for immediate use is an efficient way to keep your plants well groomed. Cut back a stray branch of rosemary or snip off a few roving sprigs of wild marjoram and use the trimmings in your kitchen. To shape a plant and also make it fuller, remove only the growing tip of a stem, a method called pinching back. You can induce dense, bushy growth on a sprawling mat of thyme, for example, by removing a few inches from the tips of scraggly branches.

How to Gather Leaves

Harvest leaves early in the morning as soon as the dew has evaporated but before the sun gets bright and hot, ideally on a dry day following a day of good weather. Choose healthy, vigorous growth with leaves unblemished by pests and disease. Using sharp pruners, scissors, or a knife, cut only as much as you'll need for the day's meals or for processing immediately for storage. Handle the leaves as little as possible to avoid bruising them.

Because herbs change in appearance as they dry, gather leaves from one type of herb at a time, keeping each kind separate and labeling the batches. Spread the cut leaves in a thin layer on a screen or in a basket; piling up herbs generates heat that makes them wilt.

Culinary Classics

Both weekend cooks and professional chefs know from experience how quickly the flavor of many herbs starts to wane once they're harvested. Widely available curly parsley, for example, is often relegated to use as a garnish because it has languished in your grocer's produce bin. But gardeners who grow it and its stronger-tasting and longer-lasting cousin—flatleaf or Italian parsley—can enjoy them to the fullest extent: When minced with garlic and lemon peel, the herbs produce a tangy *gremolata*, adding a piquant finish to soups and stews. Fines herbes, a mixture of finely chopped chives, parsley or chervil, and more pungent herbs such as tarragon, thyme, and savory, is basic to French cook-

Culling Herbs from a Clump

To harvest the leafy growth of herbs that send up stems directly from the ground, such as the Italian parsley shown here, cut off individual stems at soil level from the outside edges of the plant. This will stimulate new growth at the center of the plant, keeping it compact and laden with leaves.

Clump-Forming Herbs

Allium schoenoprasum (chives)
Allium tuberosum (garlic chives)
Angelica archangelica (angelica)
Anthriscus cerefolium (chervil)
Cymbopogon citratus (lemon grass)
Petroselinum crispum var. *crispum* (curly parsley)
Petroselinum crispum var. *neopolitanum* (Italian parsley)

ing. The mixture can be bought dried, but the fresh version tastes far better.

Another indispensable component of French cooking is the bouquet garni, which is composed of three sprigs of parsley, a bay leaf, and a few sprigs of thyme tied into a bundle with string or wrapped in cheesecloth. After a bouquet has lent its blend of flavors to, say, a simmering pot of bean soup or a beef stew, it is removed before serving.

Unlike a bouquet garni, a chiffonade is made to be eaten. To make the delicate slivers that decorate and flavor a dish, gather clean, unblemished leaves of a large-leaved herb such as sorrel, washing them only if necessary and patting them dry. Roll the leaves into a cigar shape and slice the roll crosswise at one-quarter-inch intervals into fine strips. To make a visually striking salad or pep up a vegetable dish, use a mix of herbs with different leaf colors and compatible flavors, such as basil, perilla, and mint.

Adventurous cooks can make use of *Cymbopogon citratus* (lemon grass), an herb traditional to the cuisines of Southeast Asia, whose unique flavor blends the bite of lemon with the scent of roses. The young, tender shoots of lemon grass are delectable stir-fried with chicken, stuffed into the middle of a whole fish before baking, or added to soup. Or, for a delicate hint of lemon, put them in the water when you steam broccoli or other vegetables. Where winters are cold—USDA Zone

The Growth Rate of Different Herbs

SLOW GROWERS

Laurus nobilis
(bay)
Rosmarinus officinalis
(rosemary)
Satureja montana
(winter savory)

MODERATE GROWERS

***Lavandula* spp.**
(lavender)
Origanum* x *majoricum
(hardy marjoram)
Salvia elegans
(pineapple sage)
Salvia officinalis
(common sage)
***Thymus* spp.**
(thyme)

VIGOROUS GROWERS

Artemisia dracunculus* var. *sativa
(French tarragon)
Melissa officinalis
(lemon balm)
***Mentha* spp.**
(mint)
***Ocimum* spp.**
(basil)
Origanum vulgare
(oregano)
Satureja hortensis
(summer savory)

Note: The abbreviation "spp." stands for the plural of "species"; where used in lists it means that many, but not all, of the species in a genus meet the criterion of the list.

Slow-Growing Herbs

Woody herbs, including the potted bay laurel pictured here, *grow less rapidly than their herbaceous counterparts. Pick only a few leaves their first season. Wait until the plant is fully established in the fall of its second year before cutting one-quarter off the top. Cut back to a leaf node, preferably an outward-pointing one, to stimulate growth.*

7 and colder—pot up lemon grass and bring it inside to a sunny window; its slender, pale green leaves make it an attractive houseplant.

Herbs for Storage

Fresh herbs generally have more flavor than dried or frozen ones. One exception is bay leaves, which gain flavor when dried. In climates where even tender herbs grow year round, they can always be enjoyed fresh. But in colder areas, bay leaves must be preserved for winter use.

Preserving herbs need not be mystifying or labor-intensive, especially if you begin on a small scale. Simply pluck a few leafy stems of basil, tarragon, marjoram, or any culinary herb and place them in a single layer in a colander. Set the colander in a dry, airy place out of direct sunlight. When the leaves are dry enough to crumble,

break them into pieces, discarding the stems. Store the pieces in a tightly sealed jar and crush them just before using.

Gathering Herbs to Retain Quality

To preserve large quantities of herbs, you must know when to harvest them to capture their optimal flavor, fragrance, or color and how to retain those qualities through careful processing. The right time to harvest depends on which part of the plant is to be used. The maximum flow of essential oils, which furnish flavor and fragrance, generally occurs in leaves just before the plant's flowers open. But if you are harvesting blossoms, wait until they are newly opened; that's usually when a flower is richest in essential oils.

Because plants flower at different times, the

Robust Herbs

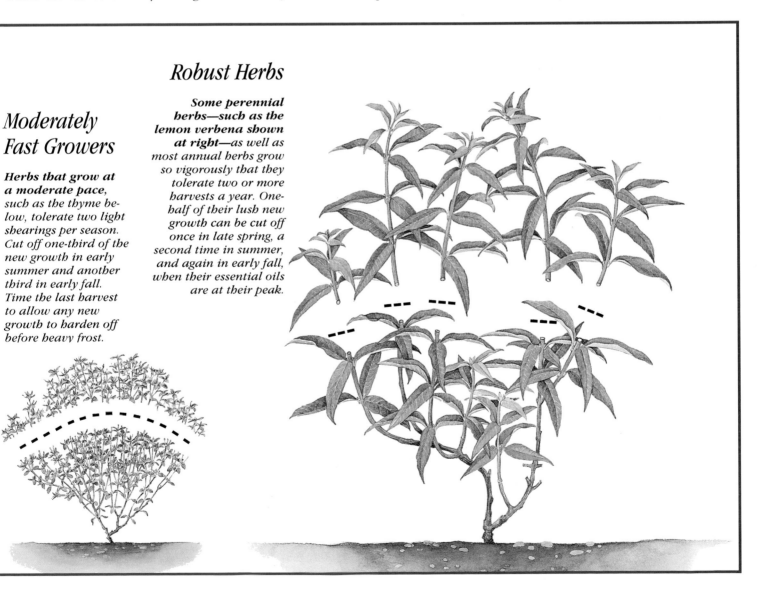

Moderately Fast Growers

Herbs that grow at a moderate pace, such as the thyme below, tolerate two light shearings per season. Cut off one-third of the new growth in early summer and another third in early fall. Time the last harvest to allow any new growth to harden off before heavy frost.

Some perennial herbs—such as the lemon verbena shown at right—as well as most annual herbs grow so vigorously that they tolerate two or more harvests a year. One-half of their lush new growth can be cut off once in late spring, a second time in summer, and again in early fall, when their essential oils are at their peak.

precise moment to harvest leaves varies from plant to plant and, of course, with a growing season's particular climate and weather conditions. In most areas, many herbs flower in midsummer. Keep an eye on your plants so you'll know when each one is ready to bloom.

When harvesting herbs, you may want to consider wearing gloves. Many people are allergic to the potent chemical compounds found in the plants. The hairy leaves of borage, for instance, can irritate sensitive skin, and angelica can cause dermatitis. Reactions are generally worse if contact occurs during the heat of the day.

Use a sharp knife or pruning shears to cut the herbs. Remove a branch or cut back part of one directly above a node, the place where the leaf grows from the stem; this will stimulate the plants to produce healthy new growth. For herbs that send up clumps of unbranched stems directly from the ground—parsley, chervil, and lemon grass, for example—cut the outer leaves at the base of the plant *(box, page 115)*. If you like, you can cut back all the stems of stalwart perennial herbs such as lovage and chives; they will promptly grow back.

Slow and Moderate Growers

How much you can safely cut from an herb at any one time depends on its vigor and growth habit. Some shrubby herbs—particularly bay, rosemary, and winter savory—grow slowly. Although you can pick a few leaves during their first year in the garden, wait until these plants are fully established before cutting them back. A few weeks before the first frost, take off one-quarter of the plants' growth. Pruning back to an outward-pointing bud encourages graceful branching *(box, page 116)*.

Herbs that grow slightly faster—lavender, marjoram, pineapple sage, common sage, and thyme, for instance—tolerate a somewhat sizable harvest once they are established. You can cut one-third off the top once, and sometimes twice, each year *(box, page 117)*. Just be sure to time your last pruning early enough in late summer or early fall so that new growth has a chance to harden off before winter.

Rambunctious growers like mint and lemon balm can withstand extensive shearing. Cut as much as one-half of the new growth off the top twice—or even three times—during the growing season *(box, page 117)*. Tarragon, while not as robust as mint and lemon balm, also tolerates severe pruning. Vigorous annuals like basil and summer savory can be cut back to 5 or 6 inches; be sure to

save the lower foliage, however, which is needed for further growth.

Picking Flowers

The flavor and color of blossoms generally peak when they have just bloomed. For example, golden yellow and orange calendula florets and showy red or pink-lavender bee balm petals—used to perk up salads or blended into soft cheese and butter for flavor and bright color—are best picked right after they have opened. (For a list of edible flowers, see page 50.)

The right time to harvest flowers for potpourri varies. Rose petals used to add scent to potpourri, for instance, should be picked when the blossoms are fresh and at the peak of fragrance. The best time to pick whole rosebuds, which combine nicely with crumbled flowers and flakes of petals, is when they are in tight bud. And lavender flowers used in potpourri should be harvested when the blossoms are fully formed and about to open. At this stage, the top of the bud will show faint color and be intensely fragrant.

Harvesting Seeds

An herb grown for its edible seeds must be watched carefully; once the plant flowers, its seedpods and seed heads will soon follow. Harvest the seed heads when the seeds start losing their green color and begin turning light brown and the plant's stems and pods—if it has any—begin to wither and look dry. After the seed heads are cut from the plant, the seeds will continue to ripen. The seeds of many herbs such as caraway, coriander, and fennel don't all ripen at the same time. With these herbs, harvest the seed heads when there are still immature seeds present. Above all, don't wait too long to gather seeds. Leaving seeds exposed to the vagaries of weather will turn them black, an indication that they have deteriorated. If you are planning to save some for spring planting, they will probably not germinate.

After a day of drying, seed heads should be checked carefully for insects. (Unwelcome pests such as tiny aphids will make their presence known by crawling away from seeds that have be-

The bright yellow and orange flowers of pot marigold mingle with the soft blue of borage in an edible planting. Pot marigold's petals and the blossoms of borage both make colorful additions to salads.

Foeniculum vulgare (fennel)

Herbs with Aromatic Seeds

Anethum graveolens
(dill)
Brassica juncea
(brown mustard)
Carum carvi
(caraway)
**Coriandrum
sativum**
(coriander)
Foeniculum vulgare
(fennel)
Nigella sativa
(black cumin)
Sesamum indicum
(sesame)

gun to lose moisture. If you see or suspect that there are insect eggs or larvae hidden in the seeds, pop them into the freezer for 48 hours.) Spread both immature and ripe seeds out on paper towels and leave them to cure in a warm, dry place. Then store the seeds in an airtight container, such as a screw-top glass jar, in a cool, dark place.

Seeds for Sowing

Seeds destined to start next year's herb garden should be allowed to ripen on the plant until no trace of green remains. This helps to ensure a higher rate of germination next spring. Some herbs—dill, German chamomile, and angelica, among others—will self-sow. Simply allow their ripe seeds to drop to the ground.

Make sure seeds to be held until spring are completely dry, then place them in an airtight glass jar with a package of commercial desiccant or an inch of powdered milk to keep the humidity low. Store the sealed jar in your refrigerator.

Saving Other Plant Parts

In addition to leaves, seeds, and flowers, the aromatic roots of herbs such as *Zingiber officinale* (ginger) and the fragrant and colorful stigmas of *Crocus sativus* (saffron crocus) are highly prized. To dry gingerroot, harvest the roots in fall, when their moisture content is low and the length of time it takes them to dry will be minimal.

Saffron, the world's most expensive spice, is the dried stigmas of the autumn-blooming saffron crocus. Labor alone accounts for its costliness, for it takes many thousands of the threadlike stigmas—which must be gathered by hand—to produce a single ounce. Fortunately, you need only a pinch to flavor cookies or rice. A few dozen bulbs grown in your garden will supply you with enough for a handful of uses. Pluck the bright orange stigmas when the flowers open over several weeks in the fall. Spread them out on a kitchen towel to dry, then store them in a tightly sealed glass container away from heat and light.

The Art of Preserving Herbs

Air-drying, the traditional way of preserving herbs, remains one of the best methods today. Speed is of the essence, because the faster an herb dries, the more flavor and color it will retain and the less likely it is to become contaminated or moldy. Conventional ovens, however, even at low temperatures, are too hot for drying herbs. Use them only in an emergency, when herbs are so wet that they are in danger of becoming moldy.

Two conditions important for drying herbs are good air circulation and a temperature that stays consistently between 80° and 85° F. Higher temperatures and sunlight dissipate an herb's essential oils. Another crucial factor in speedy drying is low humidity. For this reason, don't wash herbs unless it is absolutely necessary. Give dusty or mud-spattered herbs a shower with a garden hose a day or two before harvesting them.

The place you choose to dry your herbs will influence the finished product. In some climates, dry, breezy days in late summer render almost any room in the house ideal. In hot, muggy climates, however, you'll have to keep your herbs in an air-conditioned room or one equipped with a dehumidifier for them to dry properly. Avoid a basement that, while dry and cool, harbors stagnant air. And an attic, though airy and dry, may get too hot.

Hanging herbs in bunches tied with decorative knots of raffia and ribbon may be picturesque, but this method works well only for thyme and other tiny-leaved herbs that dry quickly. If you choose to hang-dry herbs, keep the bunches relatively small and tie them loosely; otherwise, the innermost leaves may mildew.

Most herbs, especially those with thick, fleshy leaves, should be dried in a single layer on a flat surface that allows for adequate air flow, like the shallow basket shown below. A large window screen that has been scrubbed and dried also makes an ideal drying tray. For smaller quantities, try cookie sheets or oven racks covered with kitchen towels, or hanging wicker baskets.

Freshly picked sage leaves line this flat-bottomed wicker basket, where they will dry. Their arrangement in a single layer and the coarse weave of the basket permit air to circulate around each leaf, promoting quick drying. The faster an herb dries, the more color and flavor it retains in storage.

Fleshy Leaves and Tender Tissues

Fleshy leaves such as those of scented geraniums contain a lot of moisture. To dry their thick tissues successfully, strip them from their stems to shorten the drying time and place them in a shallow basket or on a screen in one layer, with plenty of room surrounding each leaf.

Thin, tender leaves such as those of basil require great care in handling; they are easily bruised and crushed, which compromises their quality. Their fragility also makes them difficult to store without sacrificing flavor. Freezing is a good method of storage for the leaves of herbs with delicate tissues, such as basil, chervil, tarragon, lovage, and cilantro.

Helpful Appliances

Dehydrators, which force warm air through a series of screens, are excellent for drying herbs quickly. The fastest method, however, is drying with a microwave oven. Microwaves differ in power wattage, so you'll have to experiment if you choose this drying method, which works best for herbs with resinous leaves, such as rosemary, bay, and sage. Place the leaves between two sheets of paper towels and microwave on low for 20 seconds. Check the leaves for crispness; if they are still pliable, microwave them for several seconds more, then check them again. Avoid overdrying the leaves; they will be brittle and turn to powder when crumbled. You can also dry herbs between paper towels in a frost-free refrigerator. They should be dry and crisp in about 24 hours.

When your herbs are dry, remove the remaining stems, but take care to keep the leaves as intact as possible. The larger the pieces, the longer they retain their flavor in storage. Crumble them into smaller pieces right before you use them.

Herbal Teas

You don't need to be as careful when you prepare a harvest for making herbal tea, a beverage made from dried herbs steeped in hot water. Because the tea is strained before serving, whole leaves, stems, and flowers can go into it. You can make a tea of just one herb or several herbs. A particularly refreshing tea combines the dried leaves of lemon grass with other citrusy herbs such as lemon verbena and lemon balm.

Packaging and Storing Herbs

Because dried herbs can reabsorb moisture from the air, it's important to package them as soon as they are dry. Further exposure to air will cause them to lose essential oils, collect dust, and quite possibly become infested with insects. Use airtight glass or plastic containers for storage. Although clear containers let you see what's inside, opaque

The leaves of feathery chervil, broad-leaved sorrel, and sage, with blue-violet flower spikes, all taste best fresh. To keep chervil, freeze leafy stems in plastic bags or make an herb butter. Freeze shredded sorrel leaves in oil or layer them in salt. Sage can be dried or frozen and makes a delicious flavored vinegar.

or colored ones are better because they keep out damaging light. Find a cool, dark place to store your herbs; heat from any source such as an oven or stove will sap their potency.

Freezing is a quick way to preserve herbs, especially hard-to-dry herbs such as chives, chervil, parsley, and fresh coriander, or cilantro *(Coriandrum sativum)*. The easiest way to freeze these herbs is simply to enclose them in a plastic bag labeled with the contents and the date. Wait to chop a frozen herb until you are ready to use it.

You can also try freezing herbs in oil. Start with clean, dry leaves that have been stripped from their stems. Chop them and mix with just enough oil to form a paste. Then pack into containers and label, date, and store them in the freezer. You'll be able to scrape out what you need with a spoon without thawing the whole containerful, because oil doesn't freeze as hard as water.

Culinary Treats

Herbs can also be preserved in oil, butter, salt, vinegar, or wine. Each of these preparations has a specific shelf life. For example, herb butter, a mixture of ½ pound of softened butter and 3 table-spoons of finely chopped herbs such as parsley or tarragon or a combination of herbs, must be kept refrigerated. It is best used within a week unless it is frozen, in which case it should be good for as long as 2 months.

Herbal oils must be used within 2 weeks. To infuse oil with herbal essence, combine ½ cup of oil and sprigs of an herb such as rosemary, thyme, or marjoram in a metal measuring cup or small metal bowl. Simmer in the lower third of a preheated 300° oven for 1 hour to flavor the oil and destroy any bacteria that cause botulism. Strain the oil, bottle it, and keep it refrigerated at all times. Herbal vinegars, made by steeping fresh herbs in vinegar or wine, last up to a year and don't require refrigeration.

You can also use salt to dry herbs. In an airtight canning jar that will keep the salt from caking, layer leaves of herbs such as basil or lovage over salt—the large crystals of kosher salt are best—covering each layer with more salt. In a week the herbs will be ready to use.

Sweetly scented geranium leaves and rose petals can be steeped in sugar, which will absorb their aromatic oils. Discard the leaves and petals after they are dry and use the flavored sugar to make cake icings, cookies, and candy.

Herbs for Potpourri

Aloysia triphylla (lemon verbena)
Borago officinalis (borage—flowers)
Calendula officinalis (calendula—flowers)
Citrus **spp.** (orange and lemon—peel)
Cymbopogon citratus (lemon grass)
Laurus nobilis (bay)
Lavandula (lavender)
Melissa officinalis (lemon balm)
Mentha **spp.** (mint)
Origanum majorana (sweet marjoram)
Origanum vulgare (oregano)
Rosmarinus officinalis (rosemary)
Salvia **spp.** (sage)
Viola **spp.** (violet—flower)
Zingiber officinale (ginger—root)

Note: The abbreviation "spp." stands for the plural of "species"; where used in lists it means that many, but not all, of the species in a genus meet the criterion of the list.

Sage, Lavender, and Orange Peel

Decorative glass bottles hold sparkling, unclouded vinegars infused with, from left, purple basil, salad burnet, rosemary, sage, and garlic chives. Make sure herbs are free of surface moisture before steeping them in vinegar, or the infusion may become murky. To retain their full flavor, store the vinegars in a cool, dark place.

Potpourri

An aromatic potpourri—a blend of dried flowers, spices, and leaves—lends the delectable scent of a summer garden to a room. Although there are many different recipes for potpourri, there are basically just two methods: the moist and the dry. The moist method is time-consuming and results in a highly fragrant but unattractive product. The dry method is far simpler and produces a potpourri that looks as pretty as it smells.

A few culinary herbs that can also be used in potpourri are listed on page 123. If you haven't made potpourri before, a good place to begin is with this classic recipe: Prepare a quart of bone-dry rose petals or a combination of petals and rosebuds from fragrant varieties such as the fruit-scented bourbon rose 'Madame Isaac Pereire'. In-

toxicatingly fragrant gallica and damask roses such as 'Camaieux' and 'Madame Hardy' are also perfect for potpourri.

Gently stir into the roses 1 pint of completely dry scented geranium leaves, a pint of dried lavender flowers, and 2 tablespoons each of cloves, cinnamon, and allspice. Blend in a fixative—an ingredient that extends the life of potpourri by absorbing aromatic oils and releasing them slowly. You can use 1 level tablespoon of orrisroot or gum benzoin for every cup of the potpourri mixture. Another excellent fixative is vetiver root, which also adds its own woodsy fragrance to the final product. Chop the dried root and crush it slightly, but do not pulverize it; using it powdered may make the potpourri look dusty. Mix the fixative with the flowers and spices and store the potpourri in a tightly sealed container for at least a month to allow the fragrances to meld.

Extending the Harvest

Extending your garden's growing season is challenging but well worth the effort. By either protecting plants to encourage their maturation early or late in the season or planting cold-tolerant vegetables for harvesting in fall and winter, you can grow crops during the months when cold weather would usually kill them. Since every garden is a unique combination of soil, climate, cultivars, and growing methods, you should experiment with various techniques for lengthening your garden's period of productivity.

Protecting Your Plants

Simple cold frames, row covers, and plant caps, or cloches, can help maintain a consistent microclimate, protecting crops from the damage inflicted by frost, wind chill, and sudden dips in temperature. By trapping solar energy, cold frames can extend your season a month or more at each end. Cloches and row covers aren't as efficient but can

still add several weeks of growing time, allowing you to harvest warm-weather crops like tomatoes, peppers, and cucumbers even after the first frost.

You may need to try several kinds of protection—what works in your garden one year may not be as effective the next if the season is unusually cold or warm. When choosing the degree of protection you want, keep in mind that the more complicated the method, the more maintenance it will require—and even the simplest methods will need periodic monitoring. Some protective devices you can build yourself, or you can purchase readymade equipment through specialized mail-order catalogs.

Cozy Cloches

Cloches, small caps that protect a single plant or a few closely spaced small ones, can be either made or purchased to fit different crops. The very first cloches were bell-shaped glass jars used in 17th-

Polyethylene spread on a wire frame keeps a crop of greens warm on a frosty fall morning (foreground). When the day warms up, the plastic can be folded back lengthwise along the row to admit light and prevent overheating. In the background, a floating row cover of lightweight spunbonded fabric is draped directly over the plants.

century French market gardens. Today, you can choose from a variety of lightweight, portable cloches made of wax paper, plastic, glass, and polyethylene tubes filled with water *(page 57)*. You can also make cloches by recycling household articles such as gallon-sized plastic milk jugs with the bottoms cut out and the caps removed. To keep milk-jug cloches from blowing away, insert a slim stake beside the growing plant and set the jug over the plant, with the stake protruding from its mouth.

Cone-shaped cloches can be constructed from sheets of fiberglass-reinforced plastic. Cut the material into a semicircle, pull the straight edges together, and staple them to form a cone. These cloches can be made in a wide range of sizes to fit your crops and will last for a number of years. The hole on top of the cone provides some ventilation, although on warmer days you may need to remove the cloche altogether.

A tomato cage can be easily adapted for use as a cloche. Set the tomato cage over the plant and wrap it with clear plastic, taping the overlap to hold it in place. On cold nights, drape a second piece of plastic over the top and secure it with tape.

Plants covered with a cloche should be monitored closely to avoid overheating and moisture buildup. You can cut slits in the cloche for ventilation, and you should periodically remove it, especially on warm days.

Hardworking Row Covers

Row covers are one of the most effective and practical season extenders. When frost threatens, you can quickly and easily install row covers over a single row or an entire section of your garden.

Floating row covers made of spunbonded polyester can be placed directly over plants without a supporting structure. These fabric covers allow water, air, and sunlight to reach the plants while offering frost protection to around 28° F. If winds

At right, corrugated fiberglass covers a row of greens, while plastic milk jugs with the bottoms removed keep single plants snug. A cylinder of reinforced plastic tied around a whiskey-barrel planter (below, left) blocks the wind and creates a warm environment for leaf lettuce; the house wall and the paving on which the planter is set absorb heat during the day and continue to radiate it after the sun goes down. In an autumn garden (below, right), a cold frame made of cinder blocks and old windows is open on a warm day to prevent the lettuce crop from overheating.

threaten, you can bury the edges of the covers in the soil or weight them down with rocks. Floating row covers come in rolls of various sizes and are sold at most garden supply stores or through specialty mail-order catalogs.

Another material commonly used for row covers is transparent polyethylene plastic. It is too heavy to lay directly on plants, however, and must be supported by wire, PVC pipes, or wood arches. A polyethylene row cover offers a greater degree of frost protection than a row cover of spunbonded fabric, but it needs more frequent monitoring than the fabric cover to prevent overheating and excessive humidity; on a sunny day, the temperature beneath a plastic row cover may be 20° F higher than the air outside. On warm days you'll need to fold half the polyethylene sheet back lengthwise to increase air circulation and moderate the temperature. You can also buy polyethylene with slits to allow for good air circulation, but it will provide less frost protection than a solid sheet.

Cold Frames, Warm Plants

With a cold frame set in your garden, you can overwinter ready-to-harvest frost-tolerant crops, as well as seedlings that will remain dormant during the cold months, then resume growth the following spring. You can either buy a cold frame or build it yourself out of lumber. For a makeshift cold frame, simply arrange concrete blocks or bales of hay in a rectangle around the plants and use a sheet of glass, an old window, or heavy clear plastic as a lid, slanting it slightly to prevent water from collecting. When cold nights threaten, you can cover the lid with thick canvas, old blankets, or several layers of hay.

Regulating the Cold Frame's Climate

Cold frames require daily monitoring. Early in the fall, steady sun can quickly dry out and damage plants grown under glass or plastic. Check your cold frame each day, watering as necessary to keep the soil slightly moist.

You must also be diligent about monitoring the temperature inside the cold frame. Sudden temperature changes can damage plants and cause wilting or retard growth. If daytime temperatures reach 60° F or more, raise the lid or remove it and replace it at night when the temperature falls. If the outside temperature is 40° F, the lid should be propped open only a few inches and closed again at night. The need to vent the cold frame will decrease as the season advances toward winter.

If you discover that manually opening and closing the cold frame is a chore you'd rather do with-

Cold-Hardy Cultivars

Arugula

Broccoli 'Waltham', 'Green Valiant'

Brussels sprouts 'Jade Cross'

Cabbage 'Danish Ballhead', 'Savoy Ace'

Carrot 'Napoli'

Cauliflower 'Violet Queen', 'Snow Crown'

Corn salad 'Vit', 'D'Etamps'

Endive 'Salad King', 'Tres Fin' ('Fine Curled')

Kale 'Dwarf Blue Curled Scotch Vates', 'Blue Siberian', 'Winterbor'

Leek 'Alaska', 'Blue Solaise'

Lettuce 'Black-Seeded Simpson', 'Four Seasons', 'Oakleaf', 'Salad Bowl', 'Rouge d'Hiver', 'Winter Density'

Onion 'Beltsville Bunching', Egyptian onion 'Ishikura'

Radicchio 'Augusto'

Radish 'Munich Bier', 'Round Black Spanish'

Arugula

127

Tips and Techniques for a Long Season

Beets—Sow outside about 10 weeks before the average first frost date. Pick mature beets before the first hard freeze. Harvest immature beets in autumn or mulch heavily to overwinter.

Broccoli—Sow seed directly by mid-July in colder climates and by August in milder ones. Protect with floating row covers. Some cultivars can withstand temperatures below freezing as long as the weather is evenly cool. Grow all winter where temperatures remain above 40° F.

Brussels sprouts—Sow in succession for harvesting from early fall to late spring. Cold-hardy cultivars survive temperatures as low as 14° F. Freezing temperatures enhance flavor.

Cabbage—Set out cold-hardy transplants no earlier than 10 to 12 weeks before the first frost.

Carrots—Mulch with 8 to 12 inches of hay before the ground freezes. Dig all winter.

Cauliflower—Plant in time for it to mature in cool weather, but before the first frost. Or, plant frost-tolerant cultivars like 'White Sails' and protect with floating row covers.

Celeriac—Mound soil around plants and mulch heavily to continue harvest into the winter. Grow as a winter crop in mild climates.

Chard—After the first frost, protect with floating row covers or mulch deeply to extend the harvest into winter. Plant as a winter crop in a cold frame.

Garlic—Plant 2 to 4 weeks before the first frost for harvest the following summer.

Leeks—Harvest cold-hardy cultivars such as 'Blue Solaise' all winter in areas where temperatures stay above 10° F. Pull the last of the leeks before seed stalks appear in the spring.

Lettuce—Sow leaf lettuce at least 7 weeks before the first frost and heading types 10 weeks before; mulch heavily to insulate soil. Cold-hardy cultivars can be overwintered in cold frames or under row covers in mild climates.

Onions—Some varieties, including Egyptian onions and 'Walla Walla', can be overwintered with a thick layer of mulch in mild climates or in a cold frame in severe climates. For an early-spring crop of shallots in cold climates, plant after the first frost. If planted earlier, they may send up top growth that would be damaged by winter cold.

Spinach—Plant hardy cultivars such as 'Winter Bloomsdale' about a month before the first frost. Sow in late winter in a cold frame for an early-spring crop.

Mulched Lettuce

out, you can buy a thermostatic device that automatically opens and closes the lid as needed. Many prefabricated cold frames come equipped with such a device.

Hardy Plants for Cold Weather

With planning and care, you can have a thriving cold-weather garden, one that will yield fresh vegetables long after the normal season has ended. Many crops that perform well in cool spring weather and are harvested in summer can be planted a second time for a fall harvest. In general, vegetables that grow best in cool weather are leafy greens and root crops. When choosing cultivars for harvesting in the cooler temperatures and shorter days of fall and winter, look for characteristics such as cold hardiness and quick maturity. Some good candidates for the late-season garden are listed on page 127.

Timing is critical in planning the autumn garden, and it may take a season or two of trial and error to determine the best time to begin your fall plantings. Keep in mind that your goal is to schedule plantings so that crops will be mature when winter arrives, a date that will vary with your particular climate. Shorter days and colder soil and air temperatures will increase the time required to reach maturity by 20 to 40 percent. You will be able to extend your harvest by continuing to plant at 1- to 2-week intervals until approximately 6 weeks before the first frost date for your region.

Some of the cultivation practices you use during other seasons will need to be modified to suit the fall garden's special conditions. The following are among the most important things to remember:

• Seedlings should be well thinned, and plants should be spaced slightly farther apart than in spring and summer gardens to allow greater exposure to the sun.

• You may need to shade fall seedlings from the late-summer sun. You can buy black shade cloth made of polyethylene mesh from a garden center or hardware store, or improvise your own sun protection from old window screens or open snow fencing supported on cement blocks.

• Newly planted crops will need to be watered frequently if your area typically receives little rain in late summer and early fall.

And finally, try using a diluted seaweed spray on your crops for a few weeks before the first frost date. This will raise mineral levels in the leaf tissue and help prevent freezing.

Putting the Garden to Bed

As the harvest season winds down and your garden turns from green to gold, there are still a few chores to be done. Putting the garden properly to bed can yield a substantial payoff in the form of earlier, healthier spring produce. Sowing cover crops such as alfalfa and winter rye will protect your beds from erosion and compaction of the soil and will provide nutrients when they are tilled under in the spring. A clean winter garden will be less likely to harbor pests and weeds, and soil that is cultivated, fertilized, and mulched will save you valuable time and labor when planting season comes.

Cleaning and Storing Tools and Equipment

Proper storage of garden equipment prolongs its life and can also help to protect next year's garden from disease. Tools, stakes, trellises, tags, and cages should be removed from the garden and cleaned. If any of the equipment has been used near diseased or infested plants, dip it in a disinfecting solution of 1 part bleach to 10 parts water. Wipe down the metal parts of tools with mineral oil to prevent rust, and sharpen dull blades. Drain and store hoses and irrigation systems.

Remove and store sheets of plastic mulch, or recycle them if they are damaged. Carefully check cold frames for cracks and make sure that the lids fit snugly; even a small leak can expose plants to damaging cold.

Dealing with Garden Debris

Garden debris is a favorite winter home for many harmful insects, which attach eggs, cocoons, or larvae to the stems and leaves of dried and faded plants. By cleaning out your garden beds now, you will help eliminate pest and disease problems next season.

Before the ground freezes in the fall, be sure to clear your garden of all vegetation except cover crops and overwintering or perennial plants such as asparagus, rhubarb, and rosemary; vegetables and other plants left to rot will encourage insect infestation. Weeding is especially critical at this time as well, since fall is when many perennial weeds establish deep root systems and prodigiously set seed. Be thorough in your weeding—

pull out all foliage, seed heads, stems, and roots. Any weeds left in the fall garden will return with renewed vigor the following spring.

Carefully dispose of all mature weed seed heads and any plants that show signs of disease or insect infestation. Put them in a tightly sealed bag and discard according to your local ordinances for plant debris.

If you notice signs of insects or diseases on your plants as you clear the garden, consult the Troubleshooting Guide on pages 228-235, a reputable nursery, or your local Cooperative Extension Service office for an analysis of the problem and possible solutions.

Fertilized, cultivated, and mulched in fall, these raised beds will be ready for spring planting weeks earlier than a slower-to-thaw plot at ground level would be. The two smaller beds at the rear are an ideal size for accommodating temporary cold frames that can shelter the new season's first hardy crops.

The shallots planted in this raised bed in the fall will grow until cold weather arrives. Dormant over the winter months, the plants will resume growing in the spring and produce an early harvest.

Looking Ahead to Spring

If you cultivate your beds in the fall, you can plant as soon as the soil warms up in the spring. Fall is a good time to apply fertilizers that require longer periods to break down. Ground phosphate rock, greensand, and granite dust will slowly release potassium, phosphorus, and other nutrients if lightly spaded into the soil and left over the winter. Fresh manure, applied directly to your beds at the rate of 2 to 3 bushels per 100 square feet, will rot by the time you plant the following spring.

Autumn's Gift to Spring

The scattered leaves of autumn can be a true windfall for a vegetable garden's soil. Decomposed leaves are rich in potassium and micronutrients, and they also increase the soil's capacity to retain moisture. Nature will compost the leaves for you if you simply pile them in an enclosure, but this method may take several years. To hasten the process, shred the leaves with a mulching mower or a leaf shredder and add them to your compost pile *(page 25)*. Or, if you have more leaves than the compost pile can handle, make a separate mound of shredded leaves. To prevent snow and rain from leaching nutrients, cover the mound with a sheet of black polyethylene weighted down with rocks or bricks. In the spring, you will have a supply of dark, crumbly leaf compost to use as mulch or as a soil amendment.

Winter Mulch and Cover Crops

Mulch applied to the fall garden is another way of adding organic matter to the soil. It also prevents soil erosion and protects your maturing cold-hardy vegetables. Even if you mulched heavily during the growing season, the parts of your garden that are not planted with a cover crop will benefit from a thick layer of mulch in the fall. Shredded leaves, alfalfa hay, peat, straw, and buckwheat hulls are all good choices. For perennial vegetables, berries, and herbs, apply several inches of loose, airy mulch such as straw or pine needles after the soil freezes. This will protect their roots from the damaging effects of alternate freezing and thawing.

In cool climates, crops like carrots, leeks, garlic, parsnips, salsify, and turnips can be left for winter harvest if they are covered with at least 6 inches of mulch in the fall. In areas with severe winters, cover the rows with bales of straw or at least a foot of mulch just before the first hard freeze. During winter thaws you can pull up the vegetables; just be sure to harvest all of them before the next planting season.

Growing a crop specifically to nourish and reinvigorate the soil can benefit even the smallest garden. Such cover crops, as they are known, prevent erosion, choke out weeds, and keep the soil aerated. And when tilled under, these plants act as green manure—a high-powered nutrient and a soil conditioner. Your choice of a cover crop will vary depending on the result desired for your specific garden. Deep-rooted plants such as alfalfa and clover bring up nutrients from deep in the ground to the topsoil; legumes add nitrogen to your garden; and winter rye protects against erosion and keeps down weeds.

To give your cover crop time to establish itself before winter, sow seeds directly among maturing fall vegetables or fill in bare spots. Clover, vetches, and winter peas lend themselves to interplanting with end-of-season crops. Quick-growing timothy or buckwheat can fill gaps between winter squash and pumpkin vines.

You can also reap the advantages of a cover crop throughout the growing season by planting one in the paths beside your raised beds. A low-growing variety such as Dutch white clover is especially suitable for this purpose. Clover will control weeds, lower soil temperature—which encourages root growth—and help to retain soil moisture.

Updating Your Journal

Finally, update your garden journal *(page 67)*. Make notes, record observations, and reflect on how well your garden served your needs. Were the beds spaced close enough for easy cultivation and harvesting? If not, you may want to redesign your garden plot. Did you have too many vegetables of one kind and not enough of another? Note which cultivars thrived in your garden, which didn't, and why. Record cultivation techniques and interplanting combinations that worked well. Indicate periods of unusual weather. If you spent hours watering by hand, consider installing a drip-irrigation system. If weeding overwhelmed you, next year you may want to try mulching with black plastic or solarizing the soil to kill weeds *(box, page 103)*. Record any pest or disease problems you may have had, how you solved them, and what steps need to be taken in the spring to avoid those problems. Floating row covers, beneficial insects, lures, traps, botanical insecticides, and disease- and pest-resistant cultivars can all be used as part of an organic approach to disease and pest management.

Reviewing the past growing season will give you a clearer sense of your own preferences as well as the particular needs of your garden. When you make next year's choices, you will have guidelines based on conditions prevailing in *your* plot—with its unique combination of soil, climate, cultivars, growing methods, and gardening style.

A cover crop of winter rye sown in the paths beside rows of cold-hardy cabbage in this New Jersey garden quickly covers the soil. Sown in early fall, the rye controls weeds, prevents erosion, and contributes nutrients to the soil when it is tilled under in the spring.

SOIL-IMPROVING COVER CROPS			
Common Name	**Seeding Rate (lbs./1,000 Sq. Ft.)**	**When to Sow**	**Comments**
Austrian winter pea	2-4	Early spring or early fall	Winter-hardy, nitrogen building. Provides organic matter when tilled under in the spring.
Barley	2½	Early to midfall	Extensive root system prevents erosion. Winter-hardy; provides organic matter when tilled under in the spring.
Crimson clover	1	Early spring through early fall	Good for erosion control and nitrogen building. Winter-hardy and shade tolerant; can be sown under upright vegetables such as corn.
Hairy vetch	1	Late summer to early fall	Winter-hardy, nitrogen building. Provides large amounts of organic matter when tilled under.
Ryegrass	1	Early spring to late summer	Quick growing, cold tolerant. Extensive root system loosens compacted soil, protects against erosion. Dense growth chokes out weeds. Dies back during the winter in the North. Easy to till under.
Winter rye	2½	Fall	Winter-hardy, vigorous grower in a variety of soils. Extensive root system adds organic matter to the soil. Good source of straw for mulch.

Kitchen Garden Recipes

One of the greatest rewards of kitchen gardening is having fresh ingredients on hand for delicious home-cooked meals. While many people associate "homegrown produce" with tossed salads and zucchini bread, the myriad uses for fresh-picked vegetables, fruits, and herbs are limited only by your imagination.

Are you tired of slicing tomatoes for salads? Have you run out of ideas for using fresh mint? Are you wondering what to do with that rutabaga you just harvested? Do you have more blackberries than you know what to do with? On the following pages, you'll find ideas for using all of these, and more.

The 79 tasty, low-fat recipes are presented in seven sections: Appetizers, Soups & Stews, Salads, Skillet Dishes, Baked Main Dishes, Side Dishes, and Desserts. Each recipe provides nutritional information, as well as helpful hints and estimated preparation time. Interspersed throughout are illustrated tips on preparing vegetables for cooking and eating.

Bon appétit!

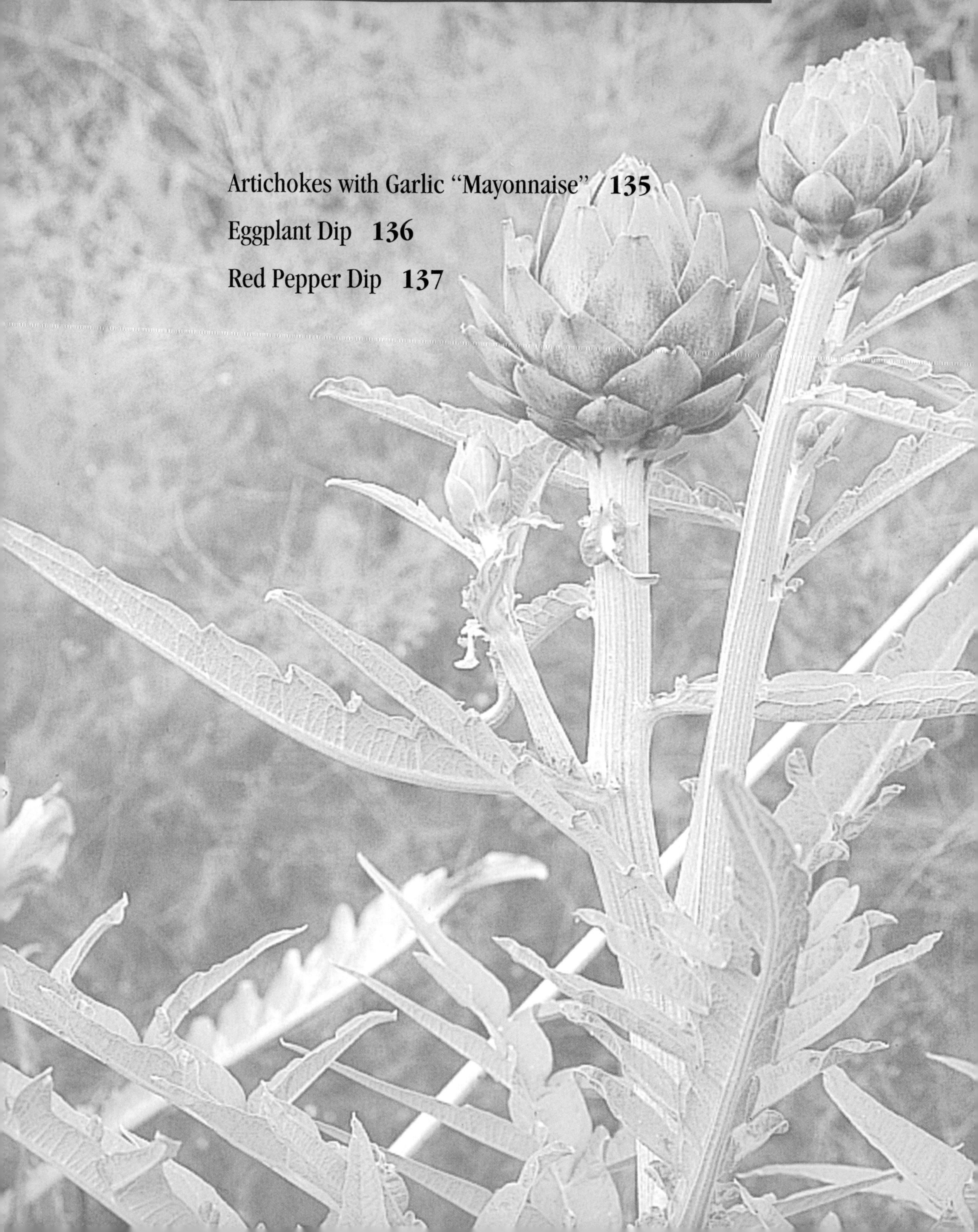

Artichokes with Garlic "Mayonnaise"

SERVES: 4
WORKING TIME: 20 MINUTES
TOTAL TIME: 45 MINUTES

1 all-purpose potato (6 ounces), peeled and thinly sliced

4 cloves garlic, peeled

¼ cup fresh lemon juice

3 tablespoons reduced-fat mayonnaise

3 tablespoons reduced-sodium chicken broth, defatted

¾ teaspoon dried rosemary

¾ teaspoon dried marjoram

½ teaspoon salt

4 large artichokes (12 ounces each)

3 tablespoons chopped fresh parsley

1. In a small pot of boiling water, cook the potato until tender, about 12 minutes. Add the garlic during the last 3 minutes of cooking. Drain. Transfer to a large bowl and mash until smooth. Add 2 tablespoons of the lemon juice, the mayonnaise, the broth, ¼ teaspoon of the rosemary, ¼ teaspoon of the marjoram, and the salt. Set aside.

2. In a large pot, combine 3½ cups of water, the remaining 2 tablespoons lemon juice, the remaining ½ teaspoon rosemary, and remaining ½ teaspoon marjoram. Bring to a boil over high heat.

3. Meanwhile, pull off the tough bottom leaves of the artichoke (see tip; top photo). With kitchen shears, snip the sharp, pointed ends from the remaining leaves (middle photo). With a paring knife, trim off the end of the stem (bottom photo). Add the artichokes to the boiling liquid, cover, and cook until the artichokes are tender, about 25 minutes. Stir the parsley into the garlic "mayonnaise" and serve with the artichokes.

Helpful hint: To eat an artichoke, pull off the outer leaves one at a time and scrape the fleshy base from each leaf by drawing it between your front teeth. When you've finished the leaves, remove the prickly "choke" from the artichoke bottom before eating it.

TIP

FAT: 3G/21%
CALORIES: 130
SATURATED FAT: 0.4G
CARBOHYDRATE: 25G
PROTEIN: 6G
CHOLESTEROL: 0MG
SODIUM: 525MG

Eggplant Dip

SERVES: 4
WORKING TIME: 15 MINUTES
TOTAL TIME: 40 MINUTES

*Similar to the Middle Eastern baba ghanouj, this smoky eggplant dip uses
just a few walnuts instead of the usual high-fat sesame paste.*

**4 slices firm-textured white
sandwich bread**

3 cloves garlic, peeled

**2 eggplants (about 1 pound each),
halved lengthwise**

**2 tablespoons coarsely chopped
walnuts**

2 tablespoons fresh lemon juice

**2 teaspoons olive oil, preferably
extra-virgin**

¾ teaspoon salt

¾ teaspoon dried oregano

¼ cup chopped fresh parsley

**2 carrots, quartered lengthwise
and cut into 2-inch-long strips**

**1 red bell pepper, cut into
2-inch-long strips**

**1 green bell pepper, cut into
2-inch-long strips**

1. Preheat the oven to 400°. Place the bread on a baking sheet and bake for
   7 minutes, or until lightly golden and crisp. Set aside.

2. Meanwhile, in a small saucepan of boiling water, cook the garlic for 2 minutes to blanch. Drain and set aside.

3. Preheat the broiler. Place the eggplant halves, cut-sides down, on the broiler
   rack and broil 6 inches from the heat for 15 minutes, or until the skins are
   charred and the eggplants are tender. Set aside to cool slightly. When cool
   enough to handle, peel the eggplants, discarding the skin.

4. Transfer the eggplants to a food processor. Add the toasts, garlic, walnuts,
   lemon juice, oil, salt, and oregano, and purée until smooth. Stir in the
   parsley. Spoon the dip into a small serving bowl and serve with the carrots
   and bell pepper strips.

*Helpful hints: Leftovers are delicious as a sandwich spread, particularly with
cooked vegetables tucked into a pita pocket. Blanching the garlic subdues the
raw taste—use this trick whenever a recipe calls for uncooked garlic.*

FAT: 7G/29%
CALORIES: 216
SATURATED FAT: 0.9G
CARBOHYDRATE: 36G
PROTEIN: 6G
CHOLESTEROL: 0MG
SODIUM: 592MG

Red Pepper Dip

SERVES: 4
WORKING TIME: 20 MINUTES
TOTAL TIME: 50 MINUTES

Garlicky and piquant with a splash of balsamic vinegar, this dip will bring your taste buds to attention. Feel free to cut back on the garlic by one or two cloves, if you like. For added body, some toasted Italian bread is puréed with the red peppers. A yellow bell pepper makes a colorful serving container, but any color pepper will work just as well.

10 thin slices diagonally cut Italian or French bread

1 tablespoon olive oil

1 large onion, halved and thinly sliced

5 cloves garlic, minced

3 red bell peppers, thinly sliced

2 tablespoons no-salt-added tomato paste

2 tablespoons balsamic or red wine vinegar

½ teaspoon salt

1 yellow bell pepper

1 green bell pepper, cut into thin strips

¾ cup cherry tomatoes

1. Preheat the oven to 400°. Place the bread on a baking sheet and bake for 7 minutes, or until lightly golden and crisp. Set aside.

2. Meanwhile, in a large nonstick skillet, heat 2 teaspoons of the oil over medium heat until hot but not smoking. Add the onion and garlic and cook, stirring frequently, until the onion is tender and golden brown, about 10 minutes.

3. Add the red peppers, cover, and cook until the peppers are very tender, about 15 minutes. Stir in the tomato paste, vinegar, salt, and remaining 1 teaspoon oil until well combined. Transfer to a food processor, add 2 slices of the toasts, and purée until smooth.

4. Slice the top off the yellow pepper, then remove and discard the seeds and ribs. Spoon the pepper dip into the yellow pepper and place on a serving platter. Serve with the remaining toasts, the green pepper, and tomatoes.

Helpful hints: The dip will keep refrigerated for up to 2 days. It's also delicious as a sandwich spread with baked ham or sliced turkey or chicken breast, and it can enliven a pasta sauce or pizza topping.

FAT: 6G/20%
CALORIES: 286
SATURATED FAT: 1.1G
CARBOHYDRATE: 50G
PROTEIN: 8G
CHOLESTEROL: 0MG
SODIUM: 699MG

Carrot and Parsnip Soup

SERVES: 4
WORKING TIME: 20 MINUTES
TOTAL TIME: 35 MINUTES

Like French onion soup, this earthy purée is partnered with cheese toasts, which are served alongside the soup rather than in it. The golden soup is a melding of potatoes, carrots, and parsnips, heightened with onion, garlic, tarragon, and orange zest. Evaporated skim milk adds creamy richness without adding any fat.

4 ounces French or Italian bread

½ cup shredded sharp Cheddar cheese (2 ounces)

2 teaspoons olive oil

1 onion, finely chopped

4 cloves garlic, minced

¾ pound all-purpose potatoes, peeled and thinly sliced

¾ pound parsnips, peeled and thinly sliced

3 carrots, thinly sliced

2 teaspoons sugar

1 teaspoon grated orange zest

¾ teaspoon dried tarragon

¼ teaspoon salt

¼ teaspoon freshly ground black pepper

2 cups reduced-sodium vegetable broth

1 cup evaporated skim milk

2 scallions, thinly sliced

1. Preheat the broiler. Slice the bread in half horizontally and place on a baking sheet. Sprinkle the Cheddar over the bread and broil until the cheese is melted, about 1 minute. Cut into 8 pieces.

2. Meanwhile, in a large saucepan, heat the oil over medium heat until hot but not smoking. Add the onion and garlic and cook, stirring, until the onion is softened, about 7 minutes. Add the potatoes, parsnips, and carrots. Sprinkle with the sugar, orange zest, tarragon, salt, and pepper, stirring to combine.

3. Add the broth and 1 cup of water to the pan and bring to a boil. Reduce to a simmer, cover, and cook until the vegetables are very tender, about 15 minutes. Transfer to a food processor and process to a smooth purée, about 1 minute. Return the soup to the saucepan, stir in the evaporated milk, and bring to a simmer. Divide the soup among 4 bowls and sprinkle the scallions on top. Serve with the cheese toasts.

Helpful hint: Instead of transferring the vegetables to a food processor, you can use a hand blender right in the pot. Run the blender in on/off pulses until the soup is a smooth purée.

FAT: 8G/19%
CALORIES: 375
SATURATED FAT: 3.6G
CARBOHYDRATE: 61G
PROTEIN: 15G
CHOLESTEROL: 17MG
SODIUM: 627MG

Irish Barley Stew

SERVES: 4

WORKING TIME: 20 MINUTES

TOTAL TIME: 35 MINUTES

There's usually lamb (or mutton) at the heart of an Irish barley stew, along with plenty of potatoes. Here, the meat is subtracted and lots more vegetables are added. Besides the potatoes, there are carrots, parsnips, turnips, green beans, and peas. This adaptation will satisfy the heartiest appetites, especially if you serve a basket of warm rolls alongside.

1 tablespoon olive oil

2 carrots, cut into 1-inch lengths

2 parsnips, peeled and cut into 1-inch lengths

2 turnips, peeled and cut into 8 wedges each

½ pound small red potatoes, quartered

⅔ cup quick-cooking barley

¾ teaspoon salt

½ teaspoon dried thyme

¼ teaspoon freshly ground black pepper

¾ pound green beans, cut into 1-inch lengths

1 cup frozen peas

1. In a large saucepan, heat the oil over medium heat until hot but not smoking. Add the carrots, parsnips, and turnips and cook, stirring frequently, until lightly browned, about 5 minutes. Add the potatoes, barley, salt, thyme, and pepper, stirring to coat. Add 3⅓ cups of water and bring to a boil. Reduce to a simmer, cover, and cook until the vegetables and barley are tender, about 10 minutes.

2. Stir the green beans into the pan, cover, and cook until the green beans are crisp-tender, about 5 minutes. Add the peas and cook, uncovered, until heated through, about 2 minutes.

Helpful hint: Quick-cooking barley, which has been precooked by steaming, is ready in less than 15 minutes, while regular pearl barley takes nearly an hour to cook.

FAT: 4G/12%

CALORIES: 299

SATURATED FAT: 0.5G

CARBOHYDRATE: 59G

PROTEIN: 9G

CHOLESTEROL: 0MG

SODIUM: 523MG

Chickpea and Spinach Soup

SERVES: 4
WORKING TIME: 20 MINUTES
TOTAL TIME: 30 MINUTES

1 tablespoon olive oil

1 onion, finely chopped

6 cloves garlic, minced

2 carrots, halved lengthwise and thinly sliced

¾ pound all-purpose potatoes, peeled and cut into ½-inch cubes

2 cups reduced-sodium vegetable broth

16-ounce can chickpeas, rinsed and drained

½ teaspoon salt

½ teaspoon grated lemon zest

¼ teaspoon freshly ground black pepper

10-ounce package fresh spinach, shredded (see tip)

1. In a large nonstick saucepan, heat the oil over medium heat until hot but not smoking. Add the onion and garlic and cook, stirring frequently, until the onion is softened, about 7 minutes. Add the carrots and cook, stirring, until the carrots are crisp-tender, about 3 minutes.

2. Add the potatoes to the pan, stirring to coat. Add the broth, 1 cup of water, the chickpeas, salt, lemon zest, and pepper, and bring to a boil. Reduce to a simmer, cover, and cook until the potatoes are firm-tender, about 7 minutes. Stir in the spinach and cook for 1 minute to wilt. Divide among 4 bowls and serve.

Helpful hint: There are three basic types of spinach. Savoy is the crinkly-leaf spinach usually sold prewashed in bags. There are also semi-Savoy (less crinkly) and smooth-leaved types. Any of the three can be used in this recipe.

TIP

The easiest way to shred spinach or other broad-leaved greens is to stack the leaves and then slice them crosswise.

FAT: 6G/23%
CALORIES: 233
SATURATED FAT: 0.6G
CARBOHYDRATE: 38G
PROTEIN: 10G
CHOLESTEROL: 0MG
SODIUM: 604MG

Cream of Broccoli Soup

SERVES: 4
WORKING TIME: 30 MINUTES
TOTAL TIME: 40 MINUTES

*With a few minor adjustments, this classic cheese-topped "cream" soup
has been transformed into healthy fare.*

---

2 teaspoons olive oil

1 onion, finely chopped

3 cloves garlic, minced

1¼ pounds broccoli

1 pound all-purpose potatoes, peeled and thinly sliced

2½ cups reduced-sodium vegetable broth

¾ teaspoon dried marjoram

½ teaspoon salt

¼ teaspoon freshly ground black pepper

1 cup evaporated skim milk

⅛ teaspoon cayenne pepper

2 tablespoons reduced-fat sour cream

2 teaspoons flour

½ cup shredded Cheddar cheese (2 ounces)

1. In a nonstick Dutch oven, heat the oil over medium heat until hot but not smoking. Add the onion and garlic and cook, stirring frequently, until the onion is softened, about 7 minutes.

2. Meanwhile, with a paring knife, separate the broccoli florets and stems; peel the stems and thinly slice them.

3. Add the potatoes to the pan, stirring well to combine. Add the broccoli stems and all but 1 cup of the broccoli florets, stirring to combine. Add the broth, 1 cup of water, the marjoram, salt, and pepper, and bring to a boil. Reduce to a simmer, cover, and cook until the potatoes and broccoli stems are tender, about 12 minutes. Meanwhile, in a small pot of boiling water, cook the reserved cup of broccoli florets for 2 minutes to blanch. Drain.

4. Transfer the vegetable mixture to a food processor and process to a smooth purée. Return the soup to the pan, stir in the evaporated milk and cayenne, and bring to a simmer. In a small bowl, stir together the sour cream and flour. Add the sour cream mixture and blanched broccoli florets to the pan and cook, stirring, until slightly thickened, about 1 minute. Divide the soup among 4 bowls, sprinkle the Cheddar on top, and serve.

Helpful hint: Adding flour to the sour cream helps keep it from curdling when added to the hot soup.

FAT: 9G/29%
CALORIES: 279
SATURATED FAT: 3.9G
CARBOHYDRATE: 37G
PROTEIN: 16G
CHOLESTEROL: 20MG
SODIUM: 636MG

Spiced Sweet Potato Soup

SERVES: 4
WORKING TIME: 30 MINUTES
TOTAL TIME: 50 MINUTES

The confetti-like garnish that tops this puréed soup consists of bell peppers, tortilla strips, and jack cheese. And despite the suave, velvety appearance of the soup itself, there's plenty of spicy excitement going on beneath the surface: The potato-rice purée is laced with jalapeño, chili sauce, and lime. Serve the soup with warmed tortillas or crisp breadsticks.

1 tablespoon olive oil

Two 6-inch corn tortillas, cut into ½-inch-wide strips

1 green bell pepper, cut into thin strips

1 red bell pepper, cut into thin strips

6 scallions, thinly sliced

1 pickled jalapeño pepper, finely chopped

1¼ pounds sweet potatoes, peeled and thinly sliced

¼ cup long-grain rice

2 cups reduced-sodium vegetable broth

¼ cup chili sauce

½ teaspoon grated lime zest

¼ cup fresh lime juice

¼ teaspoon salt

1 cup evaporated low-fat milk

½ cup shredded Monterey jack cheese (2 ounces)

1. In a large saucepan, heat the oil over medium heat until hot but not smoking. Add the tortillas and cook, turning them, until lightly crisped, about 2 minutes. With a slotted spoon, transfer the tortilla strips to paper towels.

2. Set aside ¼ cup each of the green and red bell pepper strips. Add the remaining bell pepper strips, the scallions, and jalapeño pepper to the saucepan and cook, stirring frequently, until the peppers are tender, about 5 minutes. Add the sweet potatoes and rice, stirring to combine. Add the broth, 1 cup of water, the chili sauce, lime zest, 2 tablespoons of the lime juice, and the salt, and bring to a boil. Reduce to a simmer, cover, and cook until the potatoes and rice are tender, about 17 minutes. Meanwhile, in a small pot of boiling water, cook the reserved bell pepper strips for 1 minute to blanch. Drain. When cool enough to handle, dice the peppers.

3. Transfer the soup to a food processor and process to a smooth purée. Return the soup to the pan, stir in the evaporated milk, and bring to a simmer. Stir in the remaining 2 tablespoons lime juice. Divide the soup among 4 bowls. Sprinkle with the tortilla strips, diced bell peppers, and jack cheese, and serve.

Helpful hint: Instead of transferring the vegetables to a food processor, you can use a hand blender right in the pot. Run the blender in on/off pulses until the soup is a smooth purée.

FAT: 10G/25%
CALORIES: 364
SATURATED FAT: 3.1G
CARBOHYDRATE: 58G
PROTEIN: 13G
CHOLESTEROL: 25MG
SODIUM: 728MG

Cauliflower-Cheese Soup

SERVES: 4
WORKING TIME: 25 MINUTES
TOTAL TIME: 50 MINUTES

*Take a spoonful of this rich-tasting soup and you may think it's laden with heavy cream.
Not so—the silky texture comes from the puréed potato and cauliflower, mixed with evaporated low-fat milk. The flavor has been boosted with lemon juice, cayenne pepper, and paprika.
Offer as a first course, or pair with a tossed green salad for a light lunch.*

½ **teaspoon olive oil**

1 **leek (white and light green parts only), halved lengthwise and cut into thin slices**

1 **carrot, thinly sliced**

1 **large baking potato (about 10 ounces), peeled and thinly sliced**

1 **small cauliflower, cut into florets (about 5 cups)**

2½ **cups reduced-sodium chicken broth, defatted, or reduced-sodium vegetable broth**

4 **teaspoons fresh lemon juice**

1 **teaspoon paprika, preferably sweet Hungarian**

¼ **teaspoon freshly ground black pepper**

¼ **teaspoon dry mustard**

⅛ **teaspoon cayenne pepper**

1 **cup evaporated low-fat milk**

½ **cup shredded Cheddar cheese (about 2 ounces)**

2 **tablespoons snipped fresh chives**

1. In a large saucepan, heat the oil over medium heat until hot but not smoking. Add the leek and carrot, stirring to coat. Stir in ½ cup of water and bring to a boil. Reduce to a simmer, cover, and cook until the leek is tender, about 7 minutes.

2. Add the potato and cauliflower, stirring to coat. Stir in the broth, ½ cup of water, the lemon juice, paprika, black pepper, mustard, and cayenne, and return to a boil. Reduce to a simmer, cover, and cook until the vegetables are very tender, about 25 minutes.

3. Transfer the mixture to a food processor and purée until smooth. Return the purée to the pan, stir in the evaporated milk, and bring just to a boil over medium heat.

4. Remove from the heat and stir in the cheese. Ladle the soup into 4 bowls, sprinkle the chives on top, and serve.

Helpful hint: You can prepare this soup up to 1 day ahead through Step 3 and refrigerate. Gently reheat on top of the stove or in the microwave on half power, then stir in the cheese just before serving.

FAT: 7G/28%
CALORIES: 226
SATURATED FAT: 3.1G
CARBOHYDRATE: 29G
PROTEIN: 14G
CHOLESTEROL: 25MG
SODIUM: 589MG

Greek Lemon Soup with Carrots, Leeks, and Dill

SERVES: 4

WORKING TIME: 20 MINUTES

TOTAL TIME: 45 MINUTES

This lovely starter, based on the Greek avgolemono (egg and lemon) soup, gets its body from rice instead of eggs.

---

3 cups reduced-sodium chicken broth, defatted, or reduced-sodium vegetable broth

1 teaspoon grated lemon zest

¼ cup fresh lemon juice

½ teaspoon salt

½ teaspoon ground ginger

½ teaspoon sugar

⅛ teaspoon ground nutmeg

¼ cup long-grain rice

2 carrots, halved lengthwise and cut into thin slices

1 leek (white and light green parts only), cut into fine julienne strips

½ cup snipped fresh dill

2 teaspoons cornstarch mixed with 1 tablespoon water

1. In a large saucepan, combine the broth, 2 cups of water, the lemon zest, lemon juice, salt, ginger, sugar, and nutmeg. Bring to a boil over medium heat and add the rice. Return to a boil, reduce to a simmer, cover, and cook until the rice is almost tender, about 15 minutes.

2. Stir in the carrots and leek, cover again, and simmer until the vegetables and rice are tender, about 5 minutes. Stir in the dill and cornstarch mixture, return to a boil, and cook, stirring constantly, until the soup is slightly thickened, about 1 minute longer. Ladle the soup into 4 bowls and serve.

Helpful hints: The delicate flavor of this soup is best savored as soon as it's made. If you buy dill (or any fresh herb), look for brightly colored, moist leaves or sprigs with no sign of wilting or decay. Wash the dill gently, shake off the excess water, wrap in paper towels, and refrigerate for up to 2 days.

FAT: 0G/0%

CALORIES: 110

SATURATED FAT: 0.1G

CARBOHYDRATE: 23G

PROTEIN: 5G

CHOLESTEROL: 0MG

SODIUM: 784MG

Cream of Tomato Soup

SERVES: 4

WORKING TIME: 25 MINUTES

TOTAL TIME: 40 MINUTES

1 teaspoon olive oil

4 scallions, thinly sliced

2 tablespoons flour

½ cup chopped fresh basil

¾ teaspoon salt

½ teaspoon dried oregano

½ teaspoon dried thyme

¼ teaspoon freshly ground black pepper

1½ cups reduced-sodium chicken broth, defatted, or reduced-sodium vegetable broth

1 cup evaporated low-fat milk

1½ pounds tomatoes, peeled and seeded (see tip), then finely chopped

⅓ cup no-salt-added tomato paste

2 teaspoons firmly packed light brown sugar

4 teaspoons reduced-fat sour cream

1. In a large saucepan, heat the oil over medium heat until hot but not smoking. Add the scallions and cook, stirring frequently, until the scallions are tender, about 4 minutes. Add the flour and stir well to coat. Stir in the basil, salt, oregano, thyme, and pepper. Gradually stir in the broth and evaporated milk and cook, stirring constantly, until the mixture is smooth and slightly thickened, about 5 minutes.

2. Reduce the heat to low. Stir in the tomatoes, tomato paste, and brown sugar. Cover and simmer, stirring occasionally, until the flavors have developed and the soup is thickened, about 10 minutes longer. Ladle the soup into 4 bowls, spoon the sour cream on top, and serve.

Helpful hints: Tomatoes are best stored at room temperature rather than in the refrigerator, but keep them away from direct sunlight or they may become mushy. If you don't have fresh basil on hand or can't find good-quality fresh basil, substitute chopped mint for a refreshingly different flavor.

TIP

To peel tomatoes, drop them into boiling water just until the skins begin to wrinkle, 10 to 30 seconds. Remove with a slotted spoon and, when cool enough to handle, peel them with a paring knife. To seed tomatoes, cut each in half crosswise, and scoop out the seeds with a spoon.

FAT: 4G/21%

CALORIES: 164

SATURATED FAT: 0.6G

CARBOHYDRATE: 26G

PROTEIN: 9G

CHOLESTEROL: 12MG

SODIUM: 754MG

Vegetable Soup with Pasta and Greens

SERVES: 4
WORKING TIME: 40 MINUTES
TOTAL TIME: 55 MINUTES

This garden-fresh soup is a welcome treat in any season, thanks to the year-round availability of quality produce. But keep the recipe in mind for the summer season, when basil is at peak freshness—the wonderful flavor of fresh basil makes the soup a real winner in summertime.

2 teaspoons olive oil

1 large onion, finely chopped

2 carrots, halved lengthwise and cut into thin slices

2 zucchini, halved lengthwise and cut into ¼-inch-thick slices

1 red bell pepper, diced

14½-ounce can no-salt-added stewed tomatoes, chopped with their juices

2 cups reduced-sodium chicken broth, defatted, or reduced-sodium vegetable broth

¼ cup chopped fresh basil

½ teaspoon salt

4 cups ¼-inch-wide shredded Swiss chard, spinach, or kale

½ cup ditalini pasta or small pasta shells

⅓ cup coarsely grated fresh Parmesan cheese

1. In a nonstick Dutch oven or large saucepan, heat the oil over medium heat until hot but not smoking. Add the onion and cook, stirring frequently, until the onion is softened, about 5 minutes. Add the carrots and cook, stirring frequently, until the carrots are softened, about 5 minutes.

2. Stir in the zucchini and bell pepper and cook, stirring frequently, until the pepper is tender, about 5 minutes. Add the tomatoes and their juices and cook, stirring frequently, until the liquid is slightly reduced, about 3 minutes.

3. Stir in the broth, 1½ cups of water, the basil, and salt, and bring to a boil. Stir in the Swiss chard and pasta, return to a boil, and cook until the pasta is just tender, about 10 minutes. Sprinkle the Parmesan on top and serve.

Helpful hints: For a change of pace, substitute orzo, the small rice-shaped pasta, for the ditalini. Leftovers of this soup are delicious; just add a little more broth or water when reheating, since the pasta will continue to absorb liquid as the soup sits.

FAT: 5G/24%
CALORIES: 194
SATURATED FAT: 1.7G
CARBOHYDRATE: 30G
PROTEIN: 10G
CHOLESTEROL: 6MG
SODIUM: 841MG

Root Vegetable and Apple Stew

SERVES: 4
WORKING TIME: 20 MINUTES
TOTAL TIME: 50 MINUTES

*Root vegetables are deliciously appealing in almost any culinary guise—
here, apple and nutty barley add homey goodness.*

3½ cups reduced-sodium chicken broth, defatted, or reduced-sodium vegetable broth

1 large onion, diced

3 cloves garlic, minced

⅔ cup pearl barley

2 teaspoons olive oil

1½ cups peeled rutabaga chunks (1-inch pieces)

2 carrots, halved lengthwise and cut into 2-inch-long pieces

3 turnips, cut into 1-inch-wide wedges

2 parsnips, halved lengthwise and cut into 2-inch-long pieces

2 Granny Smith apples, cored and cut into 8 wedges each

½ teaspoon dried rosemary

½ teaspoon salt

½ teaspoon freshly ground black pepper

1 tablespoon fresh lemon juice

1. In a large saucepan, combine 1 cup of the broth, 1 cup of water, the onion, and garlic. Bring to a boil and stir in the barley. Reduce to a simmer, cover, and cook until the barley is tender, about 30 minutes.

2. Meanwhile, in a nonstick Dutch oven or large pot, heat the oil over medium heat until hot but not smoking. Add the rutabaga and carrots and cook, stirring frequently, until the rutabaga is golden brown, about 5 minutes. Add the turnips and parsnips and cook, stirring frequently, until the turnips and parsnips are lightly browned, about 5 minutes.

3. Add the apples, stirring to coat. Stir in the rosemary, salt, and pepper. Add the remaining 2½ cups broth and bring to a boil. Reduce to a simmer, cover, and cook until the vegetables and apples are tender, about 15 minutes longer. Stir in the barley mixture and lemon juice. Divide the stew among 4 bowls and serve.

Helpful hint: Rutabaga is a round root vegetable with tan, green, or purple skin—color has no bearing on the quality. Select firm, unblemished rutabagas that are on the small side, because they will be sweeter than large ones. Rutabagas at the supermarket are typically waxed, so be sure to peel before cutting. If unavailable, just toss in some extra carrots, turnips, or parsnips—enough to equal 1½ cups.

FAT: 3G/1%
CALORIES: 320
SATURATED FAT: 0.5G
CARBOHYDRATE: 67G
PROTEIN: 10G
CHOLESTEROL: 0MG
SODIUM: 928MG

Hearty Cabbage Chowder

SERVES: 4
WORKING TIME: 40 MINUTES
TOTAL TIME: 1 HOUR

*Flavorfully Middle European in origin, this robust chowder is guaranteed to warm up
a chilly evening. A bit of fresh dill nicely softens the sharpness of the cider vinegar and the
sauerkraut. And a final dollop of reduced-fat sour cream adds a luxurious touch. Accompany
with a crisp green salad and, if desired, dark pumpernickel for a simple supper.*

**¾ pound baking potatoes, peeled
and cut into ½-inch cubes**

2 teaspoons olive oil

**1 large onion, halved and
thinly sliced**

3 cloves garlic, minced

2 carrots, thinly sliced

**4 cups shredded green cabbage
(about ½ head)**

**1 cup sauerkraut, rinsed
and drained**

**1 cup chopped tomatoes (fresh
or canned no-salt-added)**

**2 cups reduced-sodium chicken
broth, defatted, or reduced-
sodium vegetable broth**

1 cup snipped fresh dill

**3 tablespoons cider vinegar
or distilled white vinegar**

**½ teaspoon freshly ground
black pepper**

**3 tablespoons reduced-fat
sour cream**

1. In a large saucepan of boiling water, cook the potatoes until tender, about 10 minutes. Drain well and set aside.

2. Meanwhile, in a nonstick Dutch oven or large saucepan, heat the oil over medium heat until hot but not smoking. Add the onion and garlic and cook, stirring frequently, until the onion is softened, about 7 minutes. Stir in the carrots and cook, stirring frequently, until the carrots are tender, about 5 minutes.

3. Add the cabbage, stirring to coat. Stir in the sauerkraut and tomatoes, cover, and cook, stirring occasionally, until the cabbage is wilted, about 5 minutes. Add the potatoes, stirring to coat. Stir in the broth, 2 cups of water, ⅔ cup of the dill, the vinegar, and pepper, and bring to a boil. Reduce to a simmer, cover again, and cook until the flavors have blended, about 10 minutes.

4. Ladle the chowder into 4 bowls and sprinkle the remaining ⅓ cup dill on top. Spoon the sour cream on top and serve.

Helpful hints: This chowder can be made up to 2 days ahead through Step 3. Reheat over low heat, and add the dill and sour cream just before serving. Buy bagged sauerkraut in your supermarket refrigerator case—it has less sodium than the canned version. If you don't have fresh dill on hand, use ½ teaspoon of crushed dill seed and ½ cup of chopped parsley.

FAT: 4G/22%
CALORIES: 180
SATURATED FAT: 1.1G
CARBOHYDRATE: 32G
PROTEIN: 7G
CHOLESTEROL: 4MG
SODIUM: 506MG

Spring Vegetable Salad

SERVES: 4
WORKING TIME: 10 MINUTES
TOTAL TIME: 25 MINUTES

A favorite side dish, this deftly streamlined salad makes a hearty meatless main course when chickpeas are added for protein. In addition, sweet baby carrots, sugar snap peas, green beans, and spinach transform a simple potato salad into something quite special. The Russian dressing is made with nonfat yogurt and reduced-fat mayonnaise, and flavored with tarragon.

1½ pounds small red potatoes, quartered

½ teaspoon salt

2 cups peeled baby carrots

½ pound green beans

½ pound sugar snap peas

½ cup plain nonfat yogurt

3 tablespoons reduced-fat mayonnaise

3 tablespoons ketchup

2 tablespoons fresh lemon juice

½ teaspoon dried tarragon

19-ounce can chickpeas, rinsed and drained

10-ounce bag cleaned spinach, torn

1. In a large pot of boiling water, cook the potatoes with ¼ teaspoon of the salt until almost tender, about 10 minutes. Add the carrots and cook for 2 minutes. Add the green beans and cook for 2 minutes. Add the sugar snap peas and cook for 30 seconds. All of the vegetables should be just barely tender. Drain well.

2. Meanwhile, in a large bowl, combine the yogurt, mayonnaise, ketchup, lemon juice, tarragon, and the remaining ¼ teaspoon salt. Add the drained vegetables and chickpeas, tossing to coat with the dressing. Add the spinach, toss again, and serve.

Helpful hint: Fortunately for those who don't grow their own sugar snap peas, these delicious vegetables are becoming more widely available every year; however, if you can't get them (they do have a short season), you can substitute fresh snow peas.

FAT: 5G/12%
CALORIES: 377
SATURATED FAT: 0.6G
CARBOHYDRATE: 71G
PROTEIN: 15G
CHOLESTEROL: 1MG
SODIUM: 818MG

Caesar Salad

SERVES: 4

WORKING TIME: 15 MINUTES

TOTAL TIME: 15 MINUTES

The Italian chef Caesar Cardini devised this world-famous dish at his restaurant in Tijuana, Mexico, in the 1920s. In place of the traditional raw egg, this recipe calls for a little reduced-fat mayonnaise to add richness to the dressing. And to cut even more fat, the croutons are toasted instead of fried.

2 ounces Italian bread, cut into ½-inch cubes

3 tablespoons reduced-fat mayonnaise

2 tablespoons fresh lemon juice

2 tablespoons reduced-sodium chicken broth, defatted

1 teaspoon anchovy paste

½ teaspoon freshly ground black pepper

8 cups torn romaine lettuce

15½-ounce can red kidney beans, rinsed and drained

¼ cup grated Parmesan cheese

1. In a toaster oven or under the broiler, toast the bread cubes for about 1 minute, or until golden.

2. In a large bowl, combine the mayonnaise, lemon juice, broth, anchovy paste, and ¼ teaspoon of the pepper, whisking until smooth and blended.

3. Add the lettuce, beans, bread cubes, and Parmesan, tossing to coat thoroughly with the dressing. Sprinkle with the remaining ¼ teaspoon pepper and serve.

Helpful hint: You can make the dressing up to 12 hours in advance and store it in a covered jar. Shake or whisk the dressing again before pouring it over the salad.

FAT: 5G/23%

CALORIES: 193

SATURATED FAT: 1.5G

CARBOHYDRATE: 25G

PROTEIN: 11G

CHOLESTEROL: 5MG

SODIUM: 487MG

Three-Bean Salad with Walnuts

SERVES: 4
WORKING TIME: 15 MINUTES
TOTAL TIME: 20 MINUTES

This salad is usually served as a side dish, but since its main component is kidney beans (which are high in protein), it can make a substantial main dish, too. For variety's sake, you can mix and match the canned beans you use: One can of kidney beans and one of chickpeas, for instance, would also work well. Serve the salad with crusty rolls for a tasty meal.

2 cloves garlic, peeled

¾ pound green beans, cut into 2-inch pieces

¾ pound yellow wax beans, cut into 2-inch pieces

¾ cup plain nonfat yogurt

⅓ cup chopped fresh mint

2 tablespoons reduced-fat mayonnaise

¾ teaspoon salt

Two 16-ounce cans red kidney beans, rinsed and drained

1 cucumber, peeled, halved lengthwise, seeded, and cut into ¼-inch cubes

¼ cup chopped walnuts

16 leaves Boston, Bibb, or iceberg lettuce

1. In a large pot of boiling water, cook the garlic for 2 minutes to blanch. With a slotted spoon, remove the garlic and when cool enough to handle, chop finely.

2. Add the green beans and wax beans to the boiling water and cook until crisp-tender, about 5 minutes. Drain, rinse under cold water, and drain again.

3. In a large bowl, combine the chopped garlic, yogurt, mint, mayonnaise, and salt. Fold in the green beans, wax beans, kidney beans, cucumber, and walnuts. Divide the lettuce among 4 plates, top with the bean mixture, and serve at room temperature or chilled.

Helpful hints: The salad can be made up to 8 hours in advance; don't spoon it over the lettuce or add the walnuts until just before serving. If yellow wax beans are not available, you can substitute additional fresh green beans or frozen Italian green beans, if you like.

FAT: 8G/22%
CALORIES: 321
SATURATED FAT: 0.8G
CARBOHYDRATE: 47G
PROTEIN: 19G
CHOLESTEROL: 1MG
SODIUM: 803MG

Fresh Corn Confetti Salad with Jack Cheese

SERVES: 4
WORKING TIME: 20 MINUTES
TOTAL TIME: 20 MINUTES

Corn on the cob has an ineffable sweetness that is hard to duplicate. Here, raw kernels are sliced off the cob and tossed with colorful vegetables, cubes of jack cheese, and a tangy-sweet dressing fired up with jalapeño pepper. If you haven't discovered it already, you'll find the crunchy sweetness of raw corn to be one of the delicious pleasures of summertime.

⅓ **cup balsamic vinegar**

2 tablespoons honey

½ **teaspoon salt**

1 pickled jalapeño pepper, finely chopped

4 cups fresh corn kernels or 4 cups no-salt-added canned corn kernels, drained

2 cups cherry tomatoes, halved

2 ribs celery, thinly sliced

1 red bell pepper, cut into ½-inch squares

1 green bell pepper, cut into ½-inch cubes

1 red onion, finely chopped

¼ **cup chopped fresh parsley**

3 ounces Monterey jack cheese, cut into ¼-inch cubes

1. In a large bowl, combine the vinegar, honey, salt, and jalapeño pepper.

2. Add the corn, tomatoes, celery, bell peppers, onion, parsley, and cheese. Toss to combine, and serve at room temperature or chilled.

Helpful hints: Choose fresh ears of corn with moist green stalks and plump kernels. If you buy the corn, refrigerate it as soon as you get it home: Warmth hastens the conversion of its natural sugars to starch. Time also robs fresh corn of its sweetness, so use corn within a day or two of purchase or harvesting. If you use canned corn, be sure to get no-salt-added, which has a fresher taste and crunchier texture than regular canned corn.

FAT: 9G/28%
CALORIES: 290
SATURATED FAT: 4G
CARBOHYDRATE: 49G
PROTEIN: 12G
CHOLESTEROL: 23MG
SODIUM: 496MG

Indonesian Vegetable Salad

SERVES: 4
WORKING TIME: 20 MINUTES
TOTAL TIME: 20 MINUTES

One of Indonesia's best known dishes is "gado-gado," a salad of blanched and raw vegetables attractively arranged on a large platter. What makes it extra-special is the chilied peanut sauce that's spooned over the vegetables. Here, the oil and coconut milk have been subtracted from the sauce. Still nutty and tangy, with the bite of red pepper, it's now a far healthier dressing.

1 pound all-purpose potatoes, peeled and cut into ½-inch cubes

¾ pound green beans

¼ cup reduced-sodium soy sauce

3 tablespoons fresh lime juice

3 tablespoons smooth peanut butter

2 teaspoons firmly packed dark brown sugar

2 cloves garlic, peeled

¼ teaspoon red pepper flakes

16 Boston lettuce leaves

2 cups bean sprouts

2 tomatoes, cut into 8 wedges each

1 cucumber, peeled, halved lengthwise, seeded, and thinly sliced

2 cups juice-packed canned pineapple chunks, drained

1. In a large pot of boiling water, cook the potatoes until tender, about 7 minutes. With a slotted spoon, remove the potatoes. Add the green beans to the boiling water and cook until crisp-tender, about 4 minutes. Drain.

2. Meanwhile, in a food processor, combine the soy sauce, lime juice, peanut butter, brown sugar, garlic, red pepper flakes, and ¼ cup of water. Process to a smooth purée.

3. Line 4 plates with the lettuce leaves. Top with the bean sprouts, tomatoes, cucumber, and pineapple. Spoon the potatoes and green beans on top, drizzle the peanut sauce over the salad, and serve.

Helpful hint: To seed a cucumber, cut it in half lengthwise and use the tip of a spoon to scrape out the seeds.

FAT: 7G/20%
CALORIES: 311
SATURATED FAT. 1.1G
CARBOHYDRATE: 58G
PROTEIN: 11G
CHOLESTEROL: 0MG
SODIUM: 686MG

Mexican Salad with Salsa Vinaigrette

SERVES: 4
WORKING TIME: 15 MINUTES
TOTAL TIME: 25 MINUTES

Even with salsa's huge popularity, the idea of using it as a salad dressing may not have occurred to you. You can transform the chunky tomato-chili sauce into a pourable dressing by adding tomato-vegetable juice, lime juice, and a little olive oil. The salad features some Mexican favorites, including avocado, black beans, corn, and cilantro.

1 pound small red potatoes, halved

1½ cups peeled baby carrots

1 cup frozen corn kernels

⅔ cup mild to medium-hot prepared salsa

½ cup low-sodium tomato-vegetable juice

3 tablespoons fresh lime juice

1 tablespoon olive oil

1 yellow or red bell pepper, cut into ½-inch-wide strips

1 cup radishes, thinly sliced

19-ounce can black beans, rinsed and drained

½ cup chopped fresh cilantro or basil

¾ cup diced avocado (6 ounces)

1. In a large pot of boiling water, cook the potatoes until firm-tender, about 10 minutes. Add the carrots and cook until the potatoes and carrots are tender, about 4 minutes. Add the corn and drain well.

2. Meanwhile, in a large bowl, combine the salsa, tomato-vegetable juice, lime juice, and oil. Add the potatoes, carrots, corn, bell pepper, radishes, black beans, and cilantro, tossing well to combine. Serve at room temperature or chill for up to 8 hours. To serve, divide the salad among 4 plates and sprinkle the avocado on top.

Helpful hint: Prewashed peeled baby carrots, a wonderful convenience item, are sold in bags in most supermarkets. You can substitute thin regular carrots cut into 2-inch lengths, if you like.

FAT: 11G/28%
CALORIES: 354
SATURATED FAT: 1.6G
CARBOHYDRATE: 56G
PROTEIN: 10G
CHOLESTEROL: 0MG
SODIUM: 464MG

Potato, Leek, and Asparagus Salad

SERVES: 4
WORKING TIME: 15 MINUTES
TOTAL TIME: 25 MINUTES

1½ **pounds red potatoes, cut into 1-inch chunks**

¾ **teaspoon salt**

1¼ **pounds asparagus, trimmed and cut on the diagonal into 1-inch lengths**

3 **leeks, halved lengthwise and cut into 1-inch pieces (see tip)**

⅔ **cup reduced-sodium vegetable broth**

2 **tablespoons red wine vinegar**

1 **tablespoon Dijon mustard**

1 **tablespoon extra-virgin olive oil**

¼ **cup snipped fresh dill**

½ **pound mushrooms, thinly sliced**

½ **cup crumbled feta cheese (2 ounces)**

1. In a large pot of boiling water, cook the potatoes with ¼ teaspoon of the salt until tender, about 10 minutes. Add the asparagus and leeks during the last 2 minutes of cooking time. Drain well.

2. In a large bowl, combine the broth, vinegar, mustard, oil, and the remaining ½ teaspoon salt. Stir in the dill. Add the potatoes, asparagus, leeks, and mushrooms, tossing gently to coat. Spoon onto 4 plates, sprinkle with the feta, and serve at room temperature.

Helpful hint: If you don't grow leeks or can't get them, you can make this salad with 12 scallions, blanched for just 30 seconds and cut into 1-inch lengths.

TIP

When a recipe calls for leeks to be sliced, first trim the root end and the dark green leaves, then cut the leeks as directed. Place the cut leeks in a bowl of tepid water, let them sit for 1 to 2 minutes, then lift the leeks out of the water, leaving any dirt and grit behind in the bowl. This is easier and faster than splitting and washing whole leeks before slicing them.

FAT: 8G/24%
CALORIES: 306
SATURATED FAT: 2.7G
CARBOHYDRATE: 51G
PROTEIN: 11G
CHOLESTEROL: 13MG
SODIUM: 672MG

Pear, Watercress, and Lentil Salad

SERVES: 4
WORKING TIME: 15 MINUTES
TOTAL TIME: 50 MINUTES

A year-round delight, this lovely salad, with its pears, lentils, watercress, and goat cheese, poses sweet against earthy, tart against savory. In the dressing, pear nectar intensifies the fruit flavor and also replaces some of the oil. It's a perfect dish for both casual meals and entertaining. A loaf of French bread would be a fitting accompaniment.

1 cup reduced-sodium vegetable broth

1½ cups lentils, rinsed and picked over

2 carrots, halved lengthwise and thinly sliced

½ teaspoon salt

½ teaspoon dried tarragon

¼ teaspoon freshly ground black pepper

½ cup pear nectar

¼ cup fresh lime juice

1 tablespoon olive oil

1 tablespoon Dijon mustard

1 tablespoon mango chutney

½ cup diced red bell pepper

4 Bartlett or Bosc pears, peeled, cored, and thinly sliced

1 bunch of watercress, tough stems removed

1 cup crumbled goat cheese or feta cheese (4 ounces)

2 tablespoons coarsely chopped pecans

1. In a medium saucepan, bring the broth and 2 cups of water to a boil over medium heat. Add the lentils, carrots, salt, tarragon, and black pepper. Reduce to a simmer, cover, and cook until the lentils are firm-tender, about 25 minutes.

2. In a medium bowl, combine the pear nectar, lime juice, oil, mustard, and chutney. Add the lentil mixture, bell pepper, and pears, tossing until well coated.

3. Place the watercress on 4 plates, spoon the lentil mixture on top, sprinkle with the goat cheese and pecans, and serve.

Helpful hint: The salad can be prepared ahead of time through Step 2 and refrigerated for up to 8 hours.

FAT: 16G/25%
CALORIES: 568
SATURATED FAT: 6.6G
CARBOHYDRATE: 84G
PROTEIN: 29G
CHOLESTEROL: 22MG
SODIUM: 660MG

Italian Bread and Vegetable Salad

SERVES: 4
WORKING TIME: 30 MINUTES
TOTAL TIME: 40 MINUTES PLUS CHILLING TIME

The Tuscan dish panzanella—a rustic salad of bread, tomatoes, onions, and herbs— originated as a use for leftover bread. Here, a fresh loaf is used and the bread is toasted under the broiler. This recipe uses an oil-free dressing based on puréed peppers; be sure to let the salad stand for at least an hour to allow the bread and vegetables to absorb the dressing.

7 ounces Italian bread, halved lengthwise

2 cloves garlic, peeled and halved

5 bell peppers, mixed colors, halved lengthwise and seeded

1 tablespoon olive oil

2 yellow summer squash, halved lengthwise and cut into 1-inch pieces

2 zucchini, halved lengthwise and cut into 1-inch pieces

¾ teaspoon salt

⅓ cup red wine vinegar

½ cup reduced-sodium vegetable broth

2 tablespoons no-salt-added tomato paste

⅓ cup chopped fresh basil

3 ounces part-skim mozzarella cheese, cut into ½-inch cubes

1. Preheat the broiler. Broil the bread 6 inches from the heat until golden brown, about 30 seconds per side. When cool enough to handle, rub the toasted bread with the garlic. Cut the bread into 1-inch cubes, and transfer to a large bowl.

2. Place the bell pepper halves, cut-sides down, on the broiler rack. Broil the peppers 4 inches from the heat for 12 minutes, or until the skin is blackened. When the peppers are cool enough to handle, peel them and cut into 1-inch squares.

3. Meanwhile, in a large nonstick skillet, heat the oil over medium heat until hot but not smoking. Add the yellow squash, zucchini, and ¼ teaspoon of the salt, and cook, stirring frequently, until crisp-tender, about 7 minutes. Transfer to the bowl with the bread, tossing to combine.

4. Place ½ cup of the cut-up peppers in a food processor along with the vinegar, broth, tomato paste, and the remaining ½ teaspoon salt, and process until smooth. Add the pepper purée to the bowl, along with the remaining cut-up peppers, the basil, and mozzarella, tossing to combine. Refrigerate for 1 to 4 hours before dividing among 4 plates and serving.

Helpful hint: Either white or whole-wheat Italian bread is fine for this recipe.

FAT: 9G/28%
CALORIES: 289
SATURATED FAT: 3.1G
CARBOHYDRATE: 41G
PROTEIN: 13G
CHOLESTEROL: 12MG
SODIUM: 803MG

Pasta and Vegetable Salad with Pesto

SERVES: 4
WORKING TIME: 25 MINUTES
TOTAL TIME: 35 MINUTES

Pesto is one of those wonderful culinary creations that brings delectable flavor to all kinds of dishes—but it can harbor fat. The slimmed-down pesto in this recipe uses just a small amount of walnuts, and substitutes nonfat yogurt and reduced-fat mayonnaise for the usual olive oil. Served alone or with crusty bread, this salad makes a great lunch or light supper.

3 cloves garlic, peeled

8 ounces medium pasta shells

½ pound green beans, cut into 1-inch pieces

2 carrots, cut into 1-inch-long julienne strips

1 yellow summer squash, halved lengthwise and cut into thin slices

1 cup fresh basil leaves

½ cup plain nonfat yogurt

¼ cup grated Parmesan cheese

3 tablespoons reduced-fat mayonnaise

2 tablespoons coarsely chopped walnuts

½ teaspoon salt

1. In a large pot of boiling water, cook the garlic for 3 minutes to blanch. Reserve the boiling water for the pasta and, with a slotted spoon, transfer the garlic to a food processor and set aside.

2. Cook the pasta in the reserved boiling water for 7 minutes. Add the green beans and carrots and cook until the pasta is just tender and the beans and carrots are crisp-tender, about 3 minutes longer. Drain, rinse under cold water, and drain again. Transfer to a large bowl along with the squash.

3. Add the basil, yogurt, Parmesan, mayonnaise, walnuts, and salt to the garlic in the food processor and purée until smooth. Pour the dressing over the pasta mixture and toss to combine. Divide the salad among 4 plates and serve.

Helpful hints: This salad is equally good served at room temperature or chilled. The dressing can be made up to 2 days ahead, and then mixed with the salad just before serving. Sugar snap peas or snow peas can be substituted for the green beans, and fusilli or penne for the pasta shells.

FAT: 7G/19%
CALORIES: 357
SATURATED FAT: 1.7G
CARBOHYDRATE: 60G
PROTEIN: 14G
CHOLESTEROL: 5MG
SODIUM: 501MG

Winter Squash and Broccoli Salad

SERVES: 4
WORKING TIME: 20 MINUTES
TOTAL TIME: 30 MINUTES

Vegetable salads don't get much chunkier than this, and the combination of green broccoli, red cherry tomatoes, and orange squash provides ample color appeal as well. Both the butternut squash and the pinto beans are distinctive enough to stand up to the big flavor of the dressing—a bouncy mix of chilies, cilantro, fresh lime juice, and honey. Serve the salad with sesame breadsticks.

4 cups peeled, cut butternut squash (2 x 1-inch strips)

4 cups broccoli florets

2 cups cherry tomatoes, halved

19-ounce can pinto beans, rinsed and drained

6 tablespoons shredded Monterey jack cheese

4-ounce can chopped mild green chilies

⅓ cup chopped fresh cilantro

¼ cup fresh lime juice

2 teaspoons olive oil

½ teaspoon honey

¼ teaspoon salt

3 scallions, thinly sliced

1. In a large pot of boiling water, cook the squash for 2 minutes. Add the broccoli and cook until the squash and broccoli are crisp-tender, about 3 minutes longer. Drain, rinse under cold water, and drain again. Transfer to a large bowl along with the tomatoes, beans, and cheese.

2. In a food processor, combine the chilies, cilantro, lime juice, oil, honey, and salt, and purée until smooth. Pour the dressing over the squash mixture, add the scallions, and toss to combine. Divide the salad among 4 plates and serve.

Helpful hints: Choose a butternut squash free of cracks and bruises that feels heavy for its size—a small squash weighing 2 pounds or so will be more than enough. The squash and broccoli can be prepared up to 1 day ahead and refrigerated, as can the dressing. Other beans, such as chickpeas or red kidney beans, would also be good in this recipe.

FAT: 7G/23%
CALORIES: 265
SATURATED FAT: 2.3G
CARBOHYDRATE: 43G
PROTEIN: 14G
CHOLESTEROL: 11MG
SODIUM: 626MG

Vegetable Chef's Salad

SERVES: 4
WORKING TIME: 25 MINUTES
TOTAL TIME: 45 MINUTES

This edible palette consists of vegetables arranged in individual groupings on a bed of spinach. The dressing is a delicious blend of roasted red peppers, chicken broth, seasonings, and just a bit of extra-virgin olive oil—extra-virgin oil is preferable because of the stronger flavor, especially when the amount is restrained.

1¼ pounds small red potatoes, halved if large

1 pound asparagus, tough ends trimmed, cut into 2-inch pieces

2 red bell peppers, halved and seeded

⅓ cup reduced-sodium chicken broth, defatted, or reduced-sodium vegetable broth

3 tablespoons balsamic vinegar

2 teaspoons Dijon mustard

2 teaspoons extra-virgin olive oil

½ teaspoon salt

8 cups spinach leaves

4-ounce jar artichoke hearts, rinsed and drained

2 ounces Cheddar cheese, cut into 2-inch julienne strips

1. In a large pot of boiling water, cook the potatoes until tender, about 20 minutes. Reserve the boiling water for the asparagus and, with a slotted spoon, transfer the potatoes to a colander. Drain, rinse under cold water, and drain again. Transfer to a plate and set aside. Cook the asparagus in the reserved boiling water until crisp-tender, about 3 minutes (timing will vary depending on the thickness of the stalks). Drain, rinse under cold water, and drain again. Set aside.

2. Meanwhile, preheat the broiler. Place the pepper halves, cut-sides down, on the broiler rack and broil 6 inches from the heat for 10 minutes, or until the skin is charred. Transfer the peppers to a small bowl, cover with plastic wrap, and let stand for 5 minutes. Transfer the peppers to a cutting board, remove the skin, and cut into 1-inch-wide strips.

3. In a food processor or blender, combine ¼ cup of the pepper strips, the broth, vinegar, mustard, oil, and salt, and purée until smooth.

4. Cover 4 serving plates with the spinach. Arrange the potatoes, asparagus, remaining pepper strips, the artichokes, and cheese in separate groups on top. Drizzle the dressing over the salad and serve.

Helpful hints: All the vegetables can be prepared up to 1 day ahead and chilled separately. Bring to room temperature before serving. When using jarred artichoke hearts, be sure to rinse off the oil first.

FAT: 8G/28%
CALORIES: 251
SATURATED FAT: 3.4G
CARBOHYDRATE: 36G
PROTEIN: 12G
CHOLESTEROL: 15MG
SODIUM: 577MG

Greek Salad with White Beans

SERVES: 4
WORKING TIME: 30 MINUTES
TOTAL TIME: 30 MINUTES

Crumbly, slightly salty feta cheese, white beans, bell peppers, and juicy tomatoes—these are the refreshing components of this Greek salad. The dressing is a lively blend of fresh lemon juice, olive oil, and dill, with a pinch of cayenne pepper for some heat.

¼ **cup fresh lemon juice**

3 **tablespoons chopped fresh dill**

2 **teaspoons olive oil**

½ **teaspoon dried oregano**

¼ **teaspoon salt**

⅛ **teaspoon cayenne pepper**

2 **green bell peppers, cut into 1-inch squares**

2 **cucumbers, peeled, halved lengthwise, seeded, and cut into ½-inch-thick slices**

1 **pound tomatoes, diced**

19-**ounce can white kidney beans (cannellini), rinsed and drained**

6 **scallions, thinly sliced**

6 **cups torn romaine lettuce leaves**

2½ **ounces crumbled feta cheese**

1. In a large bowl, whisk together the lemon juice, dill, oil, oregano, salt, and cayenne. Add the bell peppers, cucumbers, tomatoes, beans, and scallions, and toss to combine.

2. Cover 4 serving plates with the lettuce. Spoon the vegetable mixture over the lettuce, sprinkle the cheese on top, and serve.

Helpful hint: Escarole leaves or even iceberg lettuce leaves can be used in place of the romaine.

FAT: 7G/29%
CALORIES: 232
SATURATED FAT: 3.1G
CARBOHYDRATE: 35G
PROTEIN: 12G
CHOLESTEROL: 16MG
SODIUM: 580MG

Green Bean Salad

SERVES: 4

WORKING TIME: 15 MINUTES

TOTAL TIME: 20 MINUTES

These delicious green beans, enlivened with dill and lemon juice, are tossed with sliced water chestnuts for a bit of crunch. The dressing is a flavorful mix of broth, lemon juice, and Dijon mustard—but not a bit of oil. This is an ideal dish for entertaining, since it looks pretty on a buffet table and will hold up at room temperature.

1¼ pounds green beans

¼ cup reduced-sodium chicken broth, defatted, or reduced-sodium vegetable broth

2 tablespoons fresh lemon juice

1 tablespoon Dijon mustard

¼ teaspoon salt

⅛ teaspoon freshly ground black pepper

1 small red onion, finely chopped

½ cup canned sliced water chestnuts, well drained

⅓ cup snipped fresh dill

1. In a large pot of boiling water, cook the green beans until crisp-tender, about 4 minutes. (The time will vary depending on the age of the beans.) Drain, rinse under cold water, and drain again.

2. In a large serving bowl, whisk together the broth, lemon juice, mustard, salt, and pepper. Add the green beans, onion, water chestnuts, and dill, toss well to combine, and serve.

Helpful hints: This salad is equally good served at room temperature or chilled. If you do decide to serve it chilled, some of the bright green color of the beans will fade, but don't worry—the taste won't.

FAT: 0.2G/3%

CALORIES: 76

SATURATED FAT: 0G

CARBOHYDRATE: 17G

PROTEIN: 4G

CHOLESTEROL: 0MG

SODIUM: 282MG

Red Cabbage Slaw

SERVES: 4
WORKING TIME: 20 MINUTES
TOTAL TIME: 20 MINUTES PLUS CHILLING TIME

⅔ **cup plain nonfat yogurt**

⅓ **cup cider vinegar**

3 **tablespoons reduced-fat mayonnaise**

1½ **teaspoons sugar**

¾ **teaspoon salt**

¼ **teaspoon celery seed**

6 **cups shredded red cabbage (see tip)**

4 **carrots, shredded (see tip)**

3 **scallions, cut into 3-inch julienne strips**

2 **Granny Smith apples, cored, quartered, and cut into thin slices**

¼ **cup snipped fresh dill**

1. In a large serving bowl, whisk together the yogurt, vinegar, mayonnaise, sugar, salt, and celery seed.

2. Add the cabbage, carrots, scallions, apples, and dill, and toss well to combine. Cover with plastic wrap and refrigerate until well chilled, about 1 hour.

Helpful hints: You can prepare this cole slaw up to 1 day ahead. Green cabbage will work just as well as the red, but with less vivid color. You will need about 1 pound of cabbage (1 medium head) to make the slaw.

TIP

You can use a food processor for shredding the vegetables, but it's often easier to use a hand grater—and there will be less to clean up. Quarter the cabbage, and then run each quarter across the coarse holes of the grater. Peel and then shred the carrots.

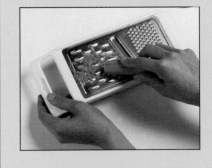

FAT: 3G/17%
CALORIES: 163
SATURATED FAT: 0.5G
CARBOHYDRATE: 33G
PROTEIN: 5G
CHOLESTEROL: 1MG
SODIUM: 571MG

Cucumber Salad

SERVES: 4
WORKING TIME: 30 MINUTES
TOTAL TIME: 30 MINUTES PLUS CHILLING TIME

This is a version of tzatziki, the yogurty cucumber salad that's a standard in Greece. Nonfat yogurt is used instead of the full-fat variety, and a little reduced-fat sour cream adds some richness while softening the flavor. Strongly accented with lime and mint, this salad can hold its own with spicy entrées of all sorts. It's also great served as a snack with crusty bread.

½ **cup plain nonfat yogurt**

2 **tablespoons reduced-fat sour cream**

½ **teaspoon grated lime zest**

1 **tablespoon fresh lime juice**

½ **teaspoon salt**

¼ **teaspoon freshly ground black pepper**

2½ **pounds cucumbers (about 5), peeled and thinly sliced**

½ **cup julienne-cut radishes**

½ **cup thinly sliced scallions**

3 **tablespoons chopped fresh mint**

1. In a large serving bowl, whisk together the yogurt, sour cream, lime zest, lime juice, salt, and pepper.

2. Add the cucumbers, radishes, scallions, and mint, and toss gently to combine. Cover with plastic wrap and refrigerate until well chilled, about 1 hour.

Helpful hints: This salad can be made and chilled up to 8 hours in advance, but no longer—further chilling may result in a watery mixture as the cucumbers release their moisture. If fresh mint is unavailable, substitute chopped fresh parsley—not the same flavor but refreshing nonetheless.

FAT: 1G/18%
CALORIES: 70
SATURATED FAT: 0.5G
CARBOHYDRATE: 12G
PROTEIN: 4G
CHOLESTEROL: 3MG
SODIUM: 319MG

Garden-Fresh Potato Salad

SERVES: 4
WORKING TIME: 25 MINUTES
TOTAL TIME: 40 MINUTES

Lots of crunchy, sliced and diced vegetables show up in this version of an American favorite. For healthful eating, the dressing has been lightened up: Nonfat yogurt and reduced-fat mayonnaise add the expected creaminess but little extra fat. For a nice presentation, line the serving bowl with crisp lettuce leaves and garnish with paprika.

1½ pounds small red potatoes, quartered

2 carrots, halved lengthwise and cut into thin slices

¼ cup distilled white vinegar

1 tablespoon Dijon mustard

¾ teaspoon salt

½ teaspoon freshly ground black pepper

6 radishes, thinly sliced

4 scallions, thinly sliced

1 red bell pepper, diced

1 rib celery, thinly sliced

¾ cup plain nonfat yogurt

2 tablespoons reduced-fat mayonnaise

1. In a large pot of boiling water, cook the potatoes for 18 minutes. Add the carrots and cook until the potatoes and carrots are tender, about 2 minutes longer. Drain well.

2. Meanwhile, in a large serving bowl, whisk together the vinegar, mustard, salt, and black pepper. Add the warm potatoes and carrots, and toss well to coat.

3. Add the radishes, scallions, bell pepper, and celery, and toss to combine. Add the yogurt and mayonnaise, stir gently to combine, and serve.

Helpful hint: Dress the salad while the potatoes are still warm so they will absorb more of the flavor as they cool.

FAT: 2G/8%
CALORIES: 215
SATURATED FAT: 0.3G
CARBOHYDRATE: 43G
PROTEIN: 7G
CHOLESTEROL: 1MG
SODIUM: 633MG

Ratatouille Stir-Fry with Goat Cheese

SERVES: 4
WORKING TIME: 30 MINUTES
TOTAL TIME: 30 MINUTES

6 ounces orzo pasta

1 tablespoon olive oil

1 red onion, coarsely diced

4 cloves garlic, finely chopped

1 red bell pepper, cut into thin strips

1 zucchini, cut into 2 x ½-inch strips

1 yellow summer squash, cut into 2 x ½-inch strips

1 small eggplant, cut into 2 x ½-inch strips (see tip)

5½-ounce can low-sodium tomato-vegetable juice

1½ cups cherry tomatoes, halved

2 teaspoons capers, rinsed and drained

¾ teaspoon dried tarragon

¾ teaspoon salt

¼ cup chopped fresh basil

3 ounces goat cheese or feta cheese, crumbled

1. In a large pot of boiling water, cook the pasta until just tender. Drain well.

2. Meanwhile, in a large nonstick skillet or wok, heat the oil over medium heat until hot but not smoking. Add the onion and garlic, and stir-fry until the onion is slightly softened, about 2 minutes. Add the bell pepper, zucchini, and yellow squash, and stir-fry until crisp-tender, about 4 minutes.

3. Add the eggplant and stir-fry until lightly browned, about 4 minutes. Add the tomato-vegetable juice, tomatoes, capers, tarragon, and salt, and cook until the tomatoes are softened, about 4 minutes. Stir in the basil. Divide the orzo among 4 plates. Spoon the vegetables over the orzo, sprinkle the cheese on top, and serve.

Helpful hint: If you can't get low-sodium tomato-vegetable juice, use regular tomato-vegetable juice and reduce the salt in the recipe to ½ teaspoon.

TIP

To cut an eggplant into strips, first cut it crosswise into ½-inch-thick slices. Stack several slices, and then cut through the stack to create ½-inch-wide strips.

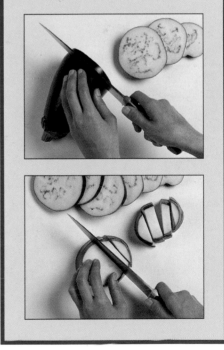

FAT: 11G/29%
CALORIES: 347
SATURATED FAT: 5G
CARBOHYDRATE: 51G
PROTEIN: 14G
CHOLESTEROL: 17MG
SODIUM: 606MG

Vegetable Chow Mein

SERVES: 4
WORKING TIME: 30 MINUTES
TOTAL TIME: 30 MINUTES

Although "chow mein" is an authentic Cantonese dish, it has been in this country for so long (probably since the early 1850s) that it has nearly achieved traditional American cuisine status. Basically a noodle stir-fry, it can include all manner of ingredients; this is a light, meatless version made with fettuccine in place of the usual fresh Chinese egg noodles.

8 ounces fettuccine

1 tablespoon dark Oriental sesame oil

6 scallions, thinly sliced

4 cloves garlic, finely chopped

2 tablespoons finely chopped fresh ginger

1 red bell pepper, cut into thin strips

1 green bell pepper, cut into thin strips

2 ribs celery, cut into ¼-inch slices

½ pound button mushrooms, halved

¼ teaspoon salt

2 teaspoons cornstarch

¾ cup reduced-sodium chicken broth, defatted

3 tablespoons reduced-sodium soy sauce

2 tablespoons dry sherry

1 tablespoon fresh lemon juice

1. In a large pot of boiling water, cook the fettuccine until just tender. Drain well.

2. Meanwhile, in a large nonstick skillet or wok, heat 2 teaspoons of the sesame oil over medium heat until hot but not smoking. Add the scallions, garlic, and ginger, and stir-fry until the scallions are crisp-tender, about 1 minute. Add the bell peppers, celery, and mushrooms, and stir-fry until the bell peppers and celery are crisp-tender, about 4 minutes. Add the pasta to the skillet and stir-fry until lightly crisped, about 1 minute.

3. In a small bowl, combine the salt, cornstarch, broth, soy sauce, sherry, lemon juice, and the remaining 1 teaspoon oil. Pour the mixture into the skillet and cook, stirring, until slightly thickened, about 1 minute.

Helpful hint: You can cut up the bell peppers and celery a few hours ahead of time; combine them in a sealable bag or a covered bowl and refrigerate until needed.

FAT: 6G/17%
CALORIES: 313
SATURATED FAT: 1G
CARBOHYDRATE: 52G
PROTEIN: 12G
CHOLESTEROL: 54MG
SODIUM: 744MG

Indian Spiced Sweet Potatoes and Cauliflower

SERVES: 4
WORKING TIME: 20 MINUTES
TOTAL TIME: 40 MINUTES

It's impossible to discuss Indian cuisine without including the infinite variety of meatless dishes. In a country with millions of vegetarians, meatless cooking is in its glory. Here, vegetables are simmered in a sweet-tart curry sauce. The curry powder is amplified with additional spices—ginger, fennel seeds, coriander, allspice, and pepper—for superb flavor.

1 cup basmati or long-grain rice

¾ teaspoon salt

2 teaspoons olive oil

2 onions, coarsely chopped

3 cloves garlic, minced

3 carrots, cut on the diagonal into ½-inch slices

1½ pounds sweet potatoes, peeled and cut into ½-inch cubes

14½-ounce can no-salt-added stewed tomatoes

1 teaspoon curry powder

1 teaspoon ground ginger

½ teaspoon fennel seeds, crushed

½ teaspoon ground coriander

¼ teaspoon ground allspice

⅛ teaspoon cayenne pepper

4 cups cauliflower florets

⅓ cup orange marmalade

1 tablespoon white wine vinegar

½ cup reduced-fat sour cream

1. In a medium saucepan, bring 2¼ cups of water to a boil. Add the rice and ¼ teaspoon of the salt, reduce to a simmer, cover, and cook until the rice is tender, about 17 minutes.

2. Meanwhile, in a large nonstick skillet, heat the oil over medium heat until hot but not smoking. Add the onions, garlic, and carrots and cook, stirring occasionally, until the onions begin to soften, about 4 minutes. Stir in the sweet potatoes, tomatoes, curry powder, ginger, fennel seeds, coriander, allspice, and cayenne. Reduce the heat to low, cover, and cook until the carrots and sweet potatoes are almost tender, about 12 minutes.

3. Add the cauliflower, marmalade, vinegar, and the remaining ½ teaspoon salt to the pan, stirring to combine. Cover and simmer until the cauliflower is tender, about 7 minutes. Divide the rice among 4 plates and spoon the vegetable mixture on top. Top with a dollop of the sour cream and serve.

Helpful hint: Fennel seeds are usually sold whole. Crush them using a mortar and pestle, or place the seeds in a plastic bag and crush them with a rolling pin.

FAT: 8G/14%
CALORIES: 533
SATURATED FAT: 2.5G
CARBOHYDRATE: 111G
PROTEIN: 14G
CHOLESTEROL: 10MG
SODIUM: 534MG

Spicy Vegetable Fried Rice

SERVES: 4
WORKING TIME: 25 MINUTES
TOTAL TIME: 40 MINUTES

Turning fried rice into a main dish is as easy as adding vegetables and tofu. This is an eggless fried rice (the tofu takes over as the protein source) laced with the flavors of fresh ginger and chilies. Unlike eggs and meat, tofu doesn't need to be cooked, so it's simply stirred into the rice until heated through and well coated with sauce.

1 cup basmati or long-grain rice

¼ teaspoon salt

1 tablespoon olive oil

1 red bell pepper, cut into thin strips

3 cups small broccoli florets

4 scallions, cut on the diagonal into ½-inch pieces

2 cloves garlic, minced

1 tablespoon grated fresh ginger

1 cup slivered snow peas

3 tablespoons reduced-sodium soy sauce

2 tablespoons chili sauce

1 tablespoon Worcestershire sauce

1 tablespoon white wine vinegar

½ teaspoon hot pepper sauce

4 ounces firm, low-fat tofu, cut into ½-inch cubes

1. In a medium saucepan, bring 2¼ cups of water to a boil. Add the rice and salt, reduce to a simmer, cover, and cook until the rice is tender, about 17 minutes.

2. In a large nonstick skillet, heat the oil over medium heat until hot but not smoking. Add the bell pepper and broccoli, cover, and cook, stirring occasionally, until the broccoli is crisp-tender, about 5 minutes. Add the scallions, garlic, and ginger, and cook, stirring, until fragrant, about 2 minutes.

3. Add the snow peas, soy sauce, chili sauce, Worcestershire sauce, vinegar, hot pepper sauce, and cooked rice to the pan, stirring to coat evenly with the sauce. Add the tofu and cook, stirring, until heated through, about 2 minutes.

Helpful hint: Another fragrant long-grain rice, such as Texmati, can be used instead of the basmati rice, which is relatively expensive.

FAT: 5G/16%
CALORIES: 275
SATURATED FAT: 0.5G
CARBOHYDRATE: 52G
PROTEIN: 13G
CHOLESTEROL: 0MG
SODIUM: 829MG

Stir-Fried Eggplant with Garlic and Cheese

SERVES: 4
WORKING TIME: 30 MINUTES
TOTAL TIME: 40 MINUTES

Rich melted cheese can transform the simplest dish into something special—but overdoing it can transform a healthy dish into one that's high in fat. However, if the recipe includes intensely flavored ingredients, such as the leeks, garlic, and rosemary used here, a moderate amount of cheese becomes an adept finishing touch rather than the main attraction.

1 pound all-purpose potatoes, peeled and cut into ½-inch chunks

1 tablespoon olive oil

1 medium eggplant, cut into ½-inch chunks

2 leeks, halved lengthwise and cut into ½-inch slices, or 4 scallions, cut into ½-inch slices

5 cloves garlic, finely chopped

1 cup reduced-sodium chicken broth, defatted

¾ teaspoon salt

½ teaspoon dried rosemary

¼ teaspoon freshly ground black pepper

½ pound green beans, cut into 1-inch lengths

1 cup evaporated skim milk

2 teaspoons flour

½ cup shredded Swiss cheese (2 ounces)

1. In a medium pot of boiling water, cook the potatoes until firm-tender, about 10 minutes. Drain.

2. In a large nonstick skillet or wok, heat the oil over medium heat until hot but not smoking. Add the eggplant and stir-fry until lightly browned, about 3 minutes. Add the leeks, garlic, and ⅓ cup of the broth, and cook, stirring frequently, until the leeks are softened, about 4 minutes. Add the potatoes, salt, rosemary, and pepper, and cook, stirring, until the leeks are tender, about 3 minutes.

3. Add the green beans to the pan and cook, stirring, until crisp-tender, about 4 minutes. In a medium bowl, whisk together the evaporated milk, the remaining ⅔ cup broth, and the flour. Add to the skillet and cook, stirring, until slightly thickened, about 2 minutes. Add the cheese and cook, stirring, until melted, about 1 minute. Divide among 4 plates and serve.

Helpful hint: A leek's many layers trap sand and dirt, and it's tricky to get a whole or split leek really clean. When a recipe calls for sliced leeks, it's easier to wash the vegetable in a bowl of water after cutting it up.

FAT: 8G/24%
CALORIES: 301
SATURATED FAT: 3.1G
CARBOHYDRATE: 46G
PROTEIN: 15G
CHOLESTEROL: 16MG
SODIUM: 709MG

Winter Vegetable Stir-Fry with Beans

SERVES: 4
WORKING TIME: 35 MINUTES
TOTAL TIME: 35 MINUTES

A creamy sauce melds the flavors of this unusual dish. It's just the thing for chilly weather and hearty appetites.

1 pound all-purpose potatoes, peeled and cut into ½-inch chunks

1 tablespoon olive oil

2 leeks, halved lengthwise and cut into ½-inch slices, or 4 scallions, cut into ½-inch slices

3 cloves garlic, finely chopped

2 carrots, halved lengthwise and cut into ½-inch pieces

1 celery root (10 ounces), peeled and cut into ½-inch chunks

2 ribs celery, cut into ½-inch slices

½ teaspoon salt

½ teaspoon dried rosemary

½ teaspoon dried tarragon

¼ teaspoon freshly ground black pepper

15-ounce can pinto beans, rinsed and drained

⅓ cup reduced-fat sour cream

¼ cup plain nonfat yogurt

2 teaspoons flour

1. In a medium pot of boiling water, cook the potatoes until firm-tender, about 7 minutes. Drain, reserving 1⅓ cups of the cooking liquid.

2. In a large nonstick skillet or wok, heat the oil over medium heat until hot but not smoking. Add the leeks and garlic, and stir-fry until the leeks are crisp-tender, about 2 minutes. Add the carrots and celery root, and stir-fry until the celery root is lightly browned, about 5 minutes. Add ⅓ cup of the reserved potato cooking liquid and cook, stirring frequently, until the celery root is crisp-tender, about 4 minutes.

3. Add the celery, salt, rosemary, tarragon, and pepper, and cook, stirring, until fragrant, about 1 minute. Add the beans, potatoes, and the remaining 1 cup potato cooking liquid and cook, stirring frequently, until the vegetables are tender, about 5 minutes.

4. Meanwhile, in a small bowl, combine the sour cream, yogurt, and flour. Add the sour cream mixture to the pan and cook, stirring, just until the vegetables are well coated, about 1 minute.

Helpful hint: Celery ribs and celery root come from two distinct varieties of celery. Celery root, also called celeriac, is grown for its knobby, baseball-sized root. It has a strong celery flavor and a texture something like a turnip.

FAT: 7G/22%
CALORIES: 283
SATURATED FAT: 1.9G
CARBOHYDRATE: 47G
PROTEIN: 10G
CHOLESTEROL: 7MG
SODIUM: 574MG

Minted Carrot Cakes

SERVES: 4
WORKING TIME: 30 MINUTES
TOTAL TIME: 50 MINUTES

Vibrantly flavored with orange juice and zest as well as with mint, these delicious carrot cakes are the perfect opener for any elegant dinner. A sauce of orange marmalade and honey underscores the sweetness of the carrots. And instead of using whole eggs to bind the cakes, this recipe calls for an egg white and flour to keep them low in fat.

1 pound carrots, thinly sliced

1 egg white

6 tablespoons chopped fresh mint

3 tablespoons flour

½ teaspoon grated orange zest

½ teaspoon baking powder

½ teaspoon salt

½ teaspoon ground coriander

⅛ teaspoon cayenne pepper

1 tablespoon olive oil

⅔ cup orange juice

1 tablespoon fresh lemon juice

1 tablespoon orange marmalade

2 teaspoons honey

1½ teaspoons cornstarch mixed with 1 tablespoon water

4 teaspoons reduced-fat sour cream

1. Place the carrots in a large saucepan and add water to cover by 1 inch. Bring to a boil, reduce to a simmer, cover, and cook until the carrots are very tender, about 20 minutes. Drain well. Transfer to a food processor and process until coarsely puréed, using on/off pulses. Add the egg white, 3 tablespoons of the mint, the flour, orange zest, baking powder, salt, coriander, and cayenne, and process until blended. Using a scant ¼ cup measure, form the mixture into 8 patties.

2. In a large nonstick skillet, heat the oil over medium heat until hot but not smoking. Add the patties and cook until they are golden brown, about 2 minutes per side.

3. Meanwhile, in a medium saucepan, stir together the orange juice, lemon juice, marmalade, and honey. Bring to a boil and cook until the mixture is slightly reduced, about 2 minutes. Stir in the cornstarch mixture, return to a boil, and cook, stirring constantly, until the sauce is slightly thickened, about 1 minute longer. Remove from the heat and stir in the remaining 3 tablespoons mint.

4. Divide the carrot cakes among 4 plates, spoon the sauce on top, and serve with the sour cream.

Helpful hint: The patties can be made earlier in the day through Step 1 and refrigerated, then cooked just before serving.

FAT: 4G/24%
CALORIES: 161
SATURATED FAT: 0.8G
CARBOHYDRATE: 29G
PROTEIN: 3G
CHOLESTEROL: 2MG
SODIUM: 394MG

Leek and Potato Sauté with Cheddar

SERVES: 4
WORKING TIME: 20 MINUTES
TOTAL TIME: 40 MINUTES

The subtle flavor of leeks is beautifully partnered with sweet pear and enriched with shredded Cheddar in this remarkably tasty dish.

½ cup lentils

1½ pounds small red potatoes, cut into ½-inch chunks

1 tablespoon olive oil

2 carrots, diced

1 leek (white and light green parts only), halved lengthwise and cut into thin slices

1 green bell pepper, diced

1½ cups reduced-sodium chicken broth, defatted, or reduced-sodium vegetable broth

½ teaspoon salt

¼ teaspoon freshly ground black pepper

1 small ripe Bartlett or Anjou pear, cored and diced

¼ cup chopped fresh parsley

¼ cup shredded sharp Cheddar cheese

1. In a large saucepan of boiling water, cook the lentils for 10 minutes. Add the potatoes and cook for 5 minutes longer (the lentils and potatoes will not be tender). Drain well.

2. Meanwhile, in a large nonstick skillet, heat the oil over medium heat until hot but not smoking. Add the carrots, leek, and bell pepper, and cook, stirring frequently, until the leek is softened, about 5 minutes. Stir in the lentils, potatoes, broth, salt, and black pepper, and bring to a boil. Reduce to a simmer, cover, and cook until the vegetables are tender, about 10 minutes.

3. Stir in the pear, cover again, and cook until the pear is tender, about 5 minutes. Stir in the parsley. Divide the leek-potato mixture among 4 plates, sprinkle the Cheddar on top, and serve.

Helpful hints: Clean leeks well because dirt can hide between the leaves. To clean, trim off the root end and blemished dark green ends, slit the leek lengthwise, and then swish in a bowl of water. Lift out the leeks, leaving the grit behind; repeat as needed with clean water. You can use other cheeses in this recipe, such as Swiss or Monterey jack.

FAT: 7G/17%
CALORIES: 341
SATURATED FAT: 2G
CARBOHYDRATE: 59G
PROTEIN: 14G
CHOLESTEROL: 3MG
SODIUM: 595MG

Mexican-Style Yellow and Green Squash

SERVES: 4
WORKING TIME: 30 MINUTES
TOTAL TIME: 35 MINUTES

*Think of this dish as a chunky vegetable chili, with some evaporated low-fat milk
stirred in for added richness.*

---

2 teaspoons olive oil

4 scallions, cut into 2-inch lengths

**2 green bell peppers, cut into
thin strips**

**2 zucchini, halved lengthwise
and cut into ½-inch-thick slices**

**2 yellow summer squash, halved
lengthwise and cut into ½-inch-
thick slices**

1 teaspoon ground coriander

¾ teaspoon ground cumin

½ teaspoon cinnamon

½ teaspoon salt

**½ teaspoon freshly ground
black pepper**

**5 plum tomatoes, coarsely
chopped**

**16-ounce can red kidney beans,
rinsed and drained**

½ cup evaporated low-fat milk

⅓ cup chopped fresh cilantro

1. In a large nonstick skillet, heat the oil over medium heat until hot but not smoking. Add the scallions and cook, stirring frequently, until the scallions are softened, about 2 minutes. Add the bell peppers and cook, stirring frequently, until the peppers are tender, about 5 minutes.

2. Stir in the zucchini, yellow squash, coriander, cumin, cinnamon, salt, and black pepper. Cover and cook, stirring occasionally, until the zucchini and yellow squash are crisp-tender, about 5 minutes.

3. Add the tomatoes and beans, increase the heat to high, and cook uncovered, stirring frequently, until the mixture is slightly thickened, about 5 minutes. Stir in the evaporated milk and cilantro and cook until the mixture is just creamy, about 2 minutes longer. Divide the squash mixture among 4 shallow bowls and serve.

Helpful hints: Black beans, pinto beans, or black-eyed peas can be substituted for the kidney beans. To make this dish ahead, prepare the recipe without the final addition of the evaporated milk and cilantro, slightly undercooking the vegetables. To serve, gently reheat until the vegetables are crisp-tender, and then stir in the milk and cilantro. You can substitute flat-leaf parsley for the cilantro.

FAT: 4G/20%
CALORIES: 184
SATURATED FAT: 0.4G
CARBOHYDRATE: 28G
PROTEIN: 11G
CHOLESTEROL: 5MG
SODIUM: 460MG

Dilled Beets, Apples, and Potatoes

SERVES: 4
WORKING TIME: 25 MINUTES
TOTAL TIME: 35 MINUTES

Deliciously sweet and sour, with a hint of smokiness from lean Canadian bacon, this skillet dish is excellent served with a green salad and crusty peasant bread for a light supper. If you want a vegetarian dish, you can easily omit the bacon. The fresh dill, in the Eastern European tradition, is a natural flavor partner for the beets.

1 tablespoon olive oil

1 Red Delicious apple, cored and diced

1 medium red onion, diced

1½ ounces Canadian bacon, diced

1 cup reduced-sodium chicken broth, defatted, or reduced-sodium vegetable broth

1½ pounds small red potatoes, halved

1 tablespoon cider vinegar

1 tablespoon honey

2 teaspoons Dijon mustard

1 teaspoon cornstarch

½ teaspoon salt

¼ teaspoon freshly ground black pepper

16-ounce can whole baby beets, drained and diced

¼ cup snipped fresh dill

1. In a large nonstick skillet, heat the oil over medium heat until hot but not smoking. Add the apple, onion, and bacon and cook, stirring frequently, until the apple and onion are softened and the bacon is lightly crisped, about 7 minutes.

2. Stir in the broth and potatoes and bring to a boil. Reduce to a simmer, cover, and cook until the potatoes are tender, about 10 minutes.

3. Meanwhile, in a small bowl, stir together the vinegar, honey, mustard, cornstarch, salt, pepper, and 2 tablespoons of water. Stir the vinegar mixture into the skillet, bring to a boil, and cook, stirring constantly, until the mixture is slightly thickened, about 1 minute. Stir in the beets and dill and cook until the beets are just warmed through, about 1 minute longer.

Helpful hints: If fresh baby beets are available, try them as a marvelous substitute for the canned. Boil them first whole, in their skins, until they are knife-tender; then peel, dice, and proceed with the recipe. For a change, use a Golden Delicious or McIntosh apple here.

FAT: 5G/15%
CALORIES: 278
SATURATED FAT: 0.7G
CARBOHYDRATE: 53G
PROTEIN: 8G
CHOLESTEROL: 5MG
SODIUM: 838MG

Cheese-Topped Vegetable Hash

SERVES: 4
WORKING TIME: 30 MINUTES
TOTAL TIME: 55 MINUTES

*Hash is an American favorite to be sure, especially in diners across the country.
And even though this version is all vegetable, winter squash and chunks of mushrooms
create a surprisingly hearty texture. This hash is kept moist and creamy by simmering
it in a little evaporated skim milk.*

1 pound all-purpose potatoes, peeled and cut into ½-inch cubes

1 pound butternut or acorn squash, peeled and cut into ½-inch cubes

1 tablespoon olive oil

½ pound mushrooms, quartered

2 green bell peppers, diced

1 large onion, chopped

1 clove garlic, minced

½ cup evaporated skim milk

½ teaspoon dried thyme

½ teaspoon salt

¼ teaspoon freshly ground black pepper

⅓ cup shredded Cheddar cheese

1. In a large pot of boiling water, cook the potatoes and squash until tender, about 10 minutes. Drain well.

2. Meanwhile, in a large ovenproof skillet, heat the oil over medium heat until hot but not smoking. Add the mushrooms, bell peppers, onion, and garlic, and cook, stirring frequently, until the peppers are tender, about 8 minutes.

3. Preheat the broiler. Stir the potatoes and squash into the skillet along with the evaporated milk, thyme, salt, and black pepper. Reduce to a simmer, cover, and cook until the flavors have blended, about 5 minutes. Uncover and cook until the liquid is absorbed, about 3 minutes longer.

4. Sprinkle the Cheddar on top of the hash and broil 4 inches from the heat for 2 to 3 minutes, or until the cheese is melted. Divide the hash among 4 plates and serve.

Helpful hints: As is frequently the case with skillet vegetable sautés, the transformation to soup is an easy one—just purée any leftovers in a food processor with enough water or reduced-sodium chicken broth to thin. To make a regular stovetop skillet ovenproof, simply wrap the handle in a double thickness of aluminum foil.

FAT: 7G/24%
CALORIES: 273
SATURATED FAT: 2.5G
CARBOHYDRATE: 46G
PROTEIN: 10G
CHOLESTEROL: 11MG
SODIUM: 384MG

Bright Summer Stir-Fry

SERVES: 4
WORKING TIME: 40 MINUTES
TOTAL TIME: 40 MINUTES

This stir-fry looks as though you've just made a trip to the vegetable garden. And the perky flavor —consisting of lime juice, fresh ginger, and soy sauce—is just as enticing. As with any stir-fry, it's best to do all of the vegetable preparation at once, since the cooking goes very quickly.

1 cup long-grain rice

1 tablespoon vegetable oil

2 cups small broccoli florets

2 ribs celery, thinly sliced on the diagonal

1 medium red onion, halved and thinly sliced

1 red bell pepper, cut into thin strips

1 yellow summer squash, halved lengthwise and cut into ½-inch-thick slices

1 cup reduced-sodium chicken broth, defatted, or reduced-sodium vegetable broth

¼ pound sugar snap peas

1 tablespoon minced fresh ginger

3 tablespoons reduced-sodium soy sauce

1 tablespoon fresh lime juice

1 tablespoon sugar

2 teaspoons cornstarch

2 tablespoons chopped fresh cilantro

1. In a medium saucepan, combine the rice and 2 cups of water. Bring to a boil over high heat, reduce to a simmer, cover, and cook until the rice is tender, about 17 minutes.

2. Meanwhile, in a large nonstick skillet, heat the oil over medium heat until hot but not smoking. Add the broccoli, celery, onion, bell pepper, and squash, and cook, stirring constantly, until the onion is softened, about 5 minutes. Stir in the broth, snap peas, and ginger and bring to a boil. Reduce to a simmer and cook until the vegetables are crisp-tender, about 5 minutes.

3. Meanwhile, in a small bowl, stir together the soy sauce, lime juice, sugar, and cornstarch. Remove the skillet from the heat and stir in the soy sauce mixture. Return the pan to medium heat and cook, stirring constantly, until the mixture boils and is slightly thickened, about 1 minute. Stir in the cilantro. Serve the stir-fry with the rice.

Helpful hint: Vary the vegetables depending on what you're growing or what looks good at the market. Just be sure to use vegetables with a similar texture— substitute green beans for the snap peas, cauliflower for the broccoli, zucchini for the yellow squash, and so on—and keep the proportions the same.

FAT: 4G/12%
CALORIES: 299
SATURATED FAT: 0.5G
CARBOHYDRATE: 58G
PROTEIN: 9G
CHOLESTEROL: 0MG
SODIUM: 682MG

Herbed Three-Bean Skillet with Tomatoes

SERVES: 4
WORKING TIME: 25 MINUTES
TOTAL TIME: 55 MINUTES

This is the ever-popular three-bean salad, dressed up in a new guise. The beans are simmered with onion, garlic, and fresh tomatoes (canned no-salt-added would be fine as well) and then spooned over brown rice for nutritional punch. Add a loaf of crusty whole-wheat bread and, if desired, slices of reduced-fat cheese—and that's it for dinner.

1 cup long-grain brown rice

1 tablespoon olive oil

1 medium onion, chopped

1 clove garlic, minced

4 large tomatoes, diced

2 tablespoons chopped fresh basil

½ teaspoon dried oregano

½ teaspoon salt

½ teaspoon sugar

⅛ teaspoon freshly ground black pepper

½ pound green beans, cut into 1-inch pieces

½ pound yellow wax beans, cut into 1-inch pieces

16-ounce can red kidney beans, rinsed and drained

1. In a medium saucepan, combine the rice and 2½ cups water. Bring to a boil over high heat, reduce to a simmer, cover, and cook until the rice is tender, about 40 minutes.

2. Meanwhile, in a large nonstick skillet, heat the oil over medium heat until hot but not smoking. Add the onion and garlic and cook, stirring frequently, until the onion is softened, about 7 minutes. Stir in the tomatoes, basil, oregano, salt, sugar, and pepper, and bring to a boil. Reduce to a simmer and cook, stirring occasionally, until the mixture is slightly thickened, about 10 minutes.

3. Meanwhile, in a large saucepan of boiling water, cook the green and yellow beans until the beans are crisp-tender, 5 to 8 minutes. Drain well.

4. Add the green and yellow beans to the tomato mixture along with the kidney beans. Cook, stirring occasionally, until the kidney beans are just warmed through, about 2 minutes. Place the rice in a large bowl, spoon the bean mixture on top, and serve.

Helpful hints: The bean-tomato mixture can be prepared up to 1 day ahead and refrigerated, and then gently reheated about 15 minutes before the rice finishes cooking. If you don't grow yellow wax beans or can't find any at the market, add another half-pound of green beans. No fresh basil? A scant teaspoon of dried basil is fine.

FAT: 6G/15%
CALORIES: 369
SATURATED FAT: 0.9G
CARBOHYDRATE: 68G
PROTEIN: 13G
CHOLESTEROL: 0MG
SODIUM: 440MG

Zucchini and Potato Pancakes

SERVES: 4
WORKING TIME: 25 MINUTES
TOTAL TIME: 35 MINUTES

Impossible but true—these crispy potato pancakes can be savored without guilt. Egg whites are used instead of whole eggs; the pancakes are browned in just a little oil to keep the fat in check. The final fat-free baking in the oven ensures that the pancakes are cooked through. Offer with tomato or split pea soup and grilled mushrooms drizzled with balsamic vinegar.

1½ cups plain nonfat yogurt

2 tablespoons reduced-fat sour cream

¾ cup snipped fresh dill

¾ cup thinly sliced scallions

¾ teaspoon salt

2 zucchini, shredded and squeezed dry in paper towels

2 large baking potatoes (about 1 pound), peeled, shredded, and squeezed dry in paper towels

2 tablespoons flour

½ teaspoon baking powder

2 egg whites

4 teaspoons olive or vegetable oil

1. In a medium bowl, stir together the yogurt, sour cream, ¼ cup of the dill, ¼ cup of the scallions, and ¼ teaspoon of the salt. Cover with plastic wrap and refrigerate until serving time.

2. In a large bowl, stir together the zucchini, potatoes, flour, baking powder, egg whites, the remaining ½ cup dill, remaining ½ cup scallions, and remaining ½ teaspoon salt.

3. Preheat the oven to 400°. In a large nonstick skillet, heat 2 teaspoons of the oil over medium heat until hot but not smoking. Using a ½ cup measure, drop the potato mixture into the skillet to form 4 pancakes, then lightly flatten to a ½-inch thickness. Cook until the pancakes are golden brown, about 2 minutes per side. Transfer to a baking sheet. Repeat with the remaining 2 teaspoons oil and remaining potato mixture, cooking 4 more pancakes. Transfer to the baking sheet.

4. Place the pancakes in the oven and bake for 7 minutes, or until the pancakes are crisp and cooked through. Divide the pancakes among 4 plates and serve with the yogurt sauce.

Helpful hints: Squeeze the potatoes and zucchini very dry, or the pancakes will steam in the pan rather than brown. If desired, prepare and bake the pancakes up to 1 day ahead and reheat in a 350° oven. You can substitute yellow squash or butternut squash for a different taste.

FAT: 6G/25%
CALORIES: 215
SATURATED FAT: 1.3G
CARBOHYDRATE: 31G
PROTEIN: 11G
CHOLESTEROL: 4MG
SODIUM: 585MG

Sautéed Vegetables with Lemon and Parsley

SERVES· 4
WORKING TIME: 35 MINUTES
TOTAL TIME: 40 MINUTES

Lemon juice enlivens the flavors in the bold mix of vegetables brought together in this sensational crunchy-topped dish.

1 tablespoon olive oil

2 carrots, thinly sliced

½ pound mushrooms, halved if small, quartered if large

½ pound asparagus, tough ends trimmed, cut into 1-inch pieces

1 clove garlic, minced

10-ounce package frozen artichoke hearts, thawed

¾ cup reduced-sodium chicken broth, defatted, or reduced-sodium vegetable broth

10-ounce package frozen lima beans, thawed

¼ cup chopped fresh parsley

1 tablespoon fresh lemon juice

¾ teaspoon dried thyme

½ teaspoon salt

⅛ teaspoon freshly ground black pepper

2 tablespoons plain dried bread crumbs

2 tablespoons grated Parmesan cheese

1. In a large nonstick ovenproof skillet, heat the oil over medium heat until hot but not smoking. Add the carrots, mushrooms, asparagus, and garlic, and cook, stirring frequently, until the mushrooms are softened, about 5 minutes.

2. Stir in the artichoke hearts and broth and bring to a boil. Reduce to a simmer and cook until the carrots are crisp-tender, about 5 minutes. Stir in the lima beans, 3 tablespoons of the parsley, the lemon juice, thyme, salt, and pepper, and cook until the vegetables are tender, about 6 minutes longer. Remove from the heat.

3. Meanwhile, preheat the broiler. In a small bowl, stir together the bread crumbs, Parmesan, and remaining 1 tablespoon parsley. Sprinkle the bread crumb mixture on top of the vegetables and broil 5 inches from the heat for 1 to 2 minutes, or until the crumbs are golden brown.

Helpful hints: If you don't grow asparagus or if you can't find good-quality fresh asparagus, substitute frozen spears, but add them toward the end of cooking when adding the lima beans. Make your regular nonstick skillet ovenproof by wrapping the handle in a double thickness of aluminum foil.

FAT: 5G/22%
CALORIES: 219
SATURATED FAT: 1.1G
CARBOHYDRATE: 34G
PROTEIN: 12G
CHOLESTEROL: 2MG
SODIUM: 557MG

Stuffed Cabbage with Dill Sauce

SERVES: 4
WORKING TIME: 25 MINUTES
TOTAL TIME: 1 HOUR

1 small head cabbage (1 pound), cored

1 teaspoon olive oil

6 scallions, thinly sliced

2 carrots, quartered lengthwise and thinly sliced

1 zucchini, halved lengthwise and thinly sliced

¼ pound mushrooms, coarsely chopped

1 cup bulgur (cracked wheat)

2 tablespoons boiling water

½ teaspoon grated lemon zest

1 tablespoon fresh lemon juice

¾ cup snipped fresh dill

½ teaspoon salt

2 tablespoons chopped pecans (¾ ounce)

2 cups reduced-sodium vegetable broth

1¼ teaspoons cornstarch mixed with 1 tablespoon water

3 tablespoons reduced-fat sour cream

FAT: 7G/24%
CALORIES: 266
SATURATED FAT: 1.3G
CARBOHYDRATE: 46G
PROTEIN: 10G
CHOLESTEROL: 4MG
SODIUM: 454MG

1. Preheat the oven to 400°. In a large pot of boiling water, cook the whole head of cabbage until it is crisp-tender and the leaves are easily separated, about 5 minutes. Drain. When cool enough to handle, separate into leaves, selecting the 12 largest leaves for stuffing. (Save the remainder for another use.)

2. In a medium saucepan, heat the oil over medium heat until hot but not smoking. Add the scallions and cook until softened, about 1 minute. Add the carrots, zucchini, and mushrooms and cook, stirring frequently, until the carrots are softened, about 4 minutes. Add the bulgur, boiling water, lemon zest, lemon juice, ⅓ cup of the dill, and the salt. Let stand until the bulgur is slightly chewy, about 10 minutes. Remove from the heat; add the pecans.

3. Using a ½-cup measuring cup as a mold, stuff the 12 cabbage leaves with the bulgur mixture and place them, seam-side down, in a 13 x 9-inch baking dish (see tip). Pour the broth on top, cover with foil, and bake for about 25 minutes, or until the leaves are tender and the filling is heated through. Transfer the cabbage packets to 4 plates. Transfer the broth from the baking dish to a small saucepan and bring to a boil. Add the cornstarch mixture and cook, stirring constantly, until slightly thickened, about 1 minute. Stir in the remaining dill. Spoon the sauce over the cabbage packets, top with a dollop of sour cream, and serve.

TIP

Fit a cabbage leaf into a ½-cup measuring cup, then spoon in the filling and fold the leaf over it to form a round packet. Invert the cup to place the cabbage packet in the baking dish.

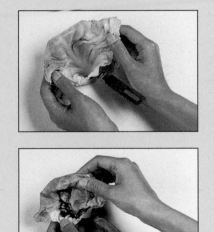

Pepper, Zucchini, and Potato Tiella

SERVES: 4
WORKING TIME: 15 MINUTES
TOTAL TIME: 35 MINUTES

The province of Apulia, which forms the "heel" of the boot-shaped Italian peninsula, is home to the layered casserole called "tiella." The dish is infinitely variable, but is almost always made with potatoes. Peppers, onions, and tomatoes are other common ingredients. In this casual tiella, the vegetables are stirred together rather than layered.

---

1 pound small red potatoes, halved

1 tablespoon olive oil

2 cloves garlic, peeled and halved

¾ teaspoon dried oregano

½ teaspoon dried rosemary

½ teaspoon dried sage

1 red onion, cut into 1-inch chunks

1 red bell pepper, cut into ½-inch-wide strips

2 zucchini, halved lengthwise and cut into 1-inch pieces

1 tomato, coarsely chopped

½ teaspoon salt

1. Preheat the oven to 400°. In a large pot of boiling water, cook the potatoes for 5 minutes to blanch. Drain well.

2. In a 13 x 9-inch baking dish, combine the oil, garlic, oregano, rosemary, and sage. Bake until the oil is hot and the herbs are fragrant, about 5 minutes. Add the potatoes, onion, bell pepper, zucchini, tomato, and salt, stirring to combine. Bake, stirring occasionally, for 25 minutes, or until the vegetables are tender. Divide among 4 plates and serve hot or at room temperature.

Helpful hint: Any kind of summer squash can go into this casserole. Golden zucchini, pattypan (white or yellow), yellow crookneck, or yellow straightneck would all work well.

FAT: 4G/22%
CALORIES: 166
SATURATED FAT: 0.5G
CARBOHYDRATE: 30G
PROTEIN: 4G
CHOLESTEROL: 0MG
SODIUM: 293MG

Three-Pepper Pizza

SERVES: 4
WORKING TIME: 10 MINUTES
TOTAL TIME: 45 MINUTES

Roasted peppers, a popular pizza topping, make for a striking pie when a mix of red, yellow, and green bell peppers is used. Char the peppers thoroughly under the broiler: That way, they'll not only be easier to peel, but they'll also have a more intensely smoky flavor. This pizza is a snap to fix because the pizza dough is store-bought.

4 bell peppers, mixed colors

1 tablespoon yellow cornmeal

1 cup chopped fresh basil

2 tablespoons grated Parmesan cheese

1 pound store-bought pizza dough

1 red onion, cut into thin rings

2 tomatoes, thickly sliced

1 cup shredded part-skim mozzarella cheese (4 ounces)

1. Preheat the broiler. Cut off the four sides of each bell pepper and remove the ribs. Broil the peppers, cut-sides down, for about 10 minutes, or until the skin is charred. When cool enough to handle, peel and cut into ½-inch-wide strips. Turn the oven to 450°.

2. Lightly dust a baking sheet with the cornmeal. Knead ½ cup of the basil and the Parmesan into the pizza dough and flatten the pizza dough into a circle. Place the dough on the cornmeal and press out to a 10-inch circle. Cover the dough with the onion and tomatoes and bake on the bottom rack of the oven for about 20 minutes, or until the crust is lightly browned.

3. Sprinkle with the mozzarella and the remaining ½ cup basil, top with the pepper strips, and bake for about 5 minutes, or until the cheese has melted and the peppers are piping hot.

Helpful hints: You can buy ready-to-use pizza dough from many pizzerias and Italian specialty stores; you may also find it in the dairy case in the super-market. Or, you can use the refrigerated dough that comes in a roll. Either type of dough can be patted out into a rectangle rather than rolled into a circle, if you like.

FAT: 10G/20%
CALORIES: 444
SATURATED FAT: 4.2G
CARBOHYDRATE: 70G
PROTEIN: 20G
CHOLESTEROL: 18MG
SODIUM: 817MG

Eggplant Stuffed with Ricotta Cheese

SERVES: 4

WORKING TIME: 20 MINUTES

TOTAL TIME: 45 MINUTES PLUS COOLING TIME

---

2 eggplants (1 pound each)

2 teaspoons olive oil

6 scallions, thinly sliced

3 cloves garlic, minced

1½ cups chopped canned no-salt-added tomatoes

15-ounce can pinto beans, rinsed and drained

½ cup chopped fresh basil

½ teaspoon salt

¼ teaspoon freshly ground black pepper

½ cup low-fat (1%) cottage cheese

½ cup part-skim ricotta cheese

1 cup unseasoned stuffing mix

1 tablespoon slivered almonds

1. Preheat the oven to 400°. Halve the eggplants lengthwise. With a paring knife, cut the pulp from the eggplants, leaving a ½-inch-thick shell (see tip; top photo). Cut the removed pulp into ½-inch chunks (bottom photo). Transfer the shells to a 13 x 9-inch glass baking dish.

2. In a large nonstick skillet, heat the oil over medium heat until hot but not smoking. Add the scallions and garlic and cook, stirring frequently, until the scallions are softened, about 1 minute. Add the diced eggplant, stirring to coat. Stir in the tomatoes, beans, basil, salt, and pepper, and bring to a boil. Reduce to a simmer and cook until slightly thickened, about 5 minutes. Transfer the eggplant mixture to a bowl and cool to room temperature.

3. Stir the cottage cheese, ricotta, stuffing mix, and almonds into the eggplant mixture. Spoon the mixture into the eggplant shells and bake for about 25 minutes, or until the filling is piping hot and the shells are tender. Divide among 4 plates and serve.

Helpful hint: Unseasoned stuffing mix is simply cubes of dried bread. If you have some stale white, Italian, or French bread on hand, you can cut it into cubes and use it instead. If the bread is not completely dry, spread the cubes on a baking sheet and bake them in a 350° oven for about 10 minutes.

FAT: 8G/23%

CALORIES: 317

SATURATED FAT: 2.4G

CARBOHYDRATE: 47G

PROTEIN: 18G

CHOLESTEROL: 11MG

SODIUM: 775MG

TIP

Use a sharp paring knife to cut the pulp from the eggplant halves, leaving a ½-inch-thick shell. Cut the pulp into strips, then cut the strips crosswise into chunks.

Polenta Vegetable Pie

SERVES: 4
WORKING TIME: 40 MINUTES
TOTAL TIME: 50 MINUTES

This is not your usual pastry-lined pie—here the crust is made from polenta, a virtually fat-free cornmeal mixture that's the Italian cousin to Southern grits. For deep, sumptuous flavor, a bit of blue cheese and reduced-fat sour cream is added. The crunchy sautéed vegetables make a delectable contrast to the smooth polenta.

1 cup yellow cornmeal

½ teaspoon salt

2 ounces crumbled blue cheese or feta cheese

2 tablespoons reduced-fat sour cream

2 teaspoons olive oil

2 yellow summer squash, halved lengthwise and cut into thin slices

¼ cup chopped fresh basil

2½ cups chopped fresh tomatoes

¾ pound sugar snap peas

1. In a small bowl, stir together 1½ cups of water, the cornmeal, and ¼ teaspoon of the salt until well combined. In a large saucepan, bring ¾ cup of water to a boil. Stir in the cornmeal mixture and cook, stirring frequently, until the mixture is thickened, about 5 minutes. Remove from the heat and stir in the cheese and sour cream. Set aside.

2. Preheat the oven to 450°. In a large nonstick skillet, heat the oil over medium heat until hot but not smoking. Add the squash and basil and cook, stirring frequently, until the squash is crisp-tender, about 5 minutes. Stir in the tomatoes and remaining ¼ teaspoon salt. Bring to a boil and cook until the mixture is slightly thickened, about 4 minutes. Stir in the snap peas and cook until the snap peas are just crisp-tender, about 1 minute longer. Remove from the heat.

3. Spoon the cornmeal mixture into a 9-inch deep-dish pie pan, pressing the mixture into the bottom and up the sides of the pan. Spoon the vegetable mixture on top and bake for 10 minutes, or until the polenta is crisp and the vegetables are piping hot.

Helpful hints: Mixing the cornmeal with cold water before stirring it into the boiling water will prevent a lumpy polenta. Try zucchini, green beans, bell peppers, or other vegetables according to the season's best.

FAT: 8G/26%
CALORIES: 298
SATURATED FAT: 3.6G
CARBOHYDRATE: 46G
PROTEIN: 11G
CHOLESTEROL: 13MG
SODIUM: 577MG

Baked Ratatouille Gratin

SERVES: 4
WORKING TIME: 20 MINUTES
TOTAL TIME: 55 MINUTES

This classic eggplant-squash mixture, reflecting the tastes of Provence, is usually fried in lots of olive oil, but not without the penalty of extra calories from fat. In this lightened version, a small amount of olive oil and garlic is heated in the oven to create a flavorful base for the vegetables. And, to trim fat even further, the recipe calls for part-skim mozzarella.

2 teaspoons olive oil

5 cloves garlic, peeled

2 zucchini, halved lengthwise and cut into ½-inch-thick slices

2 yellow summer squash, halved lengthwise and cut into ½-inch-thick slices

1 large onion, cut into ½-inch chunks

¾ pound eggplant, cut into ½-inch chunks

Two 8-ounce cans no-salt-added tomato sauce

14½-ounce can no-salt-added stewed tomatoes, chopped with their juices

1 teaspoon dried oregano

¾ teaspoon salt

⅓ cup plain dried bread crumbs

½ cup shredded part-skim mozzarella cheese

1 teaspoon chopped fresh parsley

1. Preheat the oven to 450°. In a 13 x 9-inch glass baking dish, combine the oil and garlic. Bake for 5 minutes, or until the garlic oil is fragrant and hot. Stir in the zucchini, yellow squash, onion, and eggplant, cover with foil, and bake for 20 minutes, stirring occasionally, or until the vegetables are crisp-tender.

2. Uncover and stir in the tomato sauce, tomatoes and their juices, the oregano, and salt, and bake for 10 minutes, or until the mixture is bubbly.

3. Sprinkle the bread crumbs and cheese on top and bake for 10 minutes longer, or until the gratin is piping hot and the top is lightly browned. Sprinkle with the parsley and serve.

Helpful hints: You can prepare the gratin up to 1 day ahead through Step 2. Bring the gratin to room temperature, sprinkle on the bread crumbs and cheese, and then bake as directed. This is also good served at room temperature as a salad for lunch. At the market or in the garden, choose an eggplant with tight, unblemished skin that feels heavy for its size.

FAT: 6G/23%
CALORIES: 236
SATURATED FAT: 1.9G
CARBOHYDRATE: 40G
PROTEIN: 11G
CHOLESTEROL: 8MG
SODIUM: 607MG

Overstuffed Potatoes

SERVES: 4
WORKING TIME: 25 MINUTES
TOTAL TIME: 1 HOUR

**4 large baking potatoes
(10 ounces each)**

2½ cups broccoli florets

1 red bell pepper, diced

**¾ cup shredded sharp Cheddar
cheese (about 3 ounces)**

½ cup low-fat (1%) milk

½ cup thinly sliced scallions

¾ teaspoon dried oregano

¾ teaspoon salt

**½ teaspoon freshly ground
black pepper**

1. With a fork, prick the potatoes in several places, arrange around the edge of a microwave-safe plate, and microwave on high power, turning once halfway through cooking, until the potatoes are tender, 21 to 25 minutes. (The potatoes can also be baked in a 450° oven for about 1 hour.)

2. Meanwhile, in a large saucepan of boiling water, cook the broccoli and bell pepper until the broccoli and pepper are just crisp-tender, about 3 minutes. Drain, rinse under cold water, and drain again.

3. Preheat the oven to 450°. With a fork, prick a line along the top of each potato (see tip; top photo), prick another line to form a cross, then push in the ends so the potato opens up (bottom photo). Scoop the flesh into a large bowl, reserving the potato shells. Add the cheese to the potato flesh and mash until the mixture is smooth and the cheese is melted. Stir in the broccoli, bell pepper, milk, scallions, oregano, salt, and black pepper until well combined.

4. Spoon the potato mixture back into the reserved potato shells, place the potatoes on a baking sheet with sides, and bake for 10 minutes, or until the filling is piping hot.

Helpful hints: These potatoes can be made up to 1 day ahead. Reheat leftover potatoes in the microwave on high power for about 3 minutes, or in a conventional oven at 350° for about 15 minutes.

TIP

To break open the potato, prick a cross in the top with a fork. Push from opposite ends of the potato to pop open the top so you can easily scoop out the flesh.

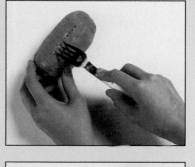

FAT: 8G/21%
CALORIES: 343
SATURATED FAT: 4.7G
CARBOHYDRATE: 57G
PROTEIN: 14G
CHOLESTEROL: 24MG
SODIUM: 596MG

Baked Spaghetti Squash with Mushroom Sauce

SERVES: 4
WORKING TIME: 30 MINUTES
TOTAL TIME: 55 MINUTES

This enticing dish looks like pasta, but it's really spaghetti squash—just scrape out the cooked strands and there's your natural spaghetti.

---

1 spaghetti squash (about 5 pounds)

2 teaspoons olive oil

5 shallots, finely chopped

3 cloves garlic, minced

1 carrot, halved lengthwise and cut into thin slices

¾ pound mushrooms, thinly sliced

1 tablespoon flour

½ cup reduced-sodium chicken broth, defatted, or reduced-sodium vegetable broth

14½-ounce can no-salt-added stewed tomatoes, chopped with their juices

1 teaspoon salt

¾ teaspoon freshly ground black pepper

½ teaspoon dried rosemary

3 tablespoons coarsely grated fresh Parmesan cheese

1. Preheat the oven to 400°. Cut the squash in half lengthwise, scoop out and discard the seeds, and place the squash, cut-sides down, on a nonstick baking sheet. With a fork, prick the squash skin all over, cover with foil, and bake for 35 minutes, or until the squash is tender when pierced with a fork.

2. Meanwhile, in a large nonstick skillet, heat the oil over medium heat until hot but not smoking. Add the shallots and garlic and cook, stirring frequently, until the shallots are softened, about 3 minutes. Add the carrot and mushrooms and cook, stirring frequently, until the carrot and mushrooms are tender, about 7 minutes.

3. Stir in the flour and cook until the vegetables are well coated, about 1 minute. Add the broth and bring to a boil. Stir in the tomatoes and their juices, the salt, pepper, and rosemary, and cook until the mixture is slightly thickened, about 5 minutes.

4. Remove the squash from the oven and let it cool slightly. With a fork, scrape out the flesh (it will form spaghetti-like strands). Place the squash in a large bowl, add the sauce, and toss to coat. Divide the squash mixture among 4 plates, sprinkle the cheese on top, and serve.

Helpful hint: Choose a pale yellow spaghetti squash for the sweetest taste.

FAT: 6G/22%
CALORIES: 251
SATURATED FAT: 1.6G
CARBOHYDRATE: 46G
PROTEIN: 8G
CHOLESTEROL: 3MG
SODIUM: 801MG

Asparagus-Cheese Puff

SERVES: 4
WORKING TIME: 20 MINUTES
TOTAL TIME: 55 MINUTES

This puff is actually a luscious soufflé in disguise, made reasonably low-fat with more egg whites than yolks. To create the illusion of richness, mashed white kidney beans are stirred into the soufflé base. Using a strongly flavored full-fat cheese means you can use less of it—in this case, a little goat cheese or feta goes a long way.

¾ pound asparagus, tough ends trimmed, cut into ½-inch pieces

3 tablespoons flour

⅔ cup low-fat (1%) milk

¾ cup canned white kidney beans (cannellini), rinsed, drained, and mashed

2 egg yolks

1½ ounces crumbled goat cheese or feta cheese

½ teaspoon dried tarragon

½ teaspoon salt

⅛ teaspoon cayenne pepper

6 egg whites

⅛ teaspoon cream of tartar

1. Preheat the oven to 375°. In a medium saucepan of boiling water, cook the asparagus until barely tender, about 2 minutes. Drain well and blot dry on paper towels.

2. Place the flour in a large saucepan over medium heat, and gradually whisk in the milk until no lumps remain. Bring to a boil and cook, whisking frequently, until the mixture is slightly thickened, about 4 minutes. Remove from the heat and stir in the beans. Whisk in the egg yolks, cheese, tarragon, ¼ teaspoon of the salt, and the cayenne until well combined.

3. In a large bowl, with an electric mixer, beat the egg whites, remaining ¼ teaspoon salt, and the cream of tartar until stiff, but not dry, peaks form. Stir about 1 cup of the egg whites into the milk mixture, then gently fold in the remaining egg whites. Gently fold in the asparagus.

4. Spoon the mixture into an 8-cup soufflé mold and bake for 30 minutes, or until the soufflé is golden brown, puffed, and just set in the center. Serve immediately.

Helpful hints: For variety, replace the asparagus with cauliflower, green beans, or broccoli. Be sure to use the cream of tartar, since it helps stabilize the beaten egg whites and increases volume as well.

FAT: 5G/29%
CALORIES: 164
SATURATED FAT: 2.9G
CARBOHYDRATE: 15G
PROTEIN: 14G
CHOLESTEROL: 63MG
SODIUM: 499MG

"Egg Roll" with Diced Vegetables

SERVES: 4

WORKING TIME: 20 MINUTES

TOTAL TIME: 35 MINUTES

¼ **cup sun-dried (not oil-packed) tomato halves**

½ **cup boiling water**

2 **tablespoons flour**

3 **whole eggs**

3 **egg whites**

6 **cups fresh spinach leaves, shredded**

2 **cups jarred roasted red peppers, rinsed, drained, and diced**

4 **scallions, thinly sliced**

½ **teaspoon salt**

¼ **cup fresh basil leaves**

1 **tablespoon no-salt-added tomato paste**

2 **tablespoons grated Parmesan cheese**

1. In a small bowl, combine the sun-dried tomatoes and boiling water and let stand until the tomatoes are softened, about 15 minutes. Drain the tomatoes, discarding the soaking liquid. Coarsely chop the tomatoes and set aside.

2. Meanwhile, preheat the oven to 400°. Spray a 15 x 11-inch jelly-roll pan with nonstick cooking spray. Place the flour in a large bowl, and whisk in the whole eggs and egg whites until the mixture is smooth. Stir in the tomatoes, spinach, 1 cup of the red peppers, the scallions, and ¼ teaspoon of the salt. Pour the mixture into the prepared pan and bake for 12 minutes, or until the top is just set.

3. Meanwhile, in a food processor, combine the remaining 1 cup red peppers, the basil, tomato paste, and remaining ¼ teaspoon salt, and purée until smooth.

4. Remove the baked egg mixture from the oven, place the pan on a wire rack, and immediately sprinkle the Parmesan on top. When cool enough to handle, beginning at one long side, roll up the mixture, jelly-roll style (see tip). Cut the egg roll into 12 slices. Divide the slices among 4 plates, drizzle the pepper sauce on top, and serve.

Helpful hints: Instead of the spinach, try Swiss chard or kale. For all your low-fat cooking, opt for dry-packed sun-dried tomatoes rather than the variety packed in oil.

TIP

When the baked egg mixture is cool enough to handle, starting from a long side, roll up as you would a jelly roll.

FAT: 5G/29%

CALORIES: 165

SATURATED FAT: 1.7G

CARBOHYDRATE: 18G

PROTEIN: 12G

CHOLESTEROL: 162MG

SODIUM: 654MG

Stuffed Peppers with Pine Nuts

SERVES: 4
WORKING TIME: 30 MINUTES
TOTAL TIME: 1 HOUR

This stuffed pepper recipe includes the usual white rice, but instead of the expected ground beef or lamb, it calls for meaty mushrooms and broccoli rabe, a pungently flavored, leafy green member of the cabbage family (you could use spinach if broccoli rabe is unavailable). For extra richness and a little texture, it also includes some pine nuts— just a smattering because nuts do add fat.

---

2 red bell peppers

2 yellow bell peppers

1½ cups cut broccoli rabe (1-inch pieces) or small broccoli florets

2 teaspoons olive oil

1 large onion, diced

3 cloves garlic, minced

2 cups mushrooms, thinly sliced

½ cup long-grain rice

1¼ cups reduced-sodium chicken broth, defatted, or reduced-sodium vegetable broth

¾ teaspoon salt

½ teaspoon freshly ground black pepper

8-ounce can no-salt-added tomato sauce

3 tablespoons orange juice

Three 3 x ½-inch strips of orange zest (optional)

⅛ teaspoon cinnamon

2 tablespoons pine nuts

1. Slice the tops off the bell peppers and set aside, then remove and discard the seeds and ribs. In a large pot of boiling water, cook the bell peppers and their tops until the peppers are crisp-tender, about 5 minutes. Reserve the boiling water for the broccoli rabe and, with a slotted spoon, transfer the peppers, cut-sides down, and their tops to paper towels to drain. Cook the broccoli rabe in the boiling water until tender, about 2 minutes. Drain well.

2. In a medium saucepan, heat the oil over medium heat until hot but not smoking. Add the onion and garlic and cook, stirring frequently, until the onion is softened, about 5 minutes. Add the mushrooms and cook until the mushrooms are softened, about 2 minutes. Stir in the rice. Add the broth, ½ teaspoon of the salt, and ¼ teaspoon of the black pepper; bring to a boil. Reduce to a simmer, cover, and cook until the rice is tender, about 17 minutes.

3. Preheat the oven to 425°. In an 8-inch square baking dish, stir together the tomato sauce, orange juice, orange zest, remaining ¼ teaspoon salt, remaining ¼ teaspoon black pepper, and the cinnamon. Stir the broccoli rabe and pine nuts into the rice mixture, then spoon the mixture into the bell peppers. Place the stuffed peppers over the sauce, replace their tops, cover with foil, and bake for 15 minutes, or until the peppers are piping hot.

Helpful hint: Use bell peppers of a similar size so everything cooks evenly.

FAT: 5G/22%
CALORIES: 220
SATURATED FAT: 0.7G
CARBOHYDRATE: 38G
PROTEIN: 8G
CHOLESTEROL: 0MG
SODIUM: 645MG

Eggplant Parmesan

SERVES: 4
WORKING TIME: 25 MINUTES
TOTAL TIME: 1 HOUR

This Italian favorite has all the taste and visual appeal you're used to, but the dish has been altered slightly in order to lower the fat. Instead of frying fat-laden breaded slices of eggplant, you dip the slices into no-fat egg whites, then bread crumbs, and then oven-bake them. And, this recipe calls for less cheese than usual.

2 egg whites

⅔ cup plain dried bread crumbs

1 pound eggplant, peeled and cut into ¼-inch-thick slices

2 cups no-salt-added tomato sauce

14½-ounce can no-salt-added stewed tomatoes, chopped with their juices

¼ cup chopped fresh mint

½ teaspoon salt

½ teaspoon freshly ground black pepper

½ teaspoon dried oregano

¾ cup shredded part-skim mozzarella cheese (about 3 ounces)

2 tablespoons grated Parmesan cheese

2 teaspoons chopped fresh parsley

1. Preheat the oven to 400°. Line a baking sheet with foil. In a shallow dish, with a fork, beat the egg whites and 2 tablespoons of water until foamy. On a plate, spread the bread crumbs. Dip the eggplant into the egg whites, then into the bread crumbs, pressing the crumbs into the eggplant. Place the eggplant on the prepared baking sheet, spray the eggplant with nonstick cooking spray, and bake for 20 minutes. Turn the eggplant and bake for 10 minutes longer, or until the eggplant is crisp and golden brown.

2. Meanwhile, in a medium bowl, stir together the tomato sauce, tomatoes and their juices, the mint, salt, pepper, and oregano. In a 9-inch square baking dish, spread 3 tablespoons of the tomato mixture. Lay half of the eggplant on top, spoon half of the remaining tomato mixture over the eggplant, and sprinkle half of the mozzarella on top. Repeat with the remaining eggplant, tomato mixture, and mozzarella.

3. Sprinkle the Parmesan on top and bake for 20 minutes, or until the eggplant is piping hot and the sauce is bubbly. Sprinkle the parsley on top and serve.

Helpful hints: If good-quality fresh mint is not available, substitute fresh basil for a tasty variation. You can bake this up to 1 day ahead, and then reheat in a 350° oven, covered, for about 20 minutes. Leftovers would be great on a French roll for lunch.

FAT: 6G/22%
CALORIES: 238
SATURATED FAT: 2.9G
CARBOHYDRATE: 35G
PROTEIN: 14G
CHOLESTEROL: 14MG
SODIUM: 649MG

Layered Tortilla Casserole

SERVES: 4
WORKING TIME: 25 MINUTES
TOTAL TIME: 45 MINUTES

*How could this casserole, oozing with cheese and other goodies, be low in fat, you may ask?
The answer: cheese in moderation, lots of vegetables, and corn tortillas, which provide
a satisfying fullness. And, the light white sauce is made by thickening low-fat milk with a little
flour, and then adding spices and herbs for assertive flavor.*

3 tablespoons flour

2 cups low-fat (1%) milk

¾ teaspoon ground cumin

½ teaspoon dried oregano

½ teaspoon salt

¼ teaspoon freshly ground black pepper

2 cups cauliflower florets

1 red bell pepper, diced

1 green bell pepper, diced

4-ounce can chopped mild green chilies, drained

1½ cups frozen corn kernels, thawed

Eight 6-inch corn tortillas

1 cup shredded jalapeño jack cheese (about 4 ounces)

1. Preheat the oven to 375°. Spray an 11 x 7-inch baking dish with nonstick cooking spray. Place the flour in a large saucepan over medium heat, and gradually whisk in the milk until no lumps remain. Bring to a boil and whisk in the cumin, oregano, salt, and black pepper. Cook, whisking frequently, until the mixture is slightly thickened, about 3 minutes.

2. Stir in the cauliflower, bell peppers, and chilies, and cook, stirring occasionally, until the cauliflower and peppers are crisp-tender, about 5 minutes. Remove from the heat and stir in the corn.

3. Place 2 of the tortillas in the prepared baking dish and spoon one-quarter of the vegetable mixture on top. Repeat 3 more times with the remaining tortillas and vegetable mixture. Sprinkle the cheese on top, cover with foil, and bake for 10 minutes, or until the casserole is piping hot. Uncover and bake for 5 minutes longer, or until the cheese is lightly browned.

Helpful hints: Vary the vegetables by using broccoli, zucchini, green beans, asparagus, and so on. If the jalapeño jack cheese is too spicy for your taste, use plain Monterey jack. The casserole can be assembled earlier in the day and refrigerated. Bring to room temperature before baking, or allow extra baking time if you are taking the pan directly from the refrigerator.

FAT: 13G/29%
CALORIES: 384
SATURATED FAT: 6G
CARBOHYDRATE: 55G
PROTEIN: 18G
CHOLESTEROL: 35MG
SODIUM: 789MG

Zucchini and Sweet Pepper Enchiladas

SERVES: 4
WORKING TIME: 30 MINUTES
TOTAL TIME: 45 MINUTES

The vegetables for these scrumptious enchiladas are treated in a special way to enhance their taste. First, they are sautéed in a small amount of oil, and then simmered in broth until the liquid has evaporated and the vegetables are infused with flavor. Serve with a refreshing salad of mixed greens, radishes, and sliced red onion.

---

2 teaspoons vegetable oil

2 zucchini, halved lengthwise and cut into thin slices

2 yellow bell peppers, cut into thin strips

1 medium onion, halved and thinly sliced

1 clove garlic, minced

¾ cup reduced-sodium beef broth, defatted, or reduced-sodium vegetable broth

1 teaspoon dried oregano or basil

2 cups no-salt-added crushed tomatoes

Eight 6-inch flour tortillas

¼ cup shredded Monterey jack cheese

¼ cup prepared salsa

1. In a large nonstick skillet, heat the oil over medium heat until hot but not smoking. Add the zucchini, bell peppers, onion, and garlic, stirring to coat. Add ¼ cup of the broth and cook, stirring frequently, until the onion is softened, about 5 minutes. Stir in the remaining ½ cup broth and the oregano, and bring to a boil. Reduce to a simmer and cook until almost all the liquid has evaporated, about 5 minutes longer. Remove from the heat.

2. Preheat the oven to 375°. Spread half of the tomatoes in a 13 x 9-inch baking dish. Spoon one-eighth of the zucchini mixture down the center of each tortilla. Roll up the tortillas tightly and place, seam-side down, over the tomatoes. Spoon the remaining tomatoes over the tortillas and sprinkle the cheese on top.

3. Cover with foil and bake for 10 minutes, or until the cheese is melted and the enchiladas are piping hot. Divide the enchiladas among 4 plates, spoon the salsa on top, and serve.

Helpful hints: If you don't have yellow bell peppers, substitute sweet red bell peppers. You can assemble the casserole earlier in the day through Step 2, and then bake just before serving.

FAT: 8G/28%
CALORIES: 248
SATURATED FAT: 2.1G
CARBOHYDRATE: 37G
PROTEIN: 9G
CHOLESTEROL: 8MG
SODIUM: 527MG

Baked Stuffed Tomatoes

SERVES: 4
WORKING TIME: 20 MINUTES
TOTAL TIME: 45 MINUTES

*A made-for-summer specialty, these hearty and delicious tomatoes are ideal
with anything barbecued or roasted.*

**4 large tomatoes (about
3 pounds)**

1 red bell pepper, diced

1 green bell pepper, diced

**1 rib celery, halved lengthwise
and cut into thin slices**

¼ cup chopped fresh parsley

¼ cup plain dried bread crumbs

**2 tablespoons no-salt-added
tomato paste**

3 cloves garlic, minced

2 teaspoons olive oil

½ teaspoon dried oregano

½ teaspoon salt

1. Preheat the oven to 400°. With a sharp paring knife, remove the core and center pulp from each tomato, leaving a thick shell. Coarsely chop ½ cup of the tomato pulp, discarding the remaining pulp. Set the tomato shells aside.

2. In a large bowl, stir together the ½ cup tomato pulp, the bell peppers, celery, parsley, bread crumbs, tomato paste, garlic, oil, oregano, and salt. Spoon the mixture into the tomato shells, mounding the tops slightly.

3. Transfer the tomatoes to a baking dish just large enough to hold them snugly and bake for 25 minutes, or until the tomatoes are piping hot and the stuffing is softened.

Helpful hints: Stuff the tomatoes earlier in the day, if desired, then bake them shortly before serving. These are also tasty served at room temperature.

FAT: 4G/25%
CALORIES: 136
SATURATED FAT: 0.5G
CARBOHYDRATE: 25G
PROTEIN: 4G
CHOLESTEROL: 0MG
SODIUM: 376MG

Roasted Potatoes with Parmesan and Herbs

SERVES: 4
WORKING TIME: 15 MINUTES
TOTAL TIME: 45 MINUTES

*When you cook potatoes in the pan along with a roast or bird, the result
is undeniably delicious but unfortunately loaded with fat. The potatoes absorb the fat
that runs off from the meat. But even with a spoonful of olive oil and a generous
sprinkling of Parmesan, these "al forno" (oven-cooked) potatoes are a healthier choice.
Try them with sage-rubbed roasted game hens.*

1½ pounds small red potatoes

1 tablespoon extra-virgin olive oil

3 cloves garlic, peeled and halved

¾ teaspoon dried rosemary

½ teaspoon dried sage

1½ teaspoons grated lemon zest

½ teaspoon salt

¼ cup grated Parmesan cheese

1. Preheat the oven to 400°. With a vegetable peeler, peel a thin band around the circumference of each potato. In a large pot of boiling water, cook the potatoes for 5 minutes. Drain.

2. In a large roasting pan, combine the oil, garlic, rosemary, and sage. Bake until the garlic is fragrant and the oil is hot, about 4 minutes. Add the potatoes, lemon zest, and salt and bake, turning occasionally, for 20 minutes, or until the potatoes are crisp, golden, and tender. Sprinkle the Parmesan over the potatoes and bake for 2 minutes, or just until the cheese is melted and golden brown.

Helpful hint: If you're in a hurry, you can skip the peeling step and roast the potatoes with all of their skins on.

FAT: 5G/23%
CALORIES: 193
SATURATED FAT: 1.4G
CARBOHYDRATE: 32G
PROTEIN: 6G
CHOLESTEROL: 4MG
SODIUM: 380MG

Asparagus Vinaigrette

SERVES: 4
WORKING TIME: 10 MINUTES
TOTAL TIME: 15 MINUTES

This tomato-based vinaigrette is scented with orange juice that showcases both the delicate flavor and the brilliant color of fresh asparagus. Be careful not to overcook the asparagus—the spears are at their best when they are still firm to the bite. Serve as part of a spring buffet menu, or as a prelude to a vegetable frittata.

1 pound asparagus, tough ends trimmed

2 tablespoons no-salt-added tomato paste

½ cup orange juice

2 tablespoons reduced-sodium chicken broth, defatted, or water

2 tablespoons red wine vinegar

1 teaspoon Dijon mustard

1 teaspoon olive oil, preferably extra-virgin

¼ teaspoon salt

1. In a large pot of boiling water, cook the asparagus until just crisp-tender, about 3 minutes. Drain well and pat dry on paper towels. Arrange the asparagus on a serving platter.

2. Place the tomato paste in a small bowl. Whisk in the orange juice, broth, vinegar, mustard, oil, and salt until well combined. Spoon the vinaigrette over the asparagus and serve.

Helpful hints: Although asparagus is available all year round, spring asparagus—preferably straight from the garden—is still the best. Select spears with moist-looking, unwrinkled stems and tight tips. If the stems are very thick, you may want to peel the tough outer skin with a vegetable peeler. Refrigerate asparagus for no more than a day or two, wrapping the bases of the stems in moist paper towels and placing them in a plastic bag.

FAT: 1G/26%
CALORIES: 47
SATURATED FAT: 0.2G
CARBOHYDRATE: 7G
PROTEIN: 2G
CHOLESTEROL: 0MG
SODIUM: 192MG

Succotash

SERVES: 4

WORKING TIME: 25 MINUTES

TOTAL TIME: 40 MINUTES

Sweet fresh corn stars in this New England classic. When scraping the kernels from the cob, be sure to include all the delicious "milk."

---

6 ears of corn

1 teaspoon olive oil

4 shallots, minced

10-ounce package frozen baby lima beans

1 pound tomatoes, seeded and coarsely chopped

¾ teaspoon dried tarragon

½ teaspoon salt

2 tablespoons chopped fresh parsley

2 teaspoons unsalted butter

1. Remove the husks and silk from the corn. With a sharp knife, working over a large bowl, cut the kernels off the cobs from the tips to the stems, making sure to catch the juices as well. Set aside.

2. In a large saucepan, heat the oil over medium heat until hot but not smoking. Add the shallots and cook, stirring frequently, until the shallots are softened, about 4 minutes. Add the lima beans and ¼ cup of water and bring to a boil. Stir in the tomatoes, tarragon, and salt and return to a boil. Reduce to a simmer, cover, and cook until the lima beans are almost tender, about 7 minutes.

3. Stir in the corn kernels and their juices, cover again, and cook until the corn and lima beans are tender, about 4 minutes. Stir in the parsley and butter and cook, uncovered, just until the butter is melted, about 1 minute longer.

Helpful hints: You can substitute frozen corn for the fresh to enjoy this dish all year round. Plan on using about 3 cups of corn kernels. If there are leftovers, stir in some reduced-sodium chicken broth, gently reheat, and you'll have a fine corn soup.

FAT: 5G/18%

CALORIES: 248

SATURATED FAT: 1.6G

CARBOHYDRATE: 46G

PROTEIN: 10G

CHOLESTEROL: 5MG

SODIUM: 339MG

Braised Leeks

SERVES: 4

WORKING TIME: 15 MINUTES

TOTAL TIME: 45 MINUTES

Simmering the leeks in a deeply fragrant orange-tomato sauce turns a simple vegetable into an extraordinary dish.

4 medium leeks

1⅔ cups reduced-sodium tomato-vegetable juice

Three 3 x ½-inch strips of orange zest

⅔ cup orange juice

½ teaspoon dried thyme

¼ teaspoon cinnamon

¼ teaspoon ground allspice

¼ teaspoon cayenne pepper

1 tablespoon extra-virgin olive oil

½ teaspoon salt

2 tablespoons diced yellow or red bell pepper

1. Trim the root ends off each leek, being careful to keep the leeks intact. Trim the tough dark green tops off, then quarter each leek lengthwise up to, but not through, the root. Swish the leeks in a bowl of lukewarm water, easing the leaves apart to remove the grit. Lift out the leeks, leaving the grit behind; repeat as needed with clean water. Set aside.

2. In a large skillet, combine the tomato-vegetable juice, orange zest, orange juice, thyme, cinnamon, allspice, and cayenne. Bring to a boil over medium heat, reduce to a simmer, and add the leeks. Cover and cook until the leeks are tender, about 30 minutes.

3. With a slotted spoon, transfer the leeks to a serving platter. Add the oil and salt to the sauce in the skillet, return to a boil over high heat, and cook, stirring constantly, for 1 minute. Spoon the sauce over the leeks, sprinkle the bell pepper on top, and serve.

Helpful hints: This can be prepared 1 day ahead and refrigerated—the leeks will absorb even more flavor. Do not add the bell pepper until just before serving. Depending on the rest of the menu, the leeks can be served hot, at room temperature, or chilled.

FAT: 4G/24%

CALORIES: 143

SATURATED FAT: 0.5G

CARBOHYDRATE: 26G

PROTEIN: 3G

CHOLESTEROL: 0MG

SODIUM: 430MG

Sweet Potato Purée

SERVES: 4

WORKING TIME: 25 MINUTES

TOTAL TIME: 40 MINUTES

Vividly orange and enticingly flavorful, these creamy potatoes are deceptively rich, but actually contain very little fat.

1¾ **pounds sweet potatoes, peeled and thinly sliced**

½ **pound baking potatoes, peeled and thinly sliced**

5 **cloves garlic, thinly sliced**

2 **cups reduced-sodium chicken broth, defatted, or reduced-sodium vegetable broth**

¼ **cup reduced-fat sour cream**

1 **tablespoon olive oil**

1 **teaspoon sugar**

¾ **teaspoon dried thyme**

¾ **teaspoon ground ginger**

½ **teaspoon salt**

½ **teaspoon freshly ground black pepper**

1. In a large saucepan, combine the sweet potatoes, baking potatoes, garlic, broth, and 1 cup of water. Bring to a boil, reduce to a simmer, cover, and cook until the potatoes are tender, about 20 minutes. Drain well, reserving the cooking liquid.

2. Transfer the potatoes to a large bowl. Add the sour cream, oil, sugar, thyme, ginger, salt, and pepper. With a potato masher or an electric beater, mash the mixture until smooth, adding enough of the reserved cooking liquid to make a creamy purée. Spoon the purée into a large bowl and serve.

Helpful hint: Turn any leftovers into a satisfying potato soup by reheating the purée over low heat and then stirring in enough reduced-sodium chicken broth to thin.

FAT: 6G/20%

CALORIES: 259

SATURATED FAT: 1.5G

CARBOHYDRATE: 47G

PROTEIN: 6G

CHOLESTEROL: 5MG

SODIUM: 626MG

Orange-Glazed Baked Acorn Squash

SERVES: 4
WORKING TIME: 15 MINUTES
TOTAL TIME: 55 MINUTES

This is so delicious you may want to double the recipe to have leftovers to enjoy the next day. Baking squash in a hot oven brings out its natural sweetness, while the orange-maple syrup glaze adds a wonderfully tangy flavor. These squash halves would look inviting on any dinner plate—for even more color, fill them with cooked peas.

2 small acorn squash (¾ pound each), halved lengthwise and seeded

½ teaspoon salt

¼ teaspoon freshly ground black pepper

¼ cup maple syrup

½ cup orange juice, preferably fresh

2 tablespoons orange marmalade

1 tablespoon fresh lemon juice

1. Preheat the oven to 450°. Sprinkle the cut sides of the squash with ¼ teaspoon of the salt and the pepper. Fill a large baking pan with 1 inch of water and place the squash, cut-sides up, in the pan. Brush 1 tablespoon of the maple syrup over the cut sides of the squash, cover with foil, and bake for 25 minutes, or until the squash is tender. Leave the oven on.

2. Meanwhile, in a small saucepan, combine the remaining 3 tablespoons maple syrup, the orange juice, marmalade, lemon juice, and remaining ¼ teaspoon salt, and bring to a boil over medium heat. Cook until the mixture is reduced to a syrup thick enough to coat the back of a spoon, about 5 minutes.

3. Remove the squash from the baking pan and discard the water. Return the squash to the pan, cut-sides up. Brush the squash with the syrup and bake for 15 minutes longer, or until the syrup is slightly reduced and the squash is lightly browned around the edges.

Helpful hints: Select acorn squash of equal size so the halves finish baking at the same time. If you'd like a bit of herb flavor, add a pinch of dried rosemary to the maple syrup mixture.

FAT: 0.2G/1%
CALORIES: 143
SATURATED FAT: 0G
CARBOHYDRATE: 37G
PROTEIN: 1G
CHOLESTEROL: 0MG
SODIUM: 285MG

Orange-Glazed Carrots

MAKES: 4 CUPS
WORKING TIME: 20 MINUTES
TOTAL TIME: 40 MINUTES

For this simple and appealing side dish, the tartness of orange deliciously underscores the sweetness of carrots. And a subtle Oriental touch has been added and the taste enlivened with a little ginger. These carrots look especially inviting on a big buffet table with other great holiday staples—orange yams, green beans, ruby red cranberry sauce, and a golden bird.

2 pounds carrots, cut lengthwise into thirds, then into 2-inch pieces

¾ teaspoon finely julienned orange zest

1½ cups fresh orange juice

2 cloves garlic, minced

⅓ cup thinly sliced scallion whites

1 tablespoon firmly packed light brown sugar

2 teaspoons unsalted butter

1 teaspoon ground ginger

½ teaspoon salt

¼ cup thinly sliced scallion greens

1. In a large saucepan, combine the carrots, orange zest, orange juice, garlic, scallion whites, brown sugar, butter, ginger, and salt. Bring to a boil over medium heat and cook gently, stirring occasionally, until the carrots are tender and glossy and the liquid is syrupy, about 20 minutes.

2. Stir in the scallion greens until well combined. Spoon the carrots into a medium bowl and serve.

Helpful hints: Plan on using 5 or 6 oranges for the amount of juice needed. This dish can be prepared up to 1 day ahead through Step 1. To serve, gently reheat, stirring occasionally, on the stovetop over low heat or in a microwave on half power. Mix in the scallion greens just before serving.

VALUES ARE PER ½ CUP
FAT: 1G/13%
CALORIES: 88
SATURATED FAT: 0.6G
CARBOHYDRATE: 19G
PROTEIN: 2G
CHOLESTEROL: 3MG
SODIUM: 179MG

Sautéed Spinach with Sun-Dried Tomatoes

SERVES: 4
WORKING TIME: 10 MINUTES
TOTAL TIME: 20 MINUTES

*Make a lovely meatless meal of a big baked potato and this garlicky spinach—
it's sautéed with bits of sweet sun-dried tomatoes.*

½ **cup sun-dried (not oil-packed) tomato halves**

1 cup boiling water

2 teaspoons olive oil

2 cloves garlic, minced

⅛ **teaspoon red pepper flakes**

2 pounds fresh spinach leaves

½ **teaspoon salt**

⅛ **teaspoon sugar**

¼ **cup reduced-sodium chicken broth, defatted**

1. In a small bowl, combine the sun-dried tomatoes and boiling water and let stand until the tomatoes have softened, about 15 minutes. Drain the tomatoes, reserving ¼ cup of the soaking liquid. Coarsely chop the tomatoes and set aside.

2. In a large nonstick skillet, heat the oil over medium heat until hot but not smoking. Add the garlic, red pepper flakes, spinach, salt, sugar, and broth, and cook just until the garlic is fragrant, about 3 minutes. Add the sun-dried tomatoes and the reserved soaking liquid. Cover and cook just until the spinach is wilted, about 4 minutes. Spoon onto 4 plates and serve.

Helpful hint: Sand and grit will rinse out of spinach more quickly if you rinse the leaves in lukewarm, rather than ice-cold, tap water.

FAT: 3G/28%
CALORIES: 98
SATURATED FAT: 0.4G
CARBOHYDRATE: 14G
PROTEIN: 8G
CHOLESTEROL: 0MG
SODIUM: 501MG

Creamy Mashed Rutabaga

MAKES: 5 CUPS
WORKING TIME: 20 MINUTES
TOTAL TIME: 45 MINUTES

The apple adds a tangy sweetness to the already subtly sweet rutabaga.
This is a natural with roast turkey or chicken.

1¾ pounds rutabaga, peeled and thickly sliced

1 Granny Smith apple, peeled, cored, and thickly sliced

3 cloves garlic, slivered

¾ teaspoon dried marjoram or oregano

½ teaspoon salt

3 tablespoons evaporated low-fat milk

2 tablespoons grated Parmesan cheese

2 teaspoons unsalted butter

1. In a large saucepan, combine the rutabaga, apple, garlic, marjoram, and ¼ teaspoon of the salt. Add cold water to cover by 1 inch and bring to a boil. Reduce to a simmer, cover, and cook until the rutabaga is tender, about 25 minutes. Drain well and transfer the mixture to a large bowl.

2. Add the evaporated milk, Parmesan, butter, and remaining ¼ teaspoon salt, and mash until the mixture is well blended but still chunky. Spoon the rutabaga mixture onto a platter and serve.

Helpful hints: This recipe can be prepared 1 day ahead through Step 1 and refrigerated. To serve, gently reheat over low heat, stirring in the remaining ingredients. If you prefer a smooth vegetable purée, mash the mixture with a potato masher or an electric beater until no lumps remain.

VALUES ARE PER ½ CUP
FAT: 1G/24%
CALORIES: 48
SATURATED FAT: 0.7G
CARBOHYDRATE: 8G
PROTEIN: 2G
CHOLESTEROL: 4MG
SODIUM: 147MG

Creamed Onions

MAKES: 4 CUPS
WORKING TIME: 20 MINUTES
TOTAL TIME: 55 MINUTES

*No holiday buffet would be complete without this all-time favorite—made with
a low-fat white sauce, not cream.*

1½ pounds small white onions, peeled

1 teaspoon unsalted butter

1 teaspoon sugar

2 tablespoons flour

2¼ cups low-fat (1%) milk

¾ teaspoon salt

½ teaspoon dried thyme

¼ teaspoon freshly ground black pepper

¼ cup finely chopped fresh parsley

1. In a large pot of boiling water, cook the onions for 2 minutes to blanch. Drain well.

2. In a large nonstick skillet, melt the butter over low heat. Add the onions, sprinkle the sugar on top, and cook, shaking the pan frequently, until the onions are lightly golden and glazed, about 5 minutes.

3. Meanwhile, place the flour in a medium saucepan, and gradually whisk in the milk over medium heat until no lumps remain. Bring to a boil and whisk in the salt, thyme, and pepper. Reduce to a simmer and cook, whisking frequently, until the sauce is slightly thickened, about 5 minutes.

4. Pour the sauce over the onions, add the parsley, and stir well to combine. Return the pan to low heat, cover, and cook until the onions are tender, about 25 minutes.

Helpful hint: The onions and white sauce can be prepared earlier in the day and stored separately in the refrigerator. To serve, proceed with Step 4.

VALUES ARE PER ½ CUP
FAT: 1G/15%
CALORIES: 76
SATURATED FAT: 0.7G
CARBOHYDRATE: 13G
PROTEIN: 4G
CHOLESTEROL: 4MG
SODIUM: 250MG

Cauliflower Milanese

SERVES: 4
WORKING TIME: 15 MINUTES
TOTAL TIME: 40 MINUTES

The bread crumbs and Parmesan that top the cauliflower are what make this "Milanese."
However, one traditional Milanese ingredient—butter—has been replaced by a touch
of olive oil for a more healthful dish.

5 cups cauliflower florets

½ cup reduced-sodium chicken broth, defatted

¾ teaspoon grated lemon zest

½ teaspoon salt

½ teaspoon dried marjoram

¼ teaspoon freshly ground black pepper

¼ cup plain dried bread crumbs

2 tablespoons grated Parmesan cheese

1 teaspoon olive oil

2 teaspoons fresh lemon juice

1. Preheat the oven to 400°. In a large pot of boiling water, cook the cauliflower for 4 minutes to blanch. Drain well.

2. Meanwhile, in a small bowl, combine the broth, lemon zest, salt, marjoram, and pepper. Set aside. In another small bowl, combine the bread crumbs and Parmesan. Set aside.

3. Spread the oil in a 13 x 9-inch baking dish and heat in the oven until hot, about 4 minutes. Add the cauliflower to the baking dish and bake, stirring occasionally, for 7 minutes, or until the cauliflower is golden. Pour the reserved broth mixture over the cauliflower and bake for 7 minutes, or until the cauliflower is tender. Sprinkle the bread crumb mixture over the cauliflower, drizzle with the lemon juice, and bake for 5 minutes, or until the topping is lightly crisped.

Helpful hint: Choose a firm cauliflower head that's creamy white with crisp, green leaves at the base. Pass up heads that have dark speckles or soft spots.

FAT: 3G/22%
CALORIES: 82
SATURATED FAT: 0.7G
CARBOHYDRATE: 12G
PROTEIN: 5G
CHOLESTEROL: 2MG
SODIUM: 478MG

Strawberry Cheesecake Mousse

SERVES: 4
WORKING TIME: 20 MINUTES
TOTAL TIME: 20 MINUTES PLUS CHILLING TIME

Compare this recipe to one for a baked cheesecake and you'll notice that both the ingredients list and the preparation time have been dramatically shortened. Of course, this isn't a cake—instead of baking the filling in a crust, you spoon it into dessert bowls. The "cheesecake" mixture has a touch of tartness, and the flavor of the strawberries is underscored with a swirl of strawberry spreadable fruit.

½ **teaspoon unflavored gelatin**

2 **pints fresh strawberries**

2 **tablespoons strawberry spreadable fruit**

8 **ounces nonfat cream cheese**

¼ **cup reduced-fat sour cream**

½ **cup sugar**

½ **cup evaporated milk, chilled**

1. Place ¼ cup of cold water in a small bowl, sprinkle the gelatin on top, and let stand until softened, about 4 minutes. Set the bowl over a small saucepan of simmering water and stir until the gelatin dissolves, about 3 minutes. Set aside to cool.

2. Meanwhile, reserving 4 whole berries for a garnish, halve the strawberries. In a medium bowl, combine the halved fresh strawberries and the spreadable fruit, tossing until well coated.

3. In a food processor, combine the cream cheese, 2 tablespoons of the sour cream, and ¼ cup of the sugar, and process until smooth. In a medium bowl, with an electric mixer, beat the evaporated milk with the remaining 2 tablespoons sour cream and remaining ¼ cup sugar until soft peaks form. Gradually beat in the cooled gelatin mixture.

4. Fold the cream cheese mixture into the evaporated milk mixture. Divide the strawberry mixture among 4 goblets or dessert bowls. Top with the "cheesecake" mixture and garnish with the reserved strawberries. Chill until set, about 1 hour, and serve.

Helpful hint: Spreadable fruit is like jam, but it is sweetened with fruit juice rather than sugar. It is used in this recipe because it is soft enough, even at room temperature, to coat the strawberries.

FAT: 5G/16%
CALORIES: 282
SATURATED FAT: 2.5G
CARBOHYDRATE: 49G
PROTEIN: 12G
CHOLESTEROL: 20MG
SODIUM: 314MG

Raspberry-Filled Chocolate Cupcakes

MAKES: 1 DOZEN
WORKING TIME: 30 MINUTES
TOTAL TIME: 50 MINUTES PLUS COOLING TIME

The cream-filled cupcakes of our childhood now have a grown-up counterpart: petite chocolate cakes with hearts of raspberry jam (which you can flavor with raspberry liqueur for a truly adult treat). The cupcakes are decorated with a swirl of semisweet chocolate and a few fresh berries. Red paper cups add a note of sophistication; look for them in kitchenware shops.

⅓ cup raspberry spreadable fruit

¾ teaspoon raspberry-flavored liqueur (optional)

1¼ cups flour

3 tablespoons unsweetened cocoa powder

½ teaspoon baking soda

⅛ teaspoon salt

¼ cup unsalted butter, at room temperature

½ cup sugar

1 large egg

⅔ cup low-fat (1%) milk

½ ounce chocolate chips (about 1 tablespoon), melted

1 cup fresh raspberries

1. Preheat the oven to 375°. Line twelve 2½-inch muffin-tin cups with paper liners or spray with nonstick cooking spray; set aside. In a small bowl, combine the raspberry spreadable fruit and the raspberry liqueur; set aside.

2. In a medium bowl, combine the flour, cocoa powder, baking soda, and salt. In a large bowl, with an electric mixer, beat the butter and sugar until light and fluffy. Add the egg and beat until well combined. Alternately beat in the flour mixture and the milk, beginning and ending with the flour mixture.

3. Spoon about 1 tablespoon of batter into each muffin cup. Make a small indentation in the batter. Dividing evenly, spoon the raspberry spreadable fruit mixture into each indentation (using about 1¼ teaspoons per cupcake). Spoon the remaining batter evenly over the raspberry mixture. Bake for 20 minutes, or until the tops of the cupcakes spring back when lightly touched. Turn the cupcakes out onto a wire rack to cool completely.

4. Spoon the melted chocolate into a small plastic bag, then snip off the very tip of one corner of the bag. Pipe the melted chocolate on top of each cupcake. Top with fresh raspberries before serving.

Helpful hint: If you like, cherry-flavored kirsch can be substituted for the raspberry-flavored liqueur.

VALUES ARE PER CUPCAKE
FAT: 5G/29%
CALORIES: 158
SATURATED FAT: 2.9G
CARBOHYDRATE: 26G
PROTEIN: 3G
CHOLESTEROL: 29MG
SODIUM: 89MG

Lemon Poppy Seed Cake

SERVES: 12
WORKING TIME: 20 MINUTES
TOTAL TIME: 1 HOUR PLUS COOLING TIME

This is one of those moist cakes that tastes better a day after baking. Delicately textured, it makes a wonderful indulgence for a special brunch or dinner, or a quiet tea break in the afternoon. Keep this recipe in mind when you need a hostess offering for a holiday party—it will always be welcome.

3 tablespoons poppy seeds

2½ cups cake flour

1½ teaspoons baking powder

½ teaspoon baking soda

¼ teaspoon salt

¼ teaspoon ground allspice

2 whole eggs

1 egg white

6 tablespoons unsalted butter

1¾ cups sugar

1 tablespoon grated lemon zest

1½ cups low-fat (1.5%) buttermilk

¼ cup fresh lemon juice

1. Preheat the oven to 350°. Spray a 10-inch angel food or tube cake pan with nonstick cooking spray. Dust with flour, shaking off the excess. Spread the poppy seeds on a baking sheet with sides and bake for 4 minutes, or until lightly crisped. Set aside to cool.

2. On a sheet of wax paper, combine the flour, baking powder, baking soda, salt, allspice, and poppy seeds. In a small bowl, whisk together the eggs and egg white. In a large bowl, with an electric mixer, beat the butter, 1½ cups of the sugar, and the lemon zest until creamy. Gradually beat in the egg mixture, 1 teaspoon at a time, until light in texture. With a rubber spatula, alternately fold in the flour mixture and buttermilk, beginning and ending with the flour mixture, until just blended. Scrape the batter into the prepared pan, smoothing the top. Bake for 35 minutes, or until a toothpick inserted in the center comes out clean. Transfer to a wire rack.

3. In a small saucepan, stir together the lemon juice and remaining ¼ cup sugar. Bring to a boil over medium heat and cook, stirring constantly, until the sugar dissolves, about 2 minutes. With a fork, prick holes in the top of the cake and pour the hot syrup over the cake. Transfer to a wire rack and cool the cake in the pan for 10 minutes. Turn out onto the rack; cool completely.

Helpful hint: For homemade buttermilk, combine 1½ tablespoons lemon juice and 1½ cups low-fat milk; let stand for 5 minutes to sour.

FAT: 8G/26%
CALORIES: 290
SATURATED FAT: 4.3G
CARBOHYDRATE: 50G
PROTEIN: 5G
CHOLESTEROL: 53MG
SODIUM: 191MG

Berry Cake

SERVES: 8
WORKING TIME: 15 MINUTES
TOTAL TIME: 50 MINUTES PLUS COOLING TIME

This irresistible buttermilk cake is a snap to make, and it comes with its own garnish to boot—fresh berries peeking out from a crispy, glossy top. It's perfect for a convivial morning coffee klatch, a gracious afternoon tea, or a casual dinner with friends. Try it in the summer, when berries are in season.

1½ cups assorted whole berries (such as blackberries, blueberries, and raspberries)

1 cup flour

¾ cup plus 1 tablespoon sugar

½ teaspoon baking soda

½ teaspoon ground ginger

¼ teaspoon salt

½ cup low-fat (1.5%) buttermilk

2 tablespoons vegetable oil

2 large eggs, lightly beaten

1. Preheat the oven to 375°. Spray an 8-inch round cake pan with nonstick cooking spray. In a small bowl, combine the berries; set aside.

2. In a medium bowl, combine the flour, ¾ cup of the sugar, the baking soda, ginger, and salt. Make a well in the center and pour in the buttermilk, oil, and eggs. Stir until no dry flour is visible.

3. Scrape the batter into the prepared pan. Spoon the berries on top and sprinkle with the remaining 1 tablespoon sugar. Bake for 35 to 40 minutes, or until a toothpick inserted in the center comes out clean. Cool in the pan on a wire rack. Remove from the pan, transfer to a plate, and serve.

Helpful hints: You can use any small berries for this recipe, except strawberries, which will add too much moisture. It's important to stir the dry ingredients thoroughly to mix them, and, conversely, to go easy on the mixing once you've added the liquid ingredients so that the cake turns out nice and tender.

FAT: 5G/22%
CALORIES: 207
SATURATED FAT: 1G
CARBOHYDRATE: 37G
PROTEIN: 4G
CHOLESTEROL: 54MG
SODIUM: 171MG

Winter Fruit Compote

SERVES: 6
WORKING TIME: 20 MINUTES
TOTAL TIME: 35 MINUTES

Warm fruit compote, redolent of ginger, is a lovely cold-weather dessert; you might offer vanilla yogurt or sour cream with the compote, and pass a plate of crisp, simple cookies. The colorful fruit mixture would also be perfect at a brunch, served with warm muffins or biscuits. Stock up on cranberries at holiday time, when they're widely available, and keep them in the freezer.

½ **cup sugar**

1-inch piece of fresh ginger, peeled and very thinly slivered

2 Granny Smith apples, peeled, cored, and cut into wedges

1 firm-ripe pear, peeled, cored, and cut into ¾-inch chunks

½ **cup dried apricots**

2 cups fresh or frozen cranberries

2 oranges, peeled and sectioned

1. In a large saucepan, combine the sugar, 1½ cups of water, and the ginger. Bring to a boil over high heat. Add the apples, pear, and apricots. Reduce the heat to low and simmer, uncovered, until the fruit is softened, about 5 minutes.

2. Add the cranberries and cook, stirring occasionally, until the cranberries pop, about 5 minutes. Stir in the orange sections and remove from the heat. Transfer the compote to a bowl and serve warm or at room temperature.

Helpful hint: You can use any flavorful apple for this recipe. Some less familiar ones to try are Empires, Ida Reds, Macouns, Jonathans, Cortlands, and Winesaps.

FAT: 1G/5%
CALORIES: 172
SATURATED FAT: 0G
CARBOHYDRATE: 44G
PROTEIN: 1G
CHOLESTEROL: 0MG
SODIUM: 2MG

Gingerbread with Lemon Sauce

SERVES: 8

WORKING TIME: 20 MINUTES

TOTAL TIME: 50 MINUTES PLUS COOLING TIME

There's nothing like the aroma of gingerbread baking to bring on the holiday spirit—
crystallized ginger gives this version a tasty twist.

1¼ cups cake flour

1¼ teaspoons ground ginger

1 teaspoon baking powder

½ teaspoon baking soda

½ teaspoon cinnamon

¼ teaspoon dry mustard

¼ teaspoon salt

3 tablespoons unsalted butter

½ cup firmly packed dark brown sugar

1 egg

2 tablespoons finely chopped crystallized ginger

2 teaspoons grated lemon zest

½ cup low-fat (1.5%) buttermilk

3 tablespoons molasses

3 tablespoons freshly brewed coffee

⅓ cup fresh lemon juice

¼ cup granulated sugar

¼ teaspoon ground nutmeg

1 teaspoon cornstarch mixed with 1 tablespoon water

1 tablespoon confectioners' sugar

1. Preheat the oven to 350°. Spray an 8-inch square cake pan with nonstick cooking spray. Dust the pan with flour, shaking off the excess. Line the bottom of the pan with a square of wax paper. On a sheet of wax paper, combine the flour, ground ginger, baking powder, baking soda, cinnamon, mustard, and salt.

2. In a large bowl, with an electric mixer, beat the butter and brown sugar until creamy. Beat in the egg, crystallized ginger, and zest. In a small bowl, mix the buttermilk, molasses, and coffee. With a rubber spatula, alternately fold the flour mixture and buttermilk mixture into the butter mixture, beginning and ending with the flour mixture, until just blended. Scrape into the prepared pan and smooth the top. Bake for 25 minutes, or until a toothpick inserted in the center comes out clean. Transfer to a wire rack and cool in the pan for 10 minutes. Turn out onto the rack; cool completely.

3. In a small saucepan, stir together the lemon juice, granulated sugar, 2 tablespoons of water, and nutmeg. Bring to a boil, reduce to a simmer, and cook until the sugar dissolves, about 2 minutes. Return to a boil, stir in the cornstarch mixture, and cook, stirring, until slightly thickened, about 1 minute. Place the cake on a plate, dust with the confectioners' sugar, and serve with the sauce.

Helpful hint: To garnish, place 2 ferns or a paper doily on the cake, dust with confectioners' sugar, then carefully lift off the pattern-maker.

FAT: 5G/20%

CALORIES: 237

SATURATED FAT: 3G

CARBOHYDRATE: 45G

PROTEIN: 3G

CHOLESTEROL: 39MG

SODIUM: 235MG

Strawberry-Topped Lemon Cheesecake

SERVES: 12
WORKING TIME: 25 MINUTES
TOTAL TIME: 1 HOUR 35 MINUTES PLUS COOLING TIME

Grandly finish a holiday dinner with this spectacular cheesecake, and do so confidently, knowing its appearance and taste belie its low-fat nature—the tricks are using low-fat cottage cheese and reduced-fat cream cheese.

---

1 cup zweiback crumbs (about 12 zweiback)

1 cup graham cracker crumbs

2 tablespoons honey

1 tablespoon canola oil

2½ cups low-fat (1%) cottage cheese

11 ounces reduced-fat cream cheese (Neufchâtel)

3 tablespoons flour

1 tablespoon grated lemon zest

2 teaspoons vanilla

1¼ cups sugar

2 whole eggs

2 egg whites

1 cup halved strawberries, stems left on if desired

2 tablespoons strawberry jelly

1. Preheat the oven to 350°. In a medium bowl, stir together all the crumbs, the honey, and oil. Firmly press the mixture into the bottom and halfway up the sides of a 9-inch springform pan.

2. In a food processor or blender, combine the cottage cheese, cream cheese, flour, lemon zest, and vanilla, and purée until smooth. Add the sugar, whole eggs, and egg whites, and process until just combined. Scrape the batter into the crust and bake for 50 minutes, or until the cheesecake is still a little jiggly in the center but set around the edges. Turn off the oven, prop the oven door open, and let the cheesecake cool in the oven for 30 minutes. Transfer to a wire rack to cool completely.

3. With a metal spatula, loosen the cheesecake from the side of the pan and remove the pan side. Place the cake on a plate and arrange the strawberries in the center. In a small saucepan, warm the jelly over low heat until melted, brush over the strawberries, and serve.

Helpful hints: Other berries—such as raspberries or blueberries—could be nicely substituted for the strawberries. The cheesecake can be prepared up to 1 day ahead and refrigerated.

FAT: 10G/29%
CALORIES: 310
SATURATED FAT: 4.7G
CARBOHYDRATE: 43G
PROTEIN: 12G
CHOLESTEROL: 58MG
SODIUM: 392MG

Answers to Common Questions

RAISED-BED GARDENING

My father planted his garden in rows with good results, and I'm inclined to do the same thing. But nowadays everyone talks about raised beds. What are the advantages of raised beds?

The main advantages are that they are more productive and take less work than conventional row gardening. Because you prepare the soil intensively with organic matter and fertilizers *(pages 25-33),* you can plant vegetables very closely, getting more crops from far less space than row gardening requires. As the leaves of the vegetables touch, they shade the soil and slow weed growth. Paths don't take up as much space in a raised-bed garden as they do when vegetables are planted in rows, so you don't have to spend as much time weeding and maintaining them.

I'm building a deck and have pressure-treated scrap wood left over. Can I use it as an edging material for raised beds, or would the chemicals used in the pressure treatment contaminate vegetables grown in the beds?

The chemicals used to pressure-treat wood are quite toxic and might very well contaminate your crops. For raised beds, use ordinary wood scrap or cheap grades of redwood, black locust, or other rot-resistant wood for longevity. You can also make raised beds without constructing edges *(pages 28-29).* They really aren't needed except to improve appearance, although they may cut down on grasses creeping into the beds.

COMPOSTING AND SOIL CONDITIONING

Is there anything I shouldn't put into my compost pile?

Yes. Don't use domestic pet or human waste, since it may carry dangerous diseases or parasites. Don't use meat or meat scraps, which attract vermin and cause a stench as they decay. Don't compost diseased portions of plants that you've cut away; dispose of them with the household trash or by burning, if that is permitted in your area. Don't use coal ashes, as these contain toxic wastes; wood ashes in moderation are fine. Don't add any synthetic materials or chemicals or any plants that have been treated with herbicides or pesticides. And don't compost weeds that have set seed, or you'll spread them around the garden when you use the compost. Manures, vegetable and fruit kitchen waste, and nonseedy plant debris are all fine.

What is sheet composting?

It's a fancy name for covering the soil with the same kinds of organic matter used in a compost pile and letting them decay slowly, without turning or watering. Sheet composting has two advantages: It adds organic matter that conditions the soil as it decays, and it acts as a mulch to keep weed growth down and the soil moist. Make sure the material contains no weed seeds or other kinds of seeds; it won't be massive enough to heat up, so seeds will remain viable. On the downside, sheet-composted material may provide a breeding ground for slugs, pill bugs, earwigs, and other unwanted insects. It may also deplete the soil of nitrogen unless high-nitrogen materials such as farmyard manure are included.

Where's the best place to build my compost pile—in the shade or in the sun? And should I cover it with black plastic?

The best place for the pile is close to the garden so the hose reaches it and you don't have to carry the finished compost very far. A shady spot is probably best because the composting organic matter won't dry out as fast as it would in sun. Covering the pile with black plastic holds in moisture and keeps the temperature in the pile higher, so it decays faster. The plastic will also prevent hard rains from dissolving and leaching nutrients from the pile.

Whenever I put my kitchen waste into the compost pile, raccoons, opossums, dogs, and who-knows-what-else tear the pile apart to get at it. Is there a convenient way I can compost my kitchen waste without having this problem?

An easy solution is to keep special garbage-eating worms called red wigglers in a container that marauding animals can't get into, and let them turn your kitchen scraps into compost. A sturdy wood box with a lid and a hardware-cloth bottom will serve nicely, or you can buy a plastic worm bin from a mail-order garden supply company, along with red wigglers.

I've tried making compost, but it doesn't heat up, and it smells bad. What's the problem?

It probably doesn't heat up because the pile doesn't have enough nitrogen-rich material such as fresh farm-animal manure. A pile that's layered with 3 or 4 parts plant debris to 1 part fresh manure and that's kept moist but not sopping wet will heat up. Your compost smells bad because little or no air is getting into the pile, and anaerobic bacteria are decomposing it. Rebuild it, adding manure and layering in straw, pine needles, or other coarse materials to get air into the pile. Aerobic bacteria will continue to decompose the pile, but it will not smell bad.

My soil is very acid, and I need to raise its pH from 5 to at least 6.5. What's the organic way to do this?

Two substances that are especially good at raising a soil's pH are leached wood ashes and ground limestone. Wood ashes work faster, but ground limestone sweetens the soil over a longer period of time. Use 10 pounds of limestone or 2 pounds of wood ashes per 100 square feet, worked into the top 6 inches of soil, to raise the pH 1 point. Don't raise it more than 1 point per year. If you use 10 pounds per 100 square feet this year and 5 pounds next year, your soil pH should increase 1.5 points to reach your target level.

PLANTING AND CARE—VEGETABLES

Is rooting hormone—the kind you use to stimulate root formation on cuttings—organic?

Yes. Rooting hormones are naturally occurring plant substances and are perfectly safe to use in an organic garden. Cuttings from sweet potato vines should be dipped in rooting hormone before planting, and you can also dip root cuttings from small bush fruits such as currants to stimulate rooting. Gardeners in areas with long growing seasons can also use the hormone to root stem cuttings of their early eggplant, tomato, and pepper crops for subsequent plantings.

Is companion planting—for example, putting beans and onions side by side because they like each other—a valid organic technique or an old wives' tale?

Companion planting is a valid technique, but not because plants "like" each other. It works for one of several reasons: because the companions have different needs and thus don't compete with one another for nutrients; because their root zones are at different levels and their roots don't compete for space; or because one of the companions helps protect the other from predatory insects.

What is manure tea and how do I use it?

Manure tea is one of the secrets to success in an organic garden. Put 1 gallon of fresh, rotted, or dried farm-animal manure or manure-based compost in a burlap or muslin bag and close it securely (use poultry, goat, horse, or cow manure only). Put the bag in a 5-gallon bucket and fill it with water. Let the manure steep for 3 days to a week. Spray this manure tea onto growing plants every 3 to 4 days. It is especially helpful when they are growing rapidly or setting flowers or fruit. You'll be amazed at how well plants respond.

I know some organic gardeners who swear by foliar seaweed spray. Is there any value in this?

Yes. Foliar seaweed spray is an extract of seaweed containing many trace elements that are essential for vigorous growth in many plants. These nutrients can be absorbed through a plant's leaves as well as its roots, so regular applications of foliar seaweed spray are certainly beneficial.

Is one kind of mulch better than another?

Organic gardeners use all sorts of materials to cover bare soil—black plastic, cardboard, leaves, shredded bark, compost, grass clippings that are free of pesticides and herbicides, farm-animal bedding, and spoiled hay are just a few of the possibilities. Even stones can serve as mulch if they cover the surface of the soil completely. For most situations, it is best to use an organic mulch because it offers multiple benefits: suppressing weeds, conserving soil moisture, acting as a fertilizer, and decomposing into soil-conditioning humus.

HERBAL DESIGN AND LANDSCAPE USE

A cottage garden would fit in perfectly outside my kitchen door. How can I achieve the look of lush informality using herbs?

Herbs are particularly well suited to a cottage garden design. But don't let the seemingly random nature of a cottage garden fool you; it takes careful planning to achieve the casual effect. Begin by listing the plants and combinations you want to include. When you plant, place herbs, annuals, and perennials close together so that bare soil is covered quickly. If some plants die or simply don't look good together, remove them and experiment until the planting pleases you. Try arranging foliage and flowers in specific color combinations such as gray and red or blue and gold. Or plant freely and see what pairings of foliage, plant shape, and flower form and color arise.

I love to grow roses and wonder if I can plant my herbs with them.

Absolutely. Roses and herbs make ideal companions. Plant sun-loving herbs such as lavender, rosemary, thyme, and sage near roses to highlight their blooms. But be sure to space the plants generously to give roses good air circulation.

I've always wanted a knot garden, but I don't have a big yard. Any suggestions?

Create a miniature knot garden in a container. Select herbs that take well to container culture, such as basil, thyme, chamomile, and rosemary, and keep them neatly pruned. Devise a knot pattern that looks good when viewed from above—star shapes and figure eights are only two of the possibilities. If you can't overwinter the miniature knot garden, harvest the herbs at the end of the growing season and start over in the spring.

PLANTING AND CARE—HERBS

Which herbs are best grown from seed and which ones should I start from plants?

Sow fast-growing, short-lived annuals such as dill, coriander, and nasturtium directly in your garden. Many biennials, including angelica and clary sage, also take best to direct-sowing. Perennial herbs can be grown from seed, division, cuttings, or layering. The method will vary depending on the plant. For example, thyme, lavender, rosemary, and mint hybridize freely and are best grown from cuttings. Other perennials such as lovage are best propagated by division.

I would like to harvest seeds from my herbs, but I don't know when or how to harvest them.

Seeds are ripe when they have just turned brown. Cut the seed heads on a dry day and place them in a brown bag. Let the seeds dry for 1 to 2 weeks, and when they are completely dry, store them in airtight jars. For more information on harvesting seeds to start next year's herb garden, as well as a list of herbs with aromatic seeds, see page 120.

When I order new herb plants, how do I know if they are correctly labeled?

First check the plants against the encyclopedia descriptions and photographs starting on page 250. If you believe a plant is labeled incorrectly but can't identify it yourself, cut a stem of the plant when it is in bloom and take both leaves and flowers to a nursery or garden center for identification. You can also press the specimen and have it identified at a later date. If there is a chance the herb in question is poisonous, be sure not to ingest it.

Are there any culinary herbs that will grow in a shady container?

Sweet cicely (*Myrrhis odorata*) and chervil (*Anthriscus cerefolium*) prefer shade; mint, angelica, and lovage grow well in light shade. Although you can grow sun-loving herbs in light shade, their flavor will be less intense and often they will not flower. In hot climates, some gardeners plant herbs in a location that gets midday shade to prevent them from being scorched by the summer sun.

Can I have a productive herb garden indoors?

Herbs generally grow best in the garden, where they can enjoy full sun, fresh air, and plenty of soil. If you want to cultivate herbs indoors, they will perform better under commercial plant lights. During warm seasons, the herbs will need more water, but take care not to overwater them in winter.

Is it true that herbs have better flavor if they are grown in poor soil?

No. Herbs have the fullest flavor when planted in moderately fertile soil that encourages healthy, strong growth. Soil that is too rich or too poor will result in herbs with compromised flavor and a greater susceptibility to disease.

Will the flavor of an herb decrease if I fertilize it? Should I limit the amount of compost applied to the soil?

Using moderate amounts of fertilizer will not diminish an herb's flavor. However, heavy fertilization will encourage weak and unhealthy growth, particularly in culinary herbs. Compost is a great soil amendment for herbs, but again, don't overdo it.

What is poultry grit? Why should I add it to the soil in which I grow herbs?

Poultry grit is finely crushed rock—usually granite—given to chickens and other poultry to aid their digestion. It is available in three sizes and can be purchased at a farm-supply store. Medium-sized poultry grit added to soil improves drainage best and increases aeration around plant roots. In heavy clay soils it works better than sand because its particles are larger than grains of sand. Since poultry grit is inorganic and does not break down over time, add it to the soil only once. Herb gardeners can also use poultry grit as a mulch, spreading a 3-inch layer over the soil surface.

Should I mulch my herbs? Which mulches do you recommend?

Like all plants, herbs should be mulched for weed control and in soils where moisture retention is a problem. But be sure to use a mulch that does not hold in too much moisture, and keep the mulch away from the crown of the plant to prevent rot. Mediterranean herbs such as rosemary, thyme, and oregano are especially prone to rotting if a heavy mulch is used. Gravel, sand, and poultry grit are good choices for herbs that like good drainage. Other options include cocoa hulls, fine pine chips, and pine needles, all of which add a handsome finish of color and texture to the garden.

When should I pinch back my herbs to make them bushier?

It varies with the life cycle of each herb. Rosemary, for example, benefits from an early, low pinching to encourage side branching. Most perennial herbs respond well to a midspring pinching back to stimulate dense growth. Annual herbs with a short life cycle, such as dill and coriander, do not require any pinching. When harvesting them, take the entire plant. Annual herbs whose leaves you plan to harvest throughout the growing season, such as basil and chervil, should be pinched back in early summer to encourage bushiness. Removing their flower buds whenever they appear will hasten the growth of new foliage.

I want to rejuvenate an established lavender plant that has grown leggy and produces few blooms. Will pruning it do the job?

Yes. Prune your lavender in early spring just as new growth emerges. To rejuvenate an old plant, cut it back close to the base instead of pruning it lightly. Although you may lose the plant completely if it has grown weak and feeble, more likely it will return stronger and healthier than before.

How do you make an herb tea?

Herb teas can be made with either fresh or dried herbs, but fresh herbs result in a more pungent brew. Place the shredded leaves, seeds, or chopped root or bark in a teapot, using about 3 teaspoons of fresh or 1 heaping teaspoon of dried ingredients per cup. Add boiling water, let the tea steep for 3 to 5 minutes, strain, and serve. If you like strong tea, use a larger quantity of herbs; brewing the tea more than 5 minutes may result in an off taste.

Which herbs should I grow for herb tea?

Delicious herb teas are made from pungent herbs such as lemon verbena, which has a tart, lemon flavor; chamomile, which is fragrant and relaxing; sage, which tastes best in the cold months because it has a warming quality; and anise seed, which possesses a warm and wonderful licorice flavor. Create blends to suit your own taste. For example, peppermint combined with spearmint makes a soothing tea.

Is there any trick to preparing herbal vinegars?

No, they are easy to make. To quickly extract herbal essences, warm up any type of vinegar—wine vinegar is a good choice—and pour it into a sterile bottle filled with your favorite culinary herbs. Avoid using metal utensils, which may react with the vinegar, producing an unpleasant taste. You can also make flavored vinegar by adding herbs to a bottle of vinegar and setting it in the sun for 2 weeks. Strain the vinegar and replace the herbs with attractive fresh ones if you plan to display the vinegar or give it as a gift. Choice herbs used to flavor vinegars include tarragon, lemon verbena, basil, garlic, and chili peppers.

Is there a fun way to teach children about the life cycle of plants from seed to harvest using herbs?

Try making a salad farm using edible herbs that grow easily from seed. As they tend the miniature farm, children will learn about seed germination, a seedling's growth cycle, plant care, and when and how to harvest. If you have seeds that were collected from the garden, show children how to separate the ripe seeds from the rest of the plant. Sow the seed in rows and label each row. Watch the plants grow, and harvest them for salads. Some of the best plants to grow from seed are coriander, corn salad, dill, lettuce, nasturtium, purple hyacinth bean, arugula, and sweet fennel.

PESTS AND DISEASES

How can I attract beneficial insects to my garden?

Reserve a portion of the garden for whatever weeds happen to appear there. Beneficial insects are adapted to the local flora, using it as a source of food, as hunting grounds for prey, and for shelter. Also, make sure you plant a number of umbelliferous plants—such as fennel, carrot, and dill—in your garden. These are nectar sources for several beneficials, including green lacewings. Finally, don't use pesticides. Beneficial insects are more susceptible to pesticides than pests and will be the first to be killed off.

I understand that rotenone, ryania, and sabadilla are all organically acceptable pesticides. Should I dust the garden routinely with them as a preventive?

No. Although these pesticides are derived from plants and are active for a comparatively short time, each of them kills a broad spectrum of insects and can do the same kind of ecological damage as chemical pesticides. The goal is not a garden free of pests—you simply want to keep their numbers to a manageable level. Try beneficial insects, the physical controls described in Chapter 6, and other, less toxic methods of organic insect control before reaching for these pesticides. They should be used only as a last resort.

I've heard that organic gardeners use homemade sprays containing hot chili peppers, garlic, or tobacco on their vegetables to ward off pests. Do they work?

Yes. Many insects won't go near a plant sprayed with these substances. But never use a tobacco spray on any vegetables of the nightshade family, which includes tomatoes, potatoes, and eggplant; tobacco is also a member of the nightshade family and harbors a mosaic virus that can be spread to these crops by spraying.

I carefully start my plants from seed, then set them in the garden. Many times I find them snipped off just above the soil line, as if they were felled like little trees, but I haven't seen any pests chewing on their stems. What's causing this?

Your problem is almost certainly cutworms, grayish brown wormlike grubs that eat through the stems of tender seedlings. The reason you haven't seen them is that they feed at night and hide in the soil, under mulch, or in other sheltered places during the day. The solution is to put protective paper collars around your seedlings at planting time. The illustration on page 60 shows how to make these barriers, which are very effective.

My beet leaves have little white trails twisting and turning on them. Eventually, the leaves turn yellow and die. What is this and how do I stop it?

The problem is leaf miners, little insect larvae that burrow through the soft tissue between the outer layers of the leaves. If there are nearby stands of lamb's-quarters, a common weed, pull them out, since they may harbor these pests. Also, cover your beets when young with a lightweight floating row cover that lets in air, water, and light; it will keep adults from laying their eggs in the beet leaves.

Most years my strawberry plants get powdery mildew on their leaves. How can I prevent this organically?

Thin your plants to increase the flow of air between them, and pick off and destroy infected foliage. You can apply lime sulfur, available at garden centers, as directed on the package, or spray plants with a solution of 1 tablespoon of baking soda in a gallon of water; adding ⅛ to ¼ teaspoon of insecticidal soap will help the spray stick to the leaves. Don't increase the proportion of baking soda, as a higher concentration can damage leaves.

Here in the West, gophers are an awful problem. They burrow through the soil, eating the roots off many plants, even pulling whole plants down into their burrows. What can I do to control them?

A king snake, black snake, or gopher snake is a great boon where gophers are a problem, and some cats are avid gopher hunters. But lacking these predators, you might try mechanical gopher traps.

I have tried growing broccoli several times, but something always eats tiny holes in the seedlings' leaves. What can I do about this?

Your problem is flea beetles, fast-moving little pests that eat holes in the leaves of many members of the cabbage family, including broccoli. Before setting out your seedlings, try planting early crops of radishes and mustard greens, which the flea beetles will attack. When these "trap crops" are full of beetles, pull the plants and destroy them. Next, place bright yellow commercial sticky traps or homemade traps *(pages 102-103)* every 10 feet in the space reserved for broccoli to attract and kill any remaining beetles. Then plant your seedlings.

The branches of my bay tree (Laurus nobilis) are often covered with a brown crust. What is the problem and what is the best way for me to get rid of it?

Piercing-sucking scale insects—shiny brown and shell-like in appearance—are a common problem on bay trees. Left untreated, scales will spread to the foliage of a bay tree and eventually kill it. To control a small infestation, try scrubbing them off with a cotton-tipped swab or soft toothbrush dipped in soapy water or a solution of 1 part each of rubbing alcohol and water. For a larger infestation, spray on a horticultural oil; once this is done, however, you must refrain from using the leaves for culinary purposes.

Some of my herbs die out in summer when the weather gets hot and humid. What is the problem and what can I do about it?

In regions of the country with extended periods of hot, humid weather, the branches of herbs may turn brown and die as a result of diseases caused by soil fungi. These disease organisms are activated when plants are stressed and the weather is humid. Removing all the diseased portions of the plant will help to revive it, but if the herb is severely infected, dispose of it entirely. Then try a new plant in a different location in soil that has been amended with poultry grit, which enhances air circulation at the root zone.

Are herbs used in companion planting? How do they benefit other plants nearby?

Yes, proponents of companion planting believe that some herbs make good neighbors. They can enhance a nearby plant's growth, repel or trap pests, or attract beneficial insects. Chamomile, for example, is sometimes referred to as a "physician plant" because it is said to revive nearby ailing plants. Herbs planted with some vegetables are said to amplify their flavor, such as basil with tomatoes, and summer savory with beans. French marigolds are said to repel nematodes, and catnip and nasturtiums are possibly effective against green peach aphids. Other herbs used to keep insects away include rue, southernwood, tansy, pennyroyal, and garlic.

What are beneficial insects and what herbs attract them?

Beneficial insects include predators that kill other insects, parasites that lay their eggs on other insects, and pollinators that carry pollen from male to female flowers. Creeping predators such as ground beetles like dense, low-growing herbs such as thyme and rosemary; flying predators such as hover flies prefer chamomile and mint. Parasitic wasps like dill, anise, and flowering members of the carrot family, such as Queen Anne's lace. Most predators and parasites are excellent pollinators, too.

Troubleshooting Guide

Even the best-tended gardens can fall prey to pests and diseases. It's always better to catch an infestation or infection at an early stage, so make it a habit to inspect your plants regularly for warning signs. Keep in mind that a lack of nutrients, improper pH levels, and other environmental conditions can cause symptoms resembling those of some infectious diseases. As a rule, if wilting or yellowing appears on neighboring plants, the cause is probably environmental; damage from pests and infectious diseases is usually more random.

This guide will help you identify some of the more common pest or disease problems you may encounter. In general, good drainage and air circulation will help prevent infection. Encourage or introduce beneficial insects that prey on pests, and use row covers, handpicking, and other nonchemical methods of control. If chemical treatment becomes necessary, treat only the affected plant or plants, use an organic insecticide or fungicide, and apply sparingly. Commercial products such as insecticidal soap and neem are the least disruptive to beneficial insects and will not destroy the soil balance that is at the foundation of a healthy organic garden.

PESTS

PROBLEM: Leaves curl, are distorted in shape, may turn yellow, and may be sticky and have a black, sooty appearance. Buds and flowers are deformed, new growth is stunted, and leaves and flowers may drop off.

CAUSE: Aphids are pear shaped, semitransparent, wingless sucking insects, about ⅛ inch long and ranging in color from green to red, pink, black, or gray. They suck plant sap and may spread viral disease. Infestations are worst in spring and early summer, when the pests cluster on tender new shoots, on the undersides of leaves, and around flower buds. Aphids secrete a sticky substance known as honeydew onto leaves, which fosters the growth of a black fungus called sooty mold.

SOLUTION: Spray plants frequently with a steady stream of water from a garden hose to knock aphids off plants and discourage them from returning. In severe cases, prune off heavily infested parts and spray with insecticidal soap, horticultural oil, or pyrethrins. Introduce beneficials such as ladybugs, green lacewings, gall midges, and syrphid flies into the garden. Do not apply excessive amounts of nitrogen fertilizer.
SUSCEPTIBLE PLANTS: MOST VEGETABLES; MANY HERBS.

PROBLEM: Holes appear in leaves, flowers, and fruits; stems may also be eaten.

CAUSE: Caterpillars, including armyworms, cabbage loopers, parsley worms, and tomato hornworms, come in varied shapes, sizes, and colors. They may be smooth, hairy, or spiny. These voracious pests are the larvae of moths and butterflies.

SOLUTION: Handpick to control small populations. The bacterial pesticide *Bacillus thuringiensis* (Bt) kills many types without harming plants. Identify the caterpillar species to determine the control options and timing of spray applications. Several species are susceptible to sprays of insecticidal soap. Introduce beneficials that prey on caterpillars, such as parasitic braconid wasps, tachinid flies, and beneficial nematodes. Destroy all visible cocoons and nests.
SUSCEPTIBLE PLANTS: MOST VEGETABLES, ESPECIALLY MEMBERS OF THE CABBAGE FAMILY; MANY HERBS, INCLUDING BEE BALM, CARAWAY, HOT PEPPER, MARIGOLD, MINT, NASTURTIUM, PARSLEY, AND PINKS.

PROBLEM: Leaves and stems have ragged holes or are skeletonized and may be covered with black droppings. Young plants may die, and older plants may be defoliated.

CAUSE: Colorado potato beetles are ⅓-inch-long, oval-shaped chewing insects with yellow-and-black-striped wing covers. Emerging from the soil in spring, they feed and then lay bright orange eggs on the undersides of leaves; eggs hatch in 1 week. The plump ⅗-inch-long larvae are orange-red with black spots. They feed, enter the soil to pupate, and emerge as adults in 1 to 2 weeks. There are one to three generations a year.

SOLUTION: Handpick eggs, beetles, and larvae, and drop into soapy water. Use a thick layer of organic mulch to prevent adults from emerging from soil. Plant resistant varieties and rotate crops. Spray with Bt San Diego strain. Introduce ladybugs and spined soldier bugs. Cultivate soil in fall to kill overwintering adults. Spray plants with neem, pyrethrins, or rotenone.
SUSCEPTIBLE PLANTS: POTATOES, EGGPLANT, PEPPERS, TOMATOES.

PROBLEM: Holes appear in leaves, stalks, or husks and at the bottom of ears of corn, breaking the stems. Ears are disfigured, and kernels are eaten. Tomatoes are eaten away inside.

CAUSE: Corn ear worms are 1- to 2-inch-long yellow, green, or white caterpillars, and European corn borers are 1- to 2-inch-long beige caterpillars with brown spots and dark heads.

SOLUTION: Plant resistant varieties. Introduce tachinid flies and parasitic wasps. Spray with Bt, neem, or pyrethrins. Place 5 drops of mineral or vegetable oil in silk whorl just as silk starts to brown. Spade soil in fall to expose pupae.
SUSCEPTIBLE PLANTS: CORN EAR WORM— CORN AND TOMATOES; EUROPEAN CORN BORER—BEANS, BEETS, CELERY, CORN, PEPPERS, POTATOES, AND TOMATOES.

PROBLEM: Large oval holes appear in leaves and flowers, and new shoots may be eaten. Older plants are stunted and weakened and may fall over. Roots may be stunted. Plants may die.

CAUSE: Cucumber beetles are ¼ inch long and yellowish green with black spots or stripes. In spring, larvae hatch in 10 days to feed on plant roots and pupate in soil. Adults emerge to feed on leaves, flowers, and fruit. There are one to four generations a year. Adults and larvae carry cucumber mosaic and bacterial wilt, diseases that can kill plants.

SOLUTION: Handpick adults. Use row covers, but remove from plants that need insect pollination when flowering begins. Plant resistant varieties. Introduce beneficial nematodes, tachinid flies, and braconid wasps. Apply rotenone and sabadilla.
SUSCEPTIBLE PLANTS: CUCUMBERS, MELONS, PUMPKINS, SQUASH, AND OTHER MEMBERS OF THE CUCUMBER FAMILY. MAY ALSO ATTACK BEANS, CORN, EGGPLANT, PEAS, POTATOES, AND TOMATOES.

PROBLEM: Stems of emerging seedlings are cut off near the ground, and the plants topple over and die. Seedlings may be completely eaten. Leaves of older plants show ragged edges and holes.

CAUSE: Cutworms, the larvae of various moths, are fat, hairless, and a soft gray-brown in color. These 1- to 2-inch-long night feeders do most of their damage in the late spring. In the daytime, they curl up into a C-shape and are found under debris or below the soil surface next to the plant stem.

SOLUTION: Place cutworm collars around base of plants. Force cutworms to the soil surface by flooding the area, then handpick them. Introduce parasitic braconid wasps, tachinid flies, and beneficial nematodes. Use diatomaceous earth (DE), crushed eggshells, wood ashes, or oak-leaf mulch around plants to discourage cutworms. Cultivate the soil in late summer and fall and again in spring.
SUSCEPTIBLE PLANTS: YOUNG SEEDLINGS AND TRANSPLANTS.

PROBLEM: Numerous tiny round holes appear in leaves, making plant look as if it has been peppered with shot. Seedlings may weaken or die.

CAUSE: Flea beetles are ⅒-inch-long black, brown, bronze, or striped chewing insects that overwinter as adults and emerge in spring to feed. Eggs are laid in the soil near the plant; the larvae—¾-inch-long white grubs with brown heads—pupate in the soil and emerge as adults, which jump when disturbed. Two to four generations are produced each year. These beetles spread several viral diseases.

SOLUTION: Use row covers and white or yellow sticky traps. Spread diatomaceous earth (DE) or wood ashes around plants. Cultivate soil often to expose eggs and larvae. Introduce beneficial nematodes, braconid wasps, and tachinid flies. Pyrethrins, rotenone, and sabadilla may be used.
SUSCEPTIBLE PLANTS: MEMBERS OF THE CABBAGE FAMILY, EGGPLANT, TOMATOES.

PROBLEM: Holes are chewed in leaves, which may be reduced to skeletons with only veins remaining. Eventually, plants may be stripped of all foliage.

CAUSE: Japanese beetles have shiny metallic blue or green bodies and copper-colored wings. Voracious in the summer, they prefer feeding in sunny locations. Eggs are laid in soil in grassy or weedy areas. The fat ¾-inch-long grubs are grayish white with dark heads. They overwinter in the soil below the frostline, where they feed on the roots of grass. They pupate in late spring or early summer and emerge as adults in May, June, and July to feed and lay eggs. One generation is produced a year.

SOLUTION: Handpick small colonies, placing them in a can filled with soapy water. Use neem as a repellent. Spray with pyrethrins or rotenone. The larval stage can be controlled with milky spore disease or beneficial nematodes, both of which can be applied to the whole garden and nearby lawn areas. Introduce or encourage parasitic wasps and tachinid flies. Keep the garden well weeded.
SUSCEPTIBLE PLANTS: ASPARAGUS, BEANS, BLACKBERRIES, CORN, OKRA, POTATOES, RASPBERRIES, RHUBARB, STRAWBERRIES, TOMATOES.

PROBLEM: Leaves are skeletonized. Pods and stems may be eaten, and plants may die.

CAUSE: Mexican bean beetles are ¼-inch-long, oval-shaped, yellowish brown to copper-colored insects. With 16 black dots forming three rows across the wing covers, they look very much like a lighter-colored version of the beneficial ladybug. The yellow to orange oval larvae have long black-tipped spines. Adults overwinter in debris and emerge in early summer to feed and lay yellow egg masses on the undersides of leaves. One to four generations are produced a year.

SOLUTION: Plant resistant cultivars. Handpick adults and larvae and remove leaves with orange egg masses; drop into a container of soapy water. Cover with floating row covers until well established. Encourage or introduce spined soldier bugs and parasitic wasps. Spray undersides of leaves thoroughly with pyrethrins, neem, sabadilla, or rotenone. In fall, remove infested plants, clean garden of debris, and cultivate soil to destroy overwintering adults.
SUSCEPTIBLE PLANTS: GREEN BEANS AND LIMA BEANS ARE ESPECIALLY SUSCEPTIBLE; BLACK-EYED PEAS, KALE, SOYBEANS.

PROBLEM: Leaves become stippled or flecked, then discolor, curl, and wither. Webbing may appear, particularly on undersides of leaves. Vegetables and fruits may be stunted.

CAUSE: Mites are pinhead-sized, spider-like sucking pests that may be reddish, pale green, yellow, or brown. They are a major problem in hot, dry weather, and several generations of mites may appear in a single season. Eggs and the adults of some species hibernate over the winter in sod and bark and on plants that retain foliage.

SOLUTION: Keep plants well watered and mulched, especially during hot, dry periods. To control nymphs and adults, spray the undersides of leaves regularly with a strong stream of water or a diluted insecticidal soap solution. Remove and destroy heavily infested leaves, stems, or entire plants. Introduce predators such as ladybugs and green lacewing larvae. In severe cases, apply horticultural oil, neem, or pyrethrins. *SUSCEPTIBLE PLANTS: ASPARAGUS, BEANS, CUCUMBERS, EGGPLANT, MELONS, SQUASH, STRAWBERRIES, SUGAR PEAS, TOMATOES; MANY HERBS, PARTICULARLY THOSE RAISED IN GREENHOUSES.*

PROBLEM: Light-colored sunken brown spots appear on the upper surfaces of leaves, or tiny holes appear in leaves and stems (these are caused by stink bugs). Foliage may wilt, discolor, and fall from plants. Shoots and flower buds may be distorted or blackened, and plants may be stunted. Vegetables may be scarred or dimpled.

CAUSE: The plant bug family of sucking insects includes the ¼-inch-long oval tarnished plant bug, mottled brown and tan with a black-tipped yellow triangle on each forewing; the ⅝-inch-long squash bug, black or brown on top and yellow, yellowish brown, or grayish underneath; and the shield-shaped ½-inch-long stink bug, which is named for its unpleasant odor and is brown, tan, green, or mottled with five segmented antennae. Adults are active from late spring to late summer. Eggs are laid on the undersides of leaves. Up to five generations are produced a year.

SOLUTION: Handpick adults and larvae, remove leaves with egg masses, and drop into soapy water. Use row covers. Trap tarnished plant bugs with white sticky traps. Introduce or encourage beneficials including tachinid flies, big-eyed bugs, parasitic wasps, and damsel bugs. Spray plants with water, diluted soap solution, or insecticidal soap. Control adults and larvae with rotenone and sabadilla. *SUSCEPTIBLE PLANTS: TARNISHED PLANT BUG—MOST VEGETABLES; SQUASH BUG— ALL MEMBERS OF THE SQUASH FAMILY, ESPECIALLY PUMPKINS AND SQUASH; STINK BUG—BEANS, CABBAGE, CORN, OKRA, PEAS, SQUASH, TOMATOES.*

PROBLEM: Plants do not develop; young plants may wilt and die; older plants may be stunted. Roots and root crops have tunnels or are hollowed out, and eventually rot.

CAUSE: Root maggots are the larvae of various small flies, including cabbage, onion, and carrot rust flies. The legless, wormlike ⅓-inch-long larvae are white to yellowish white and enter the plant through roots or underground stems. Active from spring to midsummer, they thrive in cool, moist, highly organic soil. Eggs are laid at the bases of stems.

SOLUTION: Use floating row covers. Place diatomaceous earth or wood ashes around plants. Rotate crops. Do not fertilize with fresh manure. Apply beneficial nematodes to soil before planting. In fall, remove debris and infected plants. Cultivate soil in spring and fall. *SUSCEPTIBLE PLANTS: CABBAGE MAGGOT—CABBAGE FAMILY; ONION MAGGOT— ONION FAMILY; CARROT RUST MAGGOT—CARROT FAMILY.*

PROBLEM: Ragged holes appear in leaves, especially those near the ground. New shoots and seedlings may disappear entirely. Ripe fruits are destroyed. Telltale silver streaks appear on leaves and garden paths.

CAUSE: Slugs and snails hide during the day and feed on low-hanging leaves and fruits at night or on overcast or rainy days. They prefer damp soil in a shady location and are most damaging in summer, especially in wet regions or during rainy years.

SOLUTION: Keep garden clean to minimize hiding places. Handpick the pests or trap them by placing saucers of beer, sunk into the soil, near plants. Slugs and snails will also collect under a board laid on the ground or under inverted grapefruit halves or melon rinds. Salt kills the pests but may damage plants. Surround beds with copper-foil barriers or barrier strips of wood ashes, coarse sand, cinders, or diatomaceous earth (DE). Encourage rove beetles, and turn the soil in spring.

SUSCEPTIBLE PLANTS: MOST VEGETABLES, ESPECIALLY LEAFY VEGETABLES LIKE LETTUCE, AND THE FRUIT OF TOMATOES AND STRAWBERRIES; MANY HERBS WITH TENDER FOLIAGE, PARTICULARLY BASIL, MARIGOLD, OREGANO, SAGE, SAVORY, AND VIOLET.

PROBLEM: Buds do not open, or flowers are tattered and deformed. Petals may be darkened or have brownish yellow or white streaks and small dark spots or bumps. Leaves and stems may be twisted, and plants may be stunted.

CAUSE: Thrips are quick-moving sucking insects barely visible to the naked eye; they look like tiny slivers of yellow, black, or brown wood. They emerge in early spring and are especially active in hot, dry weather. The larvae are wingless and feed on stems, leaves, and flower buds. Adults are weak fliers but are easily dispersed by wind and can therefore travel great distances.

SOLUTION: Controlling thrips is difficult, especially when they are migrating in early summer. Lacewings, minute pirate bugs, and several predaceous mites feed on them; late in the growing season, such predators often keep thrips populations under control. Remove and destroy damaged buds and foliage, and for severe cases, spray plants with an insecticidal soap.

SUSCEPTIBLE PLANTS: ARTEMISIA, MARIGOLD, MYRTLE, NASTURTIUM, ONION, POT MARIGOLD, AND ROSE.

PROBLEM: Leaves turn yellow and plants are stunted. When plants are shaken, a white cloud of insects appears.

CAUSE: Whiteflies, sucking insects $\frac{1}{16}$ inch long that look like tiny white moths, generally collect on the undersides of young leaves. Found year round in warmer climates but only in summer in colder climates, they like warm, still air. Both adults and nymphs suck sap from stems and leaves, causing an infested plant to wilt. Whiteflies are often brought home with greenhouse-raised plants and can carry viruses and secrete honeydew, which promotes a fungus called sooty mold.

SOLUTION: Inspect plants before buying. Keep the garden weeded. Spray affected plants with a strong stream of water from a garden hose. Spray with insecticidal soap or horticultural oil. Use yellow sticky traps. Introduce lacewings and parasitic wasps. Pyrethrins or rotenone can be applied.

SUSCEPTIBLE PLANTS: MOST VEGETABLES, ESPECIALLY MEMBERS OF THE SQUASH AND TOMATO FAMILIES, AND MELONS; BASIL, HOT PEPPER, NASTURTIUM, POT MARIGOLD, ROSE, ROSEMARY, AND SAGE.

PROBLEM: Plants wilt, are stunted, or die. Roots are damaged. Crops are thin and patchy.

CAUSE: Wireworms, which bore into and feed on seeds, corms, roots, and other underground plant parts, are the gray, creamy, or dark brown larvae of various species of click beetles. The ½- to 1½-inch-long jointed, shiny, tough-skinned larvae hatch in spring and may persist in the soil for up to 6 years. They are especially a problem in newly turned sod.

SOLUTION: Before planting a new crop, bury pieces of potato or carrot to trap wireworms, then dig up. Cultivate soil to a depth of 10 inches to expose larvae. Apply beneficial nematodes to soil. *SUSCEPTIBLE PLANTS: MOST VEGETABLES, ESPECIALLY CORN, LETTUCE, POTATOES, AND TURNIPS.*

PROBLEM: Overnight, young seedlings suddenly topple over and die. Stems are rotted through at the soil line.

CAUSE: Damping-off, a disease caused by several soil fungi, infects seeds and the roots of seedlings. The problem often occurs in wet, poorly drained soil with a high nitrogen content.

SOLUTION: Add fresh compost to the planting medium to provide beneficial bacteria and fungi that will compete with the damping-off fungi. Top the medium with a thin layer of sand or perlite to keep seedlings dry at soil level. Provide well-drained soil and plenty of light, and avoid overcrowding. Plants started in containers are more susceptible than those sown outdoors. Do not overwater seed flats or seedbeds. *SUSCEPTIBLE PLANTS: VIRTUALLY ALL.*

PROBLEM: In spring, brown spots ringed with yellow form a bull's-eye pattern on mature leaves. Spots merge to cover leaves, which die and drop off. Spots and cankers may appear on stems. Tomatoes may rot at the stem end and have dark, leathery, sunken areas. Potatoes develop brown, corky, dry spots. In the fall, dark irregular spots appear on leaves, and there may be a white mold on the undersides; fruits and tubers may have dark rotting spots.

CAUSE: Early blight, which occurs in the spring, and late blight, which occurs in the fall, are fungal diseases. Drought, insect damage, or nutrient deficiencies increase vulnerability to early blight. Late blight is most common when the weather is wet and nights are cool.

SOLUTION: Rotate crops and plant resistant cultivars. Treat early blight with copper fungicide. Plant only seed potatoes certified disease-free. Destroy infected plants and debris at the end of the season. *SUSCEPTIBLE PLANTS: ESPECIALLY TOMATOES AND POTATOES; ALSO EGGPLANT AND PEPPERS.*

PROBLEM: Leaves develop small yellow spots that gradually turn brown. Spots are frequently surrounded by a ring of yellow or brownish black tissue. Spots often join to produce large, irregular blotches. The entire leaf may turn yellow, wilt, and drop. Extensive defoliation can occur, weakening the plant. The problem usually starts on lower leaves and moves upward.

CAUSE: Leaf-spot diseases, caused by various fungi and bacteria, are spread by wind and splashing water. They are most prevalent from summer into fall, and thrive when humidity and rainfall are high.

SOLUTION: Destroy infected leaves as they appear; do not leave infected material in the garden over the winter. Water only in the mornings. Space and thin plants to increase air circulation. A baking-soda solution can protect healthy foliage but will not destroy fungi on infected leaves. *SUSCEPTIBLE PLANTS: BEE BALM, CELERY, HORSERADISH, PARSLEY, POT MARIGOLD, AND PRIMROSE.*

PROBLEM: Leaves become mottled with light green or yellow spots or streaks. New growth is spindly and misshapen, and plant is often stunted. Fruits and pods may be discolored or streaked.

CAUSE: Mosaic viruses can infect plants at any time during the growing season.

SOLUTION: Viral infections cannot be controlled. They spread by direct contact between plants and also by hands, tools, and insects. Plant resistant varieties. Remove and destroy infected plants. Introduce lacewings and ladybugs to control virus-transmitting aphids and leafhoppers. Don't plant susceptible crops where mosaic disease has occurred. *SUSCEPTIBLE PLANTS: BEANS, CUCUMBERS, PEPPERS, POTATOES, SQUASH, TOMATOES.*

PROBLEM: White or pale gray powdery growth appears on upper surface of leaf, eventually spreading to cover entire leaf, followed by distortion, yellowing, withering, and leaf drop. The powdery growth may also be seen on stems, buds, and shoots. Plants are stunted.

CAUSE: Powdery mildew, a fungal disease, is especially noticeable in late summer and early fall when cool, humid nights follow warm days. Unlike most fungal diseases, powdery mildew does not occur readily in wet conditions. More unsightly than harmful, it rarely kills the plant.

SOLUTION: Grow mildew-resistant varieties. Allow adequate room between susceptible plants. Spray plants daily with water to kill spores. Remove and destroy badly infected plant parts or entire plant. Spray plants with a solution of baking soda. Apply a horticultural oil or sulfur. *SUSCEPTIBLE PLANTS: ESPECIALLY BEANS, CUCUMBERS, MELONS, PUMPKINS, AND SQUASH; OCCASIONALLY EGGPLANT, PEPPERS, AND TOMATOES; MANY HERBS, INCLUDING ARTEMISIA, BEE BALM, POT MARIGOLD, AND SAGE.*

PROBLEM: Leaves turn yellow or brown or are stunted and wilted; the entire plant may wilt and die. Roots are dark brown or black, feel soft and wet to the touch, and emit a slightly foul odor.

CAUSE: Root rot, a common soil-borne disease, is caused by a variety of fungi found in moist soils.

SOLUTION: Remove and destroy affected plants and surrounding soil. Plant in well-drained soil; do not overwater; keep mulch away from base of plants. Avoid damaging roots when digging. *SUSCEPTIBLE PLANTS: VIRTUALLY ALL, PARTICULARLY LAVENDER, MARIGOLD, PINKS, POT MARIGOLD, AND ROSEMARY.*

PROBLEM: Plants wilt on warm days or are stunted, abnormally yellowish in color, or low in yield. Roots may be swollen and have knotty growths. Individual stems may die back. Plants may die.

CAUSE: Soil nematodes, microscopic roundworms that live in the soil and feed on roots, inhibit a plant's uptake of nitrogen. Damage is worst in warm, moist, sandy soils in sunny locations. Nematodes overwinter in infected roots or soil, and are spread by soil and transplants, as well as tools.

SOLUTION: Since nematodes are microscopic, only a laboratory test will confirm their presence. Be suspicious if roots are swollen or stunted. Dispose of infected plants and the soil that surrounds them, or solarize the soil *(box, page 103)*. Plant resistant species or cultivars and rotate crops. Plant a cover crop of African marigolds *(page 105)*. Add nitrogen fertilizer, especially crab or fish meal. Add compost to soil and use organic mulch to encourage fungi that prey on soil nematodes.
SUSCEPTIBLE PLANTS: VIRTUALLY ANY VEGETABLE OR FRUIT.

PROBLEM: Leaves and stems rapidly turn yellow, wilt, and die. Plants with fleshy roots quickly rot and die as well. A white cottony growth may be visible on stems and surrounding soil, and tiny tan globules about the size of mustard seeds may also be visible on or near the plant and in the surrounding soil or mulch.

CAUSE: Southern blight is a soil-borne fungal disease that occurs mainly in the eastern United States from New York south. It is most serious in the Southeast because of its rapid spread in hot, humid weather.

SOLUTION: Remove and destroy diseased plants and any white cottony growth around them. Solarize the soil of new beds *(box, page 103)*, thin plants to improve air circulation, and mulch them with a thin layer of solarized or sterile sharp sand.
SUSCEPTIBLE PLANTS: BASIL, BEE BALM, CATMINT, HOT PEPPER, LEMON VERBENA, MYRTLE, ONION, POT MARIGOLD, ROSE, AND VIOLET.

PROBLEM: One side or entire plant suddenly droops or wilts, with symptoms usually appearing first on lower and outer plant parts. Leaves may turn yellow before wilting. Plant fails to grow and eventually dies. Seedlings are stunted, wilt, and eventually die. A cut made across the stem near the base reveals dark streaks or other discoloration on the tissue inside or releases an oozing, sticky white substance.

CAUSE: Wilts, some caused by bacteria and others by fusarium or verticillium fungus, display similar symptoms. Bacterial wilt occurs in midsummer, fusarium wilt in hot weather, and verticillium wilt in cool weather. These microorganisms penetrate roots and stems and clog the water-conducting vessels. Both fungi and bacteria are long lived, remaining in the soil for years after the host plant has died.

SOLUTION: Plant resistant varieties. Fertilize and water regularly to promote vigorous growth. Immediately remove and destroy infected plants, including roots, and clear away garden debris in the fall. Wash hands and disinfect tools with a 10-percent bleach solution. Don't site susceptible plants in an area that has been infected previously. Solarize the soil *(box, page 103)*.
SUSCEPTIBLE PLANTS: CUCUMBERS, EGGPLANT, MELONS, PEPPERS, PUMPKINS, SQUASH, STRAWBERRIES, TOMATOES; BASIL, HOT PEPPER, MARIGOLD, MINT, NASTURTIUM, POPPY, AND SAGE.

Plant Selection Guide—Herbs

Organized by plant type, this chart provides information on culinary herbs as well as herbs used for ornamental and other purposes. For additional information on those plants with culinary value, refer to the encyclopedia that begins on page 250.

ANNUALS AND BIENNIALS

Plant	HARDINESS			HEIGHT				LIGHT			SOIL			BLOOM SEASON				PARTS USED				
	HARDY	HALF-HARDY	TENDER	UNDER 1 FOOT	1 TO 3 FEET	3 TO 5 FEET	OVER 5 FEET	FULL SUN	LIGHT SHADE	SHADE	DRY	WELL-DRAINED	MOIST	SPRING	SUMMER	FALL	WINTER	LEAVES	FLOWERS	ROOT/BULB	SEEDS/FRUIT	STEMS/BARK
ALOE VERA		✓	✓		✓			✓				✓			✓			✓				
AMARANTHUS HYPOCHONDRIACUS		✓				✓	✓				✓	✓			✓			✓			✓	
ANETHUM GRAVEOLENS 'MAMMOTH'		✓				✓		✓				✓			✓			✓			✓	
ANGELICA ARCHANGELICA*	✓					✓	✓	✓				✓			✓			✓			✓	
ANGELICA GIGAS*	✓					✓	✓	✓				✓			✓			✓			✓	
ANTHRISCUS CEREFOLIUM		✓		✓					✓	✓	✓				✓			✓	✓			
APIUM GRAVEOLENS*	✓				✓			✓	✓			✓	✓		✓			✓			✓	
ARTEMISIA ANNUA	✓					✓		✓			✓	✓			✓			✓	✓			
ATRIPLEX HORTENSIS	✓					✓	✓					✓	✓		✓			✓				
BORAGO OFFICINALIS 'ALBA'	✓				✓			✓				✓	✓		✓			✓	✓			
BRASSICA JUNCEA	✓					✓		✓				✓			✓			✓			✓	
CALENDULA OFFICINALIS	✓			✓				✓				✓		✓	✓	✓			✓			
CAPSICUM ANNUUM VAR. ANNUUM		✓	✓		✓			✓				✓	✓	✓							✓	
CAPSICUM CHINENSE 'HABANERO'		✓			✓			✓				✓	✓	✓							✓	
CARTHAMUS TINCTORIUS		✓			✓			✓			✓	✓			✓				✓		✓	
CARUM CARVI*	✓				✓			✓	✓			✓		✓	✓		✓			✓	✓	
CATHARANTHUS ROSEUS		✓			✓			✓	✓			✓	✓	✓	✓	✓			✓			
CENTAUREA CYANUS		✓			✓			✓				✓			✓	✓		✓	✓			
CHENOPODIUM AMBROSIOIDES	✓					✓		✓				✓			✓	✓		✓	✓		✓	
CHENOPODIUM BOTRYS	✓				✓			✓				✓			✓			✓				
COIX LACRYMA-JOBI		✓				✓	✓	✓				✓			✓			✓			✓	
CORIANDRUM SATIVUM		✓			✓			✓	✓			✓			✓			✓		✓	✓	
DIGITALIS LANATA*	✓				✓			✓	✓			✓			✓				✓			
DIGITALIS PURPUREA*	✓					✓		✓	✓			✓			✓				✓			
ERUCA VESICARIA SSP. SATIVA	✓				✓			✓	✓				✓		✓	✓		✓	✓			
FOENICULUM VULGARE 'PURPURASCENS'		✓				✓		✓				✓			✓	✓		✓		✓	✓	✓
HEDEOMA PULEGIOIDES	✓			✓				✓	✓			✓			✓			✓				
HIBISCUS SABDARIFFA			✓			✓	✓	✓				✓			✓	✓		✓			✓	

*BIENNIAL

ANNUALS AND BIENNIALS

	HARDY	HALF-HARDY	TENDER	UNDER 1 FOOT	1 TO 3 FEET	3 TO 5 FEET	OVER 5 FEET	FULL SUN	LIGHT SHADE	SHADE	DRY	WELL-DRAINED	MOIST	SPRING	SUMMER	FALL	WINTER	LEAVES	FLOWERS	ROOT/BULB	SEEDS/FRUIT	STEMS/BARK
ISATIS TINCTORIA*	✓				✓			✓				✓	✓	✓					✓			
MATRICARIA RECUTITA			✓	✓				✓				✓		✓	✓			✓	✓			
NICOTIANA RUSTICA			✓		✓			✓				✓			✓	✓		✓	✓			
NIGELLA SATIVA			✓	✓				✓				✓			✓						✓	
OCIMUM 'AFRICAN BLUE'			✓		✓			✓				✓			✓	✓		✓	✓			
OCIMUM BASILICUM 'CINNAMON'			✓	✓				✓				✓			✓			✓	✓			
OCIMUM BASILICUM 'DARK OPAL'			✓	✓				✓				✓			✓	✓		✓	✓			
OCIMUM BASILICUM 'MINIMUM'			✓	✓				✓				✓			✓			✓	✓			
OCIMUM SANCTUM			✓	✓				✓				✓			✓	✓		✓	✓			
ORIGANUM DICTAMNUS		✓			✓				✓			✓			✓	✓		✓	✓			
ORIGANUM MAJORANA		✓			✓			✓				✓			✓	✓		✓	✓			
ORIGANUM X MAJORICUM		✓			✓			✓				✓			✓	✓		✓	✓			
ORIGANUM ONITES		✓		✓				✓				✓			✓	✓		✓	✓			
PAPAVER RHOEAS			✓	✓				✓				✓		✓	✓				✓		✓	
PELARGONIUM CAPITATUM			✓	✓				✓				✓			✓			✓	✓			
PELARGONIUM X FRAGRANS 'VARIEGATUM'			✓	✓				✓				✓			✓			✓	✓			
PELARGONIUM ODORATISSIMUM			✓	✓				✓	✓			✓		✓	✓			✓	✓			
PELARGONIUM QUERCIFOLIUM			✓		✓			✓				✓		✓	✓			✓	✓			
PELARGONIUM TOMENTOSUM			✓	✓				✓	✓			✓		✓	✓			✓	✓			
PERILLA FRUTESCENS 'ATROPURPUREA'			✓	✓				✓	✓			✓			✓	✓		✓			✓	
PETROSELINUM CRISPUM VAR. CRISPUM*	✓			✓				✓				✓			✓			✓				
PETROSELINUM CRISPUM VAR. NEAPOLITANUM*	✓			✓				✓				✓			✓			✓				
PLECTRANTHUS AMBOINICUS			✓	✓				✓	✓			✓			✓			✓				
RICINUS COMMUNIS 'CARMENCITA'			✓				✓	✓				✓			✓			✓				
SALVIA COCCINEA	✓			✓				✓			✓	✓			✓			✓	✓			
SALVIA VIRIDIS*	✓			✓				✓			✓	✓			✓			✓	✓			
SATUREJA HORTENSIS	✓			✓				✓				✓			✓	✓		✓				
TAGETES LUCIDA			✓	✓				✓				✓			✓	✓		✓	✓			
TAGETES MINUTA			✓	✓				✓				✓			✓	✓		✓	✓			
TAGETES PATULA			✓	✓				✓				✓			✓	✓			✓			
TROPAEOLUM MAJUS			✓	✓	✓	✓		✓	✓			✓			✓	✓		✓	✓		✓	
VERBASCUM THAPSUS*	✓					✓		✓				✓			✓	✓		✓	✓			

*BIENNIAL

237

PERENNIALS, FERNS, AND BULBS

	ZONES								HEIGHT				LIGHT			SOIL			BLOOM SEASON				PARTS USED				
	ZONE 3	ZONE 4	ZONE 5	ZONE 6	ZONE 7	ZONE 8	ZONE 9	ZONE 10	UNDER 1 FOOT	1 TO 3 FEET	3 TO 5 FEET	OVER 5 FEET	FULL SUN	LIGHT SHADE	SHADE	DRY	WELL-DRAINED	MOIST	SPRING	SUMMER	FALL	WINTER	LEAVES	FLOWERS	ROOT/BULB	SEEDS/FRUIT	STEMS/BARK
ACHILLEA MILLEFOLIUM	✓	✓	✓	✓	✓	✓				✓			✓				✓			✓	✓		✓	✓			
ACORUS CALAMUS	✓	✓	✓	✓	✓	✓	✓	✓				✓	✓	✓				✓		✓			✓		✓		
ADIANTUM CAPILLUS-VENERIS				✓	✓	✓	✓	✓	✓					✓	✓		✓	✓					✓				
AGASTACHE FOENICULUM			✓	✓	✓	✓	✓			✓			✓				✓	✓		✓			✓	✓			
ALCEA ROSEA	✓	✓	✓	✓	✓	✓						✓	✓				✓			✓				✓			
ALCHEMILLA ALPINA	✓	✓	✓	✓	✓	✓			✓				✓	✓			✓	✓		✓			✓	✓			
ALLIUM AMPELOPRASUM VAR. AMPELOPRASUM		✓	✓	✓	✓	✓	✓			✓			✓				✓	✓	✓	✓			✓		✓		
ALLIUM SATIVUM		✓	✓	✓	✓	✓	✓			✓			✓				✓		✓	✓			✓	✓	✓	✓	✓
ALLIUM SCHOENOPRASUM	✓	✓	✓	✓	✓	✓			✓				✓	✓			✓		✓	✓			✓	✓			
ALLIUM TUBEROSUM	✓	✓	✓	✓	✓	✓				✓			✓				✓			✓	✓		✓	✓		✓	
ALTHAEA OFFICINALIS	✓	✓	✓	✓	✓	✓					✓		✓					✓		✓			✓		✓	✓	
ANTHEMIS TINCTORIA	✓	✓	✓	✓	✓	✓	✓		✓				✓				✓			✓	✓		✓	✓			
ARCTOSTAPHYLOS UVA-URSI	✓	✓	✓	✓	✓	✓	✓	✓	✓				✓				✓		✓							✓	
ARMORACIA RUSTICANA	✓	✓	✓	✓	✓	✓	✓	✓			✓		✓	✓			✓	✓	✓				✓		✓		
ARNICA MONTANA			✓	✓	✓	✓				✓			✓				✓			✓				✓			
ARTEMISIA ABSINTHIUM 'LAMBROOK SILVER'	✓	✓	✓	✓	✓	✓				✓			✓			✓	✓			✓			✓				
ARTEMISIA ARBORESCENS				✓	✓					✓			✓			✓	✓		✓	✓			✓				
ARTEMISIA DRACUNCULUS VAR. SATIVA		✓	✓	✓	✓					✓			✓			✓	✓						✓				
ARTEMISIA LUDOVICIANA 'SILVER KING'		✓	✓	✓	✓	✓					✓		✓			✓	✓						✓				
ASARUM CANADENSE	✓	✓	✓	✓	✓	✓			✓					✓	✓		✓	✓	✓				✓		✓		
ASCLEPIAS TUBEROSA	✓	✓	✓	✓	✓	✓				✓			✓			✓				✓				✓		✓	
CALAMINTHA GRANDIFLORA			✓	✓	✓	✓	✓	✓		✓			✓	✓			✓			✓			✓				
CENTELLA ASIATICA					✓	✓	✓	✓		✓			✓	✓				✓		✓			✓	✓			
CHAMAEMELUM NOBILE		✓	✓	✓	✓	✓			✓				✓	✓					✓	✓	✓			✓			
CICHORIUM INTYBUS	✓	✓	✓	✓	✓	✓	✓	✓			✓		✓				✓		✓	✓	✓		✓	✓	✓		
CIMICIFUGA RACEMOSA	✓	✓	✓	✓	✓	✓						✓	✓	✓				✓		✓				✓			
COLCHICUM AUTUMNALE			✓	✓	✓	✓	✓		✓				✓	✓				✓			✓				✓		
CONVALLARIA MAJALIS	✓	✓	✓	✓	✓	✓			✓					✓	✓			✓	✓						✓		
CROCUS SATIVUS			✓	✓	✓				✓				✓	✓			✓				✓			✓			
CYMBOPOGON CITRATUS					✓	✓	✓				✓		✓	✓			✓						✓				
DIANTHUS X ALLWOODII			✓	✓	✓	✓	✓		✓				✓	✓			✓		✓	✓	✓			✓			
DIANTHUS CARYOPHYLLUS			✓	✓	✓	✓	✓		✓				✓	✓			✓		✓	✓	✓			✓			

PERENNIALS, FERNS, AND BULBS

	ZONES								HEIGHT				LIGHT			SOIL			BLOOM SEASON				PARTS USED				
	ZONE 3	ZONE 4	ZONE 5	ZONE 6	ZONE 7	ZONE 8	ZONE 9	ZONE 10	UNDER 1 FOOT	1 TO 3 FEET	3 TO 5 FEET	OVER 5 FEET	FULL SUN	LIGHT SHADE	SHADE	DRY	WELL-DRAINED	MOIST	SPRING	SUMMER	FALL	WINTER	LEAVES	FLOWERS	ROOT/BULB	SEEDS/FRUIT	STEMS/BARK
DICTAMNUS ALBUS	✓	✓	✓	✓	✓	✓	✓			✓			✓	✓			✓	✓	✓	✓				✓		✓	
EUPATORIUM PURPUREUM	✓	✓	✓	✓	✓	✓	✓	✓			✓		✓	✓				✓		✓	✓			✓			
FILIPENDULA ULMARIA	✓	✓	✓	✓	✓	✓	✓					✓	✓	✓				✓		✓	✓		✓	✓			
GALIUM ODORATUM	✓	✓	✓	✓	✓				✓				✓	✓	✓		✓	✓	✓	✓			✓	✓			
GERANIUM MACULATUM	✓	✓	✓	✓	✓				✓				✓	✓			✓		✓				✓				
GERANIUM ROBERTIANUM	✓	✓	✓	✓	✓				✓				✓	✓			✓		✓	✓			✓				
GLYCYRRHIZA GLABRA				✓	✓	✓					✓		✓	✓				✓		✓					✓		
HELICHRYSUM ANGUSTIFOLIUM					✓	✓	✓			✓			✓			✓	✓			✓			✓	✓			
HEUCHERA AMERICANA		✓	✓	✓	✓	✓			✓					✓	✓	✓	✓		✓	✓				✓			
HIEROCHLOE ODORATA	✓	✓	✓	✓	✓	✓			✓				✓	✓			✓	✓	✓				✓				
HUMULUS LUPULUS	✓	✓	✓	✓	✓	✓						✓	✓	✓			✓	✓		✓			✓	✓			
HYDRASTIS CANADENSIS		✓	✓	✓	✓	✓			✓					✓	✓		✓	✓	✓				✓				
HYPERICUM PERFORATUM		✓	✓	✓	✓	✓				✓			✓	✓				✓		✓				✓			
HYSSOPUS OFFICINALIS	✓	✓	✓	✓	✓	✓				✓			✓	✓		✓	✓		✓	✓	✓		✓	✓			
INULA HELENIUM	✓	✓	✓	✓	✓	✓	✓					✓	✓	✓			✓	✓		✓	✓			✓	✓		
IRIS VERSICOLOR	✓	✓	✓	✓	✓					✓								✓		✓					✓		
LAVANDULA ANGUSTIFOLIA		✓	✓	✓	✓					✓			✓				✓			✓			✓	✓			
LAVANDULA LANATA				✓	✓	✓					✓		✓				✓			✓			✓	✓			
LAVANDULA STOECHAS				✓	✓	✓			✓				✓				✓			✓			✓	✓			
LEVISTICUM OFFICINALE	✓	✓	✓	✓	✓						✓	✓	✓				✓	✓	✓				✓				✓
MARRUBIUM VULGARE		✓	✓	✓	✓					✓			✓			✓	✓		✓	✓			✓				
MELISSA OFFICINALIS		✓	✓	✓	✓	✓				✓			✓	✓			✓	✓		✓	✓		✓				
MENTHA X PIPERITA		✓	✓	✓	✓	✓				✓			✓	✓			✓	✓		✓			✓				
MENTHA REQUIENII				✓	✓	✓		✓						✓				✓		✓			✓				
MENTHA SPICATA	✓	✓	✓	✓	✓	✓				✓			✓	✓			✓	✓		✓			✓				
MONARDA DIDYMA		✓	✓	✓	✓	✓	✓				✓		✓	✓				✓		✓	✓		✓	✓			
MONARDA FISTULOSA	✓	✓	✓	✓	✓	✓					✓		✓	✓		✓				✓	✓		✓	✓			
MYRRHIS ODORATA	✓	✓	✓	✓	✓					✓			✓	✓				✓	✓					✓	✓	✓	
NEPETA CATARIA	✓	✓	✓	✓	✓	✓				✓			✓	✓			✓		✓	✓	✓		✓				
ORIGANUM ONITES				✓	✓	✓			✓				✓			✓	✓			✓	✓		✓	✓			
ORIGANUM VULGARE		✓	✓	✓	✓	✓			✓				✓			✓	✓			✓			✓	✓			
PANAX PSEUDOGINSENG		✓	✓	✓	✓	✓				✓				✓	✓		✓	✓	✓	✓					✓		

PERENNIALS, FERNS, AND BULBS

	ZONES								HEIGHT				LIGHT			SOIL			BLOOM SEASON				PARTS USED				
	Zone 3	Zone 4	Zone 5	Zone 6	Zone 7	Zone 8	Zone 9	Zone 10	Under 1 foot	1 to 3 feet	3 to 5 feet	Over 5 feet	Full sun	Light shade	Shade	Dry	Well-drained	Moist	Spring	Summer	Fall	Winter	Leaves	Flowers	Root/bulb	Seeds/fruit	Stems/bark
POGOSTEMON CABLIN								✓		✓			✓	✓			✓			✓			✓				
POLYGONUM ODORATUM				✓	✓					✓				✓				✓		✓			✓				
POTERIUM SANGUISORBA	✓	✓	✓	✓	✓	✓	✓	✓		✓			✓				✓			✓			✓				
PRIMULA VERIS	✓	✓	✓	✓	✓	✓			✓				✓				✓	✓	✓				✓	✓			
PRIMULA VULGARIS	✓	✓	✓	✓	✓				✓				✓				✓	✓	✓				✓	✓			
PRUNELLA VULGARIS		✓	✓	✓	✓	✓	✓			✓			✓	✓			✓			✓	✓		✓	✓			
PULMONARIA SACCHARATA	✓	✓	✓	✓	✓	✓				✓				✓	✓		✓	✓	✓				✓				
PYCNANTHEMUM VIRGINIANUM		✓	✓	✓	✓					✓			✓				✓	✓		✓			✓				
ROSMARINUS OFFICINALIS				✓	✓	✓	✓				✓		✓				✓					✓	✓				
RUBIA TINCTORUM			✓	✓	✓	✓	✓			✓			✓				✓			✓	✓				✓		
RUMEX ACETOSA		✓	✓	✓	✓	✓				✓			✓	✓			✓			✓			✓				
RUMEX SCUTATUS		✓	✓	✓	✓					✓			✓	✓			✓			✓			✓				
RUTA GRAVEOLENS		✓	✓	✓	✓	✓				✓			✓				✓			✓			✓			✓	
SALVIA CLEVELANDII					✓	✓				✓			✓			✓	✓		✓	✓			✓	✓			
SALVIA DORISIANA								✓			✓		✓			✓	✓			✓	✓	✓	✓				
SALVIA LAVANDULIFOLIA				✓	✓	✓							✓			✓	✓			✓			✓	✓			
SALVIA OFFICINALIS		✓	✓	✓	✓	✓	✓			✓			✓			✓	✓			✓			✓	✓			
SANGUINARIA CANADENSIS	✓	✓	✓	✓	✓	✓	✓		✓					✓	✓		✓	✓	✓				✓				
SANTOLINA CHAMAECYPARISSUS				✓	✓	✓				✓			✓				✓			✓			✓				
SAPONARIA OFFICINALIS	✓	✓	✓	✓	✓	✓				✓			✓	✓			✓			✓			✓	✓	✓		✓
SATUREJA MONTANA 'NANA'		✓	✓	✓	✓				✓				✓				✓			✓	✓		✓				
SATUREJA THYMBRA					✓	✓				✓			✓				✓			✓	✓		✓				
SESAMUM INDICUM							✓			✓			✓				✓			✓						✓	
SOLIDAGO ODORA	✓	✓	✓	✓	✓	✓	✓				✓		✓			✓				✓	✓		✓	✓			
STACHYS OFFICINALIS		✓	✓	✓	✓	✓	✓			✓			✓	✓			✓	✓		✓			✓	✓			
SYMPHYTUM OFFICINALE	✓	✓	✓	✓	✓	✓	✓				✓		✓	✓				✓	✓	✓	✓		✓				
TANACETUM BALSAMITA		✓	✓	✓	✓	✓					✓		✓	✓		✓	✓			✓			✓	✓			
TANACETUM CINERARIIFOLIUM		✓	✓	✓	✓	✓				✓			✓	✓			✓	✓		✓	✓		✓				
TANACETUM PARTHENIUM		✓	✓	✓	✓	✓	✓		✓	✓			✓	✓			✓			✓			✓				
THYMUS CAPITATUS						✓	✓		✓				✓			✓	✓			✓			✓	✓			
THYMUS X CITRIODORUS			✓	✓	✓	✓	✓		✓				✓			✓	✓			✓			✓	✓			
THYMUS PRAECOX SSP. ARCTICUS		✓	✓	✓	✓	✓	✓	✓	✓				✓			✓	✓			✓			✓	✓			

		Zone 3	Zone 4	Zone 5	Zone 6	Zone 7	Zone 8	Zone 9	Zone 10	Under 1 Foot	1 to 3 Feet	3 to 5 Feet	Over 5 Feet	Full Sun	Light Shade	Shade	Dry	Well-Drained	Moist	Spring	Summer	Fall	Winter	Leaves	Flowers	Root/Bulb	Seeds/Fruit	Stems/Bark
		ZONES								**HEIGHT**				**LIGHT**			**SOIL**			**BLOOM SEASON**				**PARTS USED**				
PERENNIALS, FERNS, AND BULBS	**THYMUS SERPYLLUM**		✔	✔	✔	✔	✔			✔				✔			✔	✔			✔			✔	✔			
	THYMUS VULGARIS		✔	✔	✔	✔	✔			✔				✔			✔	✔			✔			✔	✔			
	TULBAGHIA VIOLACEA							✔	✔		✔			✔	✔			✔	✔		✔			✔	✔			
	VALERIANA OFFICINALIS		✔	✔	✔	✔	✔	✔				✔		✔	✔			✔	✔		✔				✔	✔		
	VETIVERIA ZIZANIOIDES							✔	✔				✔	✔				✔	✔		✔					✔		
	VIOLA ODORATA	✔	✔	✔	✔	✔	✔	✔	✔	✔				✔	✔			✔	✔	✔	✔		✔	✔	✔			
	VIOLA TRICOLOR	✔	✔	✔	✔	✔	✔	✔	✔	✔				✔	✔			✔	✔	✔	✔			✔	✔			
	ZINGIBER OFFICINALE							✔	✔			✔			✔			✔	✔		✔					✔		
SHRUBS AND TREES	**ALOYSIA TRIPHYLLA**							✔	✔				✔	✔				✔			✔			✔	✔			
	ARTEMISIA ABROTANUM				✔	✔	✔	✔	✔			✔		✔			✔	✔						✔				
	CEDRONELLA CANARIENSIS								✔			✔		✔				✔			✔	✔		✔	✔			
	CINNAMOMUM CAMPHORA						✔	✔	✔				✔	✔				✔	✔	✔	✔			✔				
	CINNAMOMUM ZEYLANICUM							✔	✔				✔	✔				✔	✔		✔							✔
	CITRUS AURANTIUM							✔	✔				✔	✔				✔	✔	✔	✔				✔		✔	
	CITRUS LIMON							✔	✔				✔	✔				✔	✔	✔	✔				✔		✔	
	COMPTONIA PEREGRINA	✔	✔	✔	✔	✔						✔		✔	✔			✔			✔			✔				
	EUCALYPTUS CITRIODORA							✔	✔				✔	✔				✔					✔	✔		✔	✔	✔
	GAULTHERIA PROCUMBENS	✔	✔	✔	✔	✔	✔	✔	✔	✔					✔	✔		✔	✔		✔			✔			✔	
	LAURUS NOBILIS 'AUREA'						✔	✔	✔				✔	✔	✔			✔		✔				✔				
	LINDERA BENZOIN		✔	✔	✔	✔	✔	✔					✔		✔				✔	✔				✔			✔	✔
	LIPPIA GRAVEOLENS							✔	✔				✔	✔				✔		✔				✔				
	MYRICA CERIFERA					✔	✔	✔					✔				✔		✔	✔							✔	
	MYRICA GALE	✔	✔	✔	✔	✔	✔	✔				✔							✔	✔							✔	
	MYRTUS COMMUNIS 'FLORE PLENO'							✔	✔				✔	✔	✔			✔		✔	✔			✔	✔		✔	
	PUNICA GRANATUM VAR. NANA					✔	✔	✔	✔		✔			✔				✔		✔					✔		✔	
	ROSA CANINA	✔	✔	✔	✔	✔	✔	✔					✔	✔				✔		✔	✔				✔		✔	
	ROSA DAMASCENA			✔	✔	✔	✔	✔					✔	✔				✔			✔	✔			✔		✔	
	ROSA GALLICA 'OFFICINALIS'		✔	✔	✔	✔	✔	✔			✔			✔				✔			✔	✔			✔		✔	
	ROSA GALLICA 'VERSICOLOR'		✔	✔	✔	✔	✔	✔			✔			✔				✔			✔	✔			✔		✔	
	ROSA RUGOSA	✔	✔	✔	✔	✔	✔	✔					✔	✔				✔		✔	✔				✔		✔	
	TEUCRIUM CHAMAEDRYS			✔	✔	✔	✔	✔			✔			✔	✔			✔			✔	✔		✔				
	VITEX AGNUS-CASTUS					✔	✔	✔	✔				✔	✔			✔		✔		✔	✔					✔	

Plant Selection Guide—Vegetables

This chart provides information on selected vegetables, plus a few fruits and herbs. "Days to maturity" applies to crops replanted yearly, either indoors or out, from seed, sets, roots, or tubers. For details on most of the plants listed, see the encyclopedia on pages 280-323.

	HARDINESS				LIGHT		PLANTING DEPTH			PLANT SPACING			ROW SPACING			DAYS TO MATURITY				WAYS TO USE							
	cool-season annual	warm-season annual	hot-season annual	winter-hardy	sun	partial shade	< ½ inch	½ to 2 inches	> 2 inches	< 1 foot	1 to 2 feet	> 2 feet	1 to 2 feet	2 to 4 feet	> 4 feet	< 70 days	70 to 100 days	100 to 130 days	> 130 days	fresh	frozen	canned	pickled	jam/preserves	dried	containers	landscaping
ARTICHOKE 'GREEN GLOBE'		✔	✔		✔	✔	✔					✔			✔			✔		✔	✔		✔			✔	✔
ARUGULA	✔			✔	✔	✔	✔			✔			✔			✔				✔							
ASPARAGUS 'JERSEY KNIGHT'			✔	✔					✔		✔			✔						✔	✔						✔
BASIL 'SPICY GLOBE'		✔			✔	✔		✔		✔			✔							✔	✔				✔	✔	✔
BEAN, DRY 'BLACK TURTLE'		✔			✔			✔		✔				✔			✔			✔		✔			✔		
BEAN, DRY 'FRENCH HORTICULTURAL'		✔			✔			✔		✔				✔			✔			✔	✔	✔			✔		
BEAN, FAVA 'AQUADULCE'	✔				✔			✔		✔				✔			✔			✔					✔		
BEAN, FILET 'TAVERA'		✔			✔			✔		✔			✔			✔				✔							
BEAN, GREEN 'PROVIDER'		✔			✔			✔		✔			✔			✔				✔							
BEAN, GREEN 'TENDERCROP'		✔			✔			✔		✔			✔			✔				✔	✔	✔					
BEAN, LIMA 'FORDHOOK 242'		✔			✔			✔		✔				✔			✔			✔	✔	✔			✔		
BEAN, POLE 'EMERITE'		✔			✔			✔		✔			✔			✔				✔	✔						
BEAN, POLE 'TRIONFO VIOLETTO'		✔			✔			✔		✔			✔			✔				✔	✔						
BEAN, PURPLE 'ROYAL BURGUNDY'		✔			✔			✔		✔			✔			✔				✔							
BEAN, RUNNER 'SCARLET RUNNER'	✔				✔			✔		✔				✔			✔			✔					✔		✔
BEAN, YARDLONG 'GREEN POD'		✔			✔			✔		✔				✔			✔			✔	✔						
BEAN, YELLOW 'DORABEL'		✔			✔			✔		✔			✔			✔				✔	✔						
BEET 'DETROIT DARK RED'	✔				✔			✔		✔			✔			✔				✔	✔	✔	✔				
BEET 'GOLDEN'	✔				✔			✔		✔			✔			✔				✔	✔	✔	✔				
BLACKBERRY 'RANGER'			✔	✔				✔			✔			✔						✔	✔			✔			
BLACKBERRY 'THORNFREE'			✔	✔				✔			✔			✔						✔	✔			✔			
BLACKBERRY 'YOUNG'			✔	✔				✔			✔			✔						✔	✔			✔			
BLACK-EYED PEA 'MISSISSIPPI SILVER'		✔			✔			✔		✔			✔				✔			✔	✔	✔			✔		
BROCCOLI 'EMPEROR'		✔			✔	✔		✔		✔								✔		✔	✔						
BROCCOLI RABE	✔				✔			✔		✔			✔							✔	✔						
BRUSSELS SPROUT 'PRINCE MARVEL'	✔				✔			✔		✔			✔				✔			✔	✔						
CABBAGE 'EARLY JERSEY WAKEFIELD'	✔				✔	✔		✔		✔			✔							✔			✔				
CABBAGE 'WISCONSIN ALL SEASONS'	✔				✔	✔		✔		✔			✔				✔			✔			✔				

	HARDINESS				LIGHT		PLANTING DEPTH			PLANT SPACING			ROW SPACING			DAYS TO MATURITY				WAYS TO USE							
	cool-season ANNUAL	warm-season ANNUAL	hot-season ANNUAL	winter-hardy	SUN	PARTIAL SHADE	< ½ INCH	½ TO 2 INCHES	> 2 INCHES	< 1 FOOT	1 TO 2 FEET	> 2 feet	1 TO 2 FEET	2 TO 4 FEET	> 4 FEET	< 70 DAYS	70 TO 100 DAYS	100 TO 130 DAYS	> 130 DAYS	FRESH	FROZEN	CANNED	PICKLED	JAM/PRESERVES	DRIED	CONTAINERS	LANDSCAPING
CABBAGE, CHINESE 'TWO SEASONS HYBRID'		✓			✓			✓		✓			✓							✓							
CARDOON			✓	✓	✓			✓		✓			✓						✓	✓							
CARROT 'LITTLE FINGER'	✓				✓		✓			✓			✓				✓			✓	✓	✓	✓			✓	✓
CARROT 'NAPOLI'	✓				✓		✓			✓			✓							✓	✓	✓				✓	✓
CARROT 'TENDERSWEET'	✓				✓		✓			✓			✓							✓	✓	✓				✓	✓
CAULIFLOWER 'EARLY WHITE HYBRID'	✓				✓			✓			✓		✓			✓				✓	✓		✓				
CELERIAC 'BRILLIANT'		✓			✓	✓	✓				✓		✓				✓			✓							
CELERY 'UTAH 52-70R'		✓			✓		✓			✓			✓				✓			✓					✓		
CELTUCE	✓				✓	✓		✓		✓				✓						✓							
CHARD 'RHUBARB CHARD'		✓			✓	✓		✓		✓			✓							✓	✓					✓	✓
CHAYOTE			✓		✓	✓					✓		✓					✓		✓							
CHICORY 'CERIOLO'	✓				✓	✓				✓			✓							✓							
COLLARD 'GEORGIA'	✓				✓			✓		✓			✓							✓	✓						
CORN 'EARLIVEE'		✓			✓			✓		✓			✓			✓				✓	✓	✓		✓			
CORN 'SENECA STARSHINE'		✓			✓			✓		✓			✓				✓			✓	✓	✓		✓			
CORN 'STARSTRUCK'		✓			✓			✓		✓			✓				✓			✓	✓	✓					
CORN SALAD 'COQUILLE'				✓	✓			✓		✓			✓				✓			✓							
CRESS 'WINTER CRESS'	✓				✓	✓	✓			✓			✓							✓							
CUCUMBER 'BURPLESS'		✓			✓			✓			✓		✓	✓						✓			✓				
CUCUMBER 'SALADIN'		✓			✓			✓			✓		✓	✓						✓			✓				✓
CUCUMBER 'SPACEMASTER'		✓			✓			✓			✓		✓	✓						✓			✓			✓	
EGGPLANT 'ICHIBAN'		✓			✓	✓		✓			✓			✓						✓							
ENDIVE 'TRES FIN'	✓				✓	✓		✓		✓			✓							✓							
FENNEL 'ZEFA FINO'	✓				✓	✓		✓		✓				✓						✓							
GARLIC 'ELEPHANT GARLIC'				✓	✓	✓		✓	✓	✓								✓		✓					✓		
GARLIC 'SPANISH ROJA GARLIC'				✓	✓	✓			✓	✓								✓		✓					✓		
HORSERADISH 'MALINER KREN'				✓	✓				✓		✓		✓						✓	✓							
JERUSALEM ARTICHOKE 'FRENCH MAMMOTH WHITE'				✓	✓				✓		✓		✓						✓	✓							✓
JICAMA		✓			✓				✓		✓		✓						✓	✓							
KALE 'WINTERBOR'	✓				✓	✓		✓		✓			✓	✓						✓	✓					✓	✓
KOHLRABI 'GRAND DUKE'	✓				✓	✓		✓		✓	✓		✓							✓							
LEEK 'BROAD LONDON'	✓				✓	✓	✓			✓			✓							✓	✓						

	HARDINESS				LIGHT		PLANTING DEPTH			PLANT SPACING			ROW SPACING			DAYS TO MATURITY				WAYS TO USE							
	cool-season ANNUAL	warm-season ANNUAL	hot-season ANNUAL	winter-hardy	SUN	PARTIAL SHADE	< ½ INCH	½ TO 2 INCHES	> 2 INCHES	< 1 FOOT	1 TO 2 FEET	> 2 FEET	1 TO 2 FEET	2 TO 4 FEET	> 4 FEET	< 70 DAYS	70 TO 100 DAYS	100 TO 130 DAYS	> 130 DAYS	FRESH	FROZEN	CANNED	PICKLED	JAM/PRESERVES	DRIED	CONTAINERS	LANDSCAPING
LETTUCE 'LITTLE GEM'		✔			✔	✔	✔			✔		✔	✔			✔				✔							
LETTUCE 'RUBY'		✔			✔	✔	✔			✔		✔	✔			✔				✔					✔		
LETTUCE 'SUMMERTIME'		✔			✔	✔	✔			✔		✔	✔			✔				✔							
LETTUCE 'TOM THUMB'		✔			✔	✔	✔			✔		✔	✔			✔				✔							
MELON 'CASABLANCA'		✔			✔			✔			✔			✔			✔			✔	✔						
MELON 'PANCHA'		✔			✔			✔				✔		✔			✔			✔	✔						
MELON 'VENUS'		✔			✔			✔				✔		✔			✔			✔	✔						
MUSTARD GREENS 'SOUTHERN GIANT CURLED'	✔				✔		✔			✔		✔	✔			✔				✔							
NASTURTIUM 'TIP TOP MIX'	✔				✔	✔		✔		✔		✔	✔			✔				✔			✔			✔	✔
OKRA 'CLEMSON SPINELESS'			✔		✔			✔		✔	✔		✔	✔		✔				✔							
ONION 'ISHIKURA'	✔				✔			✔		✔			✔				✔			✔	✔						
ONION 'NORTHERN OAK'	✔			✔	✔			✔		✔			✔				✔			✔	✔				✔		
ONION 'TEXAS GRANO 1015Y'	✔			✔	✔			✔		✔			✔					✔		✔					✔		
ORACH 'RED ORACH'	✔				✔			✔		✔			✔			✔				✔							
PAK-CHOI 'MEI-QUING CHOI'	✔				✔			✔			✔		✔			✔				✔							
PARSLEY 'MOSS CURLED FOREST GREEN'	✔		✔		✔	✔	✔			✔			✔				✔			✔					✔	✔	
PARSNIP 'HOLLOW CROWN'	✔				✔			✔		✔			✔					✔		✔							
PEA, GARDEN 'LITTLE MARVEL'	✔				✔			✔		✔			✔			✔				✔	✔	✔					
PEA, SNOW 'OREGON SUGAR POD II'	✔				✔			✔		✔							✔			✔	✔						
PEA, SUGAR SNAP 'SUGAR DADDY'	✔				✔			✔		✔			✔			✔				✔	✔						
PEANUT 'JUMBO VIRGINIA'			✔		✔			✔			✔		✔					✔		✔							
PEPPER, CHILI 'LARGE HOT CHERRY'		✔			✔			✔			✔		✔					✔		✔			✔				
PEPPER, SWEET 'CALIFORNIA WONDER'		✔			✔			✔			✔		✔					✔		✔	✔						
PEPPER, SWEET 'GYPSY'		✔			✔			✔			✔		✔				✔			✔							✔
POTATO 'NORGOLD RUSSET'		✔			✔				✔	✔			✔			✔				✔	✔					✔	
POTATO 'RED LA SODA'		✔			✔				✔	✔			✔				✔			✔	✔					✔	
POTATO 'RUSSET BURBANK'		✔			✔				✔	✔			✔					✔		✔	✔					✔	
PUMPKIN 'CONNECTICUT FIELD'		✔			✔			✔		✔					✔			✔		✔							
PUMPKIN 'JACK BE LITTLE'		✔			✔			✔		✔				✔				✔		✔	✔						
RADICCHIO 'CASTELFRANCO'		✔			✔			✔		✔			✔					✔		✔							
RADISH 'FRENCH BREAKFAST'	✔				✔			✔	✔	✔			✔			✔				✔							
RASPBERRY 'BLACK HAWK'				✔	✔	✔		✔			✔									✔	✔			✔			

244

	HARDINESS				LIGHT		PLANTING DEPTH			PLANT SPACING			ROW SPACING			DAYS TO MATURITY				WAYS TO USE							
	cool-season ANNUAL	warm-season ANNUAL	hot-season ANNUAL	winter-hardy	SUN	PARTIAL SHADE	< ½ INCH	½ TO 2 INCHES	> 2 INCHES	< 1 FOOT	1 TO 2 FEET	> 2 FEET	1 TO 2 FEET	2 TO 4 FEET	> 4 FEET	< 70 DAYS	70 TO 100 DAYS	100 TO 130 DAYS	> 130 DAYS	FRESH	FROZEN	CANNED	PICKLED	JAM/PRESERVES	DRIED	CONTAINERS	LANDSCAPING
RASPBERRY 'NEWBURGH'				✓	✓	✓		✓			✓				✓					✓	✓			✓			
RASPBERRY 'WINEBERRY'				✓	✓	✓		✓			✓				✓					✓	✓			✓			✓
RHUBARB 'CHERRY RED'				✓	✓			✓				✓		✓						✓	✓			✓			
RUTABAGA 'IMPROVED PURPLE TOP YELLOW'	✓				✓			✓		✓			✓				✓			✓	✓						
SALSIFY 'MAMMOTH SANDWICH ISLAND'	✓				✓		✓			✓			✓					✓		✓	✓						
SHALLOT 'SUCCESS'	✓				✓	✓		✓		✓			✓						✓	✓							
SORREL				✓	✓	✓	✓			✓			✓				✓			✓	✓					✓	
SOYBEAN 'PRIZE'		✓			✓			✓		✓			✓				✓			✓	✓				✓		
SPINACH 'MELODY'	✓				✓	✓		✓		✓			✓			✓				✓	✓						
SPINACH, MALABAR 'ALBA'		✓			✓			✓				✓	✓				✓			✓						✓	✓
SPINACH, NEW ZEALAND		✓		✓	✓			✓			✓		✓				✓			✓	✓					✓	
SQUASH, SUMMER 'PARK'S CREAMY HYBRID'		✓			✓			✓			✓			✓		✓				✓	✓						
SQUASH, SUMMER 'RAVEN'		✓			✓			✓			✓			✓		✓				✓	✓						
SQUASH, SUMMER 'SCALOPPINI'		✓			✓			✓			✓			✓		✓				✓	✓						
SQUASH, SUMMER 'SUNDANCE'		✓			✓			✓			✓			✓		✓				✓	✓						
SQUASH, WINTER 'BUTTERBUSH'		✓			✓			✓				✓		✓			✓			✓	✓						
SQUASH, WINTER 'CREAM OF THE CROP'		✓			✓			✓				✓		✓				✓		✓	✓						
SQUASH, WINTER 'SWEET DUMPLING'		✓			✓			✓				✓		✓				✓		✓	✓						
SQUASH, WINTER 'TURK'S TURBAN'		✓			✓			✓				✓		✓				✓		✓	✓						
STRAWBERRY 'ALEXANDRIA'		✓		✓	✓		✓			✓			✓					✓	✓	✓	✓			✓		✓	✓
STRAWBERRY 'PICNIC'		✓		✓	✓		✓			✓			✓					✓		✓	✓			✓	✓		
SUNFLOWER 'MAMMOTH'		✓			✓			✓			✓			✓			✓			✓							✓
SWEET POTATO 'CENTENNIAL'			✓		✓			✓		✓				✓			✓			✓	✓						
TAMPALA			✓		✓		✓			✓			✓				✓			✓							
TOMATILLO 'TOMA VERDE'		✓			✓			✓			✓			✓			✓			✓							
TOMATO 'BIG GIRL'		✓			✓		✓				✓			✓			✓			✓	✓	✓					
TOMATO 'EARLY CASCADE'		✓			✓		✓				✓			✓			✓			✓	✓						
TOMATO 'HEINZ 1439'		✓			✓		✓				✓			✓				✓		✓	✓	✓					
TOMATO 'SUGAR LUMP'		✓			✓		✓				✓			✓			✓			✓							
TOMATO 'VIVA ITALIA'		✓			✓		✓				✓			✓				✓		✓		✓			✓		
TOMATO 'YELLOW CANARY'		✓			✓		✓				✓			✓			✓			✓						✓	
TURNIP 'TOKYO CROSS'	✓				✓			✓		✓			✓			✓				✓	✓	✓					

A Zone Map of the U.S. and Canada

A plant's winter hardiness is critical in deciding whether it is suitable for your garden. The map below divides the United States and Canada into 11 climatic zones based on average minimum temperatures, as compiled by the U.S. Department of Agriculture. Find your zone and check the zone information in the plant selection guides *(pages 236-245)* or the encyclopedias *(pages 250-323)* to help you choose the plants most likely to flourish in your climate.

Zone 1: Below -50° F

Zone 2: -50° to -40°

Zone 3: -40° to -30°

Zone 4: -30° to -20°

Zone 5: -20° to -10°

Zone 6: -10° to 0°

Zone 7: 0° to 10°

Zone 8: 10° to 20°

Zone 9: 20° to 30°

Zone 10: 30° to 40°

Zone 11: Above 40°

Frost Dates in the U.S. and Canada

These maps indicate the average dates for the last spring frost and the first fall frost in various parts of the United States and Canada. Planting dates for many vegetables and herbs depend on when these frosts occur. A spring crop of radishes, for instance, can be sown 5 weeks before the last frost, while a fall crop can be sown as late as 4 weeks after the first frost. Cool-season crops like radishes can withstand some frost, but warm-season crops can be grown without protection only in the frost-free period between the year's last and first frosts. Used together, the maps and the information in the encyclopedias *(pages 250-323)* will help you choose vegetables and herbs suited to your area and determine when to plant them. Be aware that specific frost dates vary widely within each region. For more precise figures, check with your local weather bureau or Cooperative Extension Service and keep a record of temperatures in your garden from year to year.

AVERAGE DATES OF LAST SPRING FROST

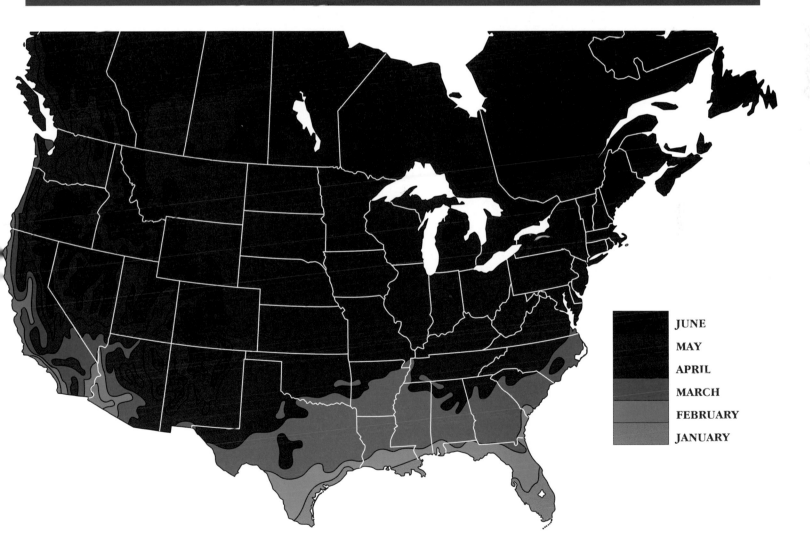

JUNE
MAY
APRIL
MARCH
FEBRUARY
JANUARY

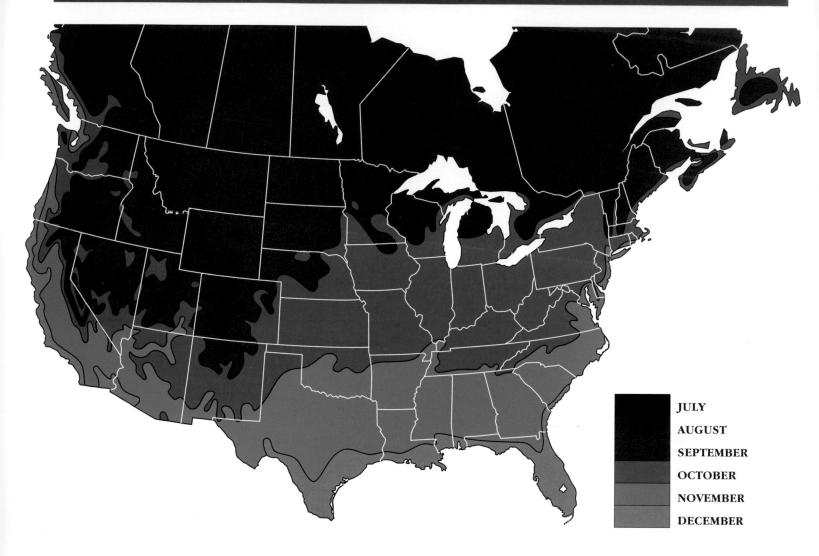

AVERAGE DATES OF FIRST FALL FROST

- JULY
- AUGUST
- SEPTEMBER
- OCTOBER
- NOVEMBER
- DECEMBER

AVERAGE DATES OF LAST SPRING FROST

- JUNE
- MAY
- APRIL

AVERAGE DATES OF FIRST FALL FROST

- JULY
- AUGUST
- SEPTEMBER

Cross-Reference Guide to Herbs

Absinthe—*Artemisia absinthium*

Balm—*Calamintha*

Balm—*Melissa*

Balm—*Monarda*

Basil—*Ocimum*

Basil—*Pycnanthemum*

Bay—*Laurus*

Bee balm—*Melissa*

Bee balm—*Monarda*

Bergamot—*Monarda*

Betony—*Stachys*

Black cumin—*Nigella sativa*

Burnet—*Poterium*

Caraway—*Carum*

Catnip—*Nepeta cataria*

Chamomile—*Chamaemelum*

Chamomile—*Matricaria*

Chervil—*Anthriscus*

Chicory—*Cichorium*

Chives—*Allium*

Cilantro—*Coriandrum*

Coriander—*Coriandrum*

Coriander—*Nigella sativa*

Cowslip—*Primula veris*

Dill—*Anethum*

Dock—*Rumex*

False saffron—*Carthamus*

Fennel—*Foeniculum*

Garlic—*Allium*

Geranium—*Pelargonium*

Ginger—*Zingiber*

Ginseng—*Panax*

Goldenrod—*Solidago*

Horehound—*Marrubium*

Horseradish—*Armoracia*

Hyssop—*Agastache*

Hyssop—*Hyssopus*

Hyssop—*Pycnanthemum*

Lamb's ears—*Stachys*

Laurel—*Laurus*

Leek—*Allium*

Lemon balm—*Melissa*

Lemon grass—*Cymbopogon*

Lemon verbena—*Aloysia*

Licorice—*Glycyrrhiza*

Lovage—*Levisticum*

Mallow—*Althaea*

Marigold—*Calendula*

Marigold—*Tagetes*

Marjoram—*Origanum*

Mint—*Agastache foeniculum*

Mint—*Mentha*

Mint—*Monarda*

Mint—*Plectranthus*

Mint—*Polygonum*

Mint—*Pycnanthemum*

Mustard—*Brassica*

Myrtle—*Myrtus*

Nasturtium—*Tropaeolum*

Nutmeg flower—*Nigella sativa*

Onion—*Allium*

Oregano—*Lippia*

Oregano—*Origanum*

Oswego tea—*Monarda*

Pansy—*Viola tricolor*

Parsley—*Petroselinum*

Pepper—*Capsicum*

Pink—*Dianthus*

Poppy—*Papaver*

Primrose—*Primula*

Prince's-feather—*Amaranthus*

Ramp—*Allium tricoccum*

Safflower—*Carthamus*

Saffron—*Crocus sativus*

Sage—*Salvia*

Savory—*Calamintha*

Savory—*Satureja*

Society garlic—*Tulbaghia*

Sorrel—*Hibiscus*

Sorrel—*Rumex*

Spicebush—*Lindera*

Sweet anise—*Foeniculum*

Sweet cicely—*Myrrhis*

Tarragon—*Artemisia dracunculus*

Thyme—*Plectranthus*

Thyme—*Thymus*

Wild celery—*Apium*

Wintergreen—*Gaultheria*

Wormwood—*Artemisia*

Encyclopedia of Herbs

Presented here is an array of herbs suitable for kitchen gardens as well as containers and borders. Each plant genus is listed alphabetically by its Latin botanical name, with the pronunciation given in parentheses. The common name of the genus follows in bold type. If you know only a plant's common name, see the cross-reference guide on page 249 or the index.

A botanical name consists of the genus and, usually, a species, both commonly written in italics. After its first mention in the entry, the Latin genus is abbreviated to an initial letter followed by a period. Species often have common names of their own, which appear in parentheses here, and many species have cultivars, whose names appear in single quotation marks. An "x" indicates plants that are hybrid offspring of two different species.

Hardiness zones for biennials, perennials, trees, and shrubs are keyed to the USDA Plant Hardiness Zone Map on page 246. For biennials, hardiness refers to their ability to survive winter after their first growing season. Hardiness for annuals refers to their ability to withstand frost after being set out in the ground in spring: Tender annuals should not be placed outdoors until all danger of frost is past; half-hardy annuals can survive a light frost; hardy annuals tolerate all but extreme cold. (See maps showing frost dates on pages 247-248.) Distinctions between annuals and perennials are not always clear-cut; some hardy annuals self-sow so readily that they perform almost like perennials, while some perennials that are hardy only in the warmest zones should be considered annuals or grown as houseplants in cooler regions.

Each entry outlines the herb's specific uses and cites the plant parts appropriate for each use. The medicinal uses of the herbs, often based on folklore or centuries-old tradition, are noted only where modern scientific support exists for them or, contrariwise, where following them is no longer advised. Note that many herbs once considered therapeutic are now known to be toxic.

Agastache
(a-GAH-sta-kee)
GIANT HYSSOP

Agastache barberi 'Tutti Frutti'

Hardiness: *Zones 4-9*

Height: *2 to 5 feet*

Light: *full sun to light shade*

Soil: *moist, well-drained*

Plant type: *perennial*

Uses: *landscaping, culinary, dried arrangements*

Clumps of erect stems lined with fragrant leaves and tipped with spikes of colorful flowers make giant hyssop a bold border accent. The nectar-filled summer flowers are edible, attract bees, and dry well for everlasting arrangements. Scatter the leaves in salad or infuse them for teas.

Selected species and varieties: *A. barberi* —red-purple flowers with a long season of bloom on stems to 2 feet tall; 'Firebird' has copper orange blooms; 'Tutti-Frutti', raspberry pink to purple flavorful flowers; Zones 6-9. *A. foeniculum* (anise hyssop, blue giant hyssop, anise mint, licorice mint)—licorice-scented leaves and purple-blue flowers on 3-foot stems; 'Alba' has white blossoms; Zones 4-9. *A. rugosa* (Korean anise hyssop)—wrinkly, mint-scented leaves and small purple flower spikes on 5-foot stems; Zones 5-9.

Growing conditions and maintenance: Start giant hyssop seeds indoors 10 to 12 weeks before the last frost, and set seedlings out 18 inches apart to bloom the first year. Established plantings self-sow; or propagate by division in spring or fall every 3 to 5 years. Hang flowers upside down in bunches to dry.

Allium
(AL-lee-um)
ONION

Allium ampeloprasum var. ampeloprasum

Hardiness: *Zones 3-9*

Height: *8 to 36 inches*

Light: *full sun to partial shade*

Soil: *rich, moist, well-drained*

Plant type: *bulb*

Uses: *culinary, landscaping, arrangements*

This large genus produces round or domed umbels of white to blue, pink, or purple flowers amid grassy leaves from summer through fall. Depending on the species, edible underground bulbs, aerial bulbils, the flat or cylindrical leaves, or young flowers provide texture, color, and a range of flavors for culinary use. Some species are suited to the flower border, others add interest to winter bouquets, and still others figure in herbal medicine.

Selected species and varieties: *A. ampeloprasum* var. *ampeloprasum* (elephant garlic)—plants to 3 feet tall with several large, mildly sweet cloves forming bulbs 4 inches or more across that can be sliced for flavoring or prepared alone as a side dish. *A. cepa* var. *proliferum* (tree onion, Egyptian onion)—stiff stalks to 3 feet tall, tipped with small aerial bulbs or bulbils from late summer through fall, grown ornamentally or for the bulbils that are used whole for cooking or pickling. *A. fistulosum* (Welsh onion, Spanish onion, ciboule, two-bladed onion)—small, cylindrical bulbs elongating into pencil-thick blanched stems topped with pungent 12- to 36-inch leaves, all parts of

which can be sliced fresh for flavoring or garnish. *A. sativum* (garlic)—up to 15 pungently flavored small cloves in bulbs 2 to 3 inches across with edible pale violet flowers tipping stems up to 36 inches tall from late summer through fall; softneck artichoke varieties have three to five layers of cloves in lumpy bulbs; softneck sil-

Allium sativum

verskin varieties, uniform bulbs that are sometimes braided into decorative ropes for storage; hardneck varieties, coiled stalks and decorative seedpods that are prized in dried arrangements; all varieties are used for flavoring. *A. schoenoprasum* (chives)—clumps of slender foot-long leaves with mild onion flavor and stalks tipped with edible pale purple flowers from summer through fall, all varieties of which are used fresh, frozen, or dried as garnishes or flavoring or planted as border accents; 'Forescate' is a particularly vigorous variety with rose-pink flowers on stalks to 18 inches. *A. scorodoprasum* (rocambole, Spanish garlic)—inch-wide bulbs with mild garlicky flavor and 3-foot stalks tipped with edible bulbils; both leaves and bulbils are used for flavoring. *A. tricoccum* (ramp, wild leek)—2-inch-wide arrow-shaped leaves that wither before white summer-to-fall flowers bloom on 12- to 18-inch stalks; the extremely pungent bulbs and leaves are used for flavoring, the flowers as ornamentals. *A. tuberosum* (garlic chives, Oriental garlic, Chinese leek)—scented white summer flowers on 1- to 1½-foot stalks grown ornamentally for fresh or dried bouquets; the summer flowers and mildly flavored flat leaves are used in cooking or salads.

Growing conditions and maintenance: Sow allium seeds indoors 10 to 12 weeks

before the last frost or outdoors in fall 8 to 12 weeks before the first frost; alliums require two growing seasons to produce eating-size bulbs from seed. For earlier harvest, plant sets of *A. fistulosum* or *A. schoenoprasum* in spring or plant the small aerial bulbils or cloves of other allium species in fall for harvest the following year; left unharvested, bulbils self-sow. Most alliums do best in moist but very well-drained organic soils; ramp prefers constantly moist soils and tolerates shade; rocambole tolerates drier soils. Set bulbs or cloves 1 to 3 inches deep. Space sets or cloves of smaller

Allium tuberosum

species such as *A. fistulosum* or *A. schoenoprasum* 4 to 6 inches apart, those of larger species such as *A. cepa* var. *proliferum, A. sativum,* or *A. ampeloprasum* var. *ampeloprasum* 8 to 10 inches apart. Wider spacing produces larger bulbs. Grow chives in containers and move indoors for harvest through the winter. Divide clumps of chives and garlic chives every 3 to 4 years to maintain vigor. Harvest allium leaves anytime during the growing season; chives do best sheared close to the ground and allowed to regrow. Harvest flowers of garlic, chives, and garlic chives for salads and garnishes just after opening. Cut seed heads of garlic chives to prevent proliferation of seedlings. Pick aerial bulbils of tree onion and rocambole in fall. Dig allium bulbs for fresh use in fall as leaves begin to wither. To dry elephant garlic or garlic for long-term storage, allow skins to dry for several days, then either braid stems or cut them off 2 inches from bulb; store with good air circulation and use within 6 to 10 months.

Aloysia
(a-LOYZ-ee-a)
LEMON VERBENA

Aloysia triphylla

Hardiness: *Zones 9-10*

Height: *2 to 8 feet*

Light: *full sun*

Soil: *average, well-drained*

Plant type: *deciduous shrub*

Uses: *potpourri, culinary, houseplant*

The lemon-lime aroma of aloysia's narrow leaves perfumes the garden from spring through fall. Its fragrance is this shrub's primary attraction; where it can be grown outdoors, it is often pinched and pruned as an espalier or standard to give it shape. Use fresh leaves in cold drinks, salads, and fish or poultry dishes or infused in liquids to flavor baked goods and puddings. Steep fresh or dried leaves for tea. Dried leaves retain their fragrance for several years in potpourri.

Selected species and varieties: *A. triphylla* (lemon verbena, cidron, limonetto)—whorls of lemon-scented leaves along open, sprawling branches growing 6 to 8 feet outdoors, 2 to 4 feet as a potted plant, and loose clusters of tiny white to lilac late-summer flowers.

Growing conditions and maintenance: Sow lemon verbena seeds 3 feet apart in spring. Where frost is a possibility, cut stems to 6 to 12 inches in fall and provide protective winter mulch. Potted plants drop their leaves in winter and do best if moved outdoors during warmer months. Propagate lemon verbena from seed or from cuttings taken in summer.

Althaea
(al-THEE-a)
MARSH MALLOW

Althaea officinalis

Hardiness: *Zones 3-9*

Height: *4 to 5 feet*

Light: *full sun*

Soil: *moist*

Plant type: *perennial*

Uses: *landscaping, culinary*

Marsh mallows create colorful border backdrops and temporary screens in marshy, wet garden sites. Tender young leaves at the tips of stems and the cup-shaped flowers growing where leaves and stems join can be tossed in salads, as can the nutlike seeds contained in the plant's ring-shaped fruits, called cheeses. Steam leaves or fry roots (after softening by boiling) and serve as a side dish. Roots release a thick mucilage after long soaking, which was once an essential ingredient in the original marshmallow confection and is sometimes used in herbal medicine.

Selected species and varieties: *A. officinalis* (marsh mallow, white mallow)—clumps of stiffly erect 4- to 5-foot-tall stems lined with velvety triangular leaves and pink or white summer flowers.

Growing conditions and maintenance: Sow seeds of marsh mallow in spring or divisions in spring or fall, setting plants 2 feet apart. Keep marsh mallow's woody taproot constantly moist. Pick leaves and flowers just as the flowers reach their peak. Dig roots of plants at least 2 years old in fall, remove rootlets, peel bark, and dry whole or in slices.

Amaranthus
(am-a-RAN-thus)
AMARANTH

Amaranthus hypochondriacus

Hardiness: *tender*

Height: *4 to 6 feet*

Light: *full sun*

Soil: *dry, well-drained*

Plant type: *annual*

Uses: *culinary, landscaping*

Flowering spikes rise from amaranth's clumps of spinachlike leaves in late summer. While amaranth can be used in the border, its primary value is as a food crop. Young leaves are steamed or boiled as a side dish. The high-protein seeds are cooked as a cereal, popped like popcorn, or ground into flour. Seed heads can also be saved as a winter treat for birds.

Selected species and varieties: *A. hypochondriacus* [also listed as *A. hybridus* var. *erythrostachys*] (golden amaranth, prince's-feather)—purple-green or golden green 6-inch leaves and tiny long-lasting deep burgundy flowers on 4- to 6-foot-tall stalks followed by red-brown or golden bronze seeds.

Growing conditions and maintenance: Sow amaranth seeds ¼ inch deep in rows 2 to 3 feet apart and thin seedlings to stand 4 to 10 inches apart. Keep soil moist until seed germinates; plants tolerate dry conditions thereafter. Harvest seeds after frost. Thresh by walking on seed heads or pushing them through ½-inch hardware cloth, then through window screening. Winnow in front of an electric fan to remove chaff.

Anethum
(a-NEE-thum)
DILL

Anethum graveolens

Hardiness: *tender*

Height: *3 to 4 feet*

Light: *full sun*

Soil: *average to rich, well-drained*

Plant type: *annual*

Uses: *culinary, dried arrangements*

Dill's aromatic feathery leaves and flat, open clusters of yellow summer flowers add delicate texture to garden beds. Dill also thrives in window-sill gardens. Snippets of tangy, fresh leaves are a culinary staple in fish, egg, meat, and vegetable dishes; immature flower heads flavor cucumber pickles; and the flat, ribbed seeds season breads and sauces.

Selected species and varieties: *A. graveolens* (dill)—soft 3- to 4-foot stems lined with fine, threadlike foliage; 'Bouquet' is a compact cultivar producing more leaves than flowers; 'Mammoth' is fast-growing with blue-green foliage.

Growing conditions and maintenance: Sow dill seed in the garden and thin seedlings to stand 8 to 10 inches apart. Plants may need staking. Dill self-sows readily; remove flower heads to prevent self-sowing and to encourage leaf production. Snip leaves and immature flower heads as needed. Harvest seed heads just before they turn brown and place in paper bags until seeds loosen and fall. Preserve leaves by freezing whole stems or drying in a microwave oven; dried conventionally, dill loses flavor.

Angelica
(an-JEL-i-ka)
ANGELICA

Angelica gigas

Hardiness: *Zones 3-9*

Height: *3 to 8 feet*

Light: *partial shade to full sun*

Soil: *rich, moist*

Plant type: *biennial or short-lived perennial*

Uses: *landscaping, culinary, potpourri*

Tall columns of coarse-textured, licorice-scented leaves make angelica a bold border specimen or backdrop. In their second year, plants produce broad, flat clusters of tiny summer flowers, then die. Fresh angelica leaves are used to flavor acidic fruits such as rhubarb; stems are steamed as a vegetable or candied for a garnish; and seeds add sweet zest to pastries. Dried leaves can be used to scent potpourri. Angelica can cause dermatitis. It should be eaten sparingly, as some herbalists believe it may be carcinogenic. Do not attempt to collect angelica in the wild, as it closely resembles poisonous water hemlock.

Selected species and varieties: *A. archangelica* (archangel, wild parsnip)—plants to 8 feet tall with 6-inch-wide clusters of greenish white flowers. *A. gigas*—specimens to 6 feet tall, with 8-inch clusters of burgundy flowers.

Growing conditions and maintenance: Sow very fresh angelica seed in the garden in spring or fall. Remove flower stalks to prolong the life of the plants. Angelica self-sows readily; transplant seedlings before taproots become established.

Anthriscus
(an-THRIS-kus)
CHERVIL

Anthriscus cerefolium

Hardiness: *tender*

Height: *1 to 2 feet*

Light: *light to full shade*

Soil: *average, well-drained*

Plant type: *annual*

Uses: *culinary, containers, arrangements*

One of the finest herbes of French cuisine, chervil's finely divided leaves resemble parsley with a hint of warm anise flavor. Chervil is an ideal outdoor container plant. Chop fresh chervil into fish, vegetable, egg, and meat dishes. Use flower stalks in fresh or dried arrangements, and add dried leaves to herbal potpourri.

Selected species and varieties: *A. cerefolium* (chervil, salad chervil)—mounds 1 to 2 feet tall of lacy bright green leaves topped by small, open clusters of tiny white flowers in summer.

Growing conditions and maintenance: Sow chervil seeds in the garden for harvestable leaves in 6 to 8 weeks. Make successive sowings for a continuous supply of fresh leaves; seeds sown in fall produce a spring crop. Remove flowers to encourage greater leaf production; alternatively, allow plants to go to seed and self-sow, producing both early- and late-summer crops. Pick leaves before flowers appear, starting when plants reach 4 inches in height, and preserve by freezing alone or mixed with butter. Flavor fades when leaves are dried. Hang flower stalks to dry for use in winter bouquets.

Apium
(AP-ee-um)
WILD CELERY

Apium graveolens

Hardiness:	*hardy*
Height:	*1 to 3 feet*
Light:	*full sun to light shade*
Soil:	*rich, moist, well-drained*
Plant type:	*biennial*
Uses:	*culinary*

The ridged stems, parsleylike leaves, and tiny seeds of wild celery all share the scent of the cultivated vegetable beloved as an aromatic culinary staple. Sprinkle stems and leaves over salads, or use fresh stems and fresh or dried leaves as a substitute for celery in soups, stews, and stuffings. Use wild celery sparingly, as it is toxic in large amounts. Proponents of herbal medicine include wild celery in various remedies.

Selected species and varieties: *A. graveolens* (wild celery, smallage)—rosettes of flat, fan-shaped leaflets with toothed edges the first year, followed by elongated, ridged, branching stems tipped with small clusters of greenish cream summer flowers the second year.

Growing conditions and maintenance: Sow wild celery seeds in sites sheltered from drying winds. Thin out the seedlings to stand 12 to 16 inches apart. Dry the leaves flat in a single layer in a shady, well-ventilated area. To obtain seed, pick flower heads as they begin to brown and store in paper bags until they dry and release seeds.

Armoracia
(ar-mo-RAH-kee-a)
HORSERADISH

Armoracia rusticana

Hardiness:	*Zones 3-10*
Height:	*2 to 4 feet*
Light:	*full sun to light shade*
Soil:	*moist, well-drained*
Plant type:	*perennial*
Uses:	*culinary*

Spring clumps of oblong leaves with ruffled, wrinkled edges grow from horseradish's fleshy taproot, followed by clusters of tiny white summer flowers. The pungent bite of fresh horseradish root grated into vinegar, cream, or mayonnaise for sauces and dressings is enjoyed in German cuisine. Chop fresh young leaves and toss in salad. Horseradish was used as a medicinal plant before it became popular as a condiment, and its dried leaves yield a yellow dye.

Selected species and varieties: *A. rusticana* (horseradish, red cole)—thick, branching white-fleshed roots a foot long or longer with leaves to 2 feet and flower stalks to 4 feet; 'Variegata' has leaves streaked white.

Growing conditions and maintenance: Plant pieces of mature root at least 6 inches long in spring or fall. Set root pieces 3 to 4 inches deep and 1 to 2 feet apart. Dig roots in fall and store in dry sand; slice and dry for later grinding, or grate into white vinegar to preserve. Horseradish can be invasive, as new plants grow from any root pieces left in the garden.

Artemisia
(ar-tem-IS-ee-a)
WORMWOOD

Artemisia absinthium 'Lambrook Silver'

Hardiness:	*hardy annual or Zones 3-10*
Height:	*1 to 6 feet*
Light:	*full sun to partial shade*
Soil:	*average, dry to moist*
Plant type:	*annual, perennial, or shrub*
Uses:	*landscaping, culinary, dried arrangements*

Artemisia's aromatic filigreed foliage in shades of green through gray-green to silver and almost white is prized as a border filler or background. The foliage dries well for use in arrangements and sachets. While most species bear inconspicuous flowers or none at all, a few produce airy sprays of tiny, fragrant, early- to late-summer blossoms useful as fillers in fresh bouquets. One variety is used as an ingredient in fines herbes, but some more bitter species contain a poisonous narcotic legally restricted in several countries, including the United States—especially *A. absinthium,* the source of absinthe, a liquor alleged to induce bizarre behavior and cause mental deterioration. Herbal tradition ascribes medicinal and insect repellent properties to wormwoods, and boiled stems yield a yellow dye.

Selected species and varieties: *A. abrotanum* (southernwood)—a deciduous subshrub or perennial 3 to 6 feet tall with gray-green camphor- or citrus-scented foliage; Zones 5-9. *A. absinthium* 'Lambrook Silver' (absinthe, common wormwood)—an evergreen shrub or perennial with filigreed silvery gray foliage in neat 18- to 36-inch-high mounds; Zones 3-9. *A. arborescens* (tree wormwood)—an evergreen or semievergreen shrub or perennial forming mounds 3 feet high and almost as wide of threadlike silvery gray leaves, with loose sprays of tiny yellow flowers from summer through fall; Zones 8-9. *A. dracunculus* var. *sativa* (French tarragon, estragon)—a sprawling perennial to 2 feet high with glossy green leaves whose peppery anise flavor is prized in cooking and seasoning; Zones 4-7. *A. ludoviciana* 'Silver King' (western mugwort, white sage)—a bushy perennial with silvery white leaves in mounds up to 4 feet high and as wide; 'Silver Queen' grows to only 2 feet with silvery white leaves; Zones 5-9. *A. pontica* (Roman wormwood)—an upright perennial 1 to 4 feet tall with feathery silvery gray leaves used to flavor vermouth; Zones 5-9.

Growing conditions and maintenance: Plant rooted stem cuttings or divisions of wormwoods 1 to 2 feet apart for low hedges, 3 to 4 feet apart as specimens or backdrop plantings, in spring or fall. Most wormwoods prefer dry, average to poor, well-drained soil, becoming leggy in fertile soils and rotting under hot, humid conditions. *A. absinthium* makes a poor companion plant, as the substance absinthin, flushed from its leaves by rain or watering, acts as a growth inhibitor to nearby plants. All wormwoods grow in full sun; French tarragon and *A. absinthium* 'Lambrook Silver' tolerate partial shade. Prune southernwood to control its size and shape, Roman wormwood to train as a hedge or curb its invasiveness. Grow French tarragon in patio containers, or pot divisions in fall, leaving them outdoors for 2 to 3 months of exposure to colder temperatures, then bringing indoors to pick fresh leaves for culinary use. Use the foliage of all wormwoods as an aromatic addition to fresh bouquets. Use dried branches in arrangements or crumble leaves into herbal mixes for potpourri and sachets.

Atriplex
(AT-ri-plex)
ORACH, SALTBUSH

![Atriplex hortensis 'Rubra']

Atriplex hortensis 'Rubra'

Hardiness:	*hardy*
Height:	*2 to 6 feet*
Light:	*full sun*
Soil:	*rich, moist, organic*
Plant type:	*annual*
Uses:	*culinary, landscaping, arrangements*

Garden orach sends up stiff stems lined with arrowhead-shaped leaves that can be massed together as an effective seasonal screen. The leaves add color and a slightly salty tang to salads. Leaves and young shoots can be boiled like spinach. Use the colorful foliage as a filler in fresh arrangements. Orach once figured in herbal medicine.

Selected species and varieties: *A. hortensis* (mountain spinach)—smooth deep green leaves and branching clusters of tiny yellow-green flowers tinged red in summer on stems to 6 feet; 'Rubra' (purple orach) has deep red leaves and stems.

Growing conditions and maintenance: Sow orach seeds in spring and thin plants to stand 8 to 12 inches apart. Orach will tolerate both saline soils and dry conditions but produces the most succulent leaves when kept constantly moist. Successive sowings every 2 weeks ensure a continuous supply of young salad leaves. Pinch out flower heads to encourage greater leaf production. Allowed to form seed, orach self-sows freely. Dip stem ends in boiling water to seal them before using in arrangements.

Borago
(bor-RAY-go)
BORAGE

Borago officinalis

Hardiness:	*hardy*
Height:	*1 to 3 feet*
Light:	*full sun*
Soil:	*rich, moist, well-drained*
Plant type:	*annual*
Uses:	*culinary, houseplant, arrangements*

Borage forms sprawling mounds of hairy, cucumber-scented oval leaves. Bees find the nodding clusters of star-shaped summer flowers with black stamens extremely attractive. Chop borage leaves into salads, soups, and dips for a cucumber flavor without gastric distress; brew leaves as tea, or sauté for a side dish. Toss flowers with salads for color, freeze them into ice cubes to garnish cool drinks, or candy them to decorate cakes and other sweets. Borage can be grown as a houseplant, and its flowers used in fresh arrangements.

Selected species and varieties: *B. officinalis* (talewort, cool-tankard)—leaves 6 to 8 inches long and deep blue flowers; 'Alba' has white blossoms.

Growing conditions and maintenance: Sow borage in the garden in spring and thin seedlings to stand 12 inches apart. Borage will tolerate dry soils but grows best with constant moisture. Plants will self-sow. Indoors, plant borage in large pots to accommodate its spreading roots. Pick rosettes of young leaves for fresh use; borage does not dry or freeze well but can be preserved in vinegar.

Brassica
(BRASS-ik-a)
MUSTARD, COLE

Brassica juncea

Hardiness: *hardy*

Height: *3 to 4 feet*

Light: *full sun*

Soil: *average, well-drained*

Plant type: *annual*

Uses: *culinary*

Mustard's pungent oval leaves add zest to salads and can be boiled or sautéed as a side dish. The four-petaled summer flowers are followed by pods filled with tiny round seeds used whole to flavor pickles and curries or ground to create mustard spread. Mustard can be grown in pots indoors for a continuous supply of young salad greens in winter.

Selected species and varieties: *B. juncea* (brown mustard, Chinese mustard, Indian mustard, mustard cabbage, mustard greens)—leaves 6 to 12 inches long, with open, branching clusters of pale yellow flowers followed by 1½-inch beaked pods filled with dark reddish brown seeds.

Growing conditions and maintenance: Sow mustard seeds ¼ inch deep in spring in rows 18 inches apart and thin plants to stand 8 inches apart. Use the thinnings in salads; young leaves are ready for salad picking in 8 to 10 days. Mustard self-sows freely for future crops. Harvest pods as they begin to brown, and finish drying them in paper bags to collect the ripening seed. Brown mustard develops its hottest flavor when ground and mixed with cold liquids.

Calamintha
(kal-a-MIN-tha)
CALAMINT

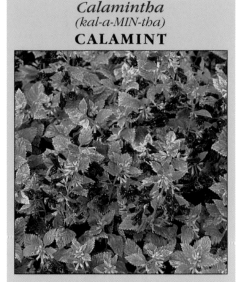

Calamintha grandiflora 'Variegata'

Hardiness: *Zones 5-10*

Height: *12 to 24 inches*

Light: *full sun to light shade*

Soil: *average, well-drained, neutral to alkaline*

Plant type: *perennial*

Uses: *landscaping, culinary, potpourri*

Calamint forms neat spreading clumps of erect stems lined with mint-scented oval leaves and tipped with spikes of tiny tubular flowers in summer. Ideal as a border edging, where a passing touch releases its aroma, calamint also grows well in patio containers. Use fresh leaves to garnish summer drinks; steep fresh or dried leaves in boiling water for tea. Mix dried leaves into herbal potpourri.

Selected species and varieties: *C. grandiflora* (mountain balm, ornamental savory)—brown-fringed, slightly hairy, deep green leaves on 12- to 18-inch-tall stems and pink flowers; 'Variegata' has a bushy habit and leaves flecked off-white. *C. nepeta* ssp. *nepeta* [also classified as *Satureja calamintha*] (lesser calamint)—shiny green leaves on 18- to 24-inch stems and pale lilac to white flowers.

Growing conditions and maintenance: Sow calamint seed in spring or fall or set out divisions in spring, spacing plants 12 inches apart. Cut stems back in fall and provide winter mulch in cooler climates. Calamint spreads by creeping rhizomes and also self-sows. Dry the leaves on screens in a shady, well-ventilated area.

Calendula
(kal-EN-dew-la)
MARIGOLD

Calendula officinalis

Hardiness: *hardy*

Height: *18 to 24 inches*

Light: *full sun*

Soil: *average, well-drained*

Plant type: *annual*

Uses: *landscaping, culinary, potpourri*

Pot marigold's thick stems lined with hairy oval leaves each bear one or two blossoms resembling zinnias from spring through frost. Their long season of bloom makes them valuable in borders, and they also grow well in patio containers or as houseplants. Pot marigolds are long lasting as cut flowers. Young leaves were once used like spinach in salads and stews. Use the fresh, slightly salty flower petals to add color to salads, soups, sandwiches, and pâtés. Dried and ground, the petals can substitute for saffron in rice dishes and baked goods. Mix dried petals into potpourri for color.

Selected species and varieties: *C. officinalis* (pot marigold, common marigold, Scotch marigold, ruddles)—coarse 2- to 3-inch leaves and 1½- to 4-inch-wide pale yellow to deep orange flowers.

Growing conditions and maintenance: Sow pot marigold seeds in early spring and thin plants to 10 inches apart. Deadhead to encourage flower production. To dry, pull petals and lay in a single layer on paper (the petals will stick to screens). Dry in a shady, well-ventilated area, and store in moisture-proof containers.

Capsicum
(KAP-si-kum)
PEPPER

Capsicum frutescens 'Tabasco'

Hardiness: *tender or Zone 10*

Height: *1 to 3 feet*

Light: *full sun*

Soil: *rich, moist, well-drained*

Plant type: *annual or short-lived perennial*

Uses: *culinary, landscaping, containers*

Peppers produce hundreds of small, colorful fruits from summer through fall, held above low clumps of narrow oval leaves. Use them as border edgings, massed in beds, or in patio containers. Chop the fiery fruits into salsa, chutneys, marinades, vinegar, salad dressings, and baked goods. The tiny peppers are even spicier when dried.

Selected species and varieties: *C. annuum* var. *annuum* 'Jalapeño' (chili pepper)—narrow, conical 2½- to 4-inch-long fruits ripening from green to red. *C. chinense* 'Habañero' (papaya chili)—extremely hot, bell-shaped 1- to 2-inch fruits ripening from green to yellow-orange. *C. frutescens* 'Tabasco' (tabasco pepper)—small, upright green fruits with a slightly smoky flavor ripening to red.

Growing conditions and maintenance: Start peppers indoors 8 to 10 weeks before the last frost and transplant to the garden when soil temperature reaches 65° F or more. Set plants 18 inches apart and mulch from midsummer on to prevent drying out. Harvest fruit when green or ripe by cutting stems. To dry, string on a line or pull entire plants and hang.

Carthamus
(KAR-tha-mus)
SAFFLOWER

Carthamus tinctorius

Hardiness: *tender*

Height: *1 to 3 feet*

Light: *full sun*

Soil: *well-drained to dry*

Plant type: *annual*

Uses: *landscaping, culinary, arrangements*

Both safflower's stiff stems lined with spiny leaves and its thistlelike summer flowers add texture and color to seasonal borders. Surrounded by a cuff of spiny bracts, the blossoms make excellent cut flowers. Dried flower petals are ground and used as a substitute for saffron in sauces, soups, and other dishes. They also yield dyes for textiles and cosmetics in shades from yellow through red. The seeds are pressed for oil.

Selected species and varieties: *C. tinctorius* (safflower, saffron thistle, false saffron, bastard saffron)—yellow to yellow-orange tousled flowers up to 1 inch across, followed by white seeds yielding polyunsaturated oil for cooking.

Growing conditions and maintenance: Sow safflower seeds in spring and thin seedlings to stand 6 inches apart. Safflowers grow best under dry conditions and are subject to disease in rainy or humid areas. Cut and dry the mature flowers, storing in airtight containers for up to a year to grind as food coloring. Alternatively, carefully pluck petals from mature blossoms and allow the oily seeds to develop so that plants can self-sow.

Carum
(KAY-rum)
CARAWAY

Carum carvi

Hardiness: *Zones 3-8*

Height: *2 feet*

Light: *full sun to light shade*

Soil: *rich, well-drained*

Plant type: *biennial*

Uses: *culinary*

Carum's feathery, aromatic carrotlike leaves grow in loose clumps from thick branching roots. In late spring or early summer of their second year, plants send up branching flower stalks tipped with flat clusters of tiny flowers followed by flavorful seeds. Chop the leaves, which have a parsley-dill flavor, into salads, and cook the roots like carrots or parsnips. Use the anise-flavored seeds in breads and cakes; add them to meat, cabbage, and apple dishes; or crystallize them in sugar for an after-dinner candy to sweeten the breath and settle the stomach.

Selected species and varieties: *C. carvi* (caraway)—ferny leaves up to 10 inches long and white flowers followed by ¼-inch dark brown seeds.

Growing conditions and maintenance: Sow caraway in the garden in spring or fall and thin seedlings to stand 8 inches apart; once established, it self-sows. Snip leaves at any time. Harvest seeds as flower clusters turn brown but before the seed capsules shatter. Hang to dry over a tray or cloth, and store the seeds in airtight containers. Dig 2-year-old roots to serve as a side dish.

Chamaemelum
(ka-mee-MAY-lum)
ROMAN CHAMOMILE

Chamaemelum nobile

Hardiness: *Zones 4-8*

Height: *1 to 6 inches*

Light: *full sun to light shade*

Soil: *dry, well-drained*

Plant type: *perennial*

Uses: *ground cover, lawn, potpourri, culinary*

Roman chamomile's feathery leaves release an apple scent when crushed. The roots spread quickly into dense mats ideal as informal ground covers or as fillers among paving stones. Dry the leaves for potpourri. The flowers that bloom from late spring through early fall can be dried and steeped for a tea. Chamomile figures in many herbal remedies.

Selected species and varieties: *C. nobile* [formerly classified as *Anthemis nobilis*] (Roman chamomile, garden chamomile) —lacy, ferny, bright green leaves and 1-inch white flowers with golden centers; 'Flore Pleno' has double-petaled cream flowers on plants 6 inches high spreading 18 inches wide; 'Treneague' is a nonflowering cultivar that grows 1 to 2 inches tall and 18 inches wide.

Growing conditions and maintenance: Sow Roman chamomile seeds in spring or fall, or plant divisions in spring; the species self-sows freely, but cultivars only come true from division. For lawns, space plants 4 to 6 inches apart and allow to spread before mowing. Harvest flowers as petals begin to fade, and dry on screens in a shady, well-ventilated area.

Chenopodium
(ken-o-PO-dee-um)
GOOSEFOOT, PIGWEED

Chenopodium ambrosioides

Hardiness: *hardy*

Height: *2 to 5 feet*

Light: *full sun*

Soil: *rich, well-drained*

Plant type: *annual*

Uses: *culinary, arrangements, potpourri*

Epazote's leaves are prized for flavoring beans, corn, and fish in Central American cuisines. They should be used sparingly, however, as the plant's oils are a potent, sometimes toxic vermifuge and insecticide. Ambrosia's fragrant foliage and plumy flower spikes are valued in both fresh and dried arrangements; leaves and seeds can be used in potpourri.

Selected species and varieties: *C. ambrosioides* (epazote)—spreading clumps of woody stems to 5 feet tall, lined with both broad, toothed, oval leaves and finely lacy leaves. *C. botrys* (ambrosia)—lobed ½- to 4-inch leaves that are deep green above and red below, and airy sprays of tiny yellow-green summer flowers without petals along arching 2-foot stems.

Growing conditions and maintenance: Sow epazote and ambrosia seeds in spring or fall, and thin seedlings to stand 12 inches apart. Pinch plants to keep them bushy. Both species self-sow freely and can become invasive weeds. Use epazote leaves either fresh or dried for cooking. For dried arrangements, hang ambrosia in a shady, well-ventilated area or stand stems in vases without water.

Cichorium
(si-KOR-ee-um)
CHICORY

Cichorium intybus

Hardiness: *Zones 3-10*

Height: *1 to 5 feet*

Light: *full sun*

Soil: *poor to average, well-drained, slightly alkaline*

Plant type: *perennial*

Uses: *culinary, landscaping, potpourri*

Chicory forms loose mounds of coarsely toothed leaves with a branching central flower stalk. Common chicory forms conical heads of young leaves called chicons. While it can be grown for ornament in a wildflower garden, chicory is most useful in the kitchen. Steam or braise young seedlings and roots. Toss bitter young leaves into salads. Roast and grind the young caramel-flavored roots to blend with coffee. Cultivars can be forced to produce blanched chicons ideal for salads or braising. Dried flowers add color to potpourri.

Selected species and varieties: *C. intybus* (common chicory, witloof, barbe-de-capuchin, succory)—daisylike 1- to 1½-inch sky blue—in rare cases white or pink— flowers the second year from seed.

Growing conditions and maintenance: Sow chicory seeds in spring and thin to 18 inches. Chicory self-sows freely. To roast, lift year-old roots in spring, slice and dry at 350° F. For blanched chicons, lift roots their first fall, cut back all but 1 inch of foliage, and shorten roots 1 inch; bury in moist, sandy compost and keep in total darkness at 50° F for 4 weeks.

Coriandrum
(kor-ree-AND-rum)
CORIANDER

Coriandrum sativum

Hardiness: *tender*

Height: *1 to 3 feet*

Light: *full sun to light shade*

Soil: *rich, well-drained*

Plant type: *annual*

Uses: *culinary, potpourri*

Coriander's pungent young leaves, commonly known as cilantro or Chinese parsley, are a staple in East Asian, Mexican, and Indian cuisines. With a hint of citrus, the round, ribbed seeds are used whole or ground in baked goods, curries, chutneys, and vegetable dishes. Add them to potpourri for a lingering lemon fragrance. The unpleasant odor of immature fruits earned coriander the nickname stinkplant; the characteristic agreeable fruity aroma develops as they ripen. Chop coriander roots into curries or steam them as a nutty vegetable.

Selected species and varieties: *C. sativum*—young leaves grow in small, scalloped fans resembling parsley; older leaves look ferny and threadlike, with flat, loose clusters of tiny white to mauve summer flowers; 'Long Standing' is a slow-to-bolt cultivar.

Growing conditions and maintenance: Sow coriander seed in spring and thin seedlings to stand 8 inches apart. Use fresh, immature leaves for best flavor; cilantro loses flavor if dried. To collect seed, cut seed heads and dry in a paper bag to catch seeds. Dig roots in fall.

Crocus
(KRO-kus)
CROCUS

Crocus sativus

Hardiness: *Zones 5-7*

Height: *6 to 12 inches*

Light: *light shade to full sun*

Soil: *well-drained*

Plant type: *bulb*

Uses: *landscaping, pot culture, culinary*

In fall, saffron crocus's bright cups open to reveal three prominent red branching stigmas. Picked and dried as saffron, they can be used to color food and textiles a delicate yellow. It takes 5,000 flowers to yield an ounce of saffron, but a dozen or so produce enough for a single recipe. *Caution:* Be careful not to confuse saffron crocus with the poisonous meadow saffron *(Colchicum autumnale),* which blooms at the same time. Mass saffron crocuses in rock gardens or scatter them in lawns. Force for indoor bloom.

Selected species and varieties: *C. sativus* (saffron crocus)—pale purple—or sometimes lavender, white, or reddish—1½- to 2-inch flowers and grassy leaves with a white midrib.

Growing conditions and maintenance: Remove cormels growing alongside mature saffron crocus corms in spring and replant 3 to 4 inches deep at 6-inch intervals. Divide corms every few years. Pick stigmas when flowers open, dry on paper, and store in airtight containers. To force, plant 12 to 18 corms in a 6-inch bulb pan. Refrigerate for at least 8 weeks, then put in a warm place to bloom.

Cymbopogon
(sim-bo-PO-gon)
OIL GRASS

Cymbopogon citratus

Hardiness: *Zones 10-11*

Height: *2 to 6 feet*

Light: *full sun to light shade*

Soil: *well-drained, sandy, slightly acid*

Plant type: *perennial grass*

Uses: *landscaping, culinary*

Lemon grass's fragrant leaves are a staple in Thai and Vietnamese cuisine. The tough stems are sliced and simmered to release their citrus flavor, then discarded before serving. Steep fresh or dried leaves for tea. Use clumps of lemon grass with its gracefully arching leaf blades in the middle of a border in warm-climate gardens. Elsewhere, grow as an annual and pot it to overwinter indoors.

Selected species and varieties: *C. citratus* (lemon grass, fever grass)—inch-wide aromatic evergreen leaves with sharp edges growing from bulbous stems in clumps to 6 feet tall and 3 feet wide.

Growing conditions and maintenance: Plant divisions of lemon grass in spring, spacing them 2 to 3 feet apart. Apply mulch both to conserve moisture in summer and to protect roots in winter. Where frost is a possibility, pot divisions in fall after cutting back to 3 inches and keep indoors over the winter, watering only sparingly to prevent root rot. Cut stems at ground level for fresh use, taking care when handling the leaf's sharp edges, and use the lower 3 to 4 inches for best flavor.

Dianthus
(dy-AN-thus)
PINK, CARNATION

![Dianthus plumarius]

Dianthus plumarius

Hardiness: *Zones 5-9*

Height: *4 to 20 inches*

Light: *full sun to light shade*

Soil: *moderately rich, well-drained, alkaline*

Plant type: *perennial*

Uses: *landscaping, arrangements, culinary*

Pinks' clove-scented flowers add fragrance to borders, beds, and rock gardens, where their evergreen foliage fills in among other plants or sprawls into ground-covering mats. Petals are often fringed, doubled, and shaded in tones of white to pink, red, purple, and yellow. The long-lasting flowers can also be dried for potpourri. Toss petals into salads or use to flavor vinegar, fruit syrup, or wine.

Selected species and varieties: *D.* x *allwoodii* (Allwood pink)—tufted blue-green foliage on 4- to 20-inch stems and 1- to 2-inch flowers. *D. caryophyllus* (carnation)—compact border varieties to 14 inches with blue-green leaves along woody stems and 2- to 3-inch flowers. *D. plumarius* (cottage pink, grass pink) —loose mats of gray-green foliage with 1½-inch flowers on 10- to 18-inch stems.

Growing conditions and maintenance: Sow seed in spring or propagate hybrids by summer cuttings or division in fall. Space plants 12 to 18 inches apart and mulch in cooler climates. Pinch to promote bushier plants, remove side buds for larger flowers, and deadhead to prolong the bloom.

Foeniculum
(fee-NIK-you-lum)
FENNEL

Foeniculum vulgare

Hardiness: *tender or Zones 9-10*

Height: *4 to 6 feet*

Light: *full sun*

Soil: *organic, well-drained*

Plant type: *perennial or annual*

Uses: *culinary, landscaping*

Fennel forms spreading clumps of succulent stems lined with feathery foliage. Flat summer-to-fall flower clusters are followed by oval seeds. Stems, leaves, and seeds all taste of anise. Substitute fresh stems for celery, or steam as a vegetable. Leaves complement seafood or garnish salads. Add seeds to baked goods, chew to freshen breath, or sprout for salads.

Selected species and varieties: *F. vulgare* (fennel, sweet anise)—branching stems to 6 feet lined with soft needlelike foliage and tipped with yellow flowers; 'Purpurascens' (copper fennel) has pink, copper, or bronze young foliage.

Growing conditions and maintenance: Fennel, though a tender perennial, is usually grown as an annual. Sow seeds successively from spring through summer for a continuous supply of leaves and stems. Left to form seed, fennel readily self-sows in fall for a spring harvest. Harvest stems as they thicken. Snip leaves anytime and use them fresh or frozen; they lose flavor on drying. Collect seed heads as they turn from yellow-green to brown and store in a paper bag until the seeds drop. Store in airtight containers.

Gaultheria
(gawl-THER-ee-a)
WINTERGREEN

Gaultheria procumbens

Hardiness: *Zones 3-10*

Height: *4 to 6 inches*

Light: *full to light shade*

Soil: *moist, organic, acid*

Plant type: *shrub*

Uses: *ground cover, culinary*

Wintergreen slowly creeps along to form low mats of glossy aromatic evergreen foliage ideal for ground cover and for use in rock gardens and wildflower gardens. Waxy summer flower bells dangle below the leaves, followed by fleshy red berries that remain on plants through the winter. Brew freshly chopped leaves or berries for a refreshing tea with hints of mint and camphor. Add a few berries to jams. Both yield an oil, now replaced by a synthetic formula, that was once used as a food flavoring and was applied externally to soothe sore muscles.

Selected species and varieties: *G. procumbens* (wintergreen, checkerberry, teaberry, ivry leaves)—leathery oval 2-inch leaves on short, erect stalks along trailing stems and ¼-inch white to pink flowers followed by edible red berries.

Growing conditions and maintenance: Propagate wintergreen from seeds sown or divisions made in spring, from rooted suckers in fall, or from cuttings taken in summer, and space plants 1 foot apart. Mulch with pine needles or leaf mold to conserve moisture. Harvest leaves anytime, berries when ripe.

Glycyrrhiza
(gly-ki-RY-za)
LICORICE

Glycyrrhiza glabra

Hardiness: *Zones 5-9*

Height: *to 3 feet*

Light: *full sun to light shade*

Soil: *rich, moist*

Plant type: *perennial*

Uses: *landscaping, culinary*

Licorice spreads in broad clumps of erect branching stems lined with long leaves composed of paired 1- to 2-inch sticky yellow-green leaflets. In summer, short flower spikes appear in leaf axils. A branching taproot contains glycyrrhizin, a compound 50 times sweeter than sugar and a source of the food flavoring. Dry root pieces to chew, or boil dried roots to extract the flavoring. *Caution:* Some people are severely allergic to glycyrrhizin.

Selected species and varieties: *G. glabra* (licorice)—yellow-green leaflets and white to blue, sometimes violet, ½-inch flowers resembling tiny sweet peas on plants growing from a 4-foot or longer taproot branching into tangled mats.

Growing conditions and maintenance: Licorice grows very slowly from seed. More often, it is grown from division of the crowns, rooted suckers, or root cuttings at least 6 inches long with two or three eyes. Space plants 18 inches apart. Wait at least 3 years before harvesting roots; root pieces left behind will sprout the next year. Dry the roots in a shady location for up to 6 months and store in a cool location in airtight containers.

Hibiscus
(hy-BIS-kus)
MALLOW, ROSE MALLOW

Hibiscus sabdariffa

Hardiness: *tender or Zones 7-11*

Height: *4 to 8 feet*

Light: *full sun*

Soil: *well-drained*

Plant type: *perennial or annual*

Uses: *landscaping, culinary*

Roselle develops round heads of broad leaves, sometimes deeply divided like the fingers on a hand, on woody stems. The dense foliage makes a handsome temporary screen. The showy flowers appearing in late summer through fall are surrounded by sepals that swell into succulent fleshy pseudofruits with a tart, acid flavor like that of cranberries. Fresh or cooked leaves taste like rhubarb. The fruits, which color dishes a deep burgundy, are used fresh or dried in herbal teas, jellies, jams, sauces, and curries. Steep leaves for tea, or roast the seeds for snacks.

Selected species and varieties: *H. sabdariffa* (roselle, sorrel, Jamaica sorrel, Indian sorrel, red sorrel)—leaves up to 6 inches across and 1½- to 2-inch-wide yellow flowers with red-purple throats on branching stems to 8 feet tall.

Growing conditions and maintenance: Sow roselle seeds outdoors after the soil warms in spring or start indoors 8 to 10 weeks before planting time. Space plants 1½ to 2 feet apart. Protect from frost, since blooms emerge only after the days gradually become shorter, and early frost will ruin fruits.

Humulus
(HEW-mew-lus)
HOP

Humulus lupulus 'Aureus'

Hardiness: *Zones 3-8*

Height: *10 to 25 feet*

Light: *full sun to light shade*

Soil: *rich, moist, well-drained*

Plant type: *perennial vine*

Uses: *landscaping, culinary, crafts*

Twining deciduous vines with coarse foliage like that of grapevines, hops quickly clamber over trellises to form dense, textured screens. In summer, female and male flowers appear on separate plants. Weave lengths of hopvine into garlands or wreaths for drying. Stuff dried female flowers, used as a bitter flavoring for beer, into herbal pillows to promote sleep. Blanch young leaves to remove bitterness and add to soups or sauces. Cook young side shoots like asparagus.

Selected species and varieties: *H. lupulus* (common hop, European hop, bine)—heart-shaped lobed leaves up to 6 inches across and female plants with paired yellow-green flowers ripening to papery scales layered in puffy cones; 'Aureus' has golden green leaves.

Growing conditions and maintenance: Because female plants are more desirable than male ones and the gender of plants grown from seed is unknown for 3 years, it is best to grow hops from tip cuttings taken from female plants, divide their roots, or remove their rooted suckers in spring. Space plants 1½ to 3 feet apart. Cut hops to the ground at season's end.

Hyssopus
(hiss-O-pus)
HYSSOP

Hyssopus officinalis

Hardiness: *Zones 3-8*

Height: *18 to 36 inches*

Light: *full sun to light shade*

Soil: *well-drained to dry*

Plant type: *perennial*

Uses: *landscaping, culinary*

Hyssop's square stems are lined with camphor-scented narrow leaves and tipped with thick spikes of tubular flowers having flared lips favored by bees and hummingbirds. Grow them as bushy specimens or plant them closely for low hedges. Add the flowers to salads; use the sagelike leaves to flavor poultry or stuffings. Use dried flowers and leaves in herbal teas or potpourri.

Selected species and varieties: *H. officinalis* (common hyssop, European hyssop)—willowlike ¾- to 1¼-inch leaves and ½-inch blue-violet flowers on plants to 3 feet; 'Albus' [also called 'Alb'] (white hyssop) has white flowers; ssp. *aristatus* (rock hyssop) produces fine leaves on 18- to 24-inch plants.

Growing conditions and maintenance: Sow hyssop from seed to bloom its second year. Otherwise, grow from stem cuttings in midsummer or from divisions taken in spring or fall. Remove spent flowers to prolong bloom. Prune mature plants to the ground in spring. Shear into formal hedges for knot gardens or for use as edgings in formal gardens. Hyssop is sometimes evergreen in milder climates.

Laurus
(LAR-us)
LAUREL, SWEET BAY

Laurus nobilis

Hardiness: *Zones 8-10*

Height: *4 to 40 feet*

Light: *full sun to light shade*

Soil: *well-drained*

Plant type: *tree or shrub*

Uses: *culinary, landscaping, dried arrangements*

In warm climates, evergreen bay laurel grows as a multistemmed shrub or tree to 40 feet; in colder climates, it reaches 4 to 6 feet as a container-grown standard. The glossy, leathery, aromatic leaves with intense flavor are prized by cooks and essential in bouquets garnis. Add leaves to potpourri, or dry branches for bouquets or wreaths. Bay laurel is a traditional medicinal and insect-repellent herb.

Selected species and varieties: *L. nobilis* (bay laurel, bay, bay tree, true laurel) —narrow, oval 2- to 4-inch gray-green leaves; 'Angustifolia' (willow-leaved bay) has extremely narrow leaves; 'Aurea', tapered golden yellow leaves.

Growing conditions and maintenance: Plant balled-and-burlapped or container-grown specimens to harvest leaves the first season. Choose sites protected from winds. To grow as standards, train plants to a single stem and prune frequently; bring plants indoors before frost. Bay laurel can be propagated from seed or from hardwood cuttings but grows very slowly. Dry the leaves in a single layer in a warm, dark place; weigh down with a board to dry them flat. Store in airtight containers.

Lavandula
(lav-AN-dew-la)
LAVENDER

Lavandula angustifolia 'Hidcote'

Hardiness: *Zones 5-10*

Height: *1 to 5 feet*

Light: *full sun*

Soil: *dry, well-drained, sandy, alkaline*

Plant type: *perennial or small shrub*

Uses: *landscaping, culinary, arrangements*

Dense spikes of intensely fragrant blue to purple, sometimes white, ¼- to ½-inch flowers bloom throughout summer on leafless stalks above cushions of gray-green foliage. Mounds of lavender make fragrant border specimens or can be used as low hedges. Aromatic oils permeate all parts of the plant but are concentrated in flowers. Use fresh flowers to flavor jellies, vinegars, and sauces; toss with salads; or crystallize as a garnish. Use fresh or dried flower stalks in bouquets, dried flowers in sachets and potpourri. Some species are reputed to have medicinal and insect-repellent properties.

Selected species and varieties: *L. angustifolia* [also listed as *L. officinalis, L. spica, L. vera*] (English lavender)—broad, compact mounds of aromatic foliage; 'Hidcote' is slow growing to 16 inches with sweetly scented deep purple flowers above silvery foliage; 'Jean Davis' has prolific pale pink flowers on 18-inch mounds; 'Munstead', early large purple flowers on compact 14-inch plants; Zones 5-9. *L. dentata* var. *candicans* (French lavender, fringed lavender)—2- to 3-foot stalks of blue flowers above pine-scented mounds of toothed leaves; Zones 9-10. *L.* x *intermedia* (lavandin)—robust, very fragrant hybrids ideal for landscaping; 'Alba' has white flower spikes on 3-foot stems; 'Dutch', very early dark violet flowers on 3-foot stems; 'Grosso', thick, 4- to 6-inch spikes of deep lavender flowers on 30-inch stems above compact 8-inch mounds of silvery foliage; 'Provence', very fragrant violet blossoms on 2-foot stems; 'Seal', pale violet flowers on vigorous plants to 5

Lavandula lanata

feet tall; Zones 6-8. *L. lanata* (woolly lavender)—deep purple flowers on 5-foot stems above mounds of white woolly foliage spreading to 4 feet; Zones 7-9. *L. pinnata*—an almost everblooming species in mild zones, with lavender to deep purple blossoms on 30-inch stems above ferny foliage; Zones 8-10. *L. stoechas* (Spanish lavender)—extremely fragrant magenta-purple butterfly-shaped flowers on 18- to 24-inch stems; Zones 6-9.

Growing conditions and maintenance: Plant rooted lavender cuttings or divisions in spring, spacing them 12 inches apart for hedges, up to 6 feet apart in borders. Poor soil intensifies fragrance. Protect fringed lavender and *L. pinnata* from frost, or grow in containers that you can move indoors. Pinch flowers the first year to encourage wider mounds. Stems become woody their second season; prune woody stems in fall, or shear entire plant to 8 to 12 inches tall. Pick lavender before the flowers are fully open, cutting early in the day before the sun dries volatile oils. Hang in bunches to dry, or remove flowers from stems and spread on screens. Stored in airtight containers, lavender retains its fragrance over many months.

Levisticum
(le-VIS-ti-kum)
LOVAGE

Levisticum officinale

Hardiness: *Zones 3-8*

Height: *3 to 6 feet*

Light: *full sun to light shade*

Soil: *organic, moist, well-drained*

Plant type: *perennial*

Uses: *culinary, landscaping*

With divided leaflets resembling flat parsley, lovage develops into towering clumps of greenish red stalks useful as specimens or to shade lower-growing herbs. Lovage's hollow stems, wedge-shaped leaves, thick roots, and ridged seeds all share an intense celery flavor and aroma. Chop leaves and stems or grate roots to garnish salads or flavor soups, potatoes, poultry, and other dishes. Steam stems as a side dish. Toss seeds into stuffings, dressings, and baked goods. Steep leaves for herbal tea.

Selected species and varieties: *L. officinale* (lovage)—deep green leaflets with toothed edges on branching stems to 6 feet topped with a flat cluster of tiny yellow-green spring-to-summer flowers.

Growing conditions and maintenance: Sow lovage seeds in fall or divide roots in spring or fall, spacing plants 2 feet apart. Top-dress annually with compost or aged manure and keep well watered during dry spells. Harvest leaves two or three times a season. Deadhead to encourage greater leaf production, or allow flowers to ripen for seeds. Dry leaves in bundles, or blanch and freeze.

Lindera
(lin-DER-a)
SPICEBUSH

Lindera benzoin

Hardiness: *Zones 4-9*

Height: *6 to 15 feet*

Light: *light shade*

Soil: *moist, acid*

Plant type: *shrub*

Uses: *landscaping, culinary, potpourri*

A round, dense deciduous shrub with erect branches, spicebush offers three-season interest, fragrance, and flavor as a specimen or in a shrub border. Flowers bloom along bare branches of both male and female plants in early spring, followed by spicy-scented leaves. On female plants, leaves color and drop in fall to reveal bright red fruits. Steep young twigs and fresh or dried leaves and berries for herbal tea. Add dried leaves and berries to woodsy potpourri, or grind dried berries as a substitute for allspice.

Selected species and varieties: *L. benzoin* (spicebush, Benjamin bush)—fragrant, tiny yellow-green flowers in clusters emerge before the 2- to 5-inch pointed, oval leaves, which turn deep gold in fall, and ½-inch oval red fruits.

Growing conditions and maintenance: Sow ripe spicebush seed in the fall before it dries out, or hold at least 4 months in the refrigerator and sow in spring. Otherwise, start new shrubs from softwood cuttings taken in summer. Collect twigs in spring, leaves throughout the growing season, and berries in fall, and use either fresh or dried.

Lippia
(LIP-ee-a)
MEXICAN OREGANO

Lippia graveolens

Hardiness: *Zones 9-11*

Height: *3 to 6 feet*

Light: *full sun*

Soil: *organic, sandy, well-drained*

Plant type: *shrub*

Uses: *culinary, containers, landscaping*

Mexican oregano's upright branches are lined with intensely aromatic, wrinkled leaves used fresh or dried to flavor tomato and other vegetable dishes as well as seafood, cheese dishes, and chili. Add them to salads and dressings, or steep them with other herbs for teas. In frost-free areas, Mexican oregano can be grown as a specimen plant or pruned into a hedge. Elsewhere, grow it as a container plant to move indoors for the winter.

Selected species and varieties: *L. graveolens* [also called *Poliomintha longiflora*] (Mexican oregano)—pointed, oval 1- to 2½-inch downy leaves and tiny yellow to white winter-to-spring flowers growing where leaves meet stems.

Growing conditions and maintenance: Sow Mexican oregano seeds anytime, or start new plants from softwood cuttings taken anytime. Keep plants slightly on the dry side. Remove deadwood in spring and prune severely to keep shrubs from sprawling. Pinch to promote branching and bushiness. Prune top growth and roots, and repot container specimens as needed to maintain their size. Pick leaves anytime and dry in a single layer.

Marrubium
(ma-ROO-bee-um)
HOREHOUND

Marrubium vulgare

Hardiness: *Zones 4-9*

Height: *18 to 24 inches*

Light: *full sun*

Soil: *poor, sandy, well-drained to dry*

Plant type: *perennial*

Uses: *landscaping, containers, culinary*

Horehound's deeply puckered, aromatic gray-green leaves, woolly with white hairs, add texture and soft color as fillers or edgings. Horehound can also be pruned into container specimens. Flowers attract bees. Use the branching foliage as a filler in fresh or dried bouquets. Steep the fresh or dried leaves, which taste slightly of thyme and menthol, for a soothing tea, or add seeds to cool drinks for flavor. Horehound is a staple in herbal cough remedies.

Selected species and varieties: *M. vulgare* (common horehound, white horehound)—pairs of 2-inch heart-shaped leaves with deeply scalloped edges along square stems, and whorls of tiny white spring-to-summer flowers.

Growing conditions and maintenance: Sow horehound seeds in spring, thinning seedlings to stand 1 foot apart. Horehound can also be grown from divisions in spring and from stem cuttings taken in summer. In addition, it self-sows easily and can be invasive. Prune before or after flowering to keep edgings or container plants compact. Dry the leaves in a single layer and store in airtight containers.

Matricaria
(mat-ri-KAY-ree-a)
GERMAN CHAMOMILE

Matricaria recutita

Hardiness: *tender*

Height: *24 to 30 inches*

Light: *full sun*

Soil: *average to poor, well-drained*

Plant type: *annual*

Uses: *landscaping, culinary, arrangements*

German chamomile's erect stems lined with feathery, finely divided leaves are crowned with numerous daisylike, honey-scented flowers from late spring to early summer. The soft foliage is excellent as a filler, especially among plants reaching their maximum size in late summer, as German chamomile tends to disappear after flowering and setting seed. The plant makes an excellent filler in fresh or dried bouquets. Its flowers make a soothing tea with an aroma of apple or pineapple.

Selected species and varieties: *M. recutita* (German chamomile, sweet false chamomile, wild chamomile)—airy clumps of fine-textured leaves and inch-wide flowers with yellow centers fringed with drooping white petals.

Growing conditions and maintenance: Sow German chamomile in fall for early-spring flowers or in early spring for summer blossoms. Thin or transplant seedlings to stand 8 to 10 inches apart. Plants self-sow freely. Hang stems in bundles to dry. Flowers for tea are best if fresh or frozen, as they lose their flavorful oils on drying.

Melissa
(mel-ISS-a)
BALM

Melissa officinalis 'All Gold'

Hardiness: *Zones 4-9*

Height: *12 to 24 inches*

Light: *full sun to light shade*

Soil: *moist, well-drained*

Plant type: *perennial*

Uses: *landscaping, culinary, potpourri*

Lemon balm's highly aromatic foliage and small flowers, growing where the paired leaves join the square stems, attract bees and perfume the garden. Though the loosely branching plants can be somewhat floppy and coarse, cultivars with colorful foliage are often sheared as ground covers. The plant's fresh leaves add a citrusy tang to salads, poultry or fish dishes, marinades, and vinegar. Dried leaves and stems scent potpourri.

Selected species and varieties: *M. officinalis* (lemon balm, bee balm, sweet balm)—1- to 3-inch pointed, oval leaves puckered by deep veins, and whorls of ½-inch white to yellow flowers in summer and fall; 'All Gold' has golden yellow foliage; 'Aurea', green-veined yellow leaves.

Growing conditions and maintenance: Sow lemon balm seeds or divide mature plants in spring or fall, spacing them 1 to 2 feet apart. Plant 'All Gold' in light shade to prevent leaf scorch, and shear 'Aurea' to prevent flower formation and greening of leaves. Lemon balm self sows readily. Contain the creeping roots by planting in bottomless pots at least 10 inches deep. Dry the leaves on screens.

Mentha
(MEN-tha)
MINT

Mentha aquatica var. crispa

Hardiness: *Zones 3-10*

Height: *1 inch to 4 feet*

Light: *full sun to light shade*

Soil: *moist, well-drained*

Plant type: *perennial*

Uses: *landscaping, culinary, potpourri*

Paired mint leaves line the characteristic square stems and lend a sharp, peppery, sweet fragrance to borders, beds, and rock gardens. Tiny white, pink, lilac, purple, or blue summer flowers appear in spiky tufts at stem tips or in whorls where leaves join stems. Mints thrive in containers and can be potted for indoor use. Low-growing species make good ground covers for potted shrubs and quickly fill niches among paving stones; mow sturdy species into an aromatic carpet. Cooks prize the hundreds of mint varieties, which vary greatly in leaf shape, size, and fragrance. Fresh leaves are the most intensely flavored, but mint can also be frozen or dried. Use sprigs of fresh mint to flavor iced drinks and accent vegetable dishes. Mint sauces and jellies are a traditional accompaniment for meats; mint syrups dress up desserts; and crystallized mint leaves make an edible garnish. Steep fresh or dried leaves in boiling water for tea, or allow the infusion to cool into a refreshing facial splash. Add to bathwater for an aromatic soak. Mix dried leaves into herbal potpourri. Mints are a traditional herbal remedy, especially as a

breath freshener and digestive aid. While pennyroyal enjoys a reputation for repelling insects, it can be toxic if ingested.

Selected species and varieties: *M. aquatica* (water mint)—heart-shaped 2-inch leaves on 1- to 2-foot stems; var. *crispa* (curly mint) has decoratively frilled leaf edges; Zones 5-10. *M. arvensis* var. *piperescens* [also spelled *piperascens*]

Mentha arvensis var. piperescens

(Japanese mint)—oval leaves with strong peppermint aroma; Zones 6-9. *M.* x *gracilis* (redmint, gingermint)—shiny red-tinged leaves and stems popular in Southeast Asian cuisine; Zones 3-9. *M. longifolia* (horsemint)—narrow, pointed, oval leaves; Zones 3-9. *M.* x *piperita* (peppermint)—characteristic 1- to 2-foot purple stems lined with intensely menthol-flavored deep green leaves yielding commercially important peppermint oil; var. *citrata* (bergamot mint, orange bergamot mint, lemon mint, eau de Cologne mint) has lemon fragrance and flavor; other varieties have aromatic overtones ranging from citrus to floral to chocolate; Zones 5-9. *M. pulegium* (pennyroyal)—round leaves to 1 inch long on 6- to 12-inch stems; 'Cunningham' (creeping pennyroyal) is a dwarf growing only 2 to 4 inches tall; Zones 6-9. *M. requienii* (Corsican mint, crème-de-menthe plant)—diminutive creeper only an inch tall forming mosslike mats of extremely aromatic ¾-inch bright green leaves; Zones 7-9. *M.* x *smithiana* (red raripila mint)-narrow red-tinged leaves on 2- to 4-foot stems; Zones 7-9. *M. spicata* (spearmint)—wrinkled, oval, pointed leaves 2 inches long with a sweet taste and fragrance lining 1- to 3-foot stems; Zones 3-9. *M. suaveolens* (apple mint, woolly mint)—hairy, wrinkled 2-inch leaves with a distinctly fruity aroma on 1- to 3-foot stems; 'Variegata' (pineapple mint, variegated apple mint) has creamy leaf edges and a pineapple scent; Zones 5-9.

Growing conditions and maintenance: Corsican mint and horsemint prefer very moist sites in partial shade. Give other mints a moist but well-drained location in full sun; they will grow in partial shade but they may be less fragrant. With the exception of pennyroyal, mints do not grow true from seed; plant divisions or rooted cuttings in spring or fall, setting them 8 to 12 inches apart. Provide Japanese mint, redmint, and apple mint with a protective winter mulch in colder zones. Restrain mint's aggressive spread by spading deeply around plants at least once annu-

Mentha x piperita

ally or, more reliably, by confining plants in bottomless plastic or clay containers sunk with their rims projecting at least 2 inches above the soil and their sides at least 10 inches deep; pull out any stems that fall to the ground and root outside this barrier. Mints can also be restrained by growing them in patio containers. Established beds of pennyroyal, peppermint, horsemint, apple mint, and spearmint tolerate mowing. The leaves are most flavorful when cut before flowers appear; shear plants when buds first form to yield about 2 cups of leaves per plant, and continue to pinch or shear at 10-day intervals to prolong fresh leaf production. Dry the leaves flat on screens, or hang stems in bunches in a warm, well-ventilated area to dry, then rub the leaves from the stems. Crystallize leaves for garnishes by simmering gently in a heavy sugar syrup.

Monarda
(mo-NAR-da)
WILD BERGAMOT

Monarda fistulosa

Hardiness:	*tender or Zones 4-10*
Height:	*1 to 4 feet*
Light:	*full sun to light shade*
Soil:	*rich, moist or dry, slightly alkaline*
Plant type:	*annual or perennial*
Uses:	*landscaping, arrangements, culinary*

Monarda's tousled, spiky, fragrant flowers in a wide array of colors attract bees and hummingbirds alike. The spreading clumps of erect, square stems are ideal as border fillers or background plants; vegetable gardeners plant bee balm to attract the bees that pollinate their crops. The ragged whorls of tiny tubular blossoms atop each stem make long-lasting cut flowers. Fresh blooms add color to salads; dried blossoms retain their fragrance well in potpourri. The pairs of fragrant, citrus-flavored gray-green leaves lining the stalks add their pungency to Earl Grey tea. Fresh leaves add flavor to fruit salads, preserves, fruit punches, and iced tea. Dried leaves are also used in tea and to scent potpourri.

Selected species and varieties: *M. citriodora* (lemon bergamot, lemon mint)—an annual to 2 feet with lemon-flavored leaves and showy purple to pink blossoms. *M. didyma* (bee balm, Oswego tea, red balm)—a perennial with deep scarlet blooms and bergamot-orange-scented leaves ideal for tea; 'Adam' grows especially prolific salmon-red blossoms on 2- to 3-foot stems; 'Croftway Pink' has soft

rose-pink blooms on 2½- to 4-foot stems; 'Mahogany', deep red-bronze blooms on 2- to 3-foot stems; 'Violet Queen', lavender to deep violet flowers on 2- to 3-foot plants; 'Snow White', pure white flowers on stems to 3 feet; Zones 4-10. *M. fistulosa* (lavender wild bergamot)—a perennial with lemon-oregano-scented leaves and lavender flowers on 4-foot plants; Zones 4-9. *M. punctata* (spotted bee balm, dotted mint, dotted horsemint)—a

Monarda punctata

short-lived perennial with mint-thyme-scented leaves and purple-flecked yellow flowers on 1- to 3-foot stems; Zones 4-9.

Growing conditions and maintenance: Sow seed of annual or perennial monardas or set out divisions of perennials in spring, spacing or thinning to 2 feet; pinch flower heads from seed-grown perennials their first year to increase root vigor. Bee balm prefers moist, rich soil; plant other monardas in dry, well-drained sites. Monardas, particularly lavender wild bergamot, will fill in garden spaces quickly and can be invasive. Weed by hand to avoid damaging the shallow roots, and thin clumps to minimize powdery mildew. Cutting stems to within 2 inches of the soil just after the flowers bloom may force a second bloom. Harvest leaves as needed, stripping them from stems and drying in a single layer on screens in a shady, well-ventilated area. Cut plants back severely in fall, and provide a protective winter mulch. Propagate monardas from seed, by transplanting the self-sown seedlings of lavender wild bergamot, or by division every 3 or 4 years in early spring, discarding the inner portion of older, mature clumps.

Myrrhis
(MIR-ris)
SWEET CICELY, MYRRH

Myrrhis odorata

Hardiness: *Zones 3-8*

Height: *2 to 3 feet*

Light: *partial shade to full sun*

Soil: *rich, moist, organic*

Plant type: *perennial*

Uses: *landscaping, culinary, crafts*

Sweet cicely's finely cut leaves perfume the garden with celery and anise when used as a filler. As flavorful as they are fragrant, the fresh leaves can be used as a sweetener for tart fruits to reduce the amount of sugar needed or to flavor salads, omelets, and soups. The spring-blooming flowers are followed by seeds that can be added either green or ripe to fruit dishes, salads, baked goods, and other dishes. The anise-scented taproot can be chopped into salads, served raw with dressing, or steamed as a vegetable.

Selected species and varieties: *M. odorata* (sweet cicely, myrrh)—fernlike leaflets along arching stems to 3 feet and flat clusters of tiny white flowers followed by ¾-inch upright, oblong, ridged green seeds ripening to brown-black.

Growing conditions and maintenance: Because sweet cicely germinates erratically, the most reliable way to grow it is to divide mature plants in fall and plant the divisions. Space seedlings or transplants 2 feet apart. Harvest fresh leaves anytime, seeds either green or ripe. Dry leaves lose their taste but can be used for crafts. Dig roots for culinary use in fall.

Myrtus
(MIR-tus)
MYRTLE

Myrtus communis 'Variegata'

Hardiness: *Zones 7-11*

Height: *5 to 20 feet*

Light: *full sun to light shade*

Soil: *average, well-drained*

Plant type: *shrub*

Uses: *landscaping, containers, culinary*

Myrtle's lustrous evergreen leaves, tiny flower buds, and white flowers with puffs of golden stamens share a spicy orange scent that has made the plant a favorite in wedding bouquets. Myrtle develops into upright specimens ideal for massing into hedges. Grown as container plants to move indoors when the weather turns cold, myrtle is often pruned into topiary. Weave fresh branches into wreaths. Toss fresh, peeled buds into salads. Use leaves and berries to flavor meats. Add dried flowers and leaves to potpourri.

Selected species and varieties: *M. communis* (sweet myrtle, Greek myrtle)—pairs of 2-inch pointed, oval glossy leaves and creamy white ¾-inch flowers followed by blue-black berries; 'Flore Pleno' has doubled petals; 'Microphylla' is a dwarf ideal for containers; 'Variegata' has leaves marbled gray-green and cream.

Growing conditions and maintenance: Start myrtle from seed sown in spring or from half-ripe cuttings taken in summer; plant in sites protected from drying winds. Myrtle will grow in light shade but prefers full sun. It tolerates severe pruning to maintain its size in containers.

Nepeta
(NEP-e-ta)
CATMINT

Nepeta x faassenii

Hardiness: *Zones 3-9*

Height: *12 to 36 inches*

Light: *full sun to light shade*

Soil: *well-drained, sandy*

Plant type: *perennial*

Uses: *landscaping, culinary*

Catmints form sprawling mounds of downy gray-green leaves along square stems tipped with spikes of tubular flowers attractive to bees. Catnip (*N. cataria*) is even more attractive to cats. Drawn by its musty, minty aroma, they go into ecstasies of rolling and rubbing. Use catmints as fillers or ground covers in an informal border. Steep dried leaves for tea or sew them into toys for cats.

Selected species and varieties: *N. cataria* (catnip)—coarse 2- to 3-inch leaves and spikes of violet to white ¼- to ½-inch summer-to-fall flowers on 2- to 3-foot plants. *N. x faassenii* (Persian ground ivy)—sprawling 2-foot mounds of 1- to 1½-inch leaves and lavender-blue early-summer flowers. *N. mussinii* 'Blue Wonder'—large 6-inch spikes of lavender-blue flowers that first emerge in spring on 12- to 18-inch plants.

Growing conditions and maintenance: Sow catmint seeds or divide mature plants in spring, spacing plants 12 to 18 inches apart. Shearing plants to remove dead flowers encourages a second bloom and keeps plants from becoming leggy. Catmint self-sows freely.

Nigella
(nye-JELL-a)
FENNEL FLOWER

Nigella sativa

Hardiness: *tender*

Height: *12 to 18 inches*

Light: *full sun*

Soil: *well-drained, slightly alkaline*

Plant type: *annual*

Uses: *landscaping, culinary, potpourri*

Black cumin forms neat clumps of erect stems lined with finely cut leaves and crowned with intricate flowers whose spidery centers are surrounded by flat, broad petals. The inflated seedpods that follow are prized in dried arrangements and yield triangular seeds with a pepper-nutmeg flavor used in curries, breads, and cakes as a substitute for caraway or cumin. It is one of the four spices included in the *quatre épices* of classic French cuisine. Black cumin is particularly effective as a specimen or edging plant in a blue garden.

Selected species and varieties: *N. sativa* (black cumin, nutmeg flower, Roman coriander)—gray-green ferny leaves and 1½-inch-wide blue flowers in summer.

Growing conditions and maintenance: Sow black cumin in the garden in fall or spring and thin seedlings to stand 4 to 6 inches apart. Black cumin does not transplant well. Plants will grow in light shade, but the color of the flowers will be less intense. Harvest seedpods for dried arrangements. Crush pods open to collect the edible seeds.

Ocimum
(OS-si-mum)
BASIL

Ocimum 'African Blue'

Hardiness: *tender*

Height: *6 inches to 3 feet*

Light: *full sun*

Soil: *rich, organic, well-drained*

Plant type: *annual*

Uses: *culinary, landscaping, potpourri*

Pointed, oval, slightly curved leaves with mixed scents of cinnamon, clove, anise, lemon, rose, orange, thyme, mint, or camphor make basil not only a classic culinary seasoning but also a choice fragrance planting. All species do well in containers, and most are ideal for window-sill pot culture throughout winter. Whorls of tiny flowers grow in spikes at the tips of stems from summer through fall. Add fresh or dried basil leaves to salads, sauces, soups, and vegetable dishes or steep them for tea. Use flowers as an edible garnish or in herbal bouquets. Add dried basil to herbal potpourri.

Selected species and varieties: *O.* 'African Blue'—resinous leaves tinged with purple-green on 3-foot stems tipped with purple flower spikes, valued as a border specimen and for fresh flowers. *O. basilicum* (common basil, sweet basil)—bushy 8- to 24-inch plants prized by cooks and ideal for garden edging, with fragrant 2- to 3-inch leaves lining stems tipped with white flowers; 'Anise' has purple-tinged licorice-scented leaves and pink flowers; 'Cinnamon', cinnamon-scented leaves especially good in tea;

'Dark Opal', deep purple leaves and pink flowers; 'Minimum' (bush basil, Greek basil) is a 6- to 12-inch dwarf with ½-inch leaves, ideal indoors; 'Minimum Purpurascens' (purple bush basil) has small purple leaves on 12-inch plants; 'Purple Ruffles', purple-black leaves whose edges are curled and frilled, excellent in pots. *O. sanctum* [also classified as *O. tenuiflorum*] (holy basil, clove basil, sri tulsi)—clove-scented 1½-inch leaves and branching spikes of tiny white flowers on stems 18 to 24 inches tall, primarily used in landscaping.

Growing conditions and maintenance: Sow basil indoors 8 to 12 weeks before the last frost or outdoors after the last

Ocimum basilicum 'Dark Opal'

frost, spacing or thinning plants to 1 to 2 feet apart. Basil can be sown in pots for indoor culture year round. It can also be propagated from cuttings, which remain true to type. Basil needs soils 50° F or warmer to thrive. Provide mulch to keep roots from drying out and to keep leaves clean. Leaves are best picked before flowers appear; to delay flowering and encourage bushiness, pinch stems back to 4 sets of leaves as flower buds form. Avoid washing basil unless necessary, as mold forms quickly on damp leaves. Preserve by blending fresh leaves into olive oil and refrigerating the oil or freezing it in small batches. Whole leaves can be layered in olive oil to preserve them, frozen flat on trays after first brushing both sides with olive oil, or layered in white vinegar; the leaves of purple bush basil give vinegar a burgundy tint. Basil can be difficult to dry successfully; lay the leaves in a single layer on trays between layers of paper towels to keep them from turning black.

Origanum
(o-RIG-a-num)
MARJORAM

Origanum majorana

Hardiness: *hardy or Zones 5-10*

Height: *6 to 24 inches*

Light: *full sun*

Soil: *rich, dry, well-drained*

Plant type: *perennial or half-hardy annual*

Uses: *culinary, landscaping, potpourri*

Fragrantly spicy small, oval leaves and branching clusters of tiny flowers on mounding or sprawling plants make marjorams useful in kitchen gardens, where leaves can be snipped to flavor meat, vegetable, cheese, and fish dishes. They can also be used as border edgings or ground covers. Tender perennial species grow as annuals in cooler climates; marjorams also do well in containers both indoors and out. Use fresh or dried marjoram leaves in cooking, dried leaves and flowers in teas and herbal potpourri.

Selected species and varieties: *O. dictamnus* (dittany-of-Crete)—tiny woolly white leaves and loose, nodding clusters of tiny pink summer-to-fall flowers on sprawling 1-foot-high plants ideal in rock gardens or hanging baskets; Zones 8-9. *O. majorana* (sweet marjoram)—spicy 1¼-inch leaves, an essential seasoning in Greek cuisine and more intensely flavored than those of *O. vulgare,* along 2-foot stems tipped with white to pink flowers; Zones 9-10. *O.* x *majoricum* (hardy marjoram, Italian oregano)—a hybrid similar to sweet marjoram but slightly hardier; Zones 7-10. *O. onites* (Greek oregano,

pot marjoram)—very mildly thyme-flavored medium-green leaves used in bouquets garnis or laid across charcoal to flavor grilled foods, and mauve to white flowers from summer to fall on 24-inch plants; Zones 8-10. *O. vulgare* (oregano, pot marjoram, wild marjoram, organy) —mildly pepper-thyme-flavored green leaves on sprawling 2-foot stems, not the same plant used in commercial dried oregano but used for flavoring and valued in landscaping for its branching clusters of white to red-purple summer flow-

Origanum vulgare 'Aureum'

ers, Zones 5-9; 'Aureum' has golden leaves, Zones 6-9; 'Aureum Crispum', round, wrinkled ½-inch golden leaves on 1-foot plants, Zones 7-9; 'Nanum' is an 8-inch dwarf with purple flowers, Zones 6-9; 'White Anniversary' has green leaves edged in white on 6- to 10-inch plants, ideal for edging or containers; Zones 8-9.

Growing conditions and maintenance: Sow marjoram seeds or plant divisions in spring or fall, spacing or thinning plants to 12 to 18 inches apart. Give golden-leaved cultivars light shade to prevent leaf scorch. Pinch stems to promote bushiness and delay flowering. Cut perennial marjorams back to two-thirds of their height before winter to promote bushier growth the following season. *O. vulgare* can be invasive. Indoors, pot up divisions or sow seeds in pots where they are to grow. Propagate marjorams from seed, from early-summer stem cuttings, or by division in spring or fall. For best flavor, harvest leaves just as flower buds begin to open. Mash leaves in oil to preserve them, layer with vinegar, or freeze. Dry leaves or flowers in a single layer in a shady, well-ventilated area.

Panax
(PAN-ax)
GINSENG

Panax quinquefolius

Hardiness: *Zones 3-8*

Height: *6 to 36 inches*

Light: *light to full shade*

Soil: *organic, moist, well-drained*

Plant type: *perennial*

Uses: *landscaping, culinary*

Ginseng's thick roots send up a single thin stalk with leaves composed of several pointed leaflets arranged like the fingers on a hand. In late spring or summer, a short flower stalk carries a cluster of tiny yellow-green flowers above the foliage, followed by red berries. In woodland gardens, ginseng slowly spreads into a lacy ground cover. Ginseng's Greek name means "all ills," reflecting its root's fame as an herbal tonic in Oriental medicine. Roots are also used in herbal teas.

Selected species and varieties: *P. pseudoginseng* [also classified as *P. ginseng*]— stems 2 to 3 feet tall with two to six leaves composed of toothed leaflets growing from a carrotlike root. *P. quinquefolius* (American ginseng)—stems 6 to 20 inches tall with leaves composed of 6-inch leaflets growing from a cigar-shaped root.

Growing conditions and maintenance: You can sow ginseng seeds in spring or fall, but division and replanting of roots in spring is often more successful, as the seeds take a year to germinate. Provide organic mulch annually. When roots are at least 6 years old, dig them up in fall to use fresh or dried for teas.

Papaver
(pa-PAY-ver)
POPPY

Papaver rhoeas

Hardiness: *tender*

Height: *8 to 36 inches*

Light: *full sun*

Soil: *well-drained*

Plant type: *annual*

Uses: *landscaping, culinary, dried arrangements*

Corn poppies decorate borders with brilliantly colored flower cups composed of crinkled petals on slender stalks lined with hairy gray-green foliage. Mass them for showy display, then harvest their bulbous seedpods to collect the tiny blue-gray seeds. The seeds, which contain none of the narcotic alkaloids found in opium poppies, add a nutty flavor to breads and cakes. Add seed heads, with interesting flat caps, to dried arrangements.

Selected species and varieties: *P. rhoeas* (corn poppy, Flanders poppy, Shirley poppy)—branching stems lined with lobed leaves carrying red to reddish purple 2- to 4-inch blossoms, sometimes double petaled, with purplish filaments and dark throats; 'Shirley Single Mixed' has a single rim of petals in shades of red, pink, salmon, orange, white, or bicolors.

Growing conditions and maintenance: Sow corn poppies in spring or fall, just pressing the seeds into the soil. Thin plants to stand 12 inches apart. Make successive sowings and deadhead plants to prolong the blooming season. Pick seed heads just before fully ripe; allowed to ripen, poppies self-sow freely.

Pelargonium
(pel-ar-GO-nee-um)
GERANIUM, STORKSBILL

Pelargonium capitatum

Hardiness: *tender or Zone 10*

Height: *12 inches to 6 feet*

Light: *full sun to light shade*

Soil: *rich, moist, well-drained*

Plant type: *annual, perennial, or shrub*

Uses: *landscaping, culinary, potpourri*

When brushed or rubbed, the foliage of scented geraniums emits a citrusy, floral, minty, or resinous perfume, depending on the species or cultivar. The kidney-shaped or broad, triangular leaves are wrinkled, lobed, frilled, or filigreed and add texture to the border. Loose, open clusters of small white, pink, mauve, or lilac flowers on branching stalks add color in spring or summer. Grown outdoors year round where they can be protected from frost, taller species serve as border specimens or background shrubs or can be pruned into standards; sprawling types can be used as ground covers or trained against trellises. Elsewhere, scented geraniums are treated like summer bedding plants or grown in containers or hanging baskets; they also do well year round as houseplants. Use fresh leaves of citrus-, floral-, or mint-scented geraniums in teas and to flavor baked goods, jam, jelly, vinegar, syrup, or sugar; use resinous leaves to flavor pâté and sausage. Toss flowers into salads for color. Add dried leaves to floral or herbal potpourri. Infuse leaves in warm water for an aromatic, mildly astringent facial splash.

Selected species and varieties: *P. capitatum* (wild rose geranium, rose-scented geranium)—a spreading plant 1 to 2 feet tall and up to 5 feet wide with crinkled, velvety 2-inch rose-scented leaves and mauve to pink summer flowers. *P. citronellum*—lemon-scented 3½-inch-wide leaves with pointed lobes and pink summer flowers streaked purple on upright shrubs to 6 feet tall and half as wide. *P. crispum* (lemon geranium)—strongly lemon-scented, kidney-shaped, ½-inch leaves, traditionally used in finger bowls, and pink to lavender flowers in spring and summer on plants 2 feet tall and half as wide; 'Variegatum' has cream-colored leaf edges. *P.* 'Fair Ellen'—finely textured lacy leaves with a balsam aroma and pale mauve summer flowers marked with pink on compact plants 1 to 2 feet tall and up to 3 feet wide. *P.* x *fragrans* 'Variegatum' (nutmeg geranium)—small, downy

Pelargonium 'Fair Ellen'

gray-green leaves smelling of nutmeg and pine, and white spring-to-summer flowers lined with red on compact plants 12 to 16 inches tall and as wide. *P. graveolens* (rose geranium)—filigreed, strongly rose-scented gray-green leaves and pale pink spring-to-summer flowers spotted purple on upright shrubs to 3 feet tall and as wide. *P.* 'Lady Plymouth'—lacy leaves with creamy edges and a rose-lemon scent with minty overtones on shrubs to 5 feet tall and as wide. *P. odoratissimum* (apple geranium)—a spreading plant 1 foot tall and twice as wide with small kidney-shaped, velvety, intensely apple-scented leaves and red-veined white spring and summer flowers on trailing flower stalks. *P.* 'Old Spice'—a compact mound 1½ to 2 feet tall and as wide with a piny aroma. *P. quercifolium* (oak-leaved geranium)—round, lobed 2- to 4-inch leaves with a resinous balsam odor and pink-purple spring-to-summer flowers on upright shrubs 1½ to 4 feet tall and up to 3 feet wide. *P.* 'Rober's Lemon Rose'—gray-green 2-inch leaves with an intense rose-lemon scent and pink summer flowers on shrubs to 5 feet tall and almost as wide. *P. tomentosum* (pepper-

Pelargonium 'Lady Plymouth'

mint geranium)—a spreading plant to 3 feet tall and twice as wide with 4- to 5-inch peppermint-scented leaves and white spring-to-summer flowers.

Growing conditions and maintenance: Sow seeds of scented geraniums indoors 10 to 12 weeks before the last frost. While all scented geraniums do best in full sun, lemon geranium, apple geranium, and peppermint geranium will tolerate light shade. Too-rich soil tends to minimize fragrance. Remove faded flowers to encourage further blooming. In containers, scented geraniums do best when slightly potbound; repot only into the next larger size pot. Indoors, provide daytime temperatures of 65° to 70° F, about 10° cooler at night, with at least 5 hours of direct sunlight daily. Keep potted plants from becoming leggy by pruning them hard after blooming or in very early spring, then feeding with any complete houseplant fertilizer. To propagate scented geraniums, cut a branch tip at least 3 inches long just below a leaf node, dip into rooting hormone, and place in clean, moist sand to root; transplant into potting soil after 2 weeks. Pick scented geranium leaves for drying anytime and lay in a single layer on screens in a shady location.

Perilla
(per-ILL-a)
PERILLA

Perilla frutescens 'Atropurpurea'

Hardiness:	*tender*
Height:	*12 to 36 inches*
Light:	*full sun to light shade*
Soil:	*average to rich, sandy*
Plant type:	*annual*
Uses:	*landscaping, culinary, dried arrangements*

Perilla forms mounds of wrinkled burgundy leaves that contrast nicely when used as a filler among gray or white foliage in an herb garden or border. The leaves and seeds, with a fragrance and flavor blending mint with cinnamon and an oil 2,000 times sweeter than sugar, are staples in Japanese cuisine. Fresh or pickled, they are used to garnish sushi and to flavor bean curd. Spikes of flower buds are batter-fried for tempura. Leaves are used to color vinegar and fruit preserves. Add the dried seed heads to herbal wreaths.

Selected species and varieties: *P. frutescens* 'Atropurpurea' (black nettle)— pairs of wrinkled oval leaves up to 5 inches long on square stems tipped with spikes of tiny white summer flowers in whorls, followed by brown nutlets.

Growing conditions and maintenance: Sow perilla seed in spring, and thin seedlings to stand 1 foot apart. Harvest leaves anytime, harvest flowers for tempura just as buds form. Pinch off spikes of flower buds to encourage bushier growth. Allowed to form seed, perilla self-sows freely.

Petroselinum
(pet-ro-se-LEE-num)
PARSLEY

Petroselinum crispum var. neapolitanum

Hardiness:	*hardy or Zones 6-9*
Height:	*12 to 24 inches*
Light:	*full sun*
Soil:	*rich, moist, well-drained*
Plant type:	*biennial*
Uses:	*culinary, landscaping, containers*

Bundled into a classic bouquet garni or chopped for use in sauces, eggs, vegetables, stuffings, and herb butters, parsley's deep green curly or flat leaves blend well with many flavors. Vitamin-rich parsley also freshens breath. Cooks consider flatleaf types more strongly flavored than curly varieties. A biennial flowering its second year, parsley is usually grown as an annual in an herb garden, as an edging plant, or in containers indoors or out.

Selected species and varieties: *P. crispum* var. *crispum* (curly parsley, French parsley)—highly frilled leaves on plants 12 to 18 inches tall. *P. crispum* var. *neapolitanum* (Italian parsley, flatleaf parsley)— flat, deeply lobed celery-like leaves on plants to 24 inches.

Growing conditions and maintenance: Soak parsley seed overnight to speed germination. Sow seed ¼ inch deep in soil warmed to at least 50° F. Thin seedlings to stand 4 to 6 inches apart. Begin harvesting leaves when plants are 6 inches tall. Dry Italian parsley in the shade, oven, or microwave. Chop curly parsley and freeze in ice cubes for best flavor.

Plectranthus
(plec-TRAN-thus)
INDIAN BORAGE

Plectranthus amboinicus 'Variegata'

Hardiness: *tender or Zones 10-11*

Height: *12 to 36 inches*

Light: *full sun to light shade*

Soil: *rich, well-drained*

Plant type: *annual*

Uses: *landscaping, culinary, containers*

The fleshy lemon-scented leaves of Indian borage have a flavor reminiscent of thyme, oregano, and savory. In tropical areas where those herbs fail to thrive, cooks grow the plant as an attractive ground cover. Elsewhere, grow it as a houseplant or a patio plant to move indoors when frost threatens. The leaves trail attractively from hanging baskets. Use fresh leaves to complement beans, meats, and other strong-flavored dishes.

Selected species and varieties: *P. amboinicus* (Indian borage, Spanish thyme, French thyme, soup mint, Mexican mint, Indian mint, country borage)—round gray-green leaves up to 4 inches across in pairs along thick stems, and whorls of tiny mintlike blue summer flowers in spikes up to 16 inches long; 'Variegata' has gray-green leaves edged in cream.

Growing conditions and maintenance: Start Indian borage from tip cuttings or divisions in spring or summer. Plants stop growing at temperatures below 50°F and are quickly killed even by light frost. Pinch tips to keep plants bushy and contain their spread. Cut leggy plants back in spring. Feed potted plants monthly.

Polygonum
(po-LIG-o-num)
KNOTWEED

Polygonum odoratum

Hardiness: *Zones 8-9*

Height: *1 to 1½ feet*

Light: *light shade*

Soil: *moist*

Plant type: *perennial*

Uses: *culinary, containers, landscaping*

Vietnamese coriander's pointed dark green leaves have a lemony, cilantro-like aroma and flavor prized in Asian cuisine, particularly in poultry and meat dishes. Where short growing seasons prevent plants from blooming and setting seed, Vietnamese coriander can be grown as a fragrant, rambling annual ground cover. Elsewhere, it is grown in indoor or outdoor containers.

Selected species and varieties: *P. odoratum* (Vietnamese coriander, Vietnamese mint)—green leaves up to 3 inches long with darker green triangular blotches along jointed 1- to 1½-foot stems that root wherever they touch the ground and, rarely, small clusters of tiny pink flowers in fall.

Growing conditions and maintenance: Start new Vietnamese coriander plants from tip cuttings taken in summer and rooted in water. In cooler climates, grow as an annual and take cuttings to root over winter as houseplants for planting outdoors the following year. Keep plants well watered, even constantly moist, and provide winter protection where they remain outdoors year round.

Poterium
(po-TEER-ee-um)
SALAD BURNET

Poterium sanguisorba

Hardiness: *Zones 3-9*

Height: *12 to 36 inches*

Light: *full sun*

Soil: *well-drained*

Plant type: *perennial*

Uses: *landscaping, culinary*

Burnet forms round mounds of delicate blue-green foliage ideal for soft, colorful edgings. In summer, tall flower stalks carry thimble-shaped clusters of tiny flowers well above the hummocks of leaves. Add the slightly nutty, cucumber-flavored young leaves to salads, coleslaw, soups, vegetables, and cool summer drinks. Preserve them in vinegar for flavorful dressings.

Selected species and varieties: *P. sanguisorba* [also classified as *Sanguisorba minor*] (burnet, garden burnet, salad burnet)—¾-inch oval leaflets with deeply scalloped edges paired along the flexible leafstalks to 1 foot long and dense ½-inch heads of minute greenish flowers tinged pink on stems to 3 feet.

Growing conditions and maintenance: Sow burnet seeds in spring or fall or divide young plants before taproots become well established. Space plants 8 to 12 inches apart. Established plants self-sow. Burnet is evergreen in milder climates; elsewhere, shear old foliage to the ground in late fall or early spring. Leaves are most flavorful when picked in early spring or late fall.

Primula
(PRIM-yew-la)
PRIMROSE

Primula veris

Hardiness: *Zones 3-8*

Height: *6 to 12 inches*

Light: *partial to full shade*

Soil: *organic, moist, well-drained*

Plant type: *perennial*

Uses: *landscaping, culinary, arrangements*

Cowslip and common primrose both produce fragrant, very early spring flowers above rosettes of oblong leaves. Use cowslip's nectar-rich flowers in jams or dry them for tea and potpourri; add the leaves to salads. Gather common primrose's flowers into posies, crystallize for decorations, add to salads, and dry for potpourri; boil the leaves as a vegetable, and add dried, powdered roots to potpourri. Both species make fine edging plants. Cowslip thrives as a houseplant.

Selected species and varieties: *P. veris* (cowslip)—clusters of tubular yellow 1- to 1½-inch-long flowers marked with orange on stalks to 12 inches above blue-green 2- to 8-inch leaves. *P. vulgaris* (common primrose)—single, flat-faced ½-inch-wide yellow, purple, or blue flowers with notched petals on 6-inch stems among 1- to 10-inch yellow-green leaves.

Growing conditions and maintenance: Sow seed when ripe in fall or divide plants after blooming, spacing them 6 to 12 inches apart. Where conditions are ideal, plants may rebloom in fall. Pick young leaves and flowers just after opening. Dig and dry the roots in fall.

Pycnanthemum
(pik-NAN-thee-mum)
MOUNTAIN MINT

Pycnanthemum virginianum

Hardiness: *Zones 4-8*

Height: *2 to 3 feet*

Light: *full sun to light shade*

Soil: *moist, well-drained*

Plant type: *perennial*

Uses: *landscaping, culinary, dried arrangements*

A sharp, peppery aroma fills gardens wherever Virginia mountain mint grows. The square stems lined with whorls of very narrow, pointed leaves branch into loose mounds. In summer, tufts of flowers growing at stem tips attract bees and butterflies in wildflower or meadow gardens. As intensely flavored as it is fragrant, Virginia mountain mint is an excellent culinary substitute for true mint. Dry the dense flower heads for arrangements, or use dried leaves and flowers to make potpourri.

Selected species and varieties: *P. virginianum* (Virginia mountain mint, wild basil, prairie hyssop)—smooth or slightly toothed, pointed, very narrow 1- to 1½-inch leaves and tiny white to lilac flowers in very dense, flat heads.

Growing conditions and maintenance: Virginia mountain mint grows best from cuttings or divisions of mature plants. Set plants out in spring or fall, spacing them 8 to 12 inches apart. Restrain their spread by spading around plants annually or by planting them in bottomless tubs and removing branches that root outside this barrier.

Rosa
(RO-za)
ROSE

Rosa canina

Hardiness: *Zones 2-10*

Height: *3 to 10 feet*

Light: *full sun*

Soil: *organic, well-drained*

Plant type: *shrub*

Uses: *landscaping, arrangements, potpourri*

Besides using roses in arrangements, try adding the petals to salads or crystallizing them as a garnish. Dry the buds and petals for potpourri. Use the fruit, or hips, for tea or jam.

Selected species and varieties: *R. canina* (dog rose, brier rose)—10-foot canes with white or pink 2-inch blooms, ¾-inch hips; Zones 4-9. *R. damascena* (damask rose)—very fragrant 3-inch blooms on 6-foot canes; 'Autumn Damask' is a double pink; 'Madame Hardy', a double white; Zones 5-9. *R. gallica* (French rose)—2- to 3-inch blooms on 3- to 4-inch plants; 'Officinalis' (apothecary rose) is a semidouble deep pink; 'Versicolor' (rosa mundi) is a semidouble pink- or red-striped white, red, or pink; Zones 4-10. *R. rugosa* (Japanese rose)—crimson 3½-inch blossoms and 1-inch hips; 'Alba' is white; 'Rubra', burgundy red; Zones 3-8.

Growing conditions and maintenance: Sow rose seeds, root hardwood cuttings, or plant commercial rootstock in fall. Mulch to conserve moisture. Prune dead or damaged wood in late winter, avoiding the previous season's growth, on which the coming season's flowers will grow.

Rosmarinus *(rose-ma-RY-nus)* **ROSEMARY**	**Rumex** *(ROO-mex)* **SORREL, DOCK**	**Salvia** *(SAL-vee-a)* **SAGE**

Rosmarinus officinalis 'Prostratus'	*Rumex crispus*	*Salvia officinalis 'Purpurea'*

Hardiness: *Zones 7-10*	**Hardiness:** *Zones 3-8*	**Hardiness:** *hardy or Zones 4-11*
Height: *6 inches to 7 feet*	**Height:** *6 inches to 5 feet*	**Height:** *1 to 4 feet*
Light: *full sun*	**Light:** *full sun to light shade*	**Light:** *full sun*
Soil: *well-drained, alkaline*	**Soil:** *well-drained*	**Soil:** *average to alkaline, dry, well-drained*
Plant type: *perennial*	**Plant type:** *perennial*	**Plant type:** *annual, biennial, perennial, or shrub*
Uses: *landscaping, culinary, potpourri*	**Uses:** *culinary, dried arrangements*	**Uses:** *landscaping, culinary, potpourri*

Rosemary's branching, stiff stems are lined with resinous, aromatic needlelike leaves. Small flowers cluster along the woody stems in winter. Grown as a ground cover or shrub in warm climates, rosemary is pot grown elsewhere. Use the piny leaves, fresh or dried, to flavor meats, sauces, vinegar, herb butter, and breads. Toss sprigs on coals for aromatic grilling or weave into wreaths. Add leaves to potpourri.

Selected species and varieties: *R. officinalis* (garden rosemary)—gray-green ⅓- to 1½-inch leaves along branches to 6 feet outdoors, 4 feet indoors, and ½-inch blue flowers; 'Arp' is very hardy, with lemon-scented leaves; 'Miss Jessup's Upright' has vertical branches; 'Prostratus' is almost everblooming, with twisting 6-inch-high, 36-inch-long branches; 'Tuscan Blue' is fast growing, with large deep blue leaves on branches to 7 feet.

Growing conditions and maintenance: Sow rosemary seed in spring, or start from summer cuttings, spacing plants 3 feet apart. Prune after flowering to encourage bushiness, removing no more than 20 percent of the plant at a time.

Sorrel's slightly sour, lemony, arrowhead-shaped leaves add zest to salads and accent soups and sauces. Use fresh leaves sparingly, as the high oxalic acid content can aggravate conditions such as gout. Boil leaves for a spinachlike vegetable, changing the water once to reduce the acid content. Birds love the tiny seeds produced at the tips of the stalks.

Selected species and varieties: *R. acetosa* (garden sorrel, sour dock)—narrow 5- to 8-inch leaves on clumps of 3-foot stems. *R. crispus* (curled dock)—extremely wavy, curly 12-inch leaves on plants 1 to 5 feet tall. *R. scutatus* (French sorrel)—thick, broad, shield-shaped leaves 1 to 2 inches long on trailing stems growing into mats 6 to 20 inches high and twice as wide.

Growing conditions and maintenance: Sow sorrel indoors 6 to 8 weeks before the last frost, outdoors after the last frost, or divide mature plants and space 8 inches apart. Leaves become bitter in hot weather, but flavor returns with cooler temperatures. Pinch out flowering stalks to encourage leaf production and control invasive self-sowing.

Puckered by a network of pronounced veins and colored a distinct gray-green hue, sage leaves bring both interesting texture and an aroma reminiscent of pine or rosemary to the border or kitchen garden. The leaves, largest at the base of the stems, are of gradually diminished size; spikes of tiny white, blue, lilac, magenta, or pink flowers appear at the stem tips. There are sages useful as edgings or throughout the border, and many do well as container plants or houseplants. Those suitable only for mild winter climates are often grown as half-hardy annuals in cooler zones. Add sage leaves and flowers to salads, or steep them for tea. Use fresh or dried leaves to flavor meat, cheese, or vegetable dishes, as well as sausages and stuffings; the dried herb is stronger than the fresh. Mix dried leaves into potpourri. Use sage in the water for a facial steam, add to the bath, or use an infusion of sage in water as a slightly astringent facial splash or aftershave or as a hair rinse. Sage is reputed to repel insects and also figures in herbal medicine; used in excess or for long periods, however, it can be toxic.

Selected species and varieties: *S. clevelandii* (blue sage, Jim sage)—an evergreen shrub with wrinkled 1-inch leaves on downy stems 2 to 3 feet tall tipped with violet or white spring-to-summer flowers, recommended for containers or as a houseplant; Zones 9-10. *S. coccinea* (Texas sage, scarlet sage)—a perennial or subshrub grown as an annual, with 2-inch heart-shaped leaves having wavy, indented edges on 3-foot stems tipped with branched spikes of red or white summer flowers that are valued in landscaping. *S. dorisiana* (fruit-scented sage)—an evergreen perennial with sweetly scented, velvety oval leaves 4 inches wide and up to 7 inches long on stems to 4 feet tall tipped with 6-inch spikes of 2-inch ma-

Salvia coccinea

genta to pink flowers in fall and winter; Zones 10-11. *S. elegans* (pineapple sage) —an evergreen perennial with fruit-scented, red-edged 3½-inch oval leaves lining 3- to 4-foot red stems tipped with late-summer red to pink 8-inch flower spikes used in cold drinks and fruit salads; Zones 8-10. *S. fruticosa* (Greek sage)—an evergreen shrub to 4½ feet with lavender-scented leaves and loose, 8-inch clusters of mauve to pink spring-to-summer flowers; Zones 8-9. *S. lavandulifolia* (Spanish sage, narrow-leaved sage)—a spreading evergreen shrub 12 to 20 inches tall with 1-inch white woolly leaves having a piny lavender aroma and red-violet summer flowers; Zones 7-9. *S. officinalis* (common sage, garden sage) —an evergreen shrub in mild climates with 2-inch velvety leaves on branching 2- to 3-foot stems tipped with edible violet to purple flower spikes in summer; 'Berggarten' is a compact 18-inch cultivar

with almost round leaves and blue-purple flowers; 'Icterina', a dwarf cultivar with yellow-splotched leaves; 'Nana', a compact cultivar with small, narrow leaves; 'Purpurea', an 18-inch plant with purple leaves; all are good for indoor winter pot culture; Zones 4-9. *S. sclarea* var.

Salvia sclarea var. turkestaniana

turkestaniana (clary sage)—a biennial producing rosettes of 6- to 9-inch oval leaves on pink stems its first year and branching 3- to 4-foot flower stalks the second year tipped with pink-and-white flowers used in tea and salads. *S. viridis* (bluebeard, painted sage)—an annual with narrow, pointed, oval leaves on erect 18-inch stems with inconspicuous summer flowers.

Growing conditions and maintenance: Sow sage seed in spring or set divisions out in spring or fall, spacing them 18 to 24 inches apart. Avoid hot, humid locations or those with too-rich soils. Provide a protective winter mulch in cooler climates. Prune sage heavily in spring to remove winter-killed stems and encourage bushy growth; cut back again immediately after flowering. Perennial sages are short lived; renew plantings every 4 or 5 years. Propagate by division or by rooting 4-inch stem cuttings taken in summer to plant in fall. Seedlings or rooted cuttings take 2 years to reach maturity for picking. Fresh leaves can be harvested anytime but are most flavorful before flowers appear. Dry leaves slowly to prevent a musty odor, laying them in a single layer on a screen or cloth; refrigerate or freeze the dried leaves, as the aromatic oils become rancid easily. To make an infusion for an aftershave or a hair rinse, steep leaves in boiling water, cool, and strain.

Satureja
(sat-yew-REE-ja)
SAVORY

Satureja hortensis

Hardiness: *hardy or Zones 5-9*

Height: *3 to 18 inches*

Light: *full sun*

Soil: *well-drained, slightly alkaline*

Plant type: *annual or perennial*

Uses: *landscaping, culinary*

Savory's aromatic needlelike leaves line erect stems tipped with whorls of tiny blossoms from summer through fall. Plant savories as border edgings, in kitchen or rock gardens, or in pots for the window sill. Use leaves fresh, dried, or frozen as fines herbes. Savory also figures in traditional herbal medicine.

Selected species and varieties: *S. hortensis* (summer savory)—a hardy annual to 18 inches tall with pink flowers. *S. montana* 'Nana' (pygmy winter savory)—6-inch plants with peppery leaves, white or lilac blooms; Zones 5-8. *S. spicigera* (creeping savory)—evergreen mats of 3-inch stems with white flowers; Zones 7-8. *S. thymbra* (goat thyme)—16-inch stems with pink blossoms; Zones 8-9.

Growing conditions and maintenance: Sow savory seeds outdoors in spring or transplant divisions of perennials in spring or fall. Pinch early growth to delay blooming, as fresh leaves are best picked before flowers emerge. For window sills, sow summer savory in fall or pot divisions of winter savory after cutting top growth back by half. Hang branches in bunches to dry, then rub leaves from stems.

Sesamum
(SES-am-um)
SESAME

Sesamum indicum

Hardiness: *tender*

Height: *18 to 36 inches*

Light: *full sun*

Soil: *well-drained*

Plant type: *perennial*

Uses: *culinary*

Each of sesame's bell-shaped flowers, which grow where leaves join the stem, produces an upright, pointed, oval capsule that bursts when ripe to release tiny nutty-tasting oily seeds, prized in Middle Eastern cuisines. The seeds are used whole in baked goods and candies and to garnish vegetables and salads. They can also be ground into dips, spreads, and sauces and pressed for cooking oil.

Selected species and varieties: *S. indicum* (sesame, benne, gingili)—square, sticky stems lined with oval, pointed 3- to 5-inch leaves and 1-inch white flowers tinged pink, yellow, or red.

Growing conditions and maintenance: Sow sesame seeds ¼ inch deep once nighttime low temperatures climb to 60° F, or start plants indoors 6 to 8 weeks in advance of this time. Space plants 6 to 8 inches apart. Plants need at least 120 days of hot weather to set seed. Harvest just as the oldest pods begin to dry, cutting stems off at ground level, and hold them in a paper bag until pods dry and release seeds. Each seed that grows produces a single stem yielding approximately 1 tablespoon of seeds.

Solidago
(sol-i-DAY-go)
GOLDENROD

Solidago odora

Hardiness: *Zones 3-9*

Height: *3 to 4 feet*

Light: *full sun*

Soil: *average to poor, dry*

Plant type: *perennial*

Uses: *landscaping, culinary, arrangements*

From late summer into fall, sweet goldenrod produces enormous clusters of tiny yellow flowers. The plant will quickly spread through a meadow garden, or you can confine it in a container as a specimen. Although folk wisdom has long held its pollen to be allergenic—the troublemaker is actually *Ambrosia* (ragweed)—the flower clusters can safely be used in fresh or dried arrangements. Brew the fresh or dried anise-scented leaves for tea. The flowers yield a yellow dye.

Selected species and varieties: *S. odora* (sweet goldenrod)—single stems lined with glossy, narrow 2- to 4-inch leaves and tipped with one-sided 8- to 12-inch plumes of ¼-inch yellow flower buttons.

Growing conditions and maintenance: Sow sweet goldenrod seeds or divide mature plants in early spring, spacing seedlings or divisions 12 to 15 inches apart. Plants begin blooming their second year and self-sow freely. Contain growth by planting in large containers or in the garden in bottomless pots, and remove spent flowers before they set seed. Shear plants to the ground in late winter or early spring, before new growth begins.

Stachys
(STAY-kis)
LAMB'S EARS, BETONY

Stachys officinalis

Hardiness: *Zones 4-8*

Height: *1 to 3 feet*

Light: *full sun to light shade*

Soil: *average, moist, well-drained*

Plant type: *perennial*

Uses: *landscaping, culinary*

Lamb's ears forms low rosettes of heart-shaped leaves and tall flower stems carrying short, dense spikes of small tubular flowers. A few sparser flowers often grow where leaves meet the square flower stems. Lamb's ears gradually spreads into low mats that provide a colorful filler in the perennial border when plants are blooming. Use the flowers in fresh bouquets. Steep the fresh or dried leaves for tea. Lamb's ears once figured prominently in herbal medicine but is now considered largely ineffective.

Selected species and varieties: *S. officinalis* (lamb's ears, common betony)— 4- to 5-inch wrinkled, coarsely toothed basal leaves, with 1-inch leaves along flower stems, and whorls of ½- to ¾-inch purple, pink, or white flowers in 1- to 3-inch spikes.

Growing conditions and maintenance: Sow seed of lamb's ears in early spring, and thin seedlings to stand 12 to 18 inches apart. Lamb's ears benefits from division every 3 or 4 years in early spring or late fall. Plants reseed themselves but are not invasive.

Tagetes
(ta-GEE-teez)
MARIGOLD

Tagetes patula

Hardiness: *tender or Zones 8-9*

Height: *6 to 36 inches*

Light: *full sun*

Soil: *organic, well-drained*

Plant type: *annual or perennial*

Uses: *landscaping, culinary, potpourri*

Primarily grown as bedding plants for their ferny, pungent foliage and clusters of flat flowers, marigolds are also valued for their root chemicals, which repel nematodes and inhibit weeds. Use leaves and flowers of some species as seasonings or to make tea; dried flower petals add color to potpourri.

Selected species and varieties: *T. lucida* (sweet mace)—a perennial to 30 inches tall with anise-scented leaves that can substitute for tarragon, and ½-inch yellow flowers; both leaves and flowers can be dried for tea; Zones 8-9. *T. minuta* (muster-John-Henry)—an annual to 3 feet with leaves lending an apple flavor; pale yellow flowers. *T. patula* (French marigold)—an annual 6 to 18 inches tall with yellow, orange, or brown flowers.

Growing conditions and maintenance: Sow annual marigold seeds indoors 4 to 6 weeks before the last frost or outdoors when the soil temperature reaches 60° F; transplant or thin to 12 inches. Deadhead to prolong bloom. Separate flower petals, and lay leaves flat to dry. Propagate sweet mace by division in spring in mild climates; grow as an annual elsewhere.

Thymus
(TY-mus)
THYME

Thymus x citriodorus 'Aureus'

Hardiness: *Zones 4-9*

Height: *2 to 18 inches*

Light: *full sun*

Soil: *average to poor, dry, well-drained, alkaline*

Plant type: *evergreen perennial or shrub*

Uses: *landscaping, culinary, potpourri*

Thyme adds pungent aroma, fine texture, and soft color to borders, rock gardens, and garden paths. Shrubby species with erect branches can be grown as specimens or low hedges. Creeping types fill niches among rocks or between paving stones, drape over walls, and sprawl into ground-covering mats. Thyme also grows well on window sills. Small clusters of ¼-inch nectar-filled summer-long flowers in a variety of shades are attractive to bees. Fresh or dried, the tiny ¼- to ½-inch narrow green to gray-green, sometimes variegated leaves are used as a basic ingredient in bouquets garnis and fines herbes and are used to make tea. Both leaves and flowers are used in potpourris and toiletries. Herbalists use thyme as an insect repellent, medicinal plant, household disinfectant, and preservative.

Selected species and varieties: *T. caespititius* [formerly classified as *T. azoricus*] (tufted thyme, Azores thyme)—a subshrub forming 6-inch-high mats of twiggy branches lined with sticky, resinous leaves and tipped with white, pink, or lilac flowers; 'Aureus' has deep yellow-green leaves and pink flowers; Zones 8-9.

T. capitatus (conehead thyme)—upright bushy plants 10 inches tall and as wide with gray leaves and pink flowers crowded into cone-shaped tufts at the tips of branches; Zone 9. *T. cilicicus* (Cilician thyme)—deep green lemon-scented leaves and clusters of pale mauve to lilac blossoms on 6-inch stems; Zones 6-8. *T.* x *citriodorus* (lemon thyme)—forms a shrubby carpet up to 2 feet wide of foot-tall branches with tiny lemon-scented leaves; 'Aureus' (golden lemon thyme) has gold-edged leaves; 'Silver Queen', leaves marbled cream and silvery gray; Zones 5-9. *T. herba-barona* (caraway thyme)—a fast-growing subshrub forming mats 4 inches tall and 2 feet across

Thymus herba-barona

with leaf flavors reminiscent of caraway, nutmeg, or lemon, and loose clusters of rose flowers; Zones 4-8. *T. mastichina* (mastic thyme)—an erect or sprawling shrub with 6- to 12-inch branches lined with gray-green eucalyptus-scented leaves; Zones 7-9. *T. praecox* ssp. *arcticus* [often sold under the name *T. serpyllum*] (creeping thyme, English wild thyme, nutmeg thyme)—2- to 3-inch-high carpets up to 18 inches wide with especially flavorful leaves and mauve to purple flowers; 'Coccineus' (crimson creeping thyme) has striking deep red blossoms; Zones 4-9. *T. pulegioides* [often sold under the name *T. serpyllum*] (broad-leaved thyme)—a shrub with large oval leaves lining 10-inch stems tipped with pink to purple flowers in broad mats; Zones 4-8. *T. serpyllum* (mother-of-thyme, wild thyme)—creeping stems only 2 to 3 inches tall in 3-foot-wide mats with cultivars in many shades of green or yellow, sometimes variegated; Zones 4-8. *T. vulgaris* (common thyme)—bushy shrubs 12 inches tall and as wide or wider with gray-green leaves used in cooking; 'Orange Balsam' has a scent recalling pine and citrus; Zones 4-8.

Growing conditions and maintenance: Plant thyme in spring, spacing transplants 12 to 24 inches apart. Select sites with average to poor soil and incorporate a small

Thymus praecox ssp. arcticus

amount of bone meal at planting time; rich or wet soils invite fungus and winterkill. To shape plants and encourage branching, prune hard in early spring before flowering or lightly after blooms appear. Remove green shoots of variegated cultivars to prevent them from reverting. Leaves are most pungent when plants are in bloom and when used fresh; dried leaves are more flavorful than fresh winter leaves. Add leaves to meat dishes, stuffings, pâtés, salad dressings, vegetable dishes, herb butter, vinegars, and mayonnaise. To dry, hang bundles of branches upside down in a shady, warm, well-ventilated location, then crumble or strip fresh leaves from stems and dry on screens; store in airtight containers for use in cooking or sachets. An infusion of thyme made by boiling fresh leaves and flowers in water, then straining the liquid, creates a soothing facial rinse; add rosemary to the infusion for a hair rinse. To propagate thyme, root softwood cuttings taken in late spring or early summer, or divide mature plants in early spring or late summer. Propagate from seed by sowing thickly in pots 6 to 8 weeks before the last frost, then set 4- to 6-inch seedlings out in clumps. Start thyme for a window-sill garden from seed, or pot divisions in late summer to bring indoors in late fall.

Tropaeolum
(tro-PEE-o-lum)
NASTURTIUM

Tropaeolum majus

Hardiness: *tender*

Height: *15 inches to 6 feet*

Light: *full sun to light shade*

Soil: *average, well-drained, sandy*

Plant type: *annual*

Uses: *landscaping, culinary, containers*

Nasturtiums bear funnel-like flowers with irregularly shaped petals from summer through frost. The flowers appear along mounding or trailing stems amid saucer-shaped leaves on twining stalks. Use dwarf, mounding nasturtiums as fillers, as houseplants, or among paving stones. Allow trailing or vining types to ramble as ground covers, cascade over walls, or trail from hanging baskets. Both the leaves and the flowers have a peppery flavor that adds zest to salads and sandwiches. Add flowers to vinegar. Substitute unripe seeds, fresh or pickled, for capers.

Selected species and varieties: *T. majus* (common nasturtium, Indian cress)—dwarf varieties to 15 inches tall, vining to 6 feet, with leaves to 6 inches across and 2½-inch flowers in yellow, orange, red, or mahogany; 'Empress of India' has vermilion blossoms amid blue-green foliage.

Growing conditions and maintenance: Sow nasturtium seeds ½ to ¾ inch deep in very early spring, spacing dwarf varieties 6 inches apart, vining types 12 inches apart. Plants growing in shade or rich soil produce more foliage and fewer flowers. Nasturtiums often self-sow.

Tulbaghia
(tul-BAJ-ee-a)
SOCIETY GARLIC

Tulbaghia violacea

Hardiness: *Zones 9-10*

Height: *1 to 2½ feet*

Light: *full sun to light shade*

Soil: *average, moist, well-drained*

Plant type: *bulb*

Uses: *landscaping, arrangements, culinary*

In summer, society garlic carries large clusters of starry flowers on tall stalks above clumps of grassy evergreen leaves. Use society garlic's neat mounds as a specimen in the perennial border, or grow the plant as an edging for garden beds or walkways. In cooler climates, society garlic grows well as a potted plant and can be wintered on a sunny window sill. Use the flowers in fresh bouquets. The leaves, with an onion or garlic aroma and a mild taste that does not linger on the breath, can be chopped and used like garlic chives as a garnish flavoring for salads, vegetables, and sauces.

Selected species and varieties: *T. violacea* (society garlic)—flat, grassy 8- to 12-inch leaves and ¾-inch white or violet flowers in clusters of eight to 16 blossoms on 1- to 2½-foot stalks; 'Silver Streak' has leaves striped cream and green.

Growing conditions and maintenance: Propagate society garlic by removing and replanting the small bulblets growing alongside mature bulbs in spring or fall. Space plants 1 foot apart. For indoor culture, plant one bulb per 6- to 8-inch pot.

Viola
(vy-O-la)
VIOLET

Viola odorata

Hardiness: *Zones 3-10*

Height: *6 to 12 inches*

Light: *partial shade to full sun*

Soil: *moist, well-drained*

Plant type: *perennial or hardy annual*

Uses: *landscaping, culinary, potpourri*

Clumps of violets with five-petaled blossoms resembling tiny faces are a staple in old-fashioned gardens as fillers among taller perennials, as edgings for beds and walkways, or in containers. Available in a wide range of shades, the small blossoms add cheer and fragrance to nosegays of fresh flowers. Their soft colors and faintly wintergreen taste accent salads, jams, and jellies. Candied violets garnish cakes, puddings, and other desserts. Violet water enhances baked goods, ices, and chilled soups, and can be used as a mouthwash or facial rinse. Add dried blossoms to potpourri. Add the slightly tangy leaves, high in vitamins A and C, to salads, or use them to perfume water for a facial steam. The flowers, leaves, and roots all figure in herbal medicine.

Selected species and varieties: *V. odorata* (sweet violet, florist's violet, English violet)—a perennial with sweetly scented deep purple or white, sometimes yellow, 1- to 1½-inch blossoms having prominent yellow centers on 6- to 8-inch stems amid quilted heart-shaped leaves in late winter to early spring in mild climates, from late spring through summer elsewhere; 'Alba' bears quantities of snow white flowers; 'Royal Robe' has extremely fragrant deep purple blossoms on 8-inch stems; Parma violets produce double rows of petals; Zones 3-10 for most except Parma violets, which are hardy only to Zone 6. *V. tricolor* (Johnny-jump-up, miniature pansy, field pansy, European wild pansy, heartsease)—hardy annual or short-lived perennial producing small, inch-wide blossoms combining purple, white, and yellow petals on 6- to 8-inch stems amid clumps of scalloped leaves throughout spring and summer.

Viola tricolor

Growing conditions and maintenance: Sow violet seeds directly in the garden in late summer or early spring, or start indoors 8 to 12 weeks before the last frost. Sweet violet grows best in partial shade, Johnny-jump-up in full sun, but either tolerates less than ideal light. Johnny-jump-up self-sows readily and behaves like a perennial in locations that favor its growth; treat sweet violet as an annual in regions with mild winters. Provide sweet violets, which spread by underground runners, with a light winter mulch. For more prolific flowering, feed violets in very early spring and remove faded flowers; shear sweet violets in late fall and remove excess runners. Divide sweet violets in fall, and space transplants 6 to 12 inches apart. For fresh use, pick flowers early in the day, leaves while still young. Candy the blossoms by dipping them in a heavy sugar syrup, then laying them flat to dry. Pour 3 ounces of boiling water over 2 ounces of leaves and petals and allow to steep for use in baking or as a cosmetic. Dry blossoms slowly in a shaded location to retain their delicate color.

Zingiber
(ZIN-ji-ber)
GINGER

Zingiber officinale

Hardiness: *Zones 9-11*

Height: *3 to 4 feet*

Light: *light shade*

Soil: *rich, moist, well-drained*

Plant type: *perennial*

Uses: *containers, culinary*

Ginger's aromatic branching roots with a spicy, citrusy bite have been prized by cooks for centuries. Fresh grated or dried ground ginger flavors baked goods, marinades, curries, chutneys, beverages, syrups, vegetables, fruit dishes, and more. Grow ginger outdoors in hot, humid regions or as a container plant elsewhere.

Selected species and varieties: *Z. officinale* (common ginger)—2- to 4-foot flat leaves composed of pointed leaflets lining reedlike stems and, rarely, yellow-petaled summer flowers with yellow-streaked purple lips in conical spikes.

Growing conditions and maintenance: Purchase gingerroot from a nursery or grocery store. Pot a section with large growth buds just below the surface in equal parts of sand, loam, peat moss, and compost. Plants grow best in warm temperatures with constant humidity and soil moisture. After 8 to 10 months, harvest the roots, retaining a small section to replant. Refrigerated, roots keep 2 to 3 months wrapped in a damp towel and plastic wrap. Alternatively, peel the roots, slice into a jar of sherry, and refrigerate indefinitely.

Encyclopedia of Vegetables

A vegetable garden that is productive throughout the growing season depends on careful planning. With the right sequence of vegetables, even a small garden can yield bountiful harvests from the last spring frost, or even before, until after the first fall frost. In fact, you may be able to harvest fresh vegetables until the beginning of the next gardening year.

Presented here is a selection of season-spanning vegetables, along with several popular fruits, for maximizing harvests. Each entry begins with hardiness information to guide garden planning. Cool-season annuals include vegetables that can be sown or transplanted outdoors when the soil is cool and can withstand spring or fall frosts. In addition to true annuals, this category includes biennials, such as Brussels sprouts and carrots, that are commonly grown as annuals. Warm-season annuals germinate best when soil temperatures reach 65° to 70° F, and will tolerate light frost. Hot-season annuals require very warm soil temperatures to germinate and both warm days and warm nights to develop and ripen. Winter-hardy vegetables are perennials in some climatic zones, where they can be left in the same site from one year to the next. Some of these perennials can also be cultivated as cool-season annuals. The frost-date maps on pages 247-248 will give you a general idea when the last hard spring frost and the first hard fall frost normally occur in your area.

To further aid the planning process, each entry also lists the number of days from seed or transplanting to harvest. Check the relative days to maturity to determine when the crop will be ready for harvest and a successive crop can be seeded or transplanted to fill the space. Plant spacings indicate how much room to allow between plants for optimum growth. The descriptions also note which varieties are disease resistant, a highly desirable characteristic, since such varieties are likely to produce well without spraying or other treatment.

ARTICHOKES

'Green Globe'

Hardiness: *Zones 8-11; warm-season annual*
Planting method: *direct sowing; rooted cuttings*
Plant spacing: *2 to 4 feet*
Light: *full sun to light shade*

Large, edible flower buds 4 to 6 inches across. Grown as perennials, artichokes are harvested in the spring; as annuals, they are harvested in the fall. The deeply lobed foliage makes artichokes attractive landscaping accents, and the buds and thistlelike flowers are prized in dried arrangements. Artichokes can be grown as container plants.

Selected varieties: 'Green Globe'—very prolific with buds in 100 days. 'Imperial Star'—spineless buds; performs well as an annual. 'Purple Sensation'—bronze-tinted buds.

Growing conditions: Artichokes need cool, moist summers and loose, constantly moist, well-drained soil enriched with manure. When grown as annuals, they need at least 100 frost-free days. Plant cuttings 6 to 8 inches deep and 2 to 4 feet apart in spring if grown as an annual; where perennial, plant in spring or fall. To grow from seed as a perennial, sow seed outdoors ½ inch deep. Thin young plants to 6 inches, then thin again to stand 2 to 4 feet apart. For annual artichokes, start seed indoors 4 to 6 weeks before last frost date and transplant when the soil temperature reaches 70° F. Renew a perennial planting every 3 to 4 years. Plants yield six to 12 buds.

ARUGULA, ROCKET

Arugula

Hardiness: *cool-season annual*

Planting method: *direct sowing*

Plant spacing: *6 inches*

Light: *full sun to light shade*

Peppery young leaves in spring or fall provide leafy salad greens or a zesty garnish for pasta or other dishes. Add the spicy flowers of bolting plants to salads for color and flavor.

Selected varieties: No named varieties; sold as arugula. Rosettes of broad oval leaves ready in 35 to 45 days.

Growing conditions: Plant seeds ½ inch deep in wide rows in early spring and again in fall 4 to 8 weeks before the first frost date. Arugula can be grown outdoors in winter where temperatures do not go below 25° F. The heat and short nights of summer cause plants to bolt and leaves to become bitter. Pick outer leaves when they are 2 to 4 inches long to encourage new growth, or harvest entire plant; small weekly sowings prolong harvest. Handpick snails and slugs or use baited traps. Interplant arugula with taller cool-season vegetables such as peas or broccoli, and fill spaces left after a spring planting is harvested with warm-season crops such as green beans or eggplant.

ASPARAGUS

'Jersey Giant'

Hardiness: *winter-hardy Zones 3-8*

Planting method: *crowns; transplants*

Plant spacing: *15 to 18 inches*

Light: *full sun*

Succulent shoots ½ inch or more in diameter tipped with tight, tender buds rise from perennial rootstocks in spring. When the year's harvest ends, allow shoots to develop into 4- to 6-foot stems with ferny leaves. Plant lettuce or other low-growing cool-season crops where asparagus foliage will shade them.

Selected varieties: 'Argenteuil'—stems especially good for blanching white. 'Jersey Giant'—a hybrid with very high yields of large spears with purplish tips; resists rust and tolerates fusarium wilt, root rot, and crown rot. 'Jersey Knight'—high-yielding hybrid adaptable to many soil types; resistant to rust and tolerant of fusarium wilt, root rot, and crown rot. 'Mary Washington'—widely available rust-resistant variety producing crisp, deep green spears over a long season. 'UC157'—hybrid especially suited to areas with mild winters; produces clumps of three to five uniform spears with some tolerance of root rot and fusarium wilt.

Growing conditions: Plant crowns in spring when the soil temperature reaches 50° F or more, or in fall. Set crowns in trenches 1 foot deep lined with 3 to 4 inches of compost or well-rotted manure. When new shoots appear, cover them with 2 to 3 inches of a mixture of equal parts of soil and compost. As the

shoots elongate, continue adding more of the mixture until the trench is filled in. Mulch heavily with compost to suppress weeds. Although planting from crowns is the easiest method, asparagus can be started outdoors or indoors from seed that has been soaked for 2 days in tepid water before sowing. Seedlings started indoors are transplanted to the garden when 10 to 12 weeks old, after all danger of frost is past. To sow outdoors, plant seed ½ inch deep when the soil reaches 70° F or more. Asparagus takes 2 years to reach full production from roots and 3 years to reach picking size from seed. Harvest about one-third of the new shoots the first year after planting roots. Harvest established beds once or twice daily, cutting or snapping off 6- to 8-inch spears just above the soil line. Pick 2- to

'Mary Washington'

3-year-old beds over 4 weeks and older beds for as long as 10 weeks. To produce white spears, blanch shoots as they emerge by covering them with 8 to 10 inches of soil or straw and harvesting when the tips peek through. Asparagus beds remain productive for 20 years or more. Control asparagus beetles and spotted asparagus beetles by handpicking them or shaking them onto a sheet and destroying them; by releasing beneficial insects such as ladybeetles or parasitic wasps; and by cleaning up garden debris in fall. Asparagus is susceptible to crown or root rot, fusarium wilt, and rust; remove and destroy affected plants. Mature plants yield 15 to 25 spears each.

BEANS, DRY

'Jacob's Cattle'

Hardiness: *warm-season annual*

Planting method: *direct sowing*

Plant spacing: *3 to 6 inches*

Light: *full sun*

Also called shelling beans. Successive plantings of bush or vining beans yield pods filled with ¼- to ¾-inch beans from summer through fall that are high in fiber and protein. Shell mature beans and use them fresh in side dishes, casseroles, and soups, or preserve them by freezing or canning. Alternatively, let pods dry on the plant, then shell and store beans. Soak dry beans to rehydrate and use like mature fresh beans.

Selected varieties: 'Adzuki'—small, dark red dry beans on 2-foot bushy plants in 118 days. 'Black Turtle'—bush variety with small black dry beans with a nutty flavor in 98 to 103 days. 'Cannellini'—vining pole bean with mildly flavored white to greenish white shelling beans in 50 to 60 days or dry beans in 80 days. 'French Horticultural'—18-inch heirloom, disease-resistant bush bean producing dry beans in 90 days. 'Great Northern'—prolific bush bean with oval, white dry beans in 85 days. 'Hutterite Soup'—heirloom bush bean with thick, yellowish white beans in 75 to 85 days. 'Jacob's Cattle', also called 'Dalmatian Bean'—heirloom 24-inch bush bean producing meaty, kidney-shaped white beans with maroon speckles, for shelling in 65 days or dry beans in 80 to 100 days. 'Pinto'—pole bean producing kidney-shaped maroon-and-white-speckled dry beans in 90 days. 'Soldier'—18-inch heirloom bush bean tolerant of both cool temperatures and drought, with slender white dry beans splotched in brown in 85 days. 'Swedish Brown'—extremely hardy 15-inch heirloom bush bean producing quantities of small oval red-brown shelling beans with a small white eye in 65 days or dry beans in 85 days. 'Tongues of Fire'—ivory pods streaked with red producing shelling beans in 70 days. 'Vermont Cranberry'—heirloom bush variety with plump, white shelling beans swirled with maroon in 60 days

'Cannellini'

and dry beans in 75 to 98 days. 'Yellow Eye'—prolific heirloom bush bean bearing white beans spotted with yellowish or tan eyes, good for shelling or for dry beans.

Growing conditions: Plant seeds outdoors after the soil temperature has reached 65° F or more and all danger of frost is past, setting them 1 to 1½ inches deep after pretreating with a bacterial legume inoculant. Make several successive weekly plantings to prolong harvest. Provide trellises or other tall supports for vining pole beans. Mulch to suppress weeds and conserve moisture, which is essential while plants are flowering and seeds are developing in the pods. To harvest beans for shelling and using fresh or for freezing or canning, pick as seeds reach maturity and fill out the pods. Continuous picking of mature pods is essential for further pod production for shelling beans; plants stop producing as soon as even a few pods become overmature. To harvest dry beans, stop watering. When at least 90 percent of the leaves have fallen and at least two-thirds of the beans are dry, pull plants and spread them on tarpaulins or hang in a well-ventilated area to finish drying. When seeds can no longer be dented when bitten, they are ready to thresh; do this by flailing them in a cloth bag. Screen or winnow to remove pod debris. Remove and discard broken beans,

'Tongues of Fire'

freeze the remainder for several hours to destroy bean weevil larvae, then store in airtight containers for up to 3 years.

BEANS, FAVA

'Broad Windsor Longpod'

Hardiness: *cool-season annual*

Planting method: *direct sowing*

Plant spacing: *4 to 6 inches*

Light: *full sun*

Also called broad beans. Large, meaty seeds mature in long pods on erect bushy plants in late spring. Shell mature fava beans for fresh use, or allow beans to dry for long-term storage.

Selected varieties: 'Aquadulce'—16-inch pods up to 2 inches wide filled with seven or eight large white beans in 85 days. 'Broad Windsor Longpod'—up to seven light green beans in 8-inch pods on heat-tolerant 3-foot plants in 85 days. 'Imperial Green Longpod'—20-inch pods in 84 days.

Growing conditions: Fava beans tolerate frost and grow best where spring weather remains cool for a long time. In hot weather, flowers will not set pods. Plant seed outdoors 4 to 6 weeks before the last spring frost, setting seeds 1 to 1½ inches deep after pretreating with a bacterial legume inoculant. Seeds may be broadcast or grown in wide rows. Provide twiggy branches or other supports among plants. Mulch to keep plants cool, suppress weeds, and conserve moisture. Continuous picking of mature pods encourages further production; plants stop producing as soon as even a few pods become overmature.

BEANS, FILET

'Tavera'

Hardiness: *warm-season annual*

Planting method: *direct sowing*

Plant spacing: *2 to 6 inches*

Light: *full sun*

Heavy crops of long, straight, elegantly thin green beans for fresh use in late spring through summer on upright, bushy plants.

Selected varieties: 'Astral'—miniature 3- to 4-inch beans on disease-resistant plants in 60 days. 'Finaud'—very thin 6- to 8-inch beans. 'Fin des Bagnols'—high yields of 7- to 8-inch beans. 'Tavera'—very thin, stringless 4- to 5-inch beans in 54 days. 'Triumph de Farcy'—straight 5- to 6-inch dark green beans in 48 days.

Growing conditions: Plant outdoors after all danger of frost is past and the soil temperature has reached 65° F, setting seeds 1 to 1½ inches deep. Mulch to conserve moisture and suppress weeds. Filet beans are best when they are ⅛ to ¼ inch in diameter. Pick every other day in hot weather and at least every 5 days, but preferably more frequently, in cool weather to prolong harvest over several weeks.

BEANS, GREEN

'Derby'

Hardiness: *warm-season annual*

Planting method: *direct sowing*

Plant spacing: *2 to 4 inches*

Light: *full sun*

Also called snap beans. Clusters of pods on compact 1- to 2-foot bushes can be harvested from early summer into fall when seed is sown in succession. Use green beans fresh or preserve them by freezing or canning.

Selected varieties: 'Blue Lake Bush'—6½-inch-long cylindrical pods produced all at once on disease-resistant plants in 58 days. 'Derby'—continuously produced cylindrical pods 7 inches long on vigorous bushes starting in 57 days over several weeks. 'Greencrop'—early crops of flat, stringless pods in 52 days. 'Harvester'—large crop of 5- to 6-inch curved, stringless pods on disease-resistant plants in 60 days. 'Jade'—large crop of straight 5- to 7-inch pods in 60 days. 'Provider'—early crop of 6-inch oval pods in 50 days on plants that resist disease, heat, and drought. 'Slenderette'—thin, stringless 5-inch pods on disease-resistant plants in 53 days. 'Stringless Greenpod'—stringless 6-inch cylindrical pods in 50 days. 'Tendercrop'—cylindrical 6-inch stringless pods on disease-resistant plants in 50 days. 'Tendergreen'—6-inch stringless pods on heat-tolerant plants.

Growing conditions: Plant outdoors after all danger of frost is past and the soil temperature has reached 65° F, setting seeds 1 to 1½ inches deep after pretreating with a bacterial legume inoculant purchased from a seed supplier. The bacteria live in nodules on the roots of the plants and extract nitrogen from the air that helps the beans grow. The shallow roots of beans are easily damaged by cultivation, so control weeds by keeping the plants well mulched. Spacing plants closely also helps to suppress weeds.

Most varieties produce a single crop all at once, so plant weekly for a month to ensure successive harvests. Harvest green beans when pods snap crisply but before seeds start to form. Continuous

'Provider'

picking of pods encourages further production; plants stop producing flowers as soon as even a few pods go to seed.

BEANS, LIMA

'Burpee's Improved Bush'

Hardiness: *warm-season annual*

Planting method: *direct sowing*

Plant spacing: *2 to 4 inches*

Light: *full sun*

Starchy, delicately flavored beans on 1½- to 2-foot bushy plants or 7- to 12-foot vining plants from early summer into fall with successive plantings. Shell lima beans for using fresh or allow them to dry on plants for long-term storage.

Selected varieties: 'Baby Fordhook'—an early baby lima bush variety with three or four small light green beans in 3-inch pods in 70 days. 'Burpee's Best'—a high-yielding pole variety with three to five beans per pod in 92 days. 'Burpee's Improved Bush'—bush variety with four or five large beans in easily shelled 5½-inch pods in 75 days. 'Fordhook 242'—midseason bush variety with three or four very large, uniform beans per pod on heat-tolerant plants in 74 days. 'Henderson's Bush'—early baby lima bush variety with three or four small white beans per pod in 65 days. 'King of the Garden'—a vining pole variety with four or five creamy white or pale green beans per pod in 88 days, good for drying.

Growing conditions: Plant outdoors after all danger of frost is past and the soil temperature has reached at least 65° F and preferably 75° F, setting seeds 1 to 1½ inches deep after pretreating with a bacterial legume inoculant, which can be purchased from most seed suppliers. Make several successive weekly plant-

ings to prolong harvesting. Plant bush lima beans in double rows and provide supports among the plants to keep leaves and pods off the ground. Provide trellises or other tall supports for vining pole varieties. If the supports have been used previously for bean crops, treat them with a mixture of 10 parts water to 1 part household bleach to kill any disease organisms that may have overwintered. Mulch plants well and keep soil moist, especially while plants are flowering and beans are developing in the pods. Continuous picking of mature pods encourages further production for shelling beans; plants stop producing as soon as even a few pods become overmature and begin to dry.

To harvest dry beans, withhold water and allow at least two-thirds of the beans to dry, then pull out plants and spread on tarps or hang in a well-ventilated area

'Fordhook 242'

to finish drying. When seeds can no longer be dented when bitten, thresh by flailing them in a cloth bag. Screen or winnow to remove pod debris, freeze for several hours to destroy bean weevil larvae, and store in airtight containers for up to 3 years.

BEANS, POLE

'Trionfo Violetto'

Hardiness: *warm-season annual*

Planting method: *direct sowing*

Plant spacing: *3 to 6 inches*

Light: *full sun*

Vines up to 12 feet long produce green, yellow, or purple pods from summer into fall with successive plantings. Pole beans produce almost twice as many beans as green bush beans, making them an ideal choice for small spaces and intensive gardening.

Selected varieties: 'Blue Lake'—early-maturing variety with straight, round, stringless 5½-inch pods in 66 days. 'Emerite'—early, very slender string-less pods on very productive vines in 55 days. 'Kentucky Wonder'—flavorful beans, with good texture for freezing, in 65 days; can also be left on vine longer for dry beans. 'Kwintus'—long, flat pods that stay tender even when mature. 'Merchant of Venice', also called 'Meraviglia di Venezia'—flat, stringless golden yellow 3-inch pods filled with black seeds in 75 days. 'Trionfo Violetto'—an heirloom variety with attractive purple flowers that make it a good landscaping plant, followed by deep purple string-less beans in 62 days.

Growing conditions: Plant outdoors after all danger of frost is past and the soil temperature has reached 65° F, setting seeds 1 to 1½ inches deep after pretreating them with a bacterial inoculant, which can be purchased from most seed suppliers. The bacteria live in nodules on the roots of the plants and extract nitrogen from the air that helps the beans grow. Provide wooden or wire trellises, netting, tepee poles, or other supports for pole beans to climb. Disease organisms can overwinter on supports; reuse supports that beans have grown on in previous years only after sterilizing them with a mixture of 10 parts water to 1 part household bleach.

Beans have shallow roots that can easily be damaged by cultivation, so keep them well mulched to control weeds. It is important to keep plants well wa-

'Kentucky Wonder'

tered, especially when they are flowering and pods are developing. Harvest beans when pods snap crisply when broken but before seeds start to form. Continuous picking of mature pods encourages further pod production; plants stop producing flowers as soon as even a few pods go to seed. For dry beans, allow pods to mature and dry on plants in the garden. Thresh seeds from pods by flailing them in a cloth bag when seeds can no longer be dented when bitten.

BEANS, PURPLE

'Royal Burgundy'

Hardiness: *warm-season annual*

Planting method: *direct sowing*

Plant spacing: *3 to 6 inches*

Light: *full sun*

Produced from early summer to fall if sown successively, the colorful pods are easy to find among the foliage. Use purple-podded beans raw to add color to salads or hors d'oeuvres; they turn green when cooked.

Selected varieties: 'Royal Burgundy'—an insect-resistant variety with deep purple stringless, slightly curved 5½-inch pods in 54 days. 'Royalty'—bright purple, curving pods in 53 days. 'Sequoia'—flat purple pods filled with large, meaty seeds.

Growing conditions: Plant outdoors after the last spring frost, setting seeds 1 to 1½ inches deep. Make successive plantings over a month's time to extend the harvest into fall. Provide supports among the plants to keep beans up off the ground. Continuous picking of mature pods encourages further production; plants stop producing as soon as even a few pods become overmature.

BEANS, RUNNER

'Scarlet Runner'

Hardiness: *Zones 7-9; cool-season annual*

Planting method: *direct sowing*

Plant spacing: *3 to 6 inches*

Light: *full sun*

Long, flat fuzzy pods filled with colorful seeds develop from large, brilliantly colored flowers on long vines in summer and fall. Plants are perennial where winters are mild. Use immature runner bean pods fresh and mature pods as shell beans. Train runner bean vines on a trellis as a flowering screen.

Selected varieties: 'Painted Lady'—red-and-white flowers followed by 12-inch pods in 90 days; 'Scarlet Emperor'—red flowers followed by tender pods in 75 days; seeds mature more slowly than other varieties. 'Scarlet Runner'—edible red flowers in clusters of 20 to 40 blossoms, followed by long, meaty pods filled with black-purple seeds in 90 days. Pods can also be picked before seeds mature and eaten fresh.

Growing conditions: Plant seeds 1 to 1½ inches deep after the last spring frost and make successive biweekly sowings to prolong harvest. Provide a trellis or other support for vines to climb, and keep mulched. Continuous picking of mature pods encourages further production; plants stop producing flowers as soon as even a few pods become overmature. Mulch heavily over winter to protect roots in Zones 7-9.

BEANS, YARDLONG

'Green-Pod Yardlong'

Hardiness: *warm-season annual*

Planting method: *direct sowing*

Plant spacing: *8 to 12 inches*

Light: *full sun*

Also called asparagus beans. Quantities of extremely long, thin pods on vining plants in late summer and fall. Yardlong beans can grow as long as their name suggests but are the most tender when they are about 10 to 12 inches long. Eat raw or cooked.

Selected varieties: 'Green-Pod Yardlong' —2- to 3-foot, pencil-thin green beans in 75 days. 'Orient Wonder'—stringless 15- to 20-inch pods in 60 days. 'Purple-Pod Yardlong'—2- to 3-foot, very slender purple pods in 75 days.

Growing conditions: Yardlong beans require a long growing season and warm temperatures. Plant seeds outdoors after the last spring frost, setting them 1 to 1½ inches deep. Provide tall trellises or other supports for the vines to climb. Mulch to conserve moisture and suppress weeds. Continuous picking of pods encourages further production; plants stop producing flowers when any pods become overmature.

BEANS, YELLOW or WAX

'Pencil Pod Wax'

Hardiness: *warm-season annual*

Planting method: *direct sowing*

Plant spacing: *3 to 6 inches*

Light: *full sun*

Delicately flavored, buttery yellow pods develop on bushy plants from summer into fall with successive plantings. Use the colorful pods raw or cooked to brighten salads and side dishes, or preserve them by freezing.

Selected varieties: 'Brittle Wax'—heavy crop of crisp 7-inch pods in 52 days. 'Cherokee'—heavy crop of stringless pods on disease-resistant plants in 50 days. 'Dorabel'—small 4- to 5-inch pods ready to pick in 57 to 60 days. 'Golden Rocky'—deep yellow 7-inch pods on cold-tolerant plants in 63 days. 'Goldenrod'—round, straight 6-inch pods with small seeds in 55 days. 'Pencil Pod Wax'—round, very crisp, slender 7-inch stringless pods in 55 days. 'Roc d'Or'—round, straight, buttery tender pods on disease-resistant plants in 57 days. 'Roma Gold'—flat, stringless pods with plump seeds in 55 days. 'Wax Romano'—broad, flat beans with meaty seeds in 59 days.

Growing conditions: Plant wax beans outdoors after all danger of frost is past and the soil temperature has reached 65° F, setting seeds 1 to 1½ inches deep. Continuous picking of mature pods encourages further production.

BEETS

'Early Wonder'

Hardiness: *cool-season annual*

Planting method: *direct sowing*

Plant spacing: *2 to 4 inches*

Light: *full sun*

Sweet, tender red, yellow, or white roots and tangy greens are harvested from summer through fall. Varieties may be globe shaped or cylindrical. Both roots and greens can be used raw or cooked. The pigment in red beets is drawn out during cooking to color dishes.

Selected varieties: 'Albina Vereduna'—globe variety with mild white flesh and wavy greens in 60 days. 'Big Red'—globe variety with fine-textured roots and disease-resistant greens in 55 days. 'Burpee's Golden'—globe variety with reddish gold roots of excellent keeping quality in 55 days. 'Chioggia'—globe variety with rosy pink skin and white flesh marked with bright pink concentric rings, and especially tasty greens. 'Cylindra'—cylindrical variety with long, 5- to 7-inch roots ideal for uniform slicing in 55 days. 'Detroit Dark Red'—globe variety with dark red roots in 60 days that store well. 'Early Wonder'—a globe variety with fine-grained 3-inch roots in 50 days. 'Formanova'—cylindrical variety with roots 6 to 8 inches long and 2½ inches in diameter in 50 days. 'Golden'—sweet, nonbleeding variety with deep yellow-orange flesh in 60 days. 'Long Season'—tapered variety with large roots and excellent storage qualities in 78 days. 'Lutz Green Leaf', also called 'Winter Keeper'—tapered variety with succulent glossy greens with white stems and very sweet dark red roots with excellent keeping quality in 80 days. 'Red Ace'—vigorous, fast-growing globe variety with exceptionally sweet, deep red roots in 53 days. 'Ruby Queen'—globe variety with smooth, deep red roots of uniform size in 54 days.

Growing conditions: Beets can be sown outdoors as soon as the soil can be worked. Soak seeds for 24 hours in warm water before setting them ½ inch deep in a loose, well-tilled soil rich in organic matter to allow growth of the long taproots. Fertilize at planting with a 5-10-10 organic fertilizer or well-rotted

'Golden'

manure. Mark rows of slow-germinating beets with quick-growing radishes for intensive cropping. Cover with floating row covers to help warm the soil and speed germination; row covers will also control insect pests on greens. Mulch to help provide the even moisture needed to produce sweet beets. Thin seedlings twice, first to stand 2 inches apart and later to stand 4 inches apart. Beets can be harvested anytime after they are half grown. For a fall crop, sow seed in mid- to late summer. Beet roots toughen when the temperature is 80° F or more. To avoid root rot, rotate beets with non-root crops.

BLACKBERRIES

'Ebony King' Blackberry

Hardiness: *winter-hardy Zones 5-10*

Planting method: *bare root; containers*

Plant spacing: *3 to 5 feet*

Light: *full sun*

Juicy, sweet-tart berries 1 to 2 inches long in midsummer and sometimes again in fall on erect or trailing canes. Except for a handful of varieties, blackberries and the closely related boysenberries, loganberries, and youngberries are notorious for the sharp thorns that line the canes. Both trailing and erect types produce canes that grow one year, then bear fruit and die the second year. The berries can be enjoyed fresh from the garden, baked into pies and other desserts, frozen, or made into preserves or wine. Blackberries and their relatives are long lived, often remaining productive for as long as 20 years.

Selected varieties: Trailing varieties include: 'Boysen'—drought-resistant canes that bear very large 1½-inch, deep red to purple-black berries with a whitish bloom. 'Logan'—deep red to dusky maroon berries 1½ inches long on semierect canes; best suited to the West Coast. 'Lucretia'—early-ripening, medium to large, jet black fruit. 'Thornless Boysen'—very large, almost seedless, black-purple berries on thornless canes. 'Young'—large, round, wine-colored berries of exceptional juiciness and sweetness; does well on both the West Coast and the Gulf Coast. All trailing varieties are hardy in Zones 7-10.

Upright blackberry varieties include: 'Comanche'—midseason crop of very large, glossy black berries. 'Darrow'—with early- to midseason crops of firm, inch-long fruits on virus-free, winter-hardy canes; Zones 5-10. 'Ebony King'—rust-resistant 3- to 4-foot canes bearing early-ripening purple-black fruits; Zones 5-10. 'Ranger'—with very early, very large yields of sweet berries ideal for fresh eating or winemaking. 'Thorn-free'—late-ripening, medium to large fruits on thornless 7- to 8-foot canes; Zones 7-10.

Growing conditions: Plant certified disease-free bare-root or container-grown plants in deep, fertile, moist but well-drained loam with a pH between 5.5 and 7.5, setting the top of the roots just be-

'Thornless Boysen'

low the soil line. From Zone 5 north, set plants out in early spring, as soon as the soil can be worked. From Zone 6 south, set plants out in fall, winter, or spring. Plant upright types 3 feet apart in rows spaced 6 feet apart; trailing types should be planted 5 feet apart in rows 8 feet apart. For both types, cut the canes of newly planted bushes back to 6 inches from the ground. Water regularly and provide a deep mulch to suppress grass and weeds. For established erect varieties, prune the side branches of canes produced the previous year back to about 18 inches in early spring to encourage heavy fruit production in the coming season; the side branches of trailing varieties should be cut back to 12 inches. For both newly planted and established bushes, pinch off the tips of any new canes that are produced during the current season when they are about

3½ feet tall; pinching is important because it stimulates the canes to produce side branches and thus helps ensure heavy production the following year.

When the fruiting season is over, cut out all the canes that produced berries. Trailing types are most productive if their canes are trained in a fan shape on a support of horizontal wires. Harvest

'Logan'

blackberries after fruits turn from pink to red and finally deep glossy black-purple; the berries should be so ripe that they drop off at the slightest touch. Leave berries that are still firmly attached to ripen fully; otherwise, they will be sour. A single plant yields 4 to 8 quarts of fruit.

BLACK-EYED PEAS

'California Blackeye #5'

Hardiness: *warm-season annual*

Planting method: *direct sowing*

Plant spacing: *2 to 4 inches*

Light: *full sun*

Also called cowpeas. White, cream, or tan ⅜- to ½-inch seeds with a dark spot, or eye, fill long clusters of pods at the top of bushy or semivining plants in summer through early fall. Harvest immature pods and cook like green beans; shell mature pods and use the peas fresh; or allow pods to dry on plants, then shell and store the beans.

Selected varieties: 'California Blackeye #5'—large seeds in pods up to 12 inches long on nematode- and wilt-resistant plants in 75 to 95 days. 'Mississippi Silver'—bears easy-to-shell cowpeas with 6-inch pods in 65 days. 'Pinkeye Purple Hull'—purple-eyed white cowpeas in 6- to 7-inch pods in 65 days; usually produces two crops a season.

Growing conditions: Plant after all danger of frost is past and the soil temperature reaches 70° F, sowing seeds ½ to 1 inch deep; seeds germinate in 10 to 14 days. Extend the harvest time with successive plantings. Fertilize soil before planting with phosphorus and potassium; adding nitrogen isn't necessary. Anthracnose, blight, powdery mildew, aphids, bean beetles, leafhoppers, mites, and nematodes may all damage black-eyed peas.

BROCCOLI

'Green Comet'

Hardiness: *warm-season annual*

Planting method: *direct sowing; transplants*

Plant spacing: *12 to 24 inches*

Light: *full sun*

Tiny flowers packed into green or blue-green heads on thick, upright stalks in summer or fall. Some broccoli varieties tend to produce a single, large central head, while others develop a smaller central head and multiple side shoots.

Selected varieties: 'Bonanza'—large central heads and many side shoots. 'De Cicco'—a very early, disease-resistant, highly productive variety with many side shoots. 'Emperor'—a heat- and disease-tolerant variety good for close spacing with dense 6- to 8-inch single heads. 'Green Comet'—a very fast-maturing, disease-resistant variety with firm blue-green central heads and abundant side shoots. 'Green Valiant'—a cold-tolerant, disease-resistant variety. 'Oktal'—early variety with large, open heads and plentiful side shoots. 'Premium Crop'—a slow-to-bolt, disease-resistant variety with a central blue-green head and no side shoots. 'Romanesco Minaret'—pale green conical heads. 'Super Dome'—very productive compact plants ideal for close spacing. 'Waltham 29'—heat-tolerant, compact variety with a single head, good for close spacing and growing in fall.

Growing conditions: Start broccoli indoors 6 to 8 weeks before the last frost and transplant to the garden 3 weeks before the last frost; otherwise, sow direct-ly in the garden 1 to 2 weeks before the last frost. Sow fall crops 3 to 4 months before the first fall frost. Set seeds ¼ to ½ inch deep in a constantly moist but not wet soil enriched with compost or other organic matter. Cold snaps while heads are forming may cause production of small buttons of buds instead of large heads, and temperatures above 80° F may cause plants to bolt. Single-head varieties are generally best for summer harvest and side-shoot types for fall.

Fertilize at planting and again as heads begin forming with fish emulsion or a balanced 10-10-10 organic fertilizer. Mulch to retain soil moisture. Use paper

'Premium Crop'

collars to foil cutworms and floating row covers or parasitic wasps to thwart cabbageworms, flea beetles, cabbage loopers, and other insect pests. Remove plant tops and roots in fall to control soil-borne diseases and wait 3 years before replanting broccoli in the same location.

To harvest, cut the large central head first to encourage production of a second crop of smaller side shoots. Soak heads in warm water with a small amount of added vinegar and salt to dislodge insects among the buds. One plant yields 1 to 2 pounds of broccoli.

BROCCOLI RABE

Broccoli Rabe

Hardiness: *cool-season annual*

Planting method: *direct sowing*

Plant spacing: *4 to 8 inches*

Light: *full sun*

Also called rapini. Tender greens with a mustardy tang and 1-inch broccoli-like florets in early summer or fall; a good choice for the winter garden in mild climates. Use the greens and florets raw in salads or cooked as a side dish. Despite its name, broccoli rabe is a member of the turnip family.

Selected varieties: None. Ruffled leaves and small florets on slender stalks ready to harvest in 40 days. Cut entire plant just as the flower buds are about to open.

Growing conditions: Start seed indoors 6 weeks before last frost or sow ½ inch deep outside in early spring; young plants tolerate light frost. Where summers are cool, plant in late summer or early fall for a late-fall crop. In milder climates, plant in late fall for a winter crop. Water generously and fertilize 2 to 3 weeks after plants are well established. In windy locations, protect stems from damage by mounding soil around the base of plants or tying plants to stakes. Broccoli rabe is a heavy feeder; rotate with legumes such as peas or beans and renew the soil with a generous amount of compost before planting. Harvest leaves when they are 4 to 6 inches long and cut florets with 2 to 3 inches of stem. A 10-foot row will produce about 3 pounds of greens over a 2- to 4-week period.

BRUSSELS SPROUTS

'Jade Cross'

Hardiness: *cool-season annual*

Planting method: *transplants; direct sowing*

Plant spacing: *18 to 24 inches*

Light: *full sun*

Firm, blue-green flower buds resembling miniature cabbages growing in a spiral up tall stalks in mid- to late fall in northern gardens and from late fall through winter in milder climates. Frost improves the flavor of the sprouts. Use them fresh or frozen cooked as a side dish.

Selected varieties: 'Jade Cross'—extremely cold-tolerant variety with abundant, closely spaced sprouts in 115 days. 'Prince Marvel'—very early crop of small, sweet sprouts with creamy white centers in 95 days. 'Rubine'—a late-maturing variety with tiny red sprouts in 130 days.

Growing conditions: Brussels sprouts require a long growing season and are best harvested after the first fall frost, so work backward from that date to determine when to sow seed outdoors or to set out transplants. Plants started indoors from seed will be ready to plant outside in 4 to 8 weeks. For direct sowing, plant seed ½ inch deep in soil enriched with compost, and mulch plants to conserve moisture. Do not plant where other members of the cabbage family have grown for at least 3 years. Harvest sprouts from the bottom of the stalk upward when they are 1 inch or more across. Fresh sprouts will keep for several weeks if the entire plant is pulled up and stored in a cool location. One plant produces 50 to 100 sprouts.

CABBAGE

'Stonehead'

Hardiness: *cool-season annual*

Planting method: *transplants; direct sowing*

Plant spacing: *12 to 24 inches*

Light: *full sun or filtered sun*

Common cabbage has firm, dense heads of succulent green or red leaves in spring, summer, or fall. Plant early varieties for spring crops of small to medium 3- to 4-pound heads; midseason varieties with medium to large heads weighing 5 to 8 pounds for spring or fall crops; or slow-maturing late varieties with large heads weighing up to 12 pounds or more for fall crops. Savoy cabbage has crinkled leaves that are more tender and milder in flavor than the common cabbage varieties.

Selected varieties: Green-leaved varieties include: 'Copenhagen Market'—midseason variety with heads in 72 days that last well in the garden. 'Danish Ballhead'—late-season variety with 6- to 8-pound heads that store well in 105 days. 'Earliana'—very early variety with 2-pound heads in 60 days. 'Early Flat Dutch'—midseason variety with split-resistant, flattened heads in 85 days. 'Early Jersey Wakefield'—disease-resistant early variety with small conical heads that tolerate close spacing in 63 days. 'Emerald Cross Hybrid'—early variety with round heads with blue-green outer leaves and creamy centers in 63 days. 'Golden Acre'—early disease-resistant variety with round light green heads in 64 days. 'Late Flat Dutch'—late variety with flat 10- to 12-pound heads in 100 days. 'Stonehead'—

early variety with blue-green leaves packed into extremely dense 3-pound heads that keep well in the garden in 60 to 70 days. 'Wisconsin All Seasons'—disease-resistant late variety with excellent storage quality in 94 days.

Red-leaved varieties include: 'Crimson'—midseason variety that stores well in the garden in 82 days. 'Lasso'—early vari-

'Ruby Ball'

ety with solid 2- to 4-pound heads in 70 days. 'Red Acre'—insect-tolerant, split-resistant midseason variety with 3- to 4-pound heads on compact plants in 76 days. 'Ruby Ball'—midseason variety with round 3- to 4-pound heads that keep well in the garden in 68 days. 'Ruby Perfection'—split-resistant midseason variety with solid, round red heads in 85 days.

Savoy varieties include: 'Chieftain Savoy'—midseason variety with round, 4- to 5-pound heads of crinkled leaves. 'Julius'—late variety with blue-green leaves in 3- to 5-pound heads with sweet flavor in 90 days. 'Savoy Ace'—midseason variety with delicately flavored leaves in 78 days.

Growing conditions: Start early cabbages for spring crops indoors 4 to 8 weeks before the last frost, planting seeds ¼ to ½ inch deep. Transplant to garden soil enriched with compost after all danger of frost is past and mulch to conserve moisture. Direct-sow midseason cabbages as soon as all danger of frost is past. For fall crops, direct-sow late cabbages at least 100 days before the first fall frost. Plant spring varieties with small heads 12 to 15 inches apart, medium-sized midseason varieties 15 to 24 inches, and large fall varieties 24 inches apart. Close spacing produces smaller heads and increases the tendency of mature heads to split.

Keep cabbages constantly moist but not soggy, and fertilize every 2 to 3 weeks with fish emulsion or other organic fertilizer with at least 10 percent nitrogen. Use paper collars to foil cutworms, water sprays to remove aphids. Use Bt, handpicking, floating row covers, or parasitic wasps to thwart cabbageworms, flea beetles, cabbage loopers, and other insect pests. To minimize clubroot and other soil-borne diseases, do not plant cabbages where other cabbage-family members have been planted for at least 3 years.

Harvest cabbages anytime after heads form. Root-pruning on one side of the plant will delay splitting and prolong garden storage; in addition, growth is slowed. Harvesting spring varieties when

'Chieftain Savoy'

the heads are softball-sized while leaving five or six large outer leaves attached to the stalk stimulates plants to produce a second crop of small heads in fall. Cabbage tolerates light frost. Heads harvested in fall will keep several weeks or more in a cool, humid place. Common green cabbages store better than red or savoy.

CABBAGE, CHINESE

'Blues'

Hardiness: *cool-season annual*

Planting method: *transplants; direct sowing*

Plant spacing: *10 to 18 inches*

Light: *full sun*

Also called celery cabbage. Vase-shaped heads of crinkly leaves with succulent ribs and mild, sweet flavor in early summer or fall. Use Chinese cabbage in salads, soups, or steamed as a side dish.

Selected varieties: 'Blues'—small disease-resistant, slow-to-bolt heads in 50 days, especially good for spring planting. 'Jade Pagoda'—disease-resistant hybrid with upright green heads with yellow hearts in 68 days. 'Monument'—tall, dense heads with creamy white centers in 80 days. 'Orient Express'—a very early, heat-resistant variety with crisp, peppery flavor in 43 days. 'Two Seasons Hybrid'— oval, slow-to-bolt heads in 62 days, good for spring or fall crops.

Growing conditions: Start Chinese cabbage indoors 8 to 10 weeks before the last frost, setting seed ½ inch deep in peat pots to transplant directly into garden soil enriched with compost. Choose locations where cabbage-family members have not grown for at least 3 years and mulch to conserve moisture. Harvest heads before the increasing length of summer days causes plants to bolt. For fall crops, sow seed for leafy varieties 7 weeks and heading varieties 10 to 12 weeks before the first frost. Tie heads loosely with string to blanch hearts for milder flavor.

CARDOON

Cardoon

Hardiness: *Zones 5-9*

Planting method: *direct sowing; transplants*

Plant spacing: *1½ to 2 feet*

Light: *full sun*

Crunchy roots and thick, succulent leaf midribs in fall on perennial thistlelike plants that can also be grown as annuals. Use mature midribs or cubed roots blanched and marinated in salads and antipasto and parboiled or battered and fried as a side dish.

Selected varieties: Usually sold without a variety name; silver-gray foliage on plants to 8 feet tall in 120 to 150 days.

Growing conditions: Start cardoon indoors 10 weeks before the last frost or sow directly in the garden 1 to 2 weeks before the last frost in a rich, constantly moist but well-drained loam. Space transplants or thin seedlings to stand 1½ to 2 feet apart. Approximately a month before first frost, when plants are 3 feet tall or more, blanch stalks by tying them together with twine and wrapping with paper or burlap; leaves will blanch in 3 to 4 weeks. Harvest by cutting stems just below the crown. Discard tough outer leaves and trim leaves from the thick midribs before cooking. Plants will grow taller and stronger the second year. If you grow cardoon as an annual, pull up the whole plant and use the roots as well as the midribs for cooking.

CARROTS

'Gold Pak'

Hardiness: *cool-season annual*

Planting method: *direct sowing*

Plant spacing: *2 to 4 inches*

Light: *full sun*

Sweet, crisp red-orange roots with fine-textured flesh surrounding a pithier core from late spring through fall and into winter with successive plantings. The deeper the color, the higher the vitamin content. Choose among several carrot shapes and sizes according to soil type. Imperator types with long, slender roots need deeply tilled, loose soils. Cylindrical Nantes types and thick, blocky Chantenay and Danvers types will grow where soils are heavy or rocky. Use the very short ball-shaped and baby varieties in extremely heavy soils. The short Nantes, Chantenay, and Danvers types can be grown in pots. Plant carrots in a border among ornamental annuals or perennials, where the lacy foliage will be an attractive filler. It also makes a pretty addition to bouquets.

Selected varieties: Long varieties include: 'Gold Pak'—pencil-thin tapered roots up to 10 inches long in 76 days. 'Imperator'—slender, tapering 8-inch roots in 77 days. 'Sweetness II'—very sweet and juicy 6- to 8-inch cylindrical roots in 73 days; 'Tendersweet'—slender, coreless roots 7 inches or longer in 75 days.

Medium varieties include: 'Artist'—thick, blunt 7- to 8-inch roots in 65 days that retain exceptional sweetness even through winter storage. 'Coreless

Nantes'—almost coreless, blunt-tipped, 6-inch roots in 65 days; 'Danvers Half Long'—crisp, cylindrical 6- to 7-inch roots that will grow in heavy soils in 75 days, good for canning and storing; 'Nantes'—small-cored cylinders of sweet flesh 1½ inches thick and 6 to 7 inches long in 65 days; 'Nantes Half Long'—slim, blunt-tipped 6- to 7-inch cylindrical roots with small cores in 70 days; 'Napoli'—with early-maturing, slim blunt

'Danvers Half Long'

7-inch roots that tolerate crowding in 66 days. 'Red Cored Chantenay', also called 'Goldinhart'—stocky, blunt-tipped 4- to 5-inch roots up to 2½ inches wide in 65 days that are good for canning and freezing and grow well in heavy soils. 'Royal Chantenay'—produces thick, tapering roots that are deep red-orange in color and up to 8 inches long in 70 days. 'Scarlet Nantes'—bright red-orange cylindrical roots with dependably sweet flavor and very small cores in 68 days. 'Touchon'—a very sweet Nantes-type carrot up to 7 inches long with high moisture content, ideal for juicing.

Ball-shaped carrot varieties include: 'Parmex'—very early ½- to 1-inch roots with exceptionally good flavor in 50 days. 'Planet'—deep orange 1½-inch roots in 55 days. 'Thumbelina'—roots ½ to 1½ inches in diameter with sweet flesh and thin skin that needs no peeling in 60 to 70 days.

Finger carrot varieties include: 'Baby Spike'—early-maturing tapered roots only 3 to 4 inches long and ½ inch in diameter in 52 days. 'Little Finger'—3½-inch roots 1 inch in diameter in 60 days. 'Minicor'—sweet, very slender, blunt-tipped 6- to 7-inch roots in 55 days.

Growing conditions: Sow carrots ¼ to ½ inch deep in well-tilled, loose loam. Begin sowing 2 to 4 weeks before the last frost, making successive sowings every 2 to 3 weeks until midsummer for continuous harvesting. To speed germination, soak seed for 24 hours, then freeze for 1 week before sowing. Mix the tiny seeds with sand for easier handling. Thin seedlings to stand 2 to 3 inches apart in blocks or rows. Use thinnings in soups or stews. Carrots can be harvested young or allowed to mature. Keep dirt mounded around shoulders to prevent them from turning green. Forked roots indicate injury by stones, hairy carrots indicate an overfertile soil, and twisted roots indicate inadequate thinning. Excessive moisture from heavy rains or heavy watering after a

'Thumbelina'

period of drought can cause roots to crack. Store carrots in the garden through the winter by covering them with a deep mulch of straw or leaves anchored with black plastic to keep the ground from freezing. A 10-foot row yields 10 to 15 pounds of carrots.

CAULIFLOWER

'Snow Crown'

Hardiness: *cool-season annual*

Planting method: *transplants; direct sowing*

Plant spacing: *18 to 36 inches*

Light: *full sun*

Mounds of immature white or purplish flower buds called curds packed tightly into broad, domed heads on upright plants in early summer or fall. Use cauliflower raw for crudités or in salads. Purple cauliflower makes a colorful raw garnish but loses its tint when cooked.

Selected varieties: 'Early Snowball'—medium-sized heads on compact plants in 60 days. 'Early White Hybrid'—early-maturing variety with tight outer leaves that naturally blanch curds in 52 days. 'Green Goddess'—easy-to-grow variety with yellow-green curds that do not require blanching. 'Self Blanche'—tight outer leaves ensure naturally creamy white curds for fall crops in 71 days. 'Snow Ball'—early-maturing variety with medium-sized heads in 55 days. 'Snow Crown'—early-maturing, vigorous variety for spring or fall crops in 50 days. 'Violet Queen'—looser, broccoli-like purple heads with milder flavor for fall harvest in 54 days.

Growing conditions: Plant heat-sensitive cauliflower for early-spring or late-fall crops when it will have the cool daytime temperatures between 57° and 68° F it requires to produce heads. For spring crops, start transplants indoors 6 to 8 weeks before the last frost date and move outdoors into a rich garden soil amended with compost or other organic matter around the time of the last frost. Light frost does not harm transplants, but after a hard frost they may produce "buttons," immature heads only an inch or two across. Mulch to conserve moisture. For a late-fall or early-winter crop, sow seeds ½ inch deep 10 to 15 weeks before the first frost.

Keep cauliflower constantly moist but not soggy, and fertilize every 2 to 3

'Snow Ball'

weeks with fish emulsion or other organic fertilizer with at least 10 percent nitrogen. Use paper collars to foil cutworms, water sprays to remove aphids. Use Bt, handpicking, floating row covers, or parasitic wasps to thwart cabbageworms, flea beetles, cabbage loopers, and other insect pests. To minimize clubroot and other soil-borne diseases, do not plant cauliflower where other members of the cabbage family have been planted for at least 3 years.

Exposure to sun will discolor the curds. When the heads of varieties that are not self-blanching reach softball size, pull the outer leaves together over the curds and secure them with a rubber band or string; this covering will blanch the curds and keep them tender. The leaves of self-blanching varieties may need to be tied over the curds if heat wilts them. Harvest as soon as heads are full and firm; overmature heads become coarse or discolored. Each cauliflower plant produces a 1- to 2-pound head. A 10-foot row produces four to seven heads, depending on spacing.

CELERIAC

'Brilliant'

Hardiness: *warm-season annual*

Planting method: *transplants*

Plant spacing: *12 inches*

Light: *light shade to full sun*

Also called celery root. Ball-shaped roots with a nutty flavor that are harvested in fall when they are 2 to 4 inches in diameter. Shred celeriac raw for salads or cook like celery, which is a close relative.

Selected varieties: 'Brilliant'—smooth 3- to 4-inch roots with a creamy white interior in 110 days. 'Large Smooth Prague'—buff-colored roots in 110 days.

Growing conditions: Sow celeriac seeds ⅛ inch deep indoors 6 to 8 weeks before the last frost and keep them covered with a damp cloth until seedlings emerge. Transplant after all danger of frost is past into a constantly moist but well-drained soil enriched with compost, setting seedlings 12 inches apart. Feed at planting time and during the growing season with a balanced organic 5-10-10 fertilizer. Celeriac requires constant, even moisture and daytime temperatures between 55° and 85° F to grow. Harvest celeriac when roots are between 2 and 4 inches in diameter. Trim leaves and stems close to roots and discard. Roots keep well in the garden under heavy mulch for up to a month after the first frost. They can also be stored in damp sand at 40° F in a root cellar or other cool location. A 10-foot row yields 6 to 10 pounds of celeriac.

CELERY

'Utah'

Hardiness: *warm-season annual*

Planting method: *transplants*

Plant spacing: *6 to 9 inches*

Light: *full sun to light shade*

Crisp, succulent stalks enclosing a pale, leafy heart in early summer or fall. Use celery in salads, for hors d'oeuvres, as a side dish, and as an aromatic flavoring in soups and stews.

Selected varieties: 'Fordhook Giant'—stocky 15- to 18-inch plants ready to harvest in 120 days. 'Giant Pascal'—thick stalks, creamy hearts, and dark green foliage on 2-foot plants in 125 days. 'Golden Self-Blanching'—very early variety with golden yellow, almost stringless 2-foot stalks in 85 days. 'Utah 52-70 R Improved'—dark green stalks with excellent keeping quality on 26-inch disease-resistant plants in 105 days.

Growing conditions: Sow celery seeds ¼ inch deep indoors 6 to 8 weeks before last frost. When seedlings are about 4 inches tall and all danger of frost is past, transplant them to a constantly moist but well-drained garden soil enriched with compost; a pH between 5.8 and 6.7 is ideal. Set seedlings 6 to 9 inches apart. Sow seed directly in the garden in late spring for a fall crop. Feed at planting and about once a month during the growing season with a balanced 5-10-10 organic fertilizer. Celery requires daytime temperatures between 55° and 85° F to grow.

CELTUCE

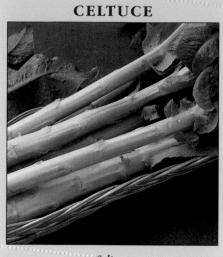

Celluco

Hardiness: *cool-season annual*

Planting method: *direct sowing; transplants*

Plant spacing: *12 inches*

Light: *full sun to light shade*

Tender spring leaves and succulent midribs on mature leaves in late spring to early summer. Use the tasty young leaves in salads or cook them as spring greens. Midribs have a consistency like that of artichoke hearts. Peel and eat them raw or cooked; they can be substituted in recipes calling for celery or asparagus. In frost-free areas, grow celtuce as a winter green.

Selected varieties: Sold only as celtuce; has rosettes of puckered, lobed leaves ready to eat in 45 days; the midribs are ready to harvest in 90 days.

Growing conditions: Start celtuce seeds indoors 4 weeks before the desired transplanting date, setting seeds ½ inch deep. Transplant outdoors as early as 4 weeks before the last frost, in time for the crop to mature before hot weather arrives. Celtuce prefers a loose soil amended with compost or other organic matter. Celtuce can also be sown directly outdoors 4 to 6 weeks before last frost for spring crops and 8 weeks before first frost for fall crops. Sow seed in wide bands and thin when seedlings are 2 inches tall. Provide ample water to keep leaves from becoming bitter and to keep midribs succulent.

CHARD, SWISS CHARD

'Rhubarb'

Hardiness: *warm-season annual*

Planting method: *direct sowing*

Plant spacing: *6 to 12 inches*

Light: *full sun to light shade*

Smooth or crinkled broad leaves with thick, crunchy midribs from late spring to fall. Actually a type of beet that lacks an edible root, chard is heat tolerant and provides a reliable crop of vitamin-rich greens throughout the summer, when many other greens bolt. Leaves have a flavor reminiscent of spinach, while the midribs are prepared like celery or asparagus. Some varieties may overwinter as perennials in milder climates. Plant chard in containers in a kitchen garden and use red-ribbed varieties in an edible landscape with carrots, nasturtiums, and other attractive vegetables and herbs.

Selected varieties: 'Fordhook Giant'—fleshy leaves with creamy white midribs up to 2½ inches across in 60 days. 'Large White Ribbed'—wide white midribs and veins on deep green, smooth leaves in 60 days. 'Lucullus'—pale green leaves and white stems in 60 days. 'Perpetual Spinach'—early variety with smooth, dark green leaves and very little midrib, ideal for cooking greens, in 50 days. 'Rhubarb'—thick, reddish green leaves and brilliant ruby red midribs and veins in 60 days. 'Swiss Chard of Geneva'—winter-hardy variety for year-round culture with large, celery-like midribs in 60 days.

Growing conditions: Sow chard outdoors just after the last frost, setting seeds ½ inch deep in well-drained soil enriched with organic matter; chard does not transplant well. It can be planted at any time throughout spring and summer up until 8 weeks before the first fall frost and is ideal for succeeding spring crops such as peas. Thin seedlings to stand 6 to 12 inches apart and use thinnings in salads and soups. Maintain a constant moisture level for the sweetest, most succulent leaves and midribs. Pick outer leaves continuously to keep new young leaves coming on, or cut entire plants 2 inches above the crown when leaves reach 6 inches or taller; plants will regrow from the deep, strong roots in 3 to 4 weeks for

'Lucullus'

harvesting again. Cutting plants back whenever leaves become too tough or coarse will stimulate them to produce tender young leaves. A 10-foot row yields approximately 5 pounds of chard.

CHAYOTE

Chayote

Hardiness: *Zones 8-10*

Planting method: *direct sowing*

Plant spacing: *10 to 15 feet*

Light: *full sun*

Also called vegetable pear. A member of the squash family with furrowed, pear-shaped green fruits on climbing vines in late summer to fall. Grow as a hot-season annual north of Zone 8. Use the mild-flavored young fruits like summer squashes and mature fruits like winter squashes. The single large seed has a nutty flavor. Harvest young shoots of established plants and prepare like asparagus or dig the large roots and use like potatoes. Also called mirliton or christophene.

Selected varieties: No named varieties; sold as chayote. Young fruits ready to harvest in 90 days and ½- to 1-pound mature fruits ready in 180 days.

Growing conditions: For each vine, plant an entire fruit, laying it at an angle with the stem end slightly exposed above the soil level. Ideal soil pH is between 5.5 and 6.5. Plant in pairs to ensure pollination needed for fruit set and provide a trellis, wall, or other support for the fast-growing vines to climb. Keep well watered. Begin harvesting when young fruits are 4 to 6 inches in length. Chayote can be stored in a cool location for up to 2 to 3 months. A well-grown vine typically bears about 35 fruits but may yield as many as 100 in ideal conditions.

COLLARDS

'Georgia'

Hardiness: *cool-season annual*

Planting method: *direct sowing*

Plant spacing: *12 to 18 inches*

Light: *full sun*

Tall rosettes of thick blue-green leaves with a mild cabbagelike flavor in summer or fall. Frost sweetens the flavor. Cook collards as a side dish or use in soups.

Selected varieties: 'Georgia'—heat-tolerant variety with loose rosettes of white-veined leaves in 70 to 80 days. 'Vates'—thick, broad leaves on compact, bolt-resistant plants in 75 days.

Growing conditions: A member of the cabbage family, collards tolerate heat better than kale and are more cold tolerant than cabbage, two closely related vegetables. Plant seed ½ inch deep outdoors 3 to 4 weeks before the last frost for harvesting from spring through summer, or in midsummer for a fall crop. Collards may overwinter in mild climates.

Keep collards constantly moist but not soggy, and fertilize every 2 to 3 weeks with fish emulsion or other organic fertilizer with at least 10 percent nitrogen. To minimize soil-borne diseases, do not plant collards where other members of the cabbage family have been planted for at least 3 years. Young leaves are ready to pick in 40 days. Twelve plants will supply a family of four with summer and fall greens.

CORN

'Silver Queen'

Hardiness: *hot-season annual*

Planting method: *direct sowing*

Plant spacing: *12 to 14 inches*

Light: *full sun*

Sweet, juicy yellow, white, or bicolored starchy kernels lining cylindrical cobs on stalks up to 9 feet tall in mid- to late summer. Plant breeders have improved both the taste and the keeping quality of sweet corn by manipulating the gene that makes sweet corn sweet to produce "sugar-enhanced" varieties that have a higher initial sugar content and a storage life 3 to 5 days longer than standard varieties. Also the result of breeding programs are "supersweet" varieties that have twice the sugar content of standard varieties and a storage life up to 10 days longer. Choose early, midseason, and late-maturing varieties for a succession of sweet corn through the end of summer. Sweet corn freezes well for long-term storage. Popcorn varieties are higher in starch and lower in sugar than sweet corn; the ears are harvested after the stalks have dried.

Selected varieties: Sweet corn varieties include: 'Burgundy Delight'—a midseason variety with bicolored kernels on 8-inch ears wrapped in burgundy-colored husks in 80 days. 'Butter and Sugar'—early variety with bicolored kernels on 7½-inch ears in 70 days. 'Earlivee'—early yellow variety with ears in 63 days, making it a good choice for short-season gardens or a succession planting to follow

spring crops such as peas or spinach. 'Golden Cross Bantam'—popular yellow hybrid with 8-inch ears in 85 days. 'Platinum Lady'—drought-resistant midseason variety with white kernels on 8-inch ears in 78 days. 'Silver Queen'—extremely sweet and tender late-season, blight- and wilt-resistant variety bearing white kernels on 9-inch ears in 92 days.

Sugar-enhanced varieties include: 'Bodacious'—midseason variety with yellow kernels on 8-inch ears in 80 days. 'Clockwork'—vigorous midseason variety that will germinate in cool soil with bicolored kernels on 8-inch ears in 78 days. 'Double Gem'—early variety that

'Lancelot'

will germinate in cool soil with tender, bicolored kernels on blocky, 8-inch ears in 70 days. 'Duet'—midseason variety with bicolored kernels on 9-inch ears wrapped in burgundy-tinged husks in 74 days. 'Lancelot'—wilt-resistant, drought-tolerant bicolored variety with 9-inch ears in 80 days. 'Miracle'—late season, rust-resistant variety with yellow kernels on large 9½-inch ears in 84 days. 'Pristine'—midseason variety with very sweet white kernels on 8½-inch ears in 76 days. 'Seneca Starshine'—early white variety with 8½-inch ears of exceptional keeping quality in 70 days. 'Sugar Buns'—early hybrid with creamy yellow kernels on 7½-inch ears in 70 days. 'Tuxedo'—wilt-resistant and drought-tolerant, midseason yellow variety with 8½-inch ears in 74 days.

Supersweet varieties include: 'Early Xtra Sweet'—early yellow hybrid with 9-inch ears in 70 days. 'How Sweet It Is'—midseason white variety with 8-inch ears in 88 days. 'Northern Xtra

Sweet'—early variety with yellow kernels on 7½-inch ears in 67 days. 'Skyline'—early bicolored variety that germinates in cool soil with very sweet kernels on 8-inch ears in 70 days. 'Starstruck'—late-maturing variety with

'Early Xtra Sweet'

bicolored kernels on 8- to 9-inch ears in 92 days.

Popcorn varieties include: 'Giant Yellow'—tender yellow kernels in 105 days. 'Mini-Blue'—stubby 2- to 4-inch ears with tiny blue kernels for decorative use or popping in 100 days. 'Robust 20-70'—late-maturing yellow variety with high popping volume in 98 days. 'White Cloud'—late white variety with 5-inch ears in 95 days. 'Yellow Hybrid'—deep yellow kernels in 89 days.

Growing conditions: Corn needs a long, hot summer for good growth; days to maturity are a less reliable measure of when a variety will ripen than the number of hot days. Plant seeds 1 to 2 inches deep when the temperature of the soil is at least 60° F, in late spring to early summer; supersweet varieties need very warm, moist soil to germinate well. Row covers help to speed the germination and growth of early varieties in cool soil. Since corn is pollinated by the wind, sow seed in blocks of at least four rows to ensure good pollination. If you are planting more than one variety, choose varieties with maturity dates at least 14 days apart to avoid cross-pollination. If space allows, you can also prevent cross-pollination by planting different varieties at least 250 feet apart.

Thin plants to stand 12 to 14 inches apart; closer spacing lowers yields and encourages fungal diseases. When the first sowing is knee high, plant a second variety to extend the harvest season. To ensure that ears on the edges of the blocks get pollinated, strip pollen from the tassels and sprinkle it on the silks. Provide ample water throughout the growing season and feed corn with a balanced 5-10-10 organic fertilizer when stalks are knee high and again when silks become visible at the tips of the ears. Rotate corn with other crops to control both pests and diseases.

Harvest sweet corn 3 weeks after silks appear; the highest ear on the stalk

'How Sweet It Is'

ripens first. Allow popcorn stalks to dry, then harvest ears, pull husks back, and hang in a well-ventilated area to finish drying. Sweet corn and popcorn produce one or two ears per stalk.

CORN SALAD, MACHE

'Vit'

Hardiness:	*winter-hardy Zones 5-9*
Planting method:	*direct sowing*
Plant spacing:	*2 inches*
Light:	*full sun*

Mounded rosettes of tender smooth greens with a mild nutty flavor prized for salads in spring or fall in northern gardens and throughout the winter in mild regions. Also called lamb's lettuce.

Selected varieties: 'Big Seed', also called 'Grosse Graine'—smooth, round, bright green leaves in 45 days. 'Coquille'—cold-tolerant variety with spoon-shaped, cupped leaves in 45 days. 'D'Etampes'—prominently veined, smooth, round leaves on compact, cold-tolerant plants good for overwintering. 'Elan'—short, smooth shiny upright leaves; especially suitable for fall and winter crops where the weather is cold and wet because of its mildew resistance. 'Verte des Cambrai'—pest-resistant and very cold-tolerant compact rosettes of 3- to 4-inch flat round leaves in 60 days. 'Vit'—very vigorous variety with long, glossy leaves and a minty flavor, especially good for overwintering.

Growing conditions: Plant corn salad ½ inch deep in very early spring 2 to 4 weeks before the last frost or in late summer to early fall; corn salad grows best at temperatures below 75° F. Keep constantly moist. Mulch fall crops lightly after frost to keep them growing into winter. Fall-planted corn salad will resume growth the following spring.

CRESS

Watercress

Hardiness:	*Zones 6-9; cool-season annual*
Planting method:	*transplants; direct sowing*
Plant spacing:	*4 inches*
Light:	*full sun to light shade*

Plants of three different species that go by the same common name because their leaves have a similar peppery flavor. Two of these cresses grow in ordinary garden soil, while the third is an aquatic plant that requires constant moisture. Use any of the cresses for garnishes, add to sandwiches for a crunchy bite, and add to salads to complement the blander taste of tender lettuces. Sprout cress seeds for use in salads, sandwiches, stir-fry dishes, and casseroles.

Selected species: Curly cress, also called broadleaf cress, garden cress, mountain grass, peppergrass *(Lepidium sativum)* —cool-season annual with finely cut, tightly frilled leaves in 10 to 21 days; seeds are especially recommended for sprouting. Watercress *(Nasturtium officinale)*—aquatic perennial with broad, mildly pungent leaves and succulent stems in 60 days. Winter cress, upland cress *(Barbarea verna)*—hardy biennial grown as a cool-season annual with smooth leaves on 6- to 8-inch stalks in 60 days.

Growing conditions: Plant curly cress 4 to 6 weeks before the last frost. Make successive sowings every 2 weeks until 2 weeks after the last frost for a continuous supply of fresh greens until plants bolt in summer heat. Sow fall crop starting 2 to

4 weeks before the first frost; plants will tolerate severe frost. Harvest by snipping stems about an inch above the plant's base; the plant will send up new growth two or three times. Indoors, sprout seeds on wet paper towels, cover with glass, and keep warm until seeds sprout, then allow to grow to about 4 inches tall, keeping towels constantly moist.

Sow winter cress ¼ inch deep in full sun to light shade in late fall or winter. Keep soil constantly moist but not wet. Thin to 4 inches. Harvest leaves from winter until

Upland Cress

late spring or early summer, when they become bitter. Seed can also be sown in early spring for harvest in 7 weeks.

Sow watercress indoors in containers, pressing seeds into the soil and covering containers with glass or plastic until seeds germinate. Transplant seedlings to individual pots, then transplant to constantly moist soil on bank of a pond or stream in full sun 2 to 4 weeks before the last frost; weight roots down with pebbles until they anchor themselves. Pinch plants back when they are 6 inches tall. Alternatively, grow watercress indoors in a container set in a saucer of water that is changed daily; when grown in soil, watercress needs indirect light to keep from becoming bitter. Pinch flower buds off; leaves become bitter if plants are allowed to bloom.

CUCUMBERS

'Marketmore 76'

Hardiness: *warm-season annual*

Planting method: *transplants; direct sowing*

Plant spacing: *12 inches*

Light: *full sun*

Oblong, cylindrical, mildly flavored succulent fruits with green skins on climbing vines or low bushy plants. Use juicy 8- to 10-inch slicing cucumbers fresh in salads and as a garnish. Crisp, stubby varieties, including dwarf cornichon types, have been specially bred for making pickles and relishes. Dwarf bush cucumbers require only one-third the space of vining types and are ideal for small garden plots or containers. Allow cucumber vines to sprawl in the garden among cornstalks or train vines on trellises or fences for edible landscaping. Gynecious varieties, which bear only female flowers, are noted for their very high yields. To ensure pollination and fruit production of gynecious cucumbers, plant at least one monoecious variety—that is, a type that bears both male and female flowers.

Selected varieties: Cornichon types include: 'Verte de Massy'—with very slim, 4-inch, bumpy fruits.

Bush types include: 'Bush Pickle'—heavy crop of early-maturing 4- to 5-inch fruits on compact 24-inch plants in 45 days. 'Salad Bush'—disease- and wilt-resistant plants with 8-inch fruits in 58 days. 'Spacemaster'—7- to 8-inch cucumbers in 62 days on compact, mosaic-resistant plants suitable for containers or hanging baskets.

Pickling types include: 'Boston'—extremely prolific vines with early crop of smooth 6- to 7-inch tapered fruits in 58 days. 'Early Green Cluster'—large crop of deep green, 5- to 6-inch fruits suitable for pickling or slicing in 55 days. 'Gherkin'—2- to 3-inch fruits ideal for sweet pickles in 60 days. 'Little Leaf'—very disease-resistant, high-yielding vines with small fruits in 70 days. 'Miss Pickler'—gynecious variety producing a large crop of uniform fruits. 'Saladin'—large crop of knobby, crisp 4- to 5-inch fruits on mildew- and disease-resistant gynecious vines in 55 days.

Slicing types include: 'Burpee Hybrid II'—gynecious plants producing straight 8-inch fruits in 55 days. 'Burpless'—somewhat disease-tolerant hybrid with 10- to 12-inch fruits that are more easily digested than those of other varieties, in

'Salad Bush'

62 days. 'Early Pride'—large crop of 8½-inch fruits on mildew- and mosaic-resistant vines in 55 days. 'Early Surecrop'—vigorous, mildew-resistant variety with 8- to 9½-inch fruits in 58 days. 'Fanfare Hybrid'—disease- and mildew-resistant semidwarf with slender, 8- to 9-inch fruits in 63 days. 'Marketmore 76'—vines with exceptional disease resistance producing 8-inch fruits in 67 days. 'Poinsett 76'—early to midseason variety with wilt and mildew resistance bearing 7½-inch fruits in 63 days. 'Slicemaster'—early crop of 8-inch fruits on disease- and wilt-resistant gynecious vines in 55 days. 'Straight Eight'—slightly striped 8-inch fruits in 63 days. 'Sweet Slice'—very mild burpless 10- to 12-inch fruits on disease- and mildew-resistant vines in 63 days. 'Sweet Success'—mildew-resistant

vines bearing seedless, burpless 14-inch fruits in 54 days.

Growing conditions: Start cucumbers indoors 4 to 6 weeks before the last frost or direct-sow 2 to 3 weeks after last frost, setting seed 1 inch deep in rows and thinning plants to stand 12 inches apart. Alternatively, plant five or six seeds in hills spaced 6 feet apart and thin to two

'Burpless'

or three plants. If you have planted a gynecious (female) variety with a monoecious pollinator, be sure to mark the pollinator so it is not accidentally thinned out. Monoecious cucumbers have green seeds, and gynecious types have beige seeds. There should be 1 pollinator plant for every 5 or 6 female plants. Provide ample water. Mulch to conserve moisture and reduce fruit rot. Plant disease-resistant varieties; remove and destroy any infected plants.

Pick cucumbers often to keep vines productive. They are ready to harvest when the flower falls off the blossom end. For best flavor and texture, pick them promptly, before seeds enlarge and toughen; a yellowish tinge at the blossom end signals an overmature fruit. Use a sharp knife to cut cucumbers from the vine to avoid injury to stems. Twenty-five plants yield approximately 30 pounds of cucumbers.

EGGPLANT

'White Egg'

Hardiness: *warm-season annual*

Planting method: *transplants; direct sowing*

Plant spacing: *18 to 24 inches*

Light: *full sun*

Glossy, smooth-skinned, shiny deep purple to lavender or white fruits with mild-flavored, soft flesh. Depending on the variety, fruits range in size from 1 to 12 inches or more. The low-growing, small-fruited varieties make excellent container plants. All parts of the plant except the fruits are poisonous.

Selected varieties: 'Bambino'—extremely heavy yields of rounded purple fruits only 1 to 2 inches in diameter on disease-resistant foot-high plants 60 days after transplanting. 'Black Beauty'—very heavy yield of glossy black-purple, almost round fruits 80 days after transplanting. 'Classic'—long, slim, glossy black-purple fruits on vigorous plants 76 days after transplanting. 'Ichiban'—slender fruits 12 inches long and 1½ inches in diameter 58 days after transplanting on bushy 3-foot plants ideal for small gardens. 'Neon'—large yield of cylindrical, dark pink fruits completely free of bitterness 60 days from transplanting. 'Slim Jim'—slender 4- to 6-inch lavender to deep purple fruits on compact plants with handsome lavender-tinged foliage 75 days after transplanting, suitable for containers. 'Violette di Firenze'—large oblong to round, deep lavender fruits, sometimes with white stripes. 'White Egg', also called 'Osterei' or 'Easter Egg'—clusters of 2- to 3-inch oval white fruits 52 days after transplanting on bushy 2-foot plants ideal for containers.

Growing conditions: Eggplant requires long, warm seasons to mature. In areas with a long growing season, sow seed ¼ to ½ inch deep directly in the garden when soil temperature is 70° F. Elsewhere, start indoors 8 to 10 weeks before last frost and set plants out about 2 to 3 weeks after the last frost, when night temperatures will remain above 50° F. Space plants 18 to 24 inches apart in

'Black Beauty'

rows 3 feet apart and stake to keep fruits growing straight. Use floating row covers to speed the growth of transplants and control insects. Feed biweekly with a side dressing of fish emulsion or manure tea and water well, especially from flowering through harvest. To control verticillium wilt, do not plant eggplant where tomatoes, peppers, or strawberries have grown the year before. Avoid working among plants after smoking to prevent introduction of tobacco mosaic virus. Harvest eggplant before the skin loses its shine; an overmature eggplant is dull and likely to be bitter. Cut the stem with shears or a knife and clip eggplant from stems; pick continuously to keep plants producing. A 10-foot row yields 7 to 8 pounds of eggplant.

ENDIVE and ESCAROLE

'Batavian'

Hardiness:	*cool-season annuals*
Planting method:	*direct sowing*
Plant spacing:	*8 to 12 inches*
Light:	*full sun to light shade*

Tender, piquant greens with distinctively different leaf shapes. Endive has rather slender, curly, finely cut leaves in loose, flat rosettes, while the broad, somewhat twisted or ruffled leaves of escarole form open, upright heads. Endive and escarole are most often used in salads but are also delicious cooked as side dishes or in soups. The gourmet vegetable called Belgian endive is actually not an endive but a type of chicory.

Selected varieties: Endive types include: 'Green Curled Ruffec'—a cold-tolerant endive good for fall planting with lacy dark green outer leaves and a creamy white heart in prostrate rosettes 15 to 17 inches across in 95 days. 'Salad King'—vigorous endive variety with deeply cut, curly dark green leaves with a pale green heart in spreading 2-foot plants that withstand light frost and are heat resistant and slow to bolt in 100 days. 'Tres Fin', also called 'Fine Curled'—lacy dark green leaves with a white midrib and creamy blanched heart in 60 to 70 days on spreading 10- to 12-inch plants that are slow to bolt.

Broad-leaved escarole types include: 'Batavian'—crumpled yellow-green outer leaves with fleshy, white midribs surrounding creamy white hearts in 85 days. 'Cornet d'Anjou'—loose head of very broad leaves with fan-shaped midribs in spring or fall that can be blanched to mellow its flavor.

Growing conditions: Plant endive and escarole for spring or fall crops; in summer leaves become bitter and plants go to seed. Sow spring crops outdoors 4 weeks before the last frost, setting seed ¼ inch deep; sow fall crops in midsummer. Space plants that will be blanched 8 inches apart; otherwise, allow 12 inches between plants. Overcrowding encourages rot. Interplant escarole and endive among herbs and lettuce or in the shade of tomatoes. Keep the soil constantly moist and side-dress biweekly with weak manure tea or fish emulsion. In warm weather, escarole types are

'Salad King'

prone to bitterness, which can be prevented by blanching. To blanch, tie the outer leaves together around the inner heart for 2 to 3 weeks. In humid climates blanching may cause rot.

To harvest, pick individual leaves or cut entire plant at the soil line. If only the central core of leaves is removed and outer leaves are left in place, plants will sprout a new, smaller center in 3 to 4 weeks.

GARLIC

'California Silverskin'

Hardiness:	*Zones 3-8*
Planting method:	*cloves*
Plant spacing:	*3 to 6 inches*
Light:	*full sun to light shade*

Plump, pungently aromatic bulbs composed of wedge-shaped cloves in midsummer. Softneck garlic varieties produce medium-sized, intensely flavored cloves surrounding several overlapping inner layers of small bulbs. These varieties have good keeping quality and are excellent for braiding. Stiffneck garlic, the most cold-hardy type, produces both underground bulbs, composed of four to six mildly flavored, easy-to-peel cloves with no inner layer, and clusters of tiny bulblets atop coiled stalks called scapes; save the bulblets for planting the next year's crop. Elephant garlic has very large, mild bulbs that are delicious raw or baked whole. Use spring greens like chives and cut flowers for bouquets.

Selected varieties: 'California Silverskin' —softneck garlic with pearly white, sometimes yellow-veined bulbs composed of up to 20 cloves; excellent keeping quality. 'Elephant Garlic'—large 2½- to 3-inch bulbs composed of four to six enormous cloves. 'German Red'—stiffneck type with bright purple ¼-pound bulbs composed of up to 12 yellow-fleshed cloves. 'German White Stiffneck'—a stiffneck type with five or six plump cloves forming large bulbs. 'Italian Purple'—stiffneck garlic producing medium-sized bulbs striped with purple;

biting flavor. 'New York Strains'—very cold-hardy softneck garlic with a purple blush on papery white skins. 'Rocambole'—stiffneck garlic type with fat, mild-flavored bulbs. 'Spanish Roja Garlic'—softneck type with a particularly sharp, biting flavor. Spring plantings of all types mature in 120 to 150 days; fall plantings mature the following summer.

Growing conditions: Separate the garlic cloves and plant them with the pointed tip up about 1½ to 2 inches deep in com-

'German White Stiffneck'

post-enriched soil starting 6 weeks before first frost and continuing until early winter; alternatively, plant in early to midspring. Mulch to prevent heaving. Garlic will grow in light shade, producing smaller bulbs than it does when grown in full sun. Spring-planted crops also yield smaller bulbs. Pinch the coiled scapes of stiffneck garlic as they appear, to produce larger bulbs instead of a dual crop of bulbs and bulblets. Harvest by forking out of ground in summer when tops begin to yellow. Use bruised bulbs immediately or freeze. Cure unblemished bulbs for several days on screens in a well-ventilated place, then braid them, hang in bunches, or put in mesh bags and store in a dry, cool area until needed.

JERUSALEM ARTICHOKES

'French Mammoth White'

Hardiness: *Zones 6-9*

Planting method: *root cuttings*

Plant spacing: *12 to 24 inches*

Light: *full sun*

Small, knobby, round tubers with a crunchy texture and nutty flavor from late summer through fall. Peel Jerusalem artichokes and slice raw for salads, use like water chestnuts, or prepare like potatoes. During the growing season the tall foliage can serve as a screen for the vegetable garden.

Selected varieties: 'French Mammoth White'—clumps of egg-sized tubers in 110 to 150 days and stout 6- to 10-foot stalks bearing 3-inch yellow blossoms resembling sunflowers.

Growing conditions: Plant small whole tubers or pieces of Jerusalem artichoke with two or three eyes each 4 to 6 inches deep in spring, allowing 3 feet between rows. Jerusalem artichoke thrives in a dry, infertile soil, so water and fertilize sparingly. Remove flower buds as they form to encourage greater root growth. Dig tubers as needed or store in sand in a cool location. They can also be mulched and stored in the ground over the winter. Jerusalem artichoke sprouts readily from tubers or pieces left in the ground and can become invasive.

JICAMA

Jicama

Hardiness: *hot-season annual*

Planting method: *transplants*

Plant spacing: *1 to 2 feet*

Light: *full sun*

Large, round tubers with crispy, sweet white flesh resembling water chestnuts in fall. Slice jicama into fruit or vegetable salads, use in place of crackers for hors d'oeuvres, or fry like potatoes. Leaves, flowers, and seeds and ripe seedpods are all poisonous.

Selected varieties: Sold only as jicama, a climbing vine with large, heart-shaped leaves, pealike purple flowers, and a single rounded to heart-shaped tuber up to 6 inches in diameter with smooth, brown-gray skin in 120 to 180 days.

Growing conditions: Start jicama seeds indoors 8 to 10 weeks before last frost and set transplants outdoors into a loose, fertile soil enriched with compost as soon as soil warms; soak seeds for best germination. Provide a trellis or other support for vines. Pinch growing tips when vines reach 3 feet and remove all flower buds to produce the largest tubers. Dig tubers before the first frost. Jicama requires a 9-month growing season to reach full size; roots grown in a shorter growing season will be proportionally smaller.

KALE

'Dwarf Blue Curled Scotch Vates'

Hardiness: *cool-season annual*

Planting method: *direct sowing; transplants*

Plant spacing: *8 to 12 inches*

Light: *full sun to light shade*

Dense rosettes of ruffled and curled succulent leaves in multiple shades of green and blue-green with a mild cabbage flavor in spring or fall; tastes best in the fall, when a touch of frost sweetens flavor. Greens can even be harvested beneath a blanket of snow for a fresh winter vegetable. Use spring thinnings and crunchy young kale leaves in salads or as a garnish. Cook greens in soups, side dishes, and casseroles, making sure to discard the tough midrib before preparing. The bold rosettes are attractive accents in beds, borders, or containers.

Selected varieties: 'Blue Siberian'—a dwarf variety with ruffled blue-green leaves in open rosettes up to 2 feet across in 70 days. 'Dwarf Blue Curled Scotch Vates'—very early variety with tightly curled leaves on low-spreading 12- to 14-inch plants from seed in 55 days; not as cold tolerant as other varieties. 'Red Russian', also called 'Ragged Jack'—heirloom variety with wavy, oak-like leaves on tall plants that turn from blue-green to deep purple-red when touched by frost in 48 days. 'Winterbor'—very cold-tolerant variety with curly green leaves in 60 days on large plants 3 feet tall and 2 feet wide that regrow vigorously when picked for a continuous harvest.

Growing conditions: For spring crops, plant seed outdoors 4 to 6 weeks before the last frost, setting seeds ½ inch deep in rows 2 to 3 feet apart. Make successive sowings that will mature before hot weather induces semidormancy and leaves become bitter and tough. For fall and winter crops, make successive sowings starting 6 to 8 weeks before the first frost. Plant kale in moist, well-drained fertile loam enriched with compost and use mulch to retain moisture. Feed growing plants every 2 weeks with fish emulsion or any other balanced organic

'Red Russian'

fertilizer that provides ample nitrogen to support leaf growth. To minimize clubroot and other soil-borne diseases, do not plant kale where other members of the cabbage family have been planted for at least 3 years.

To harvest, remove outer leaves for a continuous supply of greens or cut whole plant at the soil line. Kale can be stored over winter in the garden and harvested as needed. It will keep for several weeks after cutting if refrigerated. A 10-foot row produces about 5 pounds of kale.

KOHLRABI

'Early Purple Vienna'

Hardiness: *cool-season annual*

Planting method: *transplants; direct sowing*

Plant spacing: *4 to 6 inches*

Light: *full sun to light shade*

Pale green or purplish bulbs with a very mild cabbagelike flavor in late spring or fall. Eat young kohlrabi raw out of hand like apples, slice into salads, or steam or parboil for side dishes.

Selected varieties: 'Early Purple Vienna'—greenish white flesh beneath purple skin in 60 days, recommended for fall planting. 'Early White Vienna'—an especially cold-tolerant variety with 2-inch pale green bulbs in 55 days, recommended for fall planting. 'Grand Duke'—small bulbs with crisp, tender white flesh on compact plants in 45 days, especially recommended for spring planting.

Growing conditions: For a spring crop, sow seed indoors in peat pots 6 to 8 weeks before setting outdoors—anytime from 5 weeks before the last frost until 2 weeks after—in soil enriched with compost. For a fall crop, sow seeds ½ inch deep outdoors in mid- to late summer; light frost improves flavor. Harvest when bulbs are 2 inches across; older bulbs become woody and fibrous. Kohlrabi can be grown in light shade but if so produces elongated, rather than round, bulbs that aren't as crisp in texture. A 10-foot row yields 5 to 8 pounds of bulbs.

LEEKS

'Large American Flag'

Hardiness: *cool-season annual*

Planting method: *transplants; direct sowing*

Plant spacing: *4 to 6 inches*

Light: *full sun to light shade*

Thick white stems and broad, flat green leaves with a mild onion flavor in fall and winter. Use like onions for flavoring, garnishes, salads, soups, and side dishes.

Selected varieties: 'Alaska'—thick, sweet stems, good for overwintering, in 125 days. 'Blue Solaise'—short 4- to 6-inch stems in 140 days. 'King Richard'—early variety maturing in 75 days; will withstand frost to 20° F but is not winter hardy. 'Large American Flag', also called 'Broad London'—stems 1 to 1½ inches thick, very cold tolerant and excellent for overwintering, in 120 days. 'Winter Giant'—very tall, thick stems, good for overwintering.

Growing conditions: For fall harvest, sow leeks ¼ inch deep indoors 8 to 12 weeks before the last frost date. Bury transplants up to their leaf joints in a narrow trench 8 to 12 inches deep. As leeks grow, gradually fill trench in to develop thick, blanched stalks. For a winter or early-spring crop, sow seed of cold-hardy varieties outdoors from late spring to early summer. Where winter temperatures fall below 20° F, mulch with 12 to 18 inches of straw or leaves. Leeks will also keep for up to 8 weeks if dug before the ground freezes and packed in damp sand or sawdust in a cool place. A 10-foot row yields up to 30 pounds of leeks.

LETTUCE

'Buttercrunch'

Hardiness: *cool-season annual*

Planting method: *direct sowing; transplants*

Plant spacing: *4 to 14 inches*

Light: *full sun to light shade*

Loose rosettes or firm heads of delectable leaves from spring to early summer and again from early to late fall when a succession of different varieties is planted. Crisphead varieties have tight, firm heads that are blanched at the center. They require a very long growing season and are lowest in nutrients of all lettuce types. Butterhead or Boston varieties have tender, easily bruised leaves folded into loose heads with creamy blanched centers; they contain vitamins A and C as well as calcium and iron. Leaf or bunching varieties form open rosettes of curly, puckered leaves that are easy to grow, mature quickly, and are very nutritious, with high levels of vitamins A and C, and calcium. The stiff, erect leaves of romaine or cos varieties fold into upright heads that blanch at their centers; more heat tolerant than other types, they are similar nutritionally to leaf varieties.

Lettuce reigns as the supreme green in salads. Sauté lettuce alone or with other greens as a side dish, add whole or shredded leaves to soups, tuck into sandwiches, or use as a garnish.

Selected varieties: Crisphead varieties, also called Batavian or iceberg lettuces, include: 'Great Lakes'—a cold-tolerant, slow-to-bolt variety with crisp, juicy leaves in 82 to 90 days. 'Iceberg'—

creamy blanched centers and deep green outer leaves in 85 days. 'Ithaca'—bolt-resistant variety best for spring crops in 72 days. 'Red Grenoble'—slow-to-bolt spring lettuce with wine red leaves, to cut as needed when young or allow to develop into heads. 'Rosy'—slow-to-bolt variety with burgundy-tinged leaves in small heads. 'Summertime'—very bolt-resistant medium-sized heads of crisp leaves in 68 days.

'Green Ice'

Butterhead or Boston lettuce varieties include: 'Bibb'—3½-inch heads of deep green leaves in 75 days. 'Buttercrunch'—thick, dark green leaves in firm heads with buttery yellow centers on heat-resistant plants in 53 to 65 days. 'Dark Green Boston'—tight heads of deep green leaves in 70 days. 'Four Seasons', also called 'Merveille des Quatre Saisons'—large 16-inch heads of bronze-tinged outer leaves around a tender, pale green inner heart in 49 to 65 days; best for spring planting because of its tendency to bolt. 'Tom Thumb'—firm miniature heads of medium green leaves ideal as an individual serving in 52 to 60 days.

Leaf or bunching lettuce varieties include: 'Black-Seeded Simpson'—fast-growing, heat-tolerant variety with crisp, highly frilled leaves in 45 days. 'Green Ice'—very slow-to-bolt rosettes of sweet, deep green, crinkled leaves in 45 days. 'Oakleaf'—deeply lobed, tender leaves on slow-to-bolt plants in 45 to 55 days. 'Prizehead'—frilly red-tinged leaves in large, loose heads in 48 days. 'Red Sails'—bolt-resistant variety with large crumpled leaves fringed with red in broad, open heads up to a foot across in 45 days. 'Ruby'—heat-tolerant variety with frilled, curly leaves shading from deep burgundy to pale green in 47 days. 'Salad Bowl'—rosettes of bright green, frilly leaves in 60 days in cool weather, ideal for spring planting.

Romaine or cos lettuce varieties include: 'Cimarron Red'—compact heads with crinkled, red-tinged leaves in 58 days. 'Little Gem', also called 'Diamond Gem'—crisp miniature heads 4 inches across and 6 inches tall with creamy blanched centers in 45 to 56 days. 'Paris Island Cos'—thick-ribbed, dense 12-inch-tall heads with blanched hearts in 65 days. 'Rosalita' thick-ribbed summer lettuce with oval, curly leaves in dense heads in 62 days. 'Rouge d'Hiver'—very large heads of broad, deep red leaves enfolding crisp hearts, best for fall planting, in 60 days. 'Winter Density'—extremely frost-tolerant cross between

'Oakleaf'

cos and butterhead types, good for fall planting in 65 days.

Growing conditions: Plant lettuce seeds ¼ to ½ inch deep outdoors in a moisture-retentive, compost-enriched soil as soon as the ground can be worked in spring. In areas where the cool growing season is short, start seeds of long-season crisphead, butterhead, and romaine crops 4 to 6 weeks before the last frost date. Lettuce is very shallow rooted; keep soil evenly moist for continuous growth and sweetest flavor. Loosehead and butterhead varieties tolerate light shade, especially as summer heat approaches. Lettuce grows best in cool soil at cool temperatures. Make small successive sowings of different varieties for a continuous supply of lettuce until summer temperatures of 85° F cause plants to

bolt and leaves to become bitter. Sow again in early fall when daytime temperatures become cool again.

Proper thinning of lettuce is critical to success; thin crisphead or butterhead varieties to stand 12 to 14 inches apart, leaf or romaine varieties to stand 4 to 6 inches at first and later to 6 to 10 inches apart

'Red Sails'

depending on the variety. Use thinnings in salads or transplant to another spot for a later harvest. To harvest, pull up the entire head of crisphead or butterhead varieties. Pick outer leaves of loosehead or cos varieties as they mature, or cut entire plant off at the base; it will regrow a second, smaller crop of leaves. A 10-foot row yields 10 heads of head lettuce or 9 pounds of leaf lettuce.

MELONS

'Earlisweet' Muskmelon

Hardiness: *warm-season annual*

Planting method: *transplants; direct sowing*

Plant spacing: *18 to 36 inches*

Light: *full sun*

Round or oval fruits with sweet, juicy, often aromatic flesh enclosed in a hard rind on sprawling vines. Muskmelons, sometimes incorrectly called cantaloupes, have a deeply ribbed, heavily netted rind and orange flesh with a musky aroma. Charentais-type cantaloupes, or true cantaloupes, are small, round orange-fleshed melons with smooth rinds and no netting. Honeydew, Crenshaw, and casaba melons are large, smooth-skinned melons with pale green or orange flesh that has a fruity rather than a musky aroma. Oval or round, smooth-skinned watermelons have deliciously sweet and exceptionally juicy, crisp red or yellow flesh with seeds scattered throughout rather than in the central seed cavity found in other types of melons.

Selected varieties: Netted muskmelon types include: 'Alaska'—with very early oval melons with deep salmon flesh in 72 days. 'Ambrosia'—3- to 5-pound melons with thick peach-colored flesh and small seed cavities on disease-resistant vines in 86 days. 'Casablanca'—mildew-resistant vines bearing 4-pound melons with soft-textured, juicy, creamy white flesh tinged with pink in 85 days. 'Earlisweet'—very early-maturing 5-inch fruits with deep salmon flesh in 70 days, resistant to fusarium wilt. 'Hale's Best Jumbo'—4-pound melons with thick salmon flesh on drought-tolerant vines in 86 days. 'Hearts of Gold'—an extremely sweet salmon-fleshed variety with small seed cavities in 90 days. 'Musketeer'—compact vines only 2½ to 3 feet long bearing 3-pound fruits with fragrant, light orange flesh in 90 days. 'Super Market'—wilt- and mildew-resistant vines bearing 4-pound melons with thick, bruise-resistant rinds and juicy orange flesh in 84 days. 'Sweet Bush'—very compact vines ideal for small gardens bearing 2-pound melons in 74 days. 'Topmark'—wilt-resistant oval melons with orange flesh and a small seed cavity in 90 days.

Charentais-type cantaloupes include: 'Alienor'—round, 2-pound fruits with

'Alaska' Muskmelon

pale, smooth skins and deep orange flesh in 90 days or sooner if vines are pruned to force earlier maturity. 'Charentais'—exceptionally sweet heirloom variety from France that ripens in 75 to 85 days even in cool areas. 'Pancha'—wilt- and mildew-resistant vines bearing 2-pound fruits with aromatic flesh in 80 days. 'Savor'—2½-pound melons with pale gray-green skin and deliciously aromatic flesh on disease-resistant vines in 78 days.

Honeydew melons include: 'Earlidew' —vigorous, disease-tolerant vines recommended for gardens in the East and Midwest, with fruits that have aromatic, pale yellow-green flesh in 75 to 80 days. 'Orange Flesh'—late-maturing 4- to 6-pound round melons with sweet salmon-colored flesh in 90 days; 'Venus'—with heavy crops of 5½-inch oval fruits with a golden yellow rind enclosing bright green sweet flesh in 88 days.

Watermelon varieties include: 'Black

Diamond'—enormous round melons up to 50 pounds each with dark green skins and bright red flesh in 90 days. 'Bush Baby II'—very compact, space-saving vines bearing round 10-pound melons in 80 to 90 days. 'Charleston Gray'—wilt-

'Orange Flesh' Honeydew Melon

resistant and drought-tolerant vines with 28- to 35-pound melons that store well in 90 days. 'Crimson Sweet'—round 25-pound melons with skin striped light and dark green and firm, deep red flesh on disease-resistant vines in 80 days. 'Redball Seedless'—round 12-pound melons with glossy green skin and only a few white, edible seeds in 80 days. 'Sugar Baby'—10-inch round fruits with red flesh in 80 days. 'Yellow Baby'—small melons up to 7 inches in diameter with crisp yellow flesh in 80 days.

Miscellaneous melons include: 'Casaba Golden Beauty'—7- to 8-pound oval melon with wrinkled golden skin, white flesh, and a small seed cavity in 110 days. 'Crenshaw'—large, oval melons up to 14 pounds each with very tender peach-colored flesh and a small seed cavity in 90 days. 'Galia'—a tropical melon with pale green, very sweet flesh and a flavor reminiscent of banana in 75 days. 'Jaune des Canaries'—oval melon with slightly wrinkled green skin turning yellow when ripe and whitish green flesh in 100 to 110 days. 'Passport'—3½- to 4-pound tropical melon with thick, juicy pale green flesh with a banana-like aroma in 70 to 78 days.

Growing conditions: Start melons indoors 4 to 6 weeks before the last frost or direct-sow 2 to 3 weeks after the last frost, setting seed ½ inch deep in rows and thinning plants to stand 18 to 36 inches apart. Allow 4 to 6 feet between

rows. For direct sowing, plant five or six seeds in hills spaced 6 feet apart after the soil has warmed and thin to two or three plants. Choose compact bush-type vines for gardens that lack space for sprawling melon vines.

Melons grow best when the soil temperature is 70° F or more and need hot, dry weather in late summer and early fall to produce good fruit; air or soil temperatures below 50° F cause damage. Use black plastic mulch to warm soil and

'Crimson Sweet' Watermelon

keep fruits clean. Water well during early stages of growth and when plants are blooming and pollinating. Use floating row covers to protect young plants from insect pests, but remove row covers when plants blossom so flowers will be pollinated. After fruit sets, withhold water (unless conditions become very dry) in order to concentrate sugars in the fruits, which need 2 to 3 weeks to ripen.

Powdery mildew attacks melon seedlings and vines with heavy fruit set in cool, damp weather; once leaves become mildewed, fruit will not ripen. Melons do not ripen off the vine.

Thumb pressure at the blossom end causes ripe cantaloupes to slip from their vines. Harvest tropical melons as the deep green skin changes to buff-yellow. Watermelons are ripe when the tendril closest to the fruit stem on the vine browns or when the part of the rind resting on the ground turns yellow. Each vine produces two to four fruits.

MUSTARD GREENS

'Florida Broadleaf'

Hardiness: *cool-season annual*

Planting method: *direct sowing*

Plant spacing: *4 to 6 inches*

Light: *full sun*

Smooth or highly frilled leaves with a pungent flavor in early spring or late fall. Pick young leaves to add zest and crunch to salads; parboil mature leaves for side dishes or use as a garnish.

Selected varieties: 'Florida Broadleaf'—smooth, lobed oval leaves with a white midrib in 45 days. 'Fordhook Fancy'—heat-tolerant variety with rather mild-flavored, deeply curled and fringed leaves in 40 days. 'Green Wave'—bright green leaves with tightly frilled edges in 45 days. 'Osaka Purple'—mild-flavored, broad dark purple leaves with white veins in 40 days, extremely slow to bolt. 'Red Giant'—red and green crinkled leaves up to 18 inches tall on very productive plants in 45 days. 'Southern Giant Curled'—light green leaves with frilly edges in 45 to 50 days, cold tolerant and resistant to bolting.

Growing conditions: Sow mustard seeds outdoors ¼ to ½ inch deep in a compost-enriched soil as soon as the ground can be worked in spring. In mild-winter areas, sow a second crop 6 to 8 weeks before the first fall frost. For tender leaves, keep evenly moist and harvest leaves while young, cutting them as needed. A 10-foot row yields 10 pounds of mustard greens.

OKRA

'Annie Oakley'

Hardiness: *hot-season annual*

Planting method: *direct sowing; transplants*

Plant spacing: *18 to 24 inches*

Light: *full sun*

Smooth or ribbed pods, often with spines, on erect bushy plants. The pods thicken soups, gumbos, and stews and are delicious served as a side dish. The dried pods are lovely in dried flower arrangements.

Selected varieties: 'Annie Oakley'—large crop of pods on dwarf 3- to 4-foot plants in 55 days. 'Burgundy'—plants to 4 feet with ornamental red-veined leaves and burgundy-colored pods in 60 days that retain their color after cooking. 'Clemson Spineless'—with spineless pods on 5-foot plants in 56 to 65 days.

Growing conditions: Sow okra seed ½ inch deep outdoors after soil temperatures reach 60° F; presoaking improves their germination rate. Thin dwarf plants to stand 18 inches apart, others to 24 inches. Okra grows best at temperatures between 70° and 85° F; where the warm growing season is short, start okra seeds indoors 4 to 6 weeks before setting outdoors, and mulch with black plastic to warm the soil. Feed regularly and keep constantly moist for succulent pods. Wear gloves and a long-sleeved shirt while snipping pods from plants. Pick young, tender pods 3 to 4 inches long every 2 or 3 days to keep plants producing. A single plant produces 50 to 200 pods.

ONIONS

'Granex Yellow'

Hardiness: *Zones 3-9*

Planting method: *direct sowing; transplants; sets*

Plant spacing: *2 to 3 inches*

Light: *full sun*

Pungently sweet, crisp bulbs, thickened stems, and piquant hollow greens in summer or fall depending on the type. Onion bulb formation is sensitive to day length. Plant short-day varieties as a winter bulb crop in mild-winter areas or for small pickling onions farther north. Grow long-day varieties for bulb crops in northern gardens or for bunching onions in milder areas. Delicately flavored chives grow as a perennial in Zones 3-9. Egyptian onions form small bulbs at the tips of their stems rather than underground. Bunching onions have either very small bulbs or no bulb at all and are perennials in Zones 3-9.

Onions are the soul of many dishes. Use them as flavorings or as cases for stuffings. Cream, fry, scallop, boil, steam, or glaze them for side dishes. Slice them raw for salads, sandwiches, crudités, and garnishes. Pickle small onions or freeze chopped or whole small onions. Grow chives in pots indoors or out.

Selected varieties: Short-day varieties include: 'Granex Yellow'—very mild bulbs in 162 days. 'Red Granex'—slow-to-bolt bulbs with mild red flesh in 162 days. 'Red Hamburger'—has slightly flattened bulbs with red-and-white flesh, excellent eaten raw, in 95 days. 'Texas Early Grano'—sweet jumbo bulbs best for fresh use in

175 days. 'Texas Grano'—large disease-resistant bulbs with thick rings of soft, white flesh in 168 days. 'Texas Grano 1015Y', also called 'Texas Supersweet' —a heat- and drought-tolerant variety with very sweet softball-sized bulbs in 175 days. 'Yellow Bermuda'—extremely sweet white flesh in thick rings in 92 days.

Long-day varieties include: 'Ailsa Craig' —exceptionally large, early bulbs with pale yellow skins in 110 days. 'Early Yellow Globe'—uniform yellow onions that store well in 100 days. 'Northern Oak' —white flesh and heavy, dark brown skins with good keeping quality in 108

'Walla Walla'

days. 'Sweet Sandwich'—large globes 3½ inches across with sweet yellow flesh in 112 days. 'Walla Walla'—mildly flavored, sweet jumbo bulbs in 110 to 120 days spring seeded, 300 days fall seeded. 'White Sweet Spanish'—very mild, sweet white bulbs with good keeping quality in 110 days. 'Yellow Sweet Spanish'—very mild, sweet yellow-fleshed bulbs up to a pound each in 110 days.

Egyptian onions—very cold-hardy perennials that form small bulbs at the tips of the thick, hollow stems in lieu of flowers and a smaller number of bulbs underground in 180 days.

Green onion varieties, also called scallions or bunching onions, include: 'Beltsville Bunching'—very hardy variety for spring or fall planting in 65 days. 'Evergreen Long White', also called 'Nebuka'—good for overwintering in 60 days. 'Ishikura'—bulbless, long white stems and blue-green tops in 66 days.

Growing conditions: Grow onions from seeds, transplants, or sets, depending on the length of the growing season and the

type of onions desired. Plant short-day varieties in fall to produce bulbs the following summer; plant long-day varieties in spring for onions in fall. Plant bunching onions in spring or fall for use throughout the season. Plant perennial Egyptian onions in spring or fall; divide clumps every 3 or 4 years to maintain vigor. Sow seeds of bunching onions or long-day onions ½ inch deep in a fertile, moisture-

'Ishikura'

retentive soil enriched with compost or manure 4 to 6 weeks before last frost, as soon as the ground can be worked in spring. Thin to stand 2 to 3 inches apart in rows 1 to 2 feet apart. For larger bulbs in a shorter time, start seeds indoors 12 weeks before setting out; transplants can be moved outdoors up to a month before the last frost. Small, dry onions called sets are the most reliable way to produce large bulbs, particularly for long-day varieties. Plant sets in early spring.

Harvest bulb onions by pulling them when half of their tops have fallen over. When the tops are completely wilted, snip them off 1½ inches above the bulbs, wipe off dirt and any loose skins, and continue to dry for 2 weeks or more in a dry area with good ventilation. Store the dry onions at 35° to 50° F. Harvest Egyptian onions when the tops begin to wilt and dry; dry for storage, pickle, or freeze. Bulb and bunching onions yield about 10 pounds per 10-foot row.

PAK-CHOI or BOK CHOY

'Mei Quing Choi'

Hardiness: *cool-season annual*

Planting method: *direct sowing*

Plant spacing: *8 to 12 inches*

Light: *full sun*

Broad rosettes of upright leaves with thick, succulent stalks that have a mildly pungent flavor. Pak-choi is essential in stir-fry dishes. Uncooked, the crisp stalks can be used like celery or carrots with dips and sauces.

Selected varieties: 'Lei Choi'—heat-tolerant variety with crunchy, celery-like white 8- to 10-inch stalks and deep green leaves in 47 days. 'Mei Quing Choi'— baby pak-choi with very tender, pale green 6- to 8-inch stalks and leaves in 45 days; frost tolerant, heat tolerant, and slow to bolt.

Growing conditions: Sow pak-choi seeds outdoors as soon as ground can be worked in spring, setting seeds ½ inch deep and thinning plants to stand 8 to 12 inches apart. Pak-choi needs cool temperatures for best growth and goes to seed as days lengthen and weather warms. Plant a second crop in fall 50 to 60 days before first frost. Pak-choi will tolerate light frost. Harvest by cutting stems just above the soil line.

PARSNIPS

'Hollow Crown'

Hardiness: *cool-season annual*

Planting method: *direct sowing*

Plant spacing: *2 to 3 inches*

Light: *full sun*

Tapering white roots resembling carrots with a fine texture and sweet, nutty flavor that mature in late fall and can be stored in the garden through winter. Parsnips can be baked, steamed, grilled, sautéed, or prepared in many of the same ways as carrots or potatoes. Parboiling, however, dissolves and draws out the sugars in the roots, leaving them bland tasting.

Selected varieties: 'Harris Early Model'—short, stocky 12-inch roots with wide shoulders in 120 days. 'Hollow Crown'—exceptionally sweet, fine-grained roots up to 18 inches long in 125 days.

Growing conditions: Sow parsnip seeds in very early spring as soon as the ground can be worked. Soak seeds for 24 hours before setting them ½ to 1 inch deep in soil that has been tilled to a depth of 12 to 18 inches. Mulch to conserve moisture; lack of water causes roots to toughen. Begin harvesting after the first hard fall frost has sweetened the flavor. Store parsnips in the garden over the winter under a 12-inch mulch of hay or leaves anchored under black plastic. Harvest all of the previous season's parsnips by early spring before new growth begins; after that point, roots toughen. A 10-foot row yields about 8 pounds of parsnips.

PEANUTS

'Early Spanish'

Hardiness: *hot-season annual*

Planting method: *direct sowing; transplants*

Plant spacing: *12 inches*

Light: *full sun*

Pods or shells filled with richly flavored kernels under bushy plants. Male flowers appear among the upper leaves; the smaller female flowers, on short stalks near the plant's base. Each fertilized female flower develops a peg, or stem, that grows downward and into the soil; the pods are produced underground on the pegs. Eat shelled peanuts raw, roasted, or boiled or grind them for nut butter.

Selected varieties: 'Early Spanish'—heavy-yielding plants with early-maturing pods with two or three kernels each in 105 days. 'Jumbo Virginia'—large crop of pods with one or two large kernels on 18-inch plants in 120 to 135 days.

Growing conditions: Pretreat pods or individual peanuts with skins intact with a bacterial inoculant, and plant 1 inch deep in a heavy soil or 2 or more inches deep in a loose, sandy soil after it has warmed in the spring. Where growing seasons are short, start peanuts indoors in individual peat pots and plant out after all danger of frost is past in soil prewarmed under black plastic mulch; remove the plastic mulch to allow pegs access to the soil. Thin plants to stand 12 inches apart. Harvest after the foliage turns yellow but before the first frost, pulling plants up and hanging by roots to dry before removing pods. A single plant yields 40 to 50 pods.

PEAS

'Sugar Snap'

Hardiness: *cool-season annual*

Planting method: *direct sowing*

Plant spacing: *1 inch*

Light: *full sun*

Plump, sweet, round green seeds in long pods that are edible in some varieties, on vining or bushy plants in early spring or late fall. Garden or shelling peas have thick, stringy, inedible pods that contain long rows of up to 11 large peas. Snow peas are raised primarily for their thin, succulent edible pods. Exceptionally sweet sugar snap peas offer both plump seeds and thick-walled, edible pods. Among the first fruits of the spring garden, fresh garden peas are a tonic eaten raw out of hand or in salads; they are delicious parboiled or steamed for use in side dishes, soups, and stews. Use snow peas in Oriental cuisine or as an hors d'oeuvre. Prepare sugar snap peas like garden peas or snow peas. Freeze surplus peas for long-term storage.

Selected varieties: Garden or shelling pea varieties include: 'Alaska'—the earliest garden pea with a heavy yield of 2½-inch pods containing six to eight peas on 2-foot plants in 56 days. 'Alderman', or 'Tall Telephone'—late-maturing 5- to 6-foot vine with large peas in easy-to-shell pods in 76 days. 'Green Arrow'—large crop of 4-inch pods with up to 11 peas each on disease-resistant plants in 70 days. 'Lincoln'—vigorous 2-foot vines with 3½-inch pods filled with up to nine plump peas excellent for freezing in 67 days. 'Little Marvel'—dependable crop of very early 3-inch pods on 18-inch plants in 63 days. 'Petit Provencal'—heavy crop of 2½-inch pods filled with six or seven tiny, sweet peas, or *petit pois,* on bushy plants in 60 days. 'Progress No. 9'—4-inch pods containing up to seven peas each on short, 15-inch vines in 62 days. 'Wando'—both heat and cold tolerant with very heavy crop of 3-inch pods containing seven or eight peas in 67 days, ideal for late-season crops in northern gardens. 'Waverex'—semiclimbing 18-inch vines bearing pods filled with seven or eight tiny, sweet peas, or *petit pois.*

Snow or sugar pea varieties include:

'Green Arrow'

'Carouby de Maussane'—vigorous 5-foot vines with long, flat 5½-inch pods up to an inch wide in 65 days. 'Dwarf Gray Sugar'—pale green 2½- to 3-inch pods on 2½-foot vines in 63 days. 'Mammoth Melting Sugar'—disease-resistant 4-foot vines with broad pods in 72 days. 'Oregon Giant'—disease-resistant compact plants with broad, inch-wide pods up to 5 inches long filled with large, sweet peas in 70 days. 'Oregon Sugar Pod II'—heavy yields of crisp 4- to 5-inch pods, often in pairs, on nonclimbing dwarf vines in 70 days.

Sugar snap pea varieties include: 'Cascadia'—3-inch, thick-walled, juicy pods filled with sweet peas on compact plants in 58 days. 'Sugar Ann'—bushy, early-maturing variety with succulent 2½-inch pods on nonclimbing dwarf vines in 52 days. 'Sugar Bon'—disease-resistant, compact 2-foot plants with 3-inch pods in 56 days. 'Sugar Daddy'—stringless sugar snap peas on compact bushy 2-foot plants in 65 days. 'Sugar Snap'—3-inch pods on climbing 6-foot vines in 62

days. 'Super Sugar Mel'—thick 4-inch pods on 3-foot vines in 68 days.

Growing conditions: Sow peas ½ to 1 inch deep and 1 inch apart in spring 6 weeks before the last frost date or in fall 6 weeks before the first frost date. Sprinkle planting holes or trenches with a bacterial legume inoculant. Peas are a cool-

'Little Marvel'

weather crop that will tolerate temperatures as low as 25° F without protection and even lower temperatures when started under floating row covers. They grow best at daytime temperatures between 50° and 60° F. Do not thin; peas grow best in crowded stands. Provide trellises, netting, or other supports for vines to climb, or lay twiggy brush among bush types to support plants and keep pods off the ground. Weed carefully, as disturbing roots causes blossoms and even pods to drop.

Harvest garden peas when pods are bulging and before there is any sign of yellowing or shriveling. Pick snow peas and sugar snap peas just as seeds begin to form; overmature pods become fibrous and tough. Pick daily to encourage vining peas to continue producing; the pods of most bush varieties mature all at once for a single picking. For a continuous harvest, select varieties with different maturity dates. A 10-foot row yields approximately 5 to 10 pounds of peas.

PEPPERS

'Golden Bell'

Hardiness: *hot-season annual*

Planting method: *transplants; direct sowing*

Plant spacing: *18 to 24 inches*

Light: *full sun*

Succulent, fleshy, thin-skinned fruits, some mild and sweet, others hot, on bushy plants in late summer. Mildly flavored bell peppers are usually harvested at their immature green stage but can be left on plants to ripen to yellow, red, or purple and become even sweeter; use bell peppers as edible food cases, sliced raw in salads, or sautéed or parboiled as a flavoring. Most hot, or chili, peppers are picked after they ripen to red or yellow; use them in ethnic dishes. Surplus peppers can be chopped and frozen, dried, or pickled for long-term storage. The days to maturity for the peppers described below are counted from the date transplants are set out in the garden.

Selected varieties: Sweet bell pepper varieties include: 'Bell Boy'—a disease-resistant hybrid with thick-walled, glossy green fruits 3½ inches in diameter in 70 days that ripen to red. 'California Wonder'—thick-walled pepper 3 inches in diameter in 75 days. 'Cherry Sweet', also called 'Red Cherry'—1½-inch, slightly tapered peppers in 78 days especially recommended for pickling. 'Chocolate Belle'—blocky 4-inch fruits with chocolate brown skin and red flesh in 75 days. 'Cubanelle'—slender, tapering 6-inch-long pale green peppers 2½ inches wide at the shoulders in 65 days. 'Golden

Bell'—blocky three- or four-lobed peppers in 70 days that ripen to a deep gold. 'Gypsy'—disease-resistant variety with wedge-shaped 5-inch fruits in 65 days that mature from pale green to deep yellow. 'New Ace'—4-inch fruits in 62 days for short-season areas. 'Purple Beauty'—blocky fruits with deep purple skin in 70 days, ripening to red. 'Whopper Improved'—disease-resistant, almost square 4-inch peppers in 71 days. 'Yolo Wonder'—disease-resistant plants with 4-inch squarish peppers in 75 days.

Chili, or hot, pepper varieties include: 'Anaheim TMR 23'—with tapering, flat peppers 8 inches long by 1½ inches wide in 77 days, milder flavored than most chilies and usually picked while still green. 'Ancho', also called 'Poblano'—relatively mild with 5- to 6-inch dark green to red peppers in 65 to 75 days.

'Anaheim'

'Habañero'—extremely hot, dark green peppers 1 to 2 inches long ripening to pinkish orange in 85 to 95 days. 'Hungarian Wax'—tapering, three-lobed 6-inch-by-2-inch peppers that mature from pale yellow to bright red with a medium-hot flavor, 65 to 75 days. 'Jalapeño'—tiny, extremely hot cone-shaped peppers 3 inches long in 70 to 80 days that are usually picked green before they ripen to red. 'Large Hot Cherry'—heavy crop of hot, slightly conical 1½-inch fruits ripening from green to red in 75 days, recommended for pickling. 'Numex Big Jim'—medium-hot 10-inch red peppers in 80 days. 'Serrano Chile'—extremely hot conical peppers 2½ inches long and ½ inch across in 75 days that turn from green to red. 'Super Cayenne'—very hot, slim 4-inch peppers in 70 days that turn from green to red. 'Super Chili'—very hot, conical pale green fruits growing upright on bushes and maturing to orange then red in 70 days. 'Thai Hot'—very compact plants with extremely hot, ¾- to 1-inch green fruits that ripen to red in 75 days.

'Hungarian Wax'

Growing conditions: Start pepper plants indoors 8 to 10 weeks before night temperatures stay reliably above 55° F, setting seeds ½ inch deep; in areas with a long growing season, peppers can be sown directly in the garden. For disease prevention, avoid planting where other peppers, eggplant, or tomatoes have grown in the past 3 years. Peppers grow best when night temperatures are 62° F or more and daytime temperatures are 75° F or less. Temperatures below 55° F or above 85° F will cause blossoms to drop; although plants will recover, the crop will be smaller. Chili peppers require warmer soil for germination and growth than bell peppers; warm soil with black plastic before setting plants out in spring.

Pick bell peppers while still green and immature, while they are changing color, or when they have fully ripened to yellow, red, or purple. Fully ripe bell peppers have more sweetness and flavor than green ones. With a few exceptions, most chilies are left on plants to ripen fully before being snipped from plants. Continuous picking encourages further fruiting.

'Red La Soda'

Hardiness: *warm-season annual*
Planting method: *seed potatoes*
Plant spacing: *10 to 14 inches*
Light: *full sun*

Round or oblong firm-textured tubers, sometimes with colorful skins or flesh, from early summer to fall with successive planting of different varieties. Early-season varieties mature with thin skins tender enough to rub off when the potatoes are first harvested. Midseason and late-season or storage potatoes can be dug as thin-skinned "new" potatoes for immediate use or allowed to mature in the ground until their skins are fully set and cannot be rubbed off, then stored for fresh use over several months. Baby new potatoes are excellent boiled in their skins to eat whole or to slice into salads. Mature potatoes can be boiled, baked, fried, mashed, and scalloped in a myriad of flavorful ways. Home gardeners can enjoy potatoes with colorful yellow, blue, or purple flesh seldom available except in markets offering gourmet vegetables.

Selected varieties: Early-season varieties include: 'Irish Cobbler'—very early oblong tubers with smooth white skins and creamy white flesh in 65 days. 'Norgold Russet'—scab-resistant smooth, oblong, brown-skinned tubers with golden netting and flaky, moist flesh excellent for baking in 65 days. 'Red Norland'—scab-tolerant round potatoes with thin red skins and crisp white interiors in 65 days. 'Yukon Gold'—scab-resistant round or slightly oval potatoes with yellow skins and flavorful, buttery golden yellow flesh in 65 days with good keeping quality.

Midseason varieties include: 'Beltsville' —vigorous plants resistant to nematodes, scab, and wilt with white flesh and excellent keeping quality. 'Katahdin'— scab-resistant plants adapted to varied climate and soil conditions, producing round tubers with tan skins and white flesh. 'Kennebec'—blight-resistant plants with heavy yields of smooth-textured, round all-purpose potatoes in 80 days. 'Purple Marker'—disease-resistant plants producing medium-sized oval potatoes with deep purple-blue skins and flesh in 80 days. 'Red La Soda'—heat- and drought-tolerant round to oblong tubers

'Irish Cobbler'

with bright red skins and firm white flesh ideal for boiling in 80 days. 'Russet Burbank', also called 'Idaho Russet'—long, cylindrical, slightly flattened tubers with heavily netted brown skins and dry, flaky white flesh in 80 days. 'Russian Banana'— disease-resistant plants producing small to medium-sized fingerling potatoes with yellow skins and waxy pale yellow flesh. 'Viking Purple'—dark purple skins mottled red or pink over smooth-textured white flesh good for boiling in 80 days.

Late-season varieties include: 'Purple Peruvian'—long, narrow ½- to ¾-pound fingerling potatoes with deep purple skins, purple flesh, and purple-tinted foliage. 'Red Pontiac'—thin red skins over firm, white flesh with a light waxy texture good for boiling, midseason to late; excellent storage quality and also good harvested early for new potatoes.

Growing conditions: Use certified virus-free seed potatoes to plant a crop. An acid soil inhibits the growth of the potato scab virus. Early varieties are planted out 6 to 8 weeks before the last frost date, as soon as the ground can be worked in spring. Before planting, the seed potatoes should be sprouted, or "chitted." About 2 weeks before the date they will be set out, put them in a single layer in a

'Purple Peruvian'

shallow box with the eyes facing up. Set the box in a cool, frost-free room in indirect light until the potatoes produce short, stubby 1-inch sprouts. Plant whole seed potatoes the size of an egg or cut larger ones into egg-sized sections at least a day in advance so the cut surfaces can dry and are more resistant to rot. Set the seed potatoes 10 to 14 inches apart in trenches 6 to 8 inches deep; rows should be 2 feet apart. Cover the seed potatoes with no more than 4 inches of soil. Keep soil evenly moist. When stems are 8 inches high, hill more soil around plants, leaving 4 inches of the stems exposed. Hill twice more at 2-week intervals. Hilling in this fashion is essential because the tubers form on underground stolons produced along the stems.

Plant mid- and late-season potatoes directly in the garden, without sprouting, or chitting, 1 to 4 weeks before the last frost. Set them 3 to 4 inches deep in rows 2 feet apart. Hill the soil as described above.

Where soil is hard or rocky, potatoes can be grown under mulch. Place seed potatoes in shallow trenches and cover with a loose layer of straw, leaves, or dried grass clippings 6 to 10 inches deep; as stems elongate and plants emerge through mulch, add more mulch as though hilling soil as described above, taking care that tubers are covered at all times. Alternatively, grow potatoes in tall bottomless boxes, wooden cribs, barrels, or wire cages. Plant seed potatoes 6 to 8 inches apart and cover with 4 inches of soil; as plants grow taller, hill soil, compost, or mulch around the stems at 2-week intervals as described above.

Harvest potatoes anytime for new potatoes, carefully digging into soil to find small potatoes up to 2 inches in diameter. To harvest main-crop potatoes, cut off vines, then wait 2 weeks before digging. To dig, use a garden fork, carefully

'Red Pontiac'

lifting soil starting 1½ to 2 feet out from the plant's crown and taking care not to spear tubers. Use cut or bruised tubers immediately. Allow intact, unbruised tubers to dry for 1 to 2 weeks in a dark, well-ventilated area at 60° F, then store at 40° F in wooden boxes, burlap bags, or other well-ventilated containers. Check occasionally and remove any rotting potatoes. One plant yields between 2 and 10 pounds of potatoes.

'Big Max'

Hardiness: *warm-season annual*

Planting method: *transplants; direct sowing*

Plant spacing: *2 to 4 feet*

Light: *full sun*

Globe-shaped fruits filled with deep orange, firm-textured flesh and edible seeds on strong, sprawling vines. The large varieties are ideal for Halloween jack-o'-lanterns; the medium-sized ones, for side dishes, soups, and pies. Hollow out miniature pumpkins as containers for soups or stuffings or use them like decorative gourds in arrangements. Roasted pumpkin seeds, particularly the hull-less varieties, make a nutritious snack.

Selected varieties: 'Atlantic Giant'—huge, deeply ribbed fruits weighing up to several hundred pounds in 125 days. 'Baby Bear'—disease-resistant vines with small, slightly flattened fruits only 6 inches across and 3½ to 4 inches tall with fine-textured flesh and hull-less seeds in 105 days. 'Big Max'—enormous 50- to 100-pound fruits with thick orange flesh in 120 days, excellent for carving. 'Connecticut Field'—large 20- to 25-pound fruits with dark orange skins and slightly flattened shapes, good for carving. 'Jack Be Little'—six or seven miniature fruits only 3 inches across and 2 inches high on each vine in 95 days, ideal for decorations. 'Jack O' Lantern'—medium-sized, tall 7- to 9-pound pumpkins up to 9 inches across in 100 days. 'Lumina'—10- to 12-pound fruits up to 10 inches in diameter with creamy white skin and orange

flesh in 110 days. 'Small Sugar Pie', also called 'New England Pie', 'Early Small Sugar'—5- to 6-pound fruits with very sweet, fine-textured yellow-orange flesh, excellent for pies, in 100 days.

Growing conditions: Plant pumpkin seeds outdoors after the last frost, setting seeds ½ to 1 inch deep, and thin to stand 2 to 3 feet apart in rows 4 to 6 feet apart for bush types and 3 to 4 feet apart in rows 8 to 12 feet apart for vining types. Alternatively, plant five or six seeds in hills spaced 4 feet apart for bush types and 8 feet apart for vining types and thin to two or three plants. Pumpkin seeds can be started indoors 4 to 5 weeks before the last frost date in peat pots that are planted directly

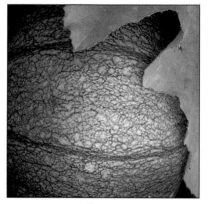

'Small Sugar Pie'

in the garden. Mulch with black plastic to warm the soil and conserve water. Water well during early growth and fruit set; standing water on maturing fruits invites rot. Ensure good pollination by transferring pollen from male to female (with swollen stems just below the blossoms) flowers with a soft brush. When vines are 2 to 3 feet long and fruits are just beginning to develop, pinch shoots to stimulate larger fruit growth. For large exhibition pumpkins, allow only one fruit to develop per vine. Raise maturing pumpkins off the ground on boards to prevent rot. Harvest pumpkins when their skins harden or after frost has killed the vines. Pumpkins will store well for up to a year if skins are undamaged.

'Castelfranco'

Hardiness: *cool-season annual*

Planting method: *direct sowing*

Plant spacing: *12 inches*

Light: *full sun*

A type of chicory with loose rosettes or small heads of green or red, slightly bitter leaves in spring, summer, or fall, depending on the region. Use as a garnish and to add color and flavor to salads.

Selected varieties: 'Augusto'—deep burgundy frost-resistant and bolt-resistant heads in 70 days. 'Castelfranco'—heirloom variety with loose red-and-white-marbled heads in 85 days. 'Early Treviso'—deep burgundy heads with white veins in 80 days. 'Giulio'—easy-to-grow white-veined burgundy heads in 80 days, ideal for spring planting. 'Red Verona'—heirloom variety with bright red, baseball-sized heads veined in white in 100 days.

Growing conditions: Sow radicchio outdoors, setting seed ½ inch deep and thinning plants to 12 inches. In Zones 3-7, plant radicchio in spring. Harvest leaves as needed during summer, then cut plants back to an inch or so above the ground in late summer or early fall to stimulate roots to produce small heads in 4 to 6 weeks. Where winter temperatures do not go below 10° F, sow seed for leaves in early spring, followed by heads in early summer. 'Castelfranco' and 'Giulio' form heads without cutting back, and 'Early Treviso' often does so. Seed can also be sown from midsummer to early fall for a fall crop.

RADISHES

'Easter Egg'

Hardiness: *cool-season annual*

Planting method: *direct sowing*

Plant spacing: *1 to 6 inches*

Light: *full sun*

Zesty roots in spring or fall. The large winter radishes, which are ready to harvest in fall, are stronger in taste and keep longer than spring varieties. Use as garnishes, hors d'oeuvres, or sliced in salads.

Selected varieties: Spring varieties include: 'Champion'—red, very cold tolerant. 'Cherry Bell'—crisp red globes. 'Giant White Globe'—white, mildly flavored. 'Early Scarlet Globe'—very early, mildly flavored red globes. 'Easter Egg'—red, white, purple, and violet roots. 'French Breakfast'—thick, cylindrical red roots with white tips. 'Plum Purple'—bright purple cylinders. 'White Icicle'—tapered white roots. All in 25 to 30 days.

Winter varieties include: 'Misato Rose'—sweet pink flesh. 'Munich Bier'—pungent white cylinders. 'Round Black Spanish'—black exterior, white flesh. 'Tokinashi'—strongly flavored white roots 8 or more inches long. All in 50 to 60 days.

Growing conditions: Sow seed ½ inch deep in fertile, moisture-retentive soil. Sow spring radishes successively from 5 weeks before the last frost until 4 weeks after; thin plants to 1 to 2 inches apart. Sow winter radishes from midsummer until 8 weeks before the first frost; thin to 4 to 6 inches apart. Keep both well watered and mulch in hot weather so roots won't be tough or unpleasantly strong.

RASPBERRIES

'Fall Red'

Hardiness: *Zones 4-7*

Planting method: *bare root; containers*

Plant spacing: *4 to 6 feet*

Light: *full sun to light shade*

Juicy, plump red, pink, golden, or black-purple berries on arching biennial canes growing from perennial rootstocks. Select varieties with maturity dates that provide fruit from early summer through frost. Standard red raspberries produce a single crop of fruit on 2-year-old canes; everbearing red raspberry canes bear fruit twice, once in the fall of their first year and again in the spring of their second year. Extremely fragile, delicately flavored yellow raspberries may be golden to pale pink. Black raspberries have a distinctly musky flavor and scent. Raspberries will spread rapidly via suckers along an underground network of rootlike stems.

Highly perishable, raspberries are most delectable straight from the garden. They can be frozen for long-term storage, although berries become mushy when thawed. Use berries in pies, desserts, jams, and jellies. Besides producing fruit, Japanese wineberry is a handsome ornamental for winter color.

Selected varieties: Red and yellow raspberry varieties include: 'Canby'—standard variety with midsummer crop of fleshy, deliciously flavored red berries on thornless canes. 'Chief'—very early crop of small red fruits, recommended for the Midwest. 'Fall Gold'—very hardy plants with golden yellow berries that have a high sugar content. 'Fall Red'—everbearing variety with large, extremely sweet berries, producing a larger crop in fall than in summer; good for areas with a short growing season. 'Heritage'—everbearing variety with firm, conical bright red berries, producing a larger crop in summer than in fall. 'Latham'—medium-

'Heritage'

sized red fruits on very hardy, adaptable plants. 'Newburgh'—standard disease-resistant variety with firm, large red berries in midsummer on short plants that need no support. 'Taylor'—standard variety with conical, somewhat tart red berries on vigorous plants that sucker freely. 'Viking'—heavy crop of red berries on very tall canes.

Black raspberry varieties include: 'Allen'—heavy crop of large, firm, very sweet berries all at once in midsummer. 'Black Hawk'—late midseason crop of large, firm, glossy berries on disease- and drought-resistant plants. 'Bristol'—large, very flavorful, nearly seedless berries on mosaic-resistant plants. 'John Robertson'—plump, juicy large berries on very hardy plants.

Hybrids include: Wineberry, also called Japanese wineberry—raspberry-blackberry hybrid with small, mildly flavored cherry red berries on attractive arching canes lined with soft red bristles that provide welcome color in the winter garden.

Growing conditions: Use only certified disease-free plants and never dig plants from the wild, since they may introduce viruses into the garden. Raspberries prefer deep, fertile loam enriched with compost. Plant rootstock with the top of the roots just below the soil line. Space plants 4 to 6 feet apart in rows 6 to 7 feet

313

apart. Water regularly and provide a deep mulch to suppress grass and weeds. For the largest yields and easier picking, provide 3-foot-high wire trellises for vines to trail over. Cover canes with coarse ¾- to 1-inch netting to protect ripening berries from birds.

Remove spent fruiting canes of standard red or yellow raspberry varieties after berries are harvested; prune the summer-fruiting canes of everbearing varieties after harvest. Remove weak suckers, leaving only two or three strong canes per foot of row.

To prune black and purple raspberries, remove old or weak canes, leaving three

'Bristol'

or four strong canes per foot of row. Prune lateral branches on the previous year's canes back to about 6 inches for black raspberries or 10 inches for purple raspberries in late winter to early spring to encourage heavy fruit production later in the season. Pinch tips of new shoots when they are about 18 to 24 inches tall to encourage lateral branching for the next season's crop.

Harvest raspberries when the fruits soften and pull away easily from the stem. Use or process immediately, as fruits are highly perishable. A mature plant yields about 1½ quarts of berries.

RHUBARB

'Cherry Red'

Hardiness: *Zones 3-8*

Planting method: *root divisions*

Plant spacing: *2 to 3 feet*

Light: *full sun*

Tart, juicy leafstalks in clumps in spring. Also called the pie plant, rhubarb is one of the earliest spring fruits for pies, cobblers, jams, and jellies. Rhubarb foliage is highly toxic and must be stripped off when the stalks are harvested.

Selected varieties: 'Cherry Red'—heavy yields of stalks that are cherry red outside, green inside. 'Valentine'—thick 12- to 24-inch stalks that retain their red color when cooked.

Growing conditions: Rhubarb needs at least 2 months of freezing weather and does not tolerate temperatures higher than 90° F. Start plants from root divisions purchased from suppliers or taken from plants at least 3 years old in late fall or very early spring; each division should have at least two eyes, or large buds. Set divisions 2 inches deep and space them 3 feet apart. Rhubarb can also be started from seed, but plants are usually not of the same quality and take a year longer to mature. Allow roots to become established the first year; harvest no more than 20 percent of the stalks the second year. Harvest stalks 1 inch or more in width from plants 3 years old or more over a 6- to 8-week period; do not remove more than half of the plant's stalks at one time. Each plant yields 10 to 20 stalks.

RUTABAGAS

'Improved Purple Top Yellow'

Hardiness: *cool-season annual*

Planting method: *direct sowing*

Plant spacing: *6 to 8 inches*

Light: *full sun*

Also called Swedish turnips. Large globe-shaped, 2- to 3-pound roots with mild, sweet, fine-grained yellow flesh and pungent leaves from fall into winter. Serve rutabaga roots mashed, baked, or fried, and boil or steam the greens.

Selected varieties: 'American Purple Top' —5- to 6-inch beige-yellow roots with purple crowns in 90 days. 'Improved Purple Top Yellow'—round to oblong roots that store well in 90 days. 'Laurentian'— round roots with pale yellow crowns that store well in 105 days.

Growing conditions: Sow rutabagas ½ inch deep 12 to 14 weeks before the first fall frost and thin seedlings to stand 6 to 8 inches apart. To control soil-borne diseases, don't plant rutabagas where they or any other members of the cabbage family have been grown within 3 years. Keep soil constantly moist but not soggy. Harvest rutabagas after several frosts have sweetened the roots, cutting off all but 1 inch of the leaves. To store roots, dip them in melted paraffin floating on top of warm water to prevent wrinkling. Store in a root cellar at 40° F. Rutabagas can also be overwintered in the garden under a thick layer of mulch but may become woody. A 10-foot row yields about 10 pounds of roots.

SALSIFY

'Mammoth Sandwich Island'

Hardiness: *cool-season annual*

Planting method: *direct sowing*

Plant spacing: *2 to 4 inches*

Light: *full sun*

Also known as oyster plant. Tapering white roots resembling parsnips from fall through winter. Salsify, which has a mild flavor reminiscent of oysters, can be boiled and mashed, fried, or added to soups.

Selected varieties: 'Mammoth Sandwich Island'—roots 8 or more inches in length and about 1½ inches in diameter in 120 days.

Growing conditions: Sow salsify ¼ to ½ inch deep in spring in loose, well-tilled soil with all stones removed. Do not use manure when preparing salsify beds because the high nitrogen content results in hairy roots. Scratching wood ashes into the soil or watering with seaweed emulsion while roots are forming encourages thicker roots. Thin seedlings to 2 to 4 inches apart and mulch to keep soil evenly moist. Frost improves the flavor of salsify. Dig roots with a garden fork or shovel and store in moist peat or sand in a root cellar at 40° F. Alternatively, store salsify roots in the garden, covering them with a 12-inch mulch of straw or leaves. Harvest all roots by the following spring before new growth begins. A 10-foot row yields 10 to 20 pounds of salsify.

SHALLOTS

'Success'

Hardiness: *Zones 6-9; cool-season annual*

Planting method: *sets*

Plant spacing: *6 inches*

Light: *full sun*

Small, round bulbs with a delicate onion flavor from summer through fall or tender scallions in spring. Shallots are prized for the unique, mild accent they add to many gourmet dishes.

Selected varieties: 'Atlantic'—clumps of plump bulbs with yellow-tan skins. 'Success'—small bulbs with reddish brown skins. Both in 120 to 150 days.

Growing conditions: Grow shallots from tiny bulbs called sets, setting them out in fall in mild climates or as soon as the ground can be worked in spring elsewhere. Place sets with their tips barely above the soil in a rich, deep garden loam enriched with compost, and keep evenly moist. Young shallots can be pulled and used like scallions. If allowed to mature, sets multiply into clusters of small bulbs each up to an inch across. When tops begin to yellow and wither in fall, pull shallots and allow to dry in a well-ventilated area. Remove dirt and loose skins, clip stems an inch above the bulbs, and store dried bulbs for up to a year. Each set produces eight to 12 shallots.

SOYBEANS

'Prize'

Hardiness: *warm-season annual*

Planting method: *direct sowing*

Plant spacing: *3 to 6 inches*

Light: *full sun*

Small, fuzzy pods in heavy clusters on bushy, erect plants in late summer. Shell mature soybeans and use them fresh or for canning or freezing. Pods can also be allowed to dry, then shelled for long-term storage. Dry soybeans are used in cooking like other dry beans and are also sprouted for salads, stir-frying, and stuffings.

Selected varieties: 'Edible Early Hakucho'—early-maturing variety 1 foot tall for fresh use in 65 days. 'Prize'—large pod clusters with two to four beans per pod, suitable for fresh use in 85 days or dried in 100 days.

Growing conditions: Dry soybeans require a long growing season, but early varieties are suitable for shelling beans in northern gardens. After all danger of frost is past and the soil temperature is 65° F or more, plant seed that has been treated with a bacterial inoculant 1 inch deep. Plant in double rows, keep well watered, and mulch to conserve moisture. In windy areas, provide supports among plants. Harvest shelling beans before seeds turn from green to yellow. Harvest dry soybeans before pods shatter and release their seeds, then thresh like other dry beans *(page 282)*.

SPINACH

'Tyee'

Hardiness: *cool-season annual*

Planting method: *direct sowing*

Plant spacing: *2 to 3 inches*

Light: *full sun to light shade*

Smooth or crinkled leaves in upright clumps from early to late spring or in fall. Use spinach in salads or for soups, side dishes, and stuffings.

Selected varieties: 'Bloomsdale Long Standing'—thick, deeply crinkled leaves on slow-to-bolt plants. 'Imperial Spring'—smooth leaves on fast-growing, upright plants resistant to mildew. 'Indian Summer'—crinkled leaves on slow-to-bolt, disease-resistant plants. 'Melody'—thick, somewhat crinkled leaves that are resistant to mold and blight. 'Space'—slow-to-bolt hybrid with smooth, deep green leaves on upright plants that are resistant to viruses and mildew. 'Tyee'—deeply crinkled leaves on upright, extremely bolt-resistant plants tolerant of mildew. All in 35 to 40 days.

Growing conditions: Sow spinach ½ inch deep outdoors in early spring, repeating every 10 days for an extended supply of greens. Keep well watered. Plant 4 to 6 weeks before the first frost for a fall crop. In mild areas it will winter over and produce a very early spring crop. Plants go to seed as weather warms and days lengthen, but bolting can be delayed by siting later sowings in the shade of taller plants. Smooth varieties require less washing than savoyed types. A 10-foot row produces 4 to 6 pounds of spinach.

SPINACH, MALABAR

'Alba'

Hardiness: *warm-season annual*

Planting method: *transplants; direct sowing*

Plant spacing: *12 inches*

Light: *full sun*

Mild-flavored 4- to 6-inch leaves on 6- to 10-foot vines throughout summer. Use Malabar spinach leaves fresh in salads, cooked like spinach, or as a thickening agent in soups or sauces. Use the handsome vines in an edible landscape, either trained on a trellis or fence or cascading from hanging baskets.

Selected varieties: 'Alba'—thick, dark green leaves. 'Rubra'—dark green leaves with red stems and veins. Both in 70 to 100 days.

Growing conditions: Start Malabar spinach indoors 8 weeks before the last frost or sow directly in the garden in late spring to early summer after the soil has warmed to at least 65 ° F. Plant seeds 1 inch deep in humus-enriched soil, and keep soil moist. Thin plants to 12 inches apart and provide supports for vines to climb. Malabar spinach requires warm temperatures to grow and will not bolt in hot weather like spinach. Begin picking young leaves for salads before vines reach maturity. Pinch tips to encourage branching, and remove any flower blossoms to prolong leaf production.

SPINACH, NEW ZEALAND

New Zealand Spinach

Hardiness: *Zones 9-11; warm-season annual*

Planting method: *direct sowing; transplants*

Plant spacing: *12 inches*

Light: *full sun*

Small clumps of thick, succulent leaves with a flavor reminiscent of spinach on trailing heat-resistant vines in summer and fall. Use New Zealand spinach fresh in salads or cooked as a hot-weather substitute for spinach. The plants are an attractive addition to an edible landscape. Use them as a ground cover, train on trellises, or plant in hanging baskets.

Selected varieties: No named varieties; sold as New Zealand spinach—mildly flavored triangular leaves on pest-free plants in 55 to 70 days.

Growing conditions: Soak seeds overnight before planting ½ to 1 inch deep. In Zones 9-11, seeds should also be chilled for 1 to 2 days before sowing directly outdoors. From Zone 8 north, sow seed outdoors 2 weeks before the last frost. For transplants, sow seed in peat pots and set them directly in the garden to minimize transplant shock, after all danger of frost is past. Pick leaves when they are young, harvesting frequently to encourage continued growth. In warm climates plants often seed themselves. A 10-foot row yields about 5 pounds of New Zealand spinach.

SQUASH, SUMMER

'Early Golden Summer'

Hardiness: *warm-season annual*

Planting method: *direct sowing; transplants*

Plant spacing: *18 inches to 7 feet*

Light: *full sun*

Mild-tasting, tender-skinned fruits on sprawling vines or compact, bushy plants ideal for small gardens. Summer squashes are grouped according to shape. The crookneck summer squashes have bumpy surfaces and narrow, curved necks. The flat, round, scallop squashes have pretty fluted edges. Straightneck varieties have narrow stem ends and bulbous blossom ends. The zucchini types are uniform cylinders, often speckled and slightly ribbed.

Summer squashes, especially the scallop varieties, are delectable harvested as baby vegetables, before seeds enlarge and harden. Whether half-grown or larger, the mild flavor of summer squashes mingles well with other vegetables in salads or hors d'oeuvres, soups, or side dishes. Use hollowed-out squashes as edible casings for a variety of meat or vegetable dishes.

Selected varieties: Crookneck squashes include: 'Crescent'—vigorous, adaptable vines bearing early-maturing bright yellow fruits in 45 days. 'Early Golden Summer'—vining variety producing a large crop of bumpy yellow fruits that freeze well in 53 days. 'Sundance'—creamy yellow, miniature oval fruits on compact, bushy plants in 50 days. 'Yellow Crookneck'—bumpy-skinned, deep yel-

low fruits with buttery flavor and firm flesh beginning in 58 days and continuing over a long season when picked often.

Scallop varieties include: 'Early White Bush', also called 'White Patty Pan'—flattened, creamy white fruits in 60 days. 'Patty Green Tint'—a very early variety with pale green fruits on bushy plants in 52 days, exceptionally tender if picked when about 2 to 3 inches across. 'Scallopini'—extremely productive compact,

'Sunburst'

bushy plants that bear early-maturing small, round dark green fruits with a nutty flavor in 50 days. 'Sunburst'—compact, bushy plants with numerous flat golden yellow fruits with a green sunburst pattern at the stem and blossom ends in 48 days.

Straightneck varieties include: 'Early Prolific'—heavy yield of yellow fruits in 50 days, best picked when about 6 inches long. 'Park's Creamy Hybrid'—compact plants only 18 inches across with heavy yields of creamy yellow 6- to 8-inch fruits in 48 days and throughout summer. 'Seneca'—high yield of cylindrical, bright yellow fruits in 51 days. 'Sundrops'—smooth-skinned golden fruits in 50 days, best harvested when 2 inches across.

Zucchini varieties include: 'Black Eagle'—very dark green, slender fruits with creamy flesh in 53 days. 'Cocozelle'—very prolific vines with fruits attractively striped in pale and dark green in 55 days. 'Condor'—early crop of glossy deep green fruits flecked with pale green on bushy plants in 48 days. 'Gold Rush'—bushy plants with bright yellow fruits in 50 days. 'Greyzini'—slightly tapered light green fruits in 50 days. 'Milano'—bushy plants bearing dark green fruits ready to

harvest in 42 days. 'Raven'—very early crop of deep green fruits in 42 days with delicate flesh even in more mature fruits.

Growing conditions: Plant seed outdoors 1 inch deep after all danger of frost is past and when soil has warmed to 70° F. Thin bush types to stand 18 to 36 inches apart and vining types to stand 3 to 7 feet apart. Alternatively, plant five or six seeds in hills 3 to 4 feet apart and thin to two or three plants. Summer squash can also be started indoors 3 to 4 weeks before the last frost. For a fall crop, sow seeds 8 to 10 weeks before the first frost. To save space, train vining varieties against trellises or fences.

Pick summer squashes while still immature for fine-textured flesh with tender seeds; mature fruits become pithy and have woody seeds that must be removed before cooking. Keep vines picked clean

'Black Eagle'

to encourage greater fruit production. Three or four vigorous summer squash plants may produce 60 to 75 pounds of summer squash over the season.

SQUASH, WINTER

'Cream of the Crop'

Hardiness: *warm-season annual*

Planting method: *direct sowing; transplants*

Plant spacing: *18 inches to 7 feet*

Light: *full sun*

Hard-skinned fruits with firm-textured flesh around a large seed cavity in an array of colors, shapes, and sizes. Acorn squash has heart-shaped, deeply ribbed fruits with sweet, somewhat dry orange flesh. Butternut squash fruits have bulbous blossom ends with small seed cavities and long, fleshy necks. Hubbard squash has teardrop- or pear-shaped fruits with rough, ribbed blue-gray skin and yellow-orange flesh. The light yellow flesh of spaghetti squash is composed of moist, slightly crunchy strands that can be served like pasta. Sweet-potato squashes have extremely sweet, fine-grained flesh. Turban squashes are flattened globes, sometimes with contrasting splotches of color and buttonlike protrusions at their blossom ends.

Bake or parboil as a side dish; hollow out smaller fruits to use as containers for a variety of dishes; or add to soups and stews. Winter squash stores well if the skin is undamaged; the cooked flesh freezes well. The colorful varieties make attractive decorations.

Selected varieties: Acorn squash varieties include: 'Bush Table'—bushy plants only 3 feet across bearing deeply ribbed, dark green 5-inch fruits with fine-textured orange flesh in 80 days. 'Cream of the Crop'—compact, bushy vines with 2-pound cream-colored fruits with a nutty flavor in 82 days. 'Table Ace'—compact plants with a very early crop of deep green fruits in 70 days. 'Table Queen'—large vines with deep green, almost black 1½-pound fruits with yellow flesh in 80 days.

Butternut varieties include: 'Butterbush'—thin-skinned fruits with deep red-orange flesh on compact, bushy

'Early Butternut'

plants 4 feet in diameter in 75 days. 'Early Butternut'—very productive vines with thick-necked, light tan fruits in 85 days. 'Ponca'—long-necked tan fruits with very small seed cavities in 83 days. 'Waltham'—fruits with sweet, dry flesh in 85 days.

Hubbard varieties include: 'Blue Hubbard'—12- to 20-pound pear-shaped blue-gray fruits with rough-textured, ribbed skin and fine-grained yellow-orange flesh in 120 days. 'Golden Hubbard'—oval, 10-pound, orange-skinned fruits in 105 days.

Spaghetti squash varieties include: 'Tivoli'—cream-colored fruits on compact, bushy plants in 100 days. 'Vegetable Spaghetti'—oblong 2- to 3-pound fruits in 100 days that store well.

Sweet-potato squash varieties include: 'Delicata'—short vines with slender, oblong 1½- to 2-pound cream-colored fruits marked with green stripes and filled with very sweet orange flesh in 100 days, good for baking, stuffing, and storage. 'Sweet Dumpling'—medium-length vines bearing small 4-inch, slightly flattened fruits with very sweet, tender flesh in 100 days, ideal for individual servings.

Turban squash varieties include: 'Buttercup'—flattened, blocky, deep green 3- to 5-pound fruits with a gray button at the blossom end and with sweet, fine-textured deep orange flesh in 105 days. 'Turk's Turban'—turban-shaped, bright orange fruits streaked green and white in 100 days.

Growing conditions: Plant winter squash outdoors after the last frost, setting seeds ½ to 1 inch deep. Thin bush types to stand 18 to 36 inches apart and vining types to stand 3 to 7 feet apart. Alternatively, plant five or six seeds in hills spaced 4 feet apart; thin each hill to two or three plants. Winter squash can also be started indoors 3 to 4 weeks before the last frost date. Mulch with black plastic to warm the soil and conserve water. Water well during early growth and fruit

'Sweet Dumpling'

set. When vines are 2 to 3 feet long and fruits are just beginning to develop, pinch shoots to stimulate the production of large fruits.

Harvest winter squashes when the skin hardens to the point where it is difficult to nick with a fingernail; leave several inches of stem attached to prevent rot during storage. Acorn, hubbard, and turban squashes bear two to four fruits per plant; spaghetti squash bears five to nine fruits per plant.

STRAWBERRIES

'Chandler'

Hardiness: *Zones 4-7*

Planting method: *direct sowing; runners*

Plant spacing: *15 inches*

Light: *full sun*

Juicy, fragrant, conical or wedge-shaped red berries in late spring, summer, or fall. Alpine strawberries form neat mounds of toothed foliage and are ideal for edging a vegetable garden or an ornamental border. Garden varieties, which send out plentiful runners that quickly spread into large mats, are categorized according to the time they set fruit. June-bearing varieties produce a single large crop of late-spring or early-summer berries. Everbearing varieties produce two crops, one in summer and another in fall; usually one crop is heavier than the other. Because they are not influenced by day length, the "day-neutral" varieties produce a continuous supply of berries from summer through fall.

Strawberries are at their best eaten fresh from the garden and are the basis of innumerable delicious desserts including shortcakes, pies, and tortes. Excess berries can be frozen or made into jams and jellies. Plant garden strawberries in containers and hanging baskets.

Selected varieties: Alpine strawberry varieties include: 'Alexandria'—inch-long, very sweet conical berries, somewhat larger than other alpine strawberries. 'Frais de Bois'—tiny golden, red, or deep crimson fruits with a fruity perfume on very cold-hardy plants. 'Reugen Im-proved'—slim, elongated, very fragrant fruits continuously from early summer through fall, with the heaviest crop in fall.

Garden varieties include: 'Big Red'—June-bearing variety with glossy conical

'Sparkle'

fruits that are a deep red throughout. 'Chandler'—an everbearing variety with flat, wedge-shaped berries on plants that produce numerous runners. 'Earli-glow'—June-bearing variety producing a large, very early spring crop of medium to large, deep red berries. 'Ever Red'—everbearing variety with large conical fruits that are deep red throughout. 'Ozark Beauty'—an everbearing variety with large, rich red, exceptionally sweet berries. 'Picnic'—everbearing strawberry that produces sweet, medium-sized fruits in just 4 months from seed. 'September Sweet'—disease-resistant day-neutral variety with very sweet, medium-sized berries from June through September, with the heaviest yield in fall. 'Serenata'—an everbearing variety with deep pink rather than the typical white flowers, followed by glossy red berries. 'Sparkle'—a single, large, late-summer crop of firm, flavorful berries on disease-resistant, hardy plants. 'Sure Crop'—June-bearing, drought-tolerant, disease-resistant variety with a reliably heavy yield of very large berries. 'Tribute'—day-neutral variety steadily producing plump, slightly acidic fruits with excellent flavor on disease-resistant plants. 'Tristar'—day-neutral variety with firm, sweet red berries on wilt- and mildew-resistant plants; ideal for hanging baskets.

Growing conditions: Select virus-free strawberry plants and set them out in spring or fall in a loose, fertile soil en-riched with organic matter. Plant in raised beds where soils are heavy or clayey. Set bare-rooted stock in the ground with the soil line where the roots and crown meet; plants set with their crowns below the soil line will rot, and those set too shallow will die because their roots are exposed. Mulch plants to control weeds and reduce rot. Alpine strawberries and some garden strawberries can also be started from seed sown indoors 2 to 3 months before the last frost, then planted outdoors.

Grow strawberries in mats or hills. For mats, set plants out 15 inches apart in rows 3 to 4 feet apart. Allow the runners

'Sure Crop'

to fill the area but keep a pathway open between rows for access. For hills, set plants 1 foot apart in double or triple rows spaced 12 inches apart; keep a pathway between each group of rows. Cut off all runners produced the first summer.

Remove old plants and renew strawberry beds when berry production slows. Everbearing varieties usually need renewing every year or every other year. June-bearing strawberries may remain productive for as long as 5 years.

SUNFLOWER

'Mammoth Russian'

Hardiness: *warm-season annual*

Planting method: *direct sowing*

Plant spacing: *18 inches*

Light: *full sun*

Tasty, oil- and protein-rich seeds from late summer to fall in heavy seed heads that follow attractive white or yellow flowers on tall stalks. Eat sunflower seeds raw or roasted as a snack, or add them to salads and breads.

Selected varieties: 'Aztec Gold'—early-maturing variety with seed heads up to 11 inches across on 6-foot plants in 68 days. 'Grey Stripe', also called 'Giant Grey Stripe'—20-inch seed heads filled with large, thin-shelled seeds on 8- to 12-foot stalks in 85 days. 'Mammoth'—seed heads crammed with thin-shelled, meaty seeds on 6- to 12-foot stalks in 80 days. 'Mammoth Russian'—disease-resistant 8- to 12-foot plants with 12-inch heads filled with large, richly flavored, striped seeds in 80 days.

Growing conditions: Plant seeds directly in the garden after all danger of frost is past, setting them ½ inch deep and thinning them to 18 inches apart. Tall stalks with heavy seed heads may need staking. Cover seed heads with cheesecloth to protect ripening seeds from birds and animals. Harvest seed heads when the back of the head dries or frost has killed foliage. Cut with 1 foot of the stalk attached and hang or lay on newspaper to finish drying in a well-ventilated area. Store seeds in airtight containers.

SWEET POTATOES

'Centennial'

Hardiness: *warm-season annual*

Planting method: *plants*

Plant spacing: *12 inches*

Light: *full sun*

Tapered tubers with sweet, moist, highly nutritious orange or red-orange flesh in fall. Enjoy baked or parboiled for side dishes, casseroles, and pies. Sweet potatoes are most easily started from small plants purchased from a nursery.

Selected varieties: 'Centennial'—fast-maturing variety with baby tubers ready to harvest in 90 to 100 days. 'Georgia Jet'—large red-skinned potatoes in 90 to 100 days. 'Jewell'—prolific variety with coppery red skins and fine-textured flesh in 100 days. 'Vardaman'—potatoes with deep orange flesh on compact, bushy plants in 100 days.

Growing conditions: Sweet potatoes are heat- and drought-resistant and need to grow where night temperatures will not drop below 60° F. Set certified virus-free plants out after all danger of frost is past and the soil is warm. Plant them in mounds of loose soil 6 to 10 inches high. Harvest sweet potatoes when vines yellow in fall. If an unseasonable frost is predicted before harvest, protect plants with floating row covers. Tubers must be harvested immediately if plants are nipped by frost. Cure tubers in a warm, humid, well-ventilated area for 8 to 10 days, then store at 55° to 60° F. A 10-foot row yields about 10 pounds of tubers.

TAMPALA

Tampala

Hardiness: *hot-season annual*

Planting method: *direct sowing*

Plant spacing: *6 inches*

Light: *full sun*

Tangy red- or green-leaved vegetable that resembles spinach but thrives in hot weather and can be sown successfully for harvesting all summer. Use tender young tampala leaves in salads, soups, and side dishes, either alone or combined with other greens.

Selected varieties: No named varieties; sold only as tampala. Heart-shaped 4-inch leaves ready to cut in 40 to 55 days on drought-tolerant, bushy plants.

Growing conditions: Sow tampala seeds ¼ inch deep after all danger of frost is past in a well-drained garden soil, working a balanced 5-10-5 organic fertilizer into the soil before planting. Tampala requires warm soil and high temperatures for best growth. When seedlings are 4 inches tall, thin to stand 6 inches apart; use thinnings in salads and soups. When plants reach 6 to 8 inches in height, harvest by cutting the entire plant at the soil line. For a continuous harvest of young, tender leaves, make successive sowings every 2 weeks until a month before the first frost date.

TOMATILLOES

Tomatillo

Hardiness: *warm-season annual*

Planting method: *transplants*

Plant spacing: *18 to 24 inches*

Light: *full sun*

Also called Mexican ground cherries. Round fruits encased in thin, papery husks on broad, bushy plants up to 4 feet tall. Tomatilloes are piquant when picked green and tangy-sweet when they ripen and turn yellow. A staple in Mexican cuisine, tomatilloes are used fresh, depending on their degree of ripeness, for savory sauces and dishes such as salsa verde or for dessert toppings, jams, and preserves. Cooked tomatilloes freeze well.

Selected varieties: 'Goldie', also called 'Golden'—¾-inch berries ripening in 75 days. 'Toma Verde'—firm-textured, 1½-inch, pale green sweet-sour berries in 60 to 80 days.

Growing conditions: Start tomatillo seeds indoors 3 to 6 weeks before the last frost, setting seeds ½ inch deep in peat pots. Transplant seedlings in their peat pots to the garden after the soil has warmed and all danger of frost is past, spacing them 18 to 24 inches apart. For firm, tart fruits, harvest when the husks turn from green to tan. For sweet, ripe fruits, wait until the fruits drop off the plant. Tomatilloes keep well in the refrigerator.

TOMATOES

'Better Boy'

Hardiness: *warm-season annual*

Planting method: *transplants; direct sowing*

Plant spacing: *3 to 4 feet*

Light: *full sun*

Juicy, meaty, red, yellow, pink, purple, or white fruits ranging from bite-sized miniatures to 2-pounders. All tomato varieties belong to one of two groups, based on the type of vine they have. The indeterminate tomatoes have tall, lanky vines and bear fruit over a long period, while the determinate tomatoes tend to be compact and bushy and to produce the season's crop all at once. Varieties mature at markedly different times. Early tomatoes set fruit in about 55 to 65 days from the time seedlings started indoors are set out in the garden, or a total of 85 to 90 days from seed; midseason tomatoes set fruit in about 65 to 75 days from the transplanting date, or 95 to 105 days from seed; and late-season tomatoes begin fruiting in 80 to 100 days after the transplanting date, or 110 to 130 days from seed.

The largest fruits are the enormous beefsteak varieties, which have a high proportion of seeds and juice to flesh. Large and medium-sized slicing tomatoes also have a high proportion of juice to pulp. Slice or chop them fresh for use in salads, sandwiches, and garnishes; stuff them, or bake, simmer, or sauté them for main or side dishes. The paste tomatoes are smaller and have a higher proportion of flesh to seeds and juice.

Ideal for cooked relishes, salsa, and sauces, they can be dried for long-term storage. Small-fruited tomato varieties have grapelike clusters of tiny sweet fruits that are good raw or cooked.

Selected varieties: Large-fruited varieties include: 'Ace 55'—broad, smooth fruits in 75 days on disease-resistant determinate vines. 'Beefmaster'—extremely large, somewhat flattened fruits in midseason on vigorous, disease-resistant indeterminate vines in 80 days. 'Beefsteak', also called 'Red Ponderosa' or 'Crimson Cushion'—meaty, thick-ribbed tomatoes weighing 2 pounds or more on indeterminate vines in 90 days. 'Better Boy'—round fruits weighing up to a pound on strong, disease-resistant indeterminate

'Early Girl'

vines in 72 days. 'Big Boy'—firm, thick-walled, aromatic fruits weighing a pound or more on indeterminate vines in 78 days. 'Big Early'—½- to 1-pound fruits with thick walls on indeterminate vines in 62 days. 'Big Girl'—large, crack-resistant fruit weighing a pound or more on disease-resistant indeterminate vines in 78 days. 'Burpee's VF'—thick-walled, crack-resistant medium-sized fruits on indeterminate vines in 72 days. 'Celebrity'—crack-resistant ½-pound fruits on compact, disease-resistant determinate vines in 75 days. 'Delicious'—record-setting fruits weighing up to 3 pounds or more each with excellent flavor on indeterminate vines in 77 days. 'Early Cascade'—large clusters of early-ripening 1½- to 2-inch heart-shaped tomatoes on disease-resistant indeterminate vines in 55 days. 'Early Girl'—offers clusters of early-ripening small, meaty, deep red fruits on indeterminate vines in 54 days.

'Fantastic'—smooth 3- to 5-inch tomatoes in 70 days on indeterminate vines. 'First Lady'—flavorful, early-ripening 4- to 6-ounce fruits on compact, indeterminate vines in 60 days. 'Heatwave'—medium-sized fruits on compact, disease-resistant determinate vines that will set

'Quick Pic'

fruit at temperatures above 90° F in 68 days. 'Heinz 1350'—crack-resistant 6-ounce fruits ideal for canning on determinate vines in 75 days. 'Heinz 1439'—meaty 6-ounce fruits good for sauces and canning on compact determinate vines in 72 days. 'Jubilee'—mild-flavored medium-sized yellow fruits on disease-resistant indeterminate vines in 80 days. 'Lady Luck'—large meaty fruits weighing up to a pound on adaptable, disease-resistant indeterminate vines in 78 days. 'Long-Keeper'—light red-orange fruits on indeterminate vines in 78 days; stores well for up to 12 weeks or more at 60° to 70° F. 'Marglobe Improved'—fruits ideal for canning on determinate vines in 75 days. 'Mountain Delight'—medium-sized fruits in clusters of three or four on disease-resistant determinate vines in 75 days. 'Northern Exposure'—half-pound flavorful fruits on compact semideterminate vines bred for cool seasons in 67 days. 'Oregon Spring'—early 4-inch tomatoes on disease-resistant, somewhat cold-tolerant determinate vines in 58 days. 'Patio'—medium to large firm, flavorful fruits on compact dwarf determinate vines suited for container growing in 60 days. 'Pilgrim'—small clusters of 7-ounce fruits on determinate vines in 65 days. 'President'—large, smooth red fruits on disease-resistant determinate vines in 68 days. 'Quick Pic'—early vari-

ety with medium-sized fruits on indeterminate vines starting in 68 days. 'Spring Giant'—large fruits with thick walls and small cores on determinate vines adaptable to many climate conditions in 65 days. 'Super Bush'—meaty fruits starting in 85 days and continuing over a long season on bushy determinate plants 38 inches tall and wide that require no pruning, staking, or caging and are ideal for containers and small gardens. 'Wonder Boy'—meaty 8-ounce fruits on vigorous indeterminate vines in 80 days.

Small-fruited varieties include: 'Florida Basket'—1- to 2-inch fruits in 70 days on very short determinate vines about 6 inches long, ideal for hanging baskets. 'Gardener's Delight', also called 'Sugar Lump'—clusters of up to a dozen bite-sized, sweet bright red fruits ripening

'Gardener's Delight'

early on indeterminate vines in 65 days. 'Red Cherry Large'—clusters of sweet, deep red 1½-inch round fruits ripening in midseason on vigorously branching indeterminate vines good for hanging baskets in 75 days. 'Sun Gold'—early apricot-colored fruits in grapelike clusters of up to 20 fruits on vigorous, disease-resistant indeterminate vines in 60 days. 'Sweet Million'—very sweet, crack-resistant 1- to 1¼-inch fruits in clusters on highly disease-resistant vines starting in 60 days and continuing for a long period. 'Sweet 100'—large elongated clusters of cherry-sized sweet fruits throughout the summer on indeterminate vines in 60 days. 'Tiny Tim'—very early variety with bite-sized tomatoes on compact 15-inch determinate vines in 45 days. 'Toy Boy' —early crop of 1½-inch fruits on 14-inch determinate vines in 58 days.

Paste tomato varieties include: 'Italian Gold'—firm, thick-walled golden-orange fruits on determinate vines in 82 days. 'La Roma'—very large crop of meaty 3- to 4-ounce fruits ideal for canning on determinate vines in 62 days. 'La Rossa'—pear-shaped 3½-inch fruits with thick flesh and thin skins in 75 days, ideal for

'Sweet Million'

fresh use as well as for cooking. 'Mama Mia'—heavy crop of small pear-shaped fruits on determinate disease-resistant vines in 62 days. 'Roma VF'—heavy crop of meaty, medium-sized, pear-shaped fruits on disease-resistant determinate vines in 75 days. 'San Marzano'—large crop of elongated, pear-shaped 3½-inch tomatoes in 80 days on indeterminate vines. 'Viva Italia'—sweet, meaty 3-ounce fruits that can be stored for 2 to 3 weeks, on vigorous, disease-resistant, heat-tolerant vines in 80 days.

Yellow tomato varieties include: 'Golden Boy'—large, mildly flavored golden yellow fruits on indeterminate vines in 80 days. 'Husky Gold'—half-pound deep yellow fruits on compact 4½-foot disease-resistant indeterminate vines that require no pinching or pruning in 70 days. 'Lemon Boy'—lemon yellow, low-acid 6- to 7-ounce fruits on disease-resistant indeterminate vines in 72 days. 'Yellow Canary'—clusters of bite-sized golden fruits on compact branching determinate vines only 6 inches long, ideal for containers and hanging baskets, in 63 days. 'Yellow Pear'—long clusters of tiny pear-shaped yellow fruits 2 inches long and an inch across, ideal for salads and relishes, on bushy, indeterminate vines good for container culture in 112 days.

White tomato varieties include: 'White

Wonder'—medium-sized, 6- to 8-ounce, very low-acid fruits with creamy white flesh and skin on indeterminate vines in 115 days.

Growing conditions: Tomatoes can be directly sown when the soil temperature reaches 50° F or more, but they do best when started indoors 4 to 6 weeks before the last frost and transplanted into compost-enriched garden loam about a week after the last frost, when soil has warmed. Set transplants deeply, burying the lower portion of the stem to stimulate it to form new roots. Cover with plant caps or cloches if frost threatens.

'Sweet 100'

Tomatoes set fruit best when nighttime temperatures are 76° F or higher and daytime temperatures are below 90° F. If nighttime temperatures drop below 50° F or daytime temperatures rise above 90° F, vines will not set fruit.

Plant bushy determinate varieties 24 inches apart. Plant indeterminate varieties that will be allowed to sprawl on the ground 4 feet apart. Allow 18 inches between plants that will be staked and 2½ to 3 feet between plants that will be supported with cages. Indeterminate vines that sprawl tend to produce more but smaller fruits, while those that are supported produce larger but fewer fruits.

Fertilize tomato plants when they are set out, and again when the fruits begin to set, with a balanced 5-10-10 organic fertilizer or manure tea. Foliar sprays of fish emulsion increase yields. Periods of wet or dry weather can stunt growth and cause blossom end rot. Mulch to maintain constant moisture levels, to suppress weeds, and to help keep the fruits of sprawling vines clean and free of decay.

If you grow indeterminate tomatoes in cages or tied to stakes, you may want to pinch off the suckers that grow at the junction of stems and side branches. Removing the suckers hastens fruiting, encourages sturdier vines, and forces more uniform ripening of larger fruits.

'Lemon Boy'

Use floating row covers to protect young plants from flea beetles. Use Bt to ward off tomato hornworms. Rotate tomato planting sites every 3 years to avoid nematode damage; when planning crop rotation, group tomatoes with eggplant, peppers, and potatoes, and follow them with a legume such as peas or beans. To prevent disease problems, choose disease-resistant varieties, prune lower branches to increase air circulation, and remove and destroy all garden debris at the end of the season.

Harvest tomatoes when they are fully ripe if the temperature is under 90° F. When the temperature is higher, pick tomatoes just before they reach full ripeness and finish the ripening process indoors at temperatures of 70° F or more. Allow tomatoes to ripen fully before refrigerating for short-term storage. Dry or can tomatoes or cook and freeze them for long-term storage; because of their high water content, tomatoes become mushy if frozen fresh. Save the seed of open-pollinated varieties for planting the following season. Hybrid varieties generally do not breed true.

TURNIP

'Purple-Top White Globe'

Hardiness: *cool-season annual*

Planting method: *direct sowing*

Plant spacing: *3 to 5 inches*

Light: *full sun*

Rumpled leaves and globe-shaped roots with a mild, sweet flavor in spring and fall. Enjoy turnip roots raw, cooked in side dishes, or cubed in stews. Cook the greens as you would spinach or collards.

Selected varieties: 'Purple-Top White Globe'—3- to 4-inch white globes with purple shoulders, fine-textured flesh, and dark green leaves in 55 days. 'Royal Crown'—early variety with deep purple shoulders and deep green tops in 52 days. 'Tokyo Cross'—disease-resistant variety with white 2- to 6-inch roots and glossy green tops in 40 days.

Growing conditions: For a late-spring crop, sow seed ¼ to ½ inch deep in spring as soon as the ground can be worked. Sow again in late summer for a fall crop. Frost increases sweetness. Keep turnips constantly moist but not soggy. Use floating row covers or introduce parasitic wasps to prevent damage from flea beetles, cabbage loopers, and other insect pests that attack members of the cabbage family. To minimize soil-borne diseases, do not plant turnips where other brassicas have grown for at least 3 years. For tender turnip greens, pick when they are small, no more than 12 inches in height. Roots can be harvested when they are an inch or more in diameter. A 10-foot row of turnips yields 30 to 40 pounds.

Picture Credits

Index

Time-Life Books is a division of **TIME LIFE INC.**

TIME LIFE INC.
PRESIDENT and CEO: George Artandi

TIME-LIFE CUSTOM PUBLISHING

Vice President and Publisher: Terry Newell
Vice President of Sales and Marketing: Neil Levin
Director of Acquisitions: Jennifer Pearce
Director of Special Markets: Liz Ziehl
Editor: Linda Bellamy
Production Manager: Carolyn M. Clark
Quality Assurance Manager: James King

Editorial Staff for
The Big Book of Kitchen Gardens

Project Manager: Lynn McGowan
Design: Kathleen Mallow
Picture Coordinator: David Cheatham
Special Contributors: Celia Beattie (proofreader),
Lina B. Burton (index), Ruth Goldberg (cover copy)

Editor: Janet Cave
Administrative Editor: Roxie France-Nuriddin
Art Directors: Cindy Morgan-Jaffe, Alan Pitts, Sue Pratt
Picture Editors: Jane Jordan, Jane A. Martin
Text Editors: Sarah Brash, Darcie Conner Johnston, Paul Mathless
Associate Editors/Research and Writing: Megan Barnett,
Sharon Kurtz, Katya Sharpe, Robert Speziale, Karen Sweet,
Mary-Sherman Willis
Senior Copyeditor: Anne Farr

First printing. Printed in U.S.A.
Pre-Press Services, Time-Life Imaging Center

TIME-LIFE is a trademark of Time Warner Inc. U.S.A.

Library of Congress Cataloging-in-Publication Data
The big book of kitchen gardens : a guide to growing
vegetables and herbs, including over 40 delicious recipes
/ by the editors of Time-Life Books.
p. cm.
Includes index.
ISBN 0-7370-0600-5
1. Vegetable gardening. 2. Kitchen gardens. 3. Herb gardening. 4. Cookery. I. Time-Life Books. II. Title:
Kitchen gardens.
SB321.B534 1999 635—dc21 98-40833 CIP